When should I travel to
Where do I go for answers  *questions?*
What's the best and easiest way to plan and book my trip?

frommers.travelocity.com

Frommer's, the travel guide leader, has teamed up with **Travelocity.com**, the leader in online travel, to bring you an in-depth, easy-to-use resource designed to help you plan and book your trip online.

At **frommers.travelocity.com**, you'll find free online updates about your destination from the experts at Frommer's plus the outstanding travel planning and purchasing features of Travelocity.com. Travelocity.com provides reservations capabilities for 95 percent of all airline seats sold, more than 47,000 hotels, and over 50 car rental companies. In addition, Travelocity.com offers more than 2,000 exciting vacation and cruise packages. Travelocity.com puts you in complete control of your travel planning with these and other great features:

> **Expert travel guidance from Frommer's** - over 150 writers reporting from around the world!

> **Best Fare Finder** - an interactive calendar tells you when to travel to get the best airfare

> **Fare Watcher** - we'll track airfare changes to your favorite destinations

> **Dream Maps** - a mapping feature that suggests travel opportunities based on your budget

> **Shop Safe Guarantee** - 24 hours a day / 7 days a week live customer service, and more!

Whether traveling on a tight budget, looking for a quick weekend getaway, or planning the trip of a lifetime, Frommer's guides and Travelocity.com will make your travel dreams a reality. You've bought the book, now book the trip!

Toronto
2001

by Hilary Davidson

IDG Books Worldwide, Inc.
An International Data Group Company
Foster City, CA • Chicago, IL • Indianapolis, IN • New York, NY

ABOUT THE AUTHOR

Hilary Davidson divides her time between her hometown of Toronto and New York City. She is a restaurant critic for *Toronto Life* magazine and has worked for *Discover, Harper's, The Globe and Mail, Chatelaine, Profit,* and *WeddingBells*. She is also a contributor to *Frommer's Canada*. Her recent travels have taken her to Northern Ireland, Wales, and Spain, though her most exciting trips have been of the aquatic variety—since learning to scuba dive, she has explored shipwrecks in Eastern Ontario and swum with reef sharks in the Bahamas. She can be reached at hilary@hilarydavidson.com.

IDG BOOKS WORLDWIDE, INC.

An International Data Group Company
909 Third Avenue
New York, NY 10022

Find us online at **www.frommers.com**

ISBN 0-7645-6173-1
ISSN 1047-7853

Editor: Myka Carroll
Production Editor: Donna Wright
Photo Editor: Richard Fox
Design by Michele Laseau
Cartographer: Roberta Stockwell
Production by IDG Books Indianapolis Production Department

SPECIAL SALES

For general information on IDG Books Worldwide's books in the U.S., please call our Consumer Customer Service department at 1-800-762-2974. For reseller information, including discounts, bulk sales, customized editions, and premium sales, please call our Reseller Customer Service department at 1-800-434-3422.

Manufactured in the United States of America

5 4 3 2 1

Contents

List of Maps   vii

1 The Best of Toronto   1

1 Frommer's Favorite Toronto
   Experiences   4
2 Best Hotel Bets   5

3 Best Dining Bets   6
   Toronto Today   7
4 Famous Torontonians   8

2 Planning a Trip to Toronto: The Basics   11

1 Visitor Information & Entry
   Requirements   11
2 Money   12
   What Things Cost in Toronto   13
   The Canadian Dollar, the U.S.
   Dollar & the British Pound   14

3 When to Go   14
   Toronto Calendar of Events   15
4 Travel Insurance   19
5 Tips for Travelers with Special
   Needs   20
6 Getting There   21

Planning Your Trip: An Online Directory   24

3 Getting to Know Toronto   36

1 Orientation   36
   Neighborhoods in Brief   40

2 Getting Around   42
   Fast Facts: Toronto   45

4 Accommodations   50

1 Downtown   51
   Family-Friendly Hotels   58
2 Midtown   61

3 Uptown   66
4 East Toronto   67
5 At the Airport   68

5 Dining   71

1 Restaurants by Cuisine   72
2 Downtown West   74
   Family-Friendly Restaurants   83
3 Downtown East   86
4 Midtown West   89
   Great Greasy Spoons   99

5 Midtown East/The East End   99
   Sleepless in Toronto: What to Do
   When the Midnight Munchies
   Attack   102
6 Uptown   103
7 North of the City   108

6   What to See & Do in Toronto   109

Suggested Itineraries   109

1 The Top Attractions   110

2 More Museums   121

3 Exploring the
  Neighborhoods   123

4 Architectural Highlights   125

5 Historic Buildings   126

6 For Sports Fans   128

7 Markets   129

8 Parks & Gardens   129

9 Cemeteries   130

10 Especially for Kids   130

11 Guided Tours   132

12 Outdoor Activities   134

13 Spectator Sports   138

7   City Strolls   140

*Walking Tour 1:
Harbourfront*   140

*Walking Tour 2: The Financial
District*   142

*Walking Tour 3: St. Lawrence &
Downtown East*   149

*Walking Tour 4: Chinatown &
Kensington Market*   153

8   Shopping   159

1 The Shopping Scene   159

2 Great Shopping Areas   159

3 Shopping A to Z   160

9   Toronto After Dark   183

1 The Performing Arts   186

2 The Club & Music Scene   192

3 The Bar Scene   199

  Cueing Up   203

4 The Gay & Lesbian Scene   206

Cyberfun: Internet Cafes   207

5 Cinemas & Movie Houses   207

*Sweet Treats: Toronto's Dessert
Cafes*   208

6 Coffeehouses   208

10   Side Trips from Toronto   210

1 Stratford   210

2 Niagara-on-the-Lake   219

3 Niagara Falls   227

4 Hamilton   236

Appendix: Toronto in Depth   240

Index   249

General Index   249

Accommodations Index   257

Restaurant Index   258

List of Maps

Metropolitan Toronto   2

Underground Toronto   38

The TTC Subway System   43

Downtown Toronto
   Accommodations   52

Midtown Toronto
   Accommodations   62

Downtown Toronto Dining   76

Midtown Toronto Dining   92

Dining—Chinatown to Bloor
   Street   101

Downtown Toronto Attractions   112

Midtown Toronto Attractions   118

Walking Tour—Harbourfront   142

Walking Tour—Financial District   145

Walking Tour—St. Lawrence &
   Downtown East   151

Walking Tour—Chinatown &
   Kensington Market   155

Shopping Highlights—Bloor/
   Yorkville   163

Shopping Highlights—Queen Street
   West   165

Downtown After Dark   184

After Dark—Chinatown to Bloor
   Street   201

Side Trips from Toronto   211

Stratford   213

Niagara-on-the-Lake   221

Niagara Falls   229

Hamilton   237

ACKNOWLEDGMENTS

Many thanks to my editor, Myka Carroll, and to the rest of the team at Frommer's, who expertly shepherded this project from manuscript to book. Thanks also to my mother, Sheila Davidson, who never turned away a page in need of proofreading. And deepest gratitude to my husband, Daniel Distler, whose tireless enthusiasm carried me throughout this project.

AN INVITATION TO THE READER

In researching this book, we discovered many wonderful places—hotels, restaurants, shops, and more. We're sure you'll find others. Please tell us about them, so we can share the information with your fellow travelers in upcoming editions. If you were disappointed with a recommendation, we'd love to know that, too. Please write to:

Frommer's Toronto 2001
IDG Books Worldwide, Inc.
909 Third Avenue
New York, NY 10022

AN ADDITIONAL NOTE

Please be advised that travel information is subject to change at any time—and this is especially true of prices. We therefore suggest that you write or call ahead for confirmation when making your travel plans. The author, editors, and publisher cannot be held responsible for the experiences of readers while traveling. Your safety is important to us, however, so we encourage you to stay alert and be aware of your surroundings. Keep a close eye on cameras, purses, and wallets, all favorite targets of thieves and pickpockets.

WHAT THE SYMBOLS MEAN

✪ Frommer's Favorites

Our favorite places and experiences—outstanding for quality, value, or both.

The following abbreviations are used for credit cards:

AE	American Express	EC	Eurocard
CB	Carte Blanche	JCB	Japan Credit Bank
DC	Diners Club	MC	MasterCard
DISC	Discover	V	Visa
ER	enRoute		

FIND FROMMER'S ONLINE

www.frommers.com offers up-to-the-minute listings on almost 200 cities around the globe—including the latest bargains and candid, personal articles updated daily by Arthur Frommer himself. No other Web site offers such comprehensive and timely coverage of the world of travel.

The Best of Toronto

Chances are that even if you've never set foot in Toronto, you've seen the city a hundred times over. Known for the past decade as Hollywood North, Toronto has stood in for international centers from European capitals to New York. Rarely does it play itself. Self-deprecating Torontonians embody a paradox: Proud of their city's architectural, cultural, and culinary charms, they are unsure whether it's all up to international snuff.

After spending a single afternoon wandering around Toronto, you might wonder why this is a question at all. The sprawling city boasts lush parks, renowned architecture, and excellent galleries. There's no shortage of skyscrapers, particularly in the downtown core. Still, many visitors marvel at the number of Torontonians who live in houses on tree-lined boulevards that are a walk or a bike ride away from work.

Out-of-towners can see the fun side of the place, but Torontonians aren't so sure. They recall the stuffiness of the city's past. Often called "Toronto the Good," it was a town where you could walk down any street in safety, but you couldn't get a drink on Sunday.

Then a funny thing happened on the way through the 1970s. Canada loosened its immigration policies and welcomed waves of Italians, Greeks, Chinese, Vietnamese, Jamaicans, Indians, Somalians, and others, many of whom settled in Toronto. Political unrest in Quebec drove out Anglophones, many into the waiting arms of Toronto. The city's economy flourished, which in turn gave its cultural side a boost.

Natives and visitors alike feel the benefits of this rich cultural mosaic. More than 5,000 restaurants are scattered across the city, serving everything from simple Greek souvlaki to five-star, Asian-accented fusion cuisine. Festivals such as Caribana and Caravan draw tremendous crowds to celebrate heritage through music and dance. Its newfound cosmopolitanism has made Toronto a key player on the arts scene, too. The Toronto International Film Festival in September and the International Festival of Authors in October draw top stars of the film and publishing worlds. The theater scene rivals London's and New York's.

Toronto now ranks at or near the top of any international urban quality-of-life study. The city has accomplished something rare, expanding and developing its daring side while holding on to its traditional strengths. It's a great place to visit, but watch out: You might just end up wanting to live here.

Metropolitan Toronto

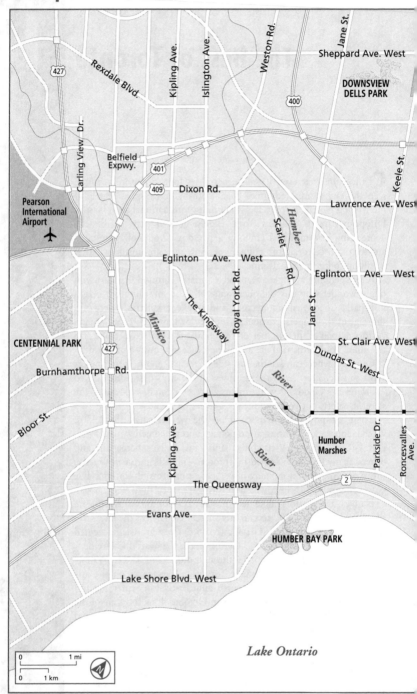

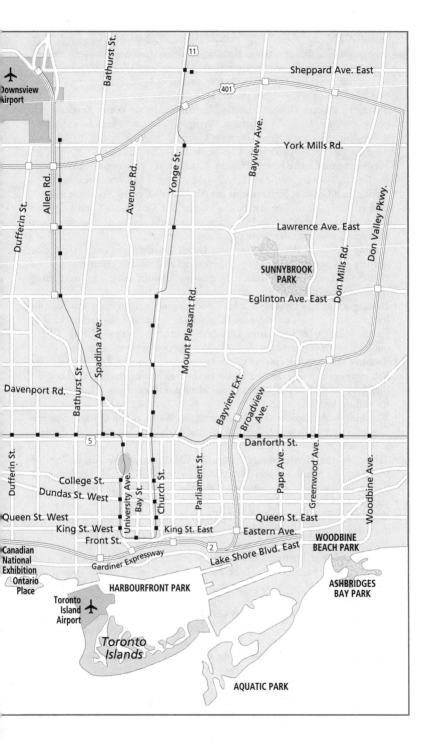

1 Frommer's Favorite Toronto Experiences

- **Horseback Riding in Sunnybrook Park.** One of Toronto's proudest features is its amazing expanses of green. In the 600-acre Sunnybrook Park system, 20 minutes from downtown, you can explore trails on horseback.
- **Taking in a Local Theater.** Toronto likes its blockbuster shows: Residents will proudly tell you how *Show Boat* and *Ragtime* got their start here *before* heading to Broadway. But the offerings from the Canadian Stage Company, the Tarragon Theatre, and the Young Peoples Theatre are consistently excellent, too.
- **Picnicking on Centre Island.** Hop on the ferry and escape to the islands. Viewing the city from across the water will make you see it in a whole new light.
- **Taking In a Game at SkyDome or the Air Canada Centre.** SkyDome is home base for the Toronto Blue Jays baseball team. The Air Canada Centre is where the Maple Leafs (hockey) and the Raptors (basketball) play. Torontonians love their teams and come out to support them in droves.
- **Staying Up Until the Wee Hours in Greek Tavernas.** No one's saying that Toronto is a city that never sleeps, but you can make such a claim about lively-at-all-hours Greektown. At 4am, upbeat bouzouki music can still be heard along the Danforth.
- **Busting a Gut at a Comedy Club.** Maybe it's something in the water: Toronto has produced more than its share of top-notch comedians, including the shagadelic Mike Myers, Jim Carrey, Dan Aykroyd, and the late John Candy. Check out local talent or international stand-up stars at one of the many comedy clubs.
- **Treasure Hunting for Vintage Clothing and Accessories in Kensington Market.** How can one small area have a dozen vintage-clothing vendors? And how do they keep prices low and quality good? Haphazard Kensington Market is a joy for bargain hunters.
- **Watching Kids Explore the Wonders of the World at the Ontario Science Centre.** You don't have to be a tyke to appreciate the amazing interactive displays about biology, ecology, and technology.
- **Taking In the Henry Moore Sculpture Collection at the Art Gallery of Ontario.** The British sculptor Henry Moore so loved Toronto that he bestowed his greatest works on this museum. Kids have been known to swing from the gigantic works in front of the gallery.
- **Wandering Through the Riverdale Farm.** In case you need more proof that Toronto is a very green city, it has a working farm in its midst. Cows, sheep, pigs, goats, and other critters call it home.
- **Cafe Hopping at Trattorias in Little Italy.** Several magazines have zeroed in on this neighborhood as one of the *haute*-est spots in North America. Trendy, yes, but it's also a lot of fun to stop by the many cafes and wine bars, and to dine on outstanding food.
- **Dining Alfresco on One of the City's Endless Patios.** Any piece of sidewalk might be appropriated for open-air dining at any time. If you can't beat 'em, join 'em.
- **Viewing the World from the Top of the CN Tower.** Most Toronto natives will tell you they've never gone to the top of their most famous landmark. It's a pity, because the view is inspiring. On any reasonably clear day, you can see Niagara Falls.
- **Exploring Harbourfront.** There's always something going on—the International Festival of Authors, art exhibits, cultural celebrations, and an antiques market, just to name a few.

Impressions

In the eyes of the rest of the country Toronto is a kind of combination Sodom and Mecca.

—Pierre Berton (1961)

- **Shopping—or Window-Shopping—in Chic Yorkville.** Once home to the city's bohemian community, Yorkville is an enclave of exclusive shops, art galleries, and upscale cafes.
- **Visiting Niagara-on-the-Lake or Stratford for a Day.** Niagara-on-the-Lake is Ontario's wine country, and home of the Shaw Festival. Picturesque Stratford has its own theater festival.

2 Best Hotel Bets

- **Best Historic Hotel:** The (gloved) hands-down winner is **Le Royal Meridien King Edward** (☎ **416/863-9700**), which was built in 1903 and in the past few years has been restored to its former glory. The lobby, with its pink marble columns and ornate frescoes, has seen the crème de la crème of society trot through over the years. In the 1960s, the Beatles holed up in the King Eddy while 3,000 fans stormed the lobby.
- **Best for a Romantic Rendezvous:** The **Park Hyatt Toronto** (☎ **800/ 268-4927**) has it all: a beautifully renovated art-deco building, top-notch service, and one of the best views in the city from its rooftop terrace lounge. This is the place to relax and let yourself be pampered.
- **Best for Business Travelers:** The **Metropolitan Hotel** (☎ **416/977-5000**) is just a few minutes from the Financial District, and its amenities are competitive with those of its pricier competitors. Standard features include fax-modem hookups, large work desks, and cordless two-line phones. There is also a 24-hour business center. The restaurants, Hemispheres and Lai Wah Heen (see chapter 5), are favorite sites for business lunches.
- **Best for Families:** The **Delta Chelsea Inn** (☎ **800/243-5732**) is a longtime family favorite. It offers children's programs, a day-care center, and kid-friendly restaurants. There are two pools, one for tykes and one for adults, and many rooms have refrigerators or kitchenettes.
- **Best Moderately Priced Hotel:** Given the location and amenities, it's hard to beat the **Holiday Inn on King** (☎ **800/263-6364**) for price. Close to the Theater District, Chinatown, and SkyDome, double rooms start at C$179 (US$121.72) per night.
- **Best Budget Accommodations:** Victoria University (☎ **416/585-4524**) rents out its student residences from mid-May until late August. It's in an excellent location, with clean rooms and great facilities, including tennis courts and a pool. All this for C$65 (US$44.20) a night.
- **Best Service:** At the **Four Seasons** (☎ **800/268-6282**), ask and you shall receive. The high staff-to-guest ratio means that there's always someone around to do your bidding.
- **Best Hotel Dining:** The **Toronto Hilton's** new and very grand dining room, Tundra (☎ **416/860-6800**), is a treat for all the senses. Across the lobby, the breakfast nook, Ovo, serves up gourmet vittles to start off the day.

- **Best Gay-Friendly Hotel:** Everyone comes to the **Hotel Selby** (☎ 800/387-4788). In a Victorian building in a predominantly gay neighborhood, this hotel draws gay, lesbian, and straight travelers with belle-époque style and individually decorated rooms.
- **Best for Travelers with Disabilities:** The **Royal York** (☎ 800/441-1414) looks monolithic, but it pays a lot of attention to accessibility. The adaptations accommodate wheelchair users, the visually impaired, and the hearing impaired.

3 Best Dining Bets

- **Best for a Business Lunch:** The always-hopping **Jump Café and Bar,** 1 Wellington St. W. (☎ 416/363-3400), in the heart of the Financial District, is a longtime favorite for deal-makers and traders. Another sure bet is **Canoe,** in the Toronto Dominion Tower at 66 Wellington St. W. (☎ 416/364-0054), a see-and-be-seen spot for local and visiting power brokers.
- **Best for a Celebration:** The atmosphere at **Veni Vidi Vici,** 650 College St. (☎ 416/536-8550), is celebratory every night of the week. The glamorous private dining room at the back provides swank elegance for parties of up to twelve.
- **Best for a Romantic Dinner:** The setting, the music, the food—everything caters to your five senses at **Senses,** 15 Bloor St. W. (☎ 416/935-0400). Relax and let the pampering begin.
- **Best Decor:** Everyone in town knows that **Monsoon,** 100 Simcoe St. (☎ 416/979-7172), has an award-winning interior design by Toronto firm Yabu Pushelberg. The brown-on-black Zen-sedate setting steals attention from the impressive kitchen.
- **Best View:** The obvious choice is **360 Revolving Restaurant,** in the CN Tower, 301 Front St. (☎ 416/362-5411). Still, **Scaramouche,** 1 Benvenuto Place (☎ 416/961-8011), offers serious competition with its floor-to-ceiling windows overlooking the downtown skyline.
- **Best Wine List:** For a truly international selection, it's hard to beat **Centro,** 2472 Yonge St. (☎ 416/483-2211). The basement is a wine bar with Italian, Californian, and Australian vintages by the glass; upstairs, the dining room boasts more than 600 bottles from around the world. Prices range from C$32 (US$21.75) into four figures.
- **Best Bistro:** Bistros often do well with comfort foods, but **Stork on the Roof,** 2009 Yonge St. (☎ 416/483-3747), warms up classic dishes with some exotic ingredients.
- **Best Italian:** **Il Posto Nuovo,** 148 Yorkville Ave. (☎ 416/968-0469), serves up fine modern Italian cuisine in elegant digs—and the efficient, knowledgeable wait staff make everyone feel at home.
- **Best Portuguese:** Standing alone on Italian-dominated College Street, **Chiado,** 484 College St. (☎ 416/538-1910), serves modern Portuguese cuisine. The seafood is flown in daily.
- **Best Greek:** The cooking at **Pan on the Danforth,** 516 Danforth Ave. (☎ 416/466-8158), will convince you that Pan was *really* the god of food. This is Greek cuisine updated with panache.
- **Best Desserts:** Dufflet Rosenberg bakes up a storm at **Dufflet Pastries,** 787 Queen St. W. (☎ 416/504-2870). You'll find her name on the dessert list at some of the city's top restaurants. Also, the lemon meringue mille-feuille at **North 44,** 2537 Yonge St. (☎ 416/487-4897), gets me every time.
- **Best Late-Night Dining:** In Greektown along the Danforth, the restaurants stay open almost all night. One of the best is **Avli,** 401 Danforth Ave.

Toronto Today

The past several years have been a tumultuous time for Toronto. The merger of its separate municipalities, rapid population growth, and provincial government budget slashing have all had a serious impact on the life of the city. It has also been a boom time, with construction of new arts and sports facilities, and a burgeoning dining and entertainment scene. Toronto is still the city of choice for arriving immigrants: 300,000 Hong Kong émigrés have joined Toronto's Chinese community, and there have been influxes of nationals from Somalia, Eastern Europe, India, Pakistan, and Central America.

MEGACITY MANIA   The dust has just started to settle—a little bit, at least. In January 1998, the six interdependent cities that made up Metro Toronto amalgamated into one monolithic megacity. The merger was anything but voluntary—two-thirds of the citizenry voted against it in a referendum. (It was widely agreed that the city's structure needed reform, but no consensus on how to go about it.) Still, the Conservative provincial government (the "Tories"), under the leadership of Premier Mike Harris, forged ahead and forced the issue. The result was pandemonium: Services and standards had varied from municipality to municipality, and creating a common denominator was no mean feat. The mayor of formerly independent North York, Mel Lastman, was elected mayor of the new megacity, and he assumed the unenviable task of restructuring and reorganizing civic government. He has succeeded in smoothing down most of the ruffled feathers, though his relationship with the provincial government has often been acrimonious.

TROUBLE ON THE HOME FRONT   Toronto has few friends in the provincial government (perhaps because its citizens vote against it whenever given the opportunity). In addition to forcing the megacity merger through, the Tories have cut social spending and reclaimed the land it was supposed to sell to the city for its new opera house. The most frequent complaint heard in Toronto is that the city's municipal taxes aren't reinvested in the city's infrastructure, but instead end up being funneled to less-populous parts of the province. Funding hasn't even been guaranteed yet for the much-needed subway line under Sheppard Avenue; miles of new tunnel have been dug out, but Toronto is still waiting to find out if the government will allot any money for tracks and platforms. Stay tuned.

BUILDING THE FUTURE   Toronto's future plans are in flux at the moment. The realization that no new opera house would be built came as a blow to the city's Canadian Opera Company and to the wider arts community. The collapse of Garth Drabinsky's Livent company caused shock waves in Toronto's theater scene, and no impresario has yet stepped in to take its place. But at the same time, Toronto is a hive of activity. The Air Canada Centre opened in 1999 as the new home of the Maple Leafs hockey team and the Raptors basketball team. And there are plans under consideration for the revitalization of the Waterfront area. Again, stay tuned.

(☎ **416/461-9577**), a raucous taverna that serves excellent fare at all hours. In Chinatown, **Happy Seven,** 358 Spadina Ave. (☎ **416/971-9820**), cooks Cantonese dishes until 4am.

- **Best People Watching:** Across from the Sutton Place Hotel is **Bistro 990,** 990 Bay St. (☎ **416/921-9990**), a restaurant where everyone in Toronto but me has had a celebrity sighting. And even I have seen the rich and famous dining at **La Bruschetta,** 1317 St. Clair Ave. W. (☎ **416/656-8622**), an out-of-the-way Italian trattoria that treats everyone like a VIP.
- **Best Value: Messis,** 97 Harbord St. (☎ **416/920-2186**), has acted as a training ground for some of the best chefs in Toronto. It's a popular, moderately priced spot where you can check out the up-and-comers.
- **Best for Kids: Millie's Bistro,** 1980 Avenue Rd. (☎ **416/481-1247**), is a family favorite. It has sunny dining rooms, a smoke-free environment, and a special children's menu. An inexpensive option is **Fran's,** 21 St. Clair Ave. W. (☎ **416/925-6337**). The 1940s-era diner is open 24 hours a day, has a children's menu, and supplies kids with pencils, crayons, and drawing paper.
- **Best Steak House: Barberian's,** 7 Elm St. (☎ **416/597-0335**), has been boosting the level of protein in Torontonians' diets since 1959. It also serves great martinis and desserts, but what everyone comes here for is the meat.
- **Best Pizza:** A cubbyhole-sized eatery in midtown, **Serra,** 378 Bloor St. W. (☎ **416/922-6999**), makes thin-crust pizzas laden with gourmet ingredients like goat cheese, prosciutto, and black olives.
- **Best Sushi:** There's only one possible answer—**Hiro Sushi,** 171 King St. E. (☎ **416/304-0550**). Chef Hiro Yoshida offers up classically prepared sushi as well as a few unique specialties.
- **Best Afternoon Tea:** For tea with all the finger sandwiches, pastries, and clotted cream you can handle, head to the **Four Seasons Hotel,** 21 Avenue Rd. (☎ **416/964-0411**).
- **Best If You Have Only One Meal in Toronto and Price Is No Object:** While I hate to go along with the crowd, the common wisdom is on the money with **North 44,** 2537 Yonge St. (☎ **416/487-4897**). Great food, great staff, great setting.
- **Best If You Have Only One Meal in Toronto and Price *Is* an Object:** Look no further than the moderately priced **Goldfish,** 372 Bloor St. W. (☎ **416/513-0077**). The minimalist Scandinavian design might not be to everyone's taste, but the inspired cooking and attentive service hit the mark every time.
- **Best Chinese: Lai Wah Heen,** at the Metropolitan Hotel, 110 Chestnut St. (☎ **416/977-9899**), serves deluxe Cantonese and Szechwan specialties, including a variety of shark's-fin soups and abalone dishes. It features several good-value prix fixe specials at lunch and dinner.
- **Best Brunch:** Who needs bacon and eggs when you can have *torta rustica* with layers of ricotta, mozzarella, leeks, peas, and smoked trout? This and other glamorous offerings are available at **Agora,** at the Art Gallery of Ontario, 317 Dundas St. W. (☎ **416/977-0414**).
- **Best Vegetarian: Annapurna Vegetarian Restaurant,** 1085 Bathurst St. (☎ **416/537-8513**), is a vegetarian venue that herbivores and their meat-eating friends can enjoy together. It features nicely spiced Indian veggie dishes and you-won't-believe-it's-tofu burgers.

4 Famous Torontonians

Margaret Atwood (b. 1939)   Author, literary critic, and poet. Atwood is best known for her futuristic novel *The Handmaid's Tale,* which was made into a Hollywood film. Perhaps Canada's most famous literary star—her books have been translated into more than twenty languages, and there's a university in Sweden that teaches a course just in the use of comedy in her novels. Atwood's oeuvre includes *The Edible Woman, The Robber Bride,* and *Alias Grace.*

Sir Frederick Banting (1891–1941)   Nobel laureate, scientist, and artist. Banting was a Renaissance man in his day. He was the co-discoverer of insulin at the University of Toronto; in 1923 he was awarded the Nobel Prize for his life-saving research. Banting also distinguished himself as a captain in the Army Medical Corps in World War I and, later in life, as an artist.

John Candy (1950–1994)   Actor and comedian. The beloved funnyman and Toronto native got his start in comedy with the local Second City troupe, playing a succession of crazy characters on *SCTV.* In Hollywood, he made a succession of popular films that included *Only the Lonely, Uncle Buck,* and *Planes, Trains, and Automobiles.* He was also a co-owner of the Toronto Argonauts football team.

Jim Carrey (b. 1962)   Actor and comedian. Before he became a $20 million man in Hollywood with movies like *The Mask, Ace Ventura: Pet Detective, Dumb and Dumber, The Truman Show,* and *Me, Myself, and Irene,* Carrey lit up the stage at local comedy clubs.

David Cronenberg (b. 1943)   Filmmaker, director, and screenwriter. Cronenberg knows how to shock audiences—witness his 1996 film *Crash,* which explored violent injury fetishes and won the Jury Prize at the Cannes Film Festival. His eerie body of work includes *The Fly, The Dead Zone, Dead Ringers, Naked Lunch,* and *eXistenZ.*

Atom Egoyan (b. 1960)   Filmmaker and director. His films—including *Exotica, The Sweet Hereafter,* and *Felicia's Journey*—have been critical successes. Born in Cairo and raised in western Canada, Egoyan originally came to Toronto to study at the University of Toronto. He and his wife, actress Arsinee Khanjian, still call it home.

Barbara Gowdy (b. 1950)   Author and editor. Born in Windsor, Ontario, Gowdy moved to Toronto with her family at the age of 4. She worked as an editor at the local publishing house of Lester & Orpen Dennys in the 1970s, but her greatest successes have been as an author. Her critically acclaimed novels include *We So Seldom Look On Love* and *The White Bone.*

Norman Jewison (b. 1926)   Academy Award-winning filmmaker and director. What award or honor hasn't Jewison won? With a raft of Oscars and Emmys, as well as an Order of Canada, Jewison is one of the most important filmmakers of our time. His films include *Fiddler on the Roof, The Cincinnati Kid, Jesus Christ Superstar, Agnes of God,* and *Moonstruck.* In 1986 the Toronto native established the Canadian Centre for Film Studies in his hometown.

Edward Lennox (1854–1933)   Architect. Lennox is responsible for designing much of the face that Toronto presents to the world. His legacy includes Old City Hall, Casa Loma, the King Edward Hotel, and the West Wing of Queen's Park, the seat of the Ontario legislature.

Marshall McLuhan (1911–1980)   Media theorist and critic. The man who is best known for coining the phrases "the medium is the message" and "the global village" was a professor of English and the director of the Centre for Culture and Technology at the University of Toronto. His seminal works include *The Gutenberg Galaxy, Understanding Media,* and *War and Peace in the Global Village.*

Agnes McPhail (1890–1954)   Activist and politician. McPhail became the first woman Member of Parliament when she was elected to the House of Commons in 1921. She proposed Canada's first pay equity legislation, encouraged reform of the penal system, and served on the League of Nations, the precursor to the United Nations.

Lucy Maud Montgomery (1874–1942)   Author. Her most famous creation, *Anne of Green Gables,* was set in Prince Edward Island, Montgomery's own birthplace. But most of her Anne books—and all of her *Emily of New Moon* series—were written after she settled in Ontario, first in Uxbridge and then in Toronto.

Mike Myers (b. 1963)   Actor, comedian, and screenwriter. Myers became a celebrity when he starred on *Saturday Night Live* from 1989 to 1994 playing a series of characters that included metalhead rocker Wayne Campbell and German aesthete Dieter. On the big screen, Myers has struck gold writing and starring in films like *Wayne's World* and *Austin Powers* (and their respective sequels).

Michael Ondaatje (b. 1943)   Author, editor, and poet. Ondaatje's name will forever be linked to his novel *The English Patient,* which was adapted into an Oscar-winning film. Born in Sri Lanka, Ondaatje has taught at Toronto's York University since 1971. His acclaimed body of work includes *Running in the Family, In the Skin of a Lion,* and *Anil's Ghost.*

Lester B. Pearson (1897–1972)   Prime Minister, Nobel laureate, and international statesman. Born, raised, and educated in Toronto, Pearson's career as a diplomat took him to London and Washington. He was a strong proponent of an alliance of Western powers, and his proposals formed part of the groundwork for the creation of NATO. In 1957 he was awarded the Nobel Prize for creating the United Nations emergency force in the Suez Canal crisis. He was elected Prime Minister in 1963, and held that position until he retired in 1968. But he continued his work on the world stage, establishing the United Nations peacekeeping forces.

Mary Pickford (1893–1979)   Actress, Academy Award winner and film studio founder. Known in the Jazz Age as "America's Sweetheart," Pickford was born and raised in Toronto. While she made some memorable films, including *Little Lord Fauntleroy* and *Coquette,* her most important role was of movie magnate: In 1919, Pickford, her husband Douglas Fairbanks, and Charlie Chaplin founded the United Artists film studio.

John Polanyi (b. 1929)   Nobel laureate and chemist. Polanyi, a University of Toronto professor, was awarded the Nobel Prize in Chemistry in 1996 for his use of chemiluminescence of molecules to highlight energy relationships in chemical reactions. Sound confusing? The fruit of his research has been the creation of vibrational and chemical lasers, the most powerful sources of infrared radiation currently known.

Joe Shuster (1914–1992)   Creator of Superman. Poor Joe Shuster—if only he and his co-creator Jerome Siegel had known what a success their cartoon character would be one day, they wouldn't have sold the rights to D.C. Comics for a pittance in 1940. Shuster had been a newspaper boy for the *Toronto Star,* and in the early Superman strips, Clark Kent worked for the *Daily Star* (later rechristened as the *Daily Planet*). Toronto purportedly served as the model for the city of Metropolis.

Michael Snow (b. 1929)   Sculptor, painter and filmmaker. While galleries like New York's Museum of Modern Art and Paris's Musée d'Art Moderne feature Snow's installations, Toronto residents can appreciate the public works of art he created for his hometown, including the flock of fiberglass geese at the Eaton Centre and the sculpted caricatures of sports fans at SkyDome. Other notable works include his series of "Walking Women" paintings, and his acclaimed art film *Wavelength.*

2

Planning a Trip to Toronto: The Basics

Whether you're traveling on a whim or charting your course months in advance, it's important to do some planning to make the most of your trip. You may already be asking how you'll get there and how much it will cost. There are many different sides of Toronto, so you'll need to figure out what kind of trip you want. This chapter will help you find the answers.

1 Visitor Information & Entry Requirements

VISITOR INFORMATION

FROM NORTH AMERICA The best source for Toronto-specific information is **Tourism Toronto, Metro Toronto Convention & Visitors Association,** Queen's Quay Terminal at Harbourfront, 207 Queen's Quay W., Toronto, ON M5J 1A7 (☎ **800/363-1990** from the continental United States, or 416/203-2600; www.tourism-toronto.com). Call before you leave and ask for the free information package, which includes sections on accommodations, sights, and dining. If you can, try to visit the Web site, which includes up-to-the-minute events information.

There are a couple of other Web sites you should check. Surf over to Toronto.com (www.toronto.com), operated by the *Toronto Star* newspaper, for extensive listings of events, accommodations, and shopping. The *Toronto Life* magazine Web site (www.torontolife.com) has extensive restaurant listings. See "Planning Your Trip: An Online Directory" in this guide to find other top Web sites for Toronto.

For information about Ontario, contact **Tourism Ontario,** P.O. Box 104, Toronto, ON M5B 2H1 (☎ **800/ONTARIO** or 416/314-0944), or visit the travel center in the Eaton Centre on Level 1 at Yonge and Dundas. It's open Monday to Friday 10am to 9pm, Saturday 9:30am to 6pm, Sunday noon to 5pm. You can view the Web site at www.travelinx.com.

The Canadian consulates in the United States do not provide tourist information. They will refer you to the offices above. Consular offices in Buffalo, Detroit, Los Angeles, New York, Seattle, and Washington, D.C., deal with visas and other political and immigration issues.

FROM ABROAD The following consulates can provide information or refer you to the appropriate offices.

U.K. and Ireland: The **Canadian High Commission,** MacDonald House, 1 Grosvenor Sq., London W1X 0AB (☎ **0171/258-6600;** fax 0171/258-6384).

Australia: The **Canadian High Commission,** Commonwealth Avenue, Canberra, ACT 2600 (☎ **02/6273-3844**), or the **Consulate-General of Canada,** Level 5, Quay West Building, 111 Harrington St., Sydney, NSW 2000 (☎ **02/9364-3000**). The consulate-general also has offices in Melbourne and Perth.

New Zealand: The **Canadian High Commission,** 3rd floor, 61 Molesworth St., Thomdon, Wellington (☎ **04/473-9577**), or the **Consulate of Canada,** Level 9 Jetset Centre, 44–48 Emily Place, Auckland (☎ **09/309-3690**).

South Africa: The **Canadian High Commission,** 1103 Arcadia St., Hatfield 0083, Pretoria (☎ **012/342-6923**). The commission also has offices in Cape Town and Johannesburg.

ENTRY REQUIREMENTS

DOCUMENTS U.S. citizens and legal residents do not need passports or visas to enter Canada, but must show proof of citizenship (birth or voter's certificate, naturalization certificates, or green card). Every person under 19 years of age is required to produce a letter from a parent or guardian granting permission to travel to Canada. The letter must state the traveler's name and the duration of the trip. It is essential for teenagers to carry proof of citizenship; otherwise their letters are useless at the border.

Citizens of Australia, New Zealand, the United Kingdom, and Ireland must have valid passports. Citizens of many other countries need visas, which must be applied for in advance at the local Canadian embassy or consulate. For detailed information, call your local Canadian consulate or embassy.

CUSTOMS Most customs regulations are generous, but they get complicated when it comes to firearms, plants, meat, and pets. Fishing tackle poses no problem (provided the lures are not made of restricted materials—specific feathers, for example), but the bearer must possess a nonresident license for the province or territory where he or she plans to use it. You can bring in free of duty up to 50 cigars, 200 cigarettes, and 2 pounds of tobacco, provided you're at least 18 years of age. You are also allowed 40 ounces (1.14ml) of liquor or wine as long as you're of age in the province you're visiting (19 in Ontario). There are no restrictions on what you can bring out. If you're thinking of bringing Cuban cigars back to the United States, beware—they can be confiscated, and you could face a fine.

For more information about customs regulations, write to **Revenue Canada,** 875 Heron Rd., Ottawa, ON K1A 0L8.

2 Money

Canadians use **dollars** and **cents,** but with a distinct advantage for U.S. visitors—the Canadian dollar has been fluctuating between 65 and 68¢ in U.S. money, give or take a couple of points' daily variation. In effect, your American money gets you 32% more the moment you exchange it for local currency. Obviously, this will make a difference in your budget, and because the nominal prices of many goods are roughly on par with those in the United States, the difference is real, not imaginary. Keep in mind that sales taxes are higher, though you should be able to recoup at least part of them (see "Taxes" under "Fast Facts," in chapter 3).

What Things Cost in Toronto	U.S.$
Taxi from the airport to downtown	25.50
Subway/bus from the airport to downtown	6.80
Local telephone call	.17
Double at the Park Hyatt (very expensive)	204.00
Double at the Delta Chelsea Inn (moderate)	95.20
Double at Victoria University (inexpensive)	44.20
Two-course lunch for one at Stork on the Roof (moderate)*	15.00
Two-course lunch for one at Kalendar (inexpensive)*	10.60
Three-course dinner for one at North 44 (very expensive)*	50.40
Three-course dinner for one at Goldfish (moderate)*	28.30
Three-course dinner for one at the Rivoli (inexpensive)*	16.30
Pint of beer	3.50
Coca-Cola	1.00
Cup of coffee	1.00
Roll of ASA 1100 Kodacolor film, 36 exposures	5.40
Admission to the Royal Ontario Museum	6.80
Movie ticket at a Silver City multiplex	7.50
Ticket for the Royal Alexandra Theatre	27.20–74.80
*Includes tax and tip, but not wine.	

Paper currency comes in $5, $10, $20, $50, and $100 denominations. (There are $1,000 bills, too, but these are currently being phased out of existence.) Coins come in 1-, 5-, 10-, and 25-cent, 1- and 2-dollar denominations (there may be another on the way: The government is considering introducing a $5 coin, possibly in 2002). The gold-colored $1 coin is a "loonie" (it sports a loon on its "tails" side), and the large gold-and-silver-colored $2 coin is a "toonie." If you find these names somewhat, ah, colorful, just remember that there's no swifter way to reveal that you're a tourist than to say "one-dollar coin."

You can bring in or take out any amount of money, but if you are importing or exporting $5,000 or more, you must file a report of the transaction with Canadian Customs. Most tourist establishments in Canada will take U.S. cash, though at an anemic exchange rate. To get the best rate, withdraw cash from a Canadian ATM (most accept Cirrus or Plus) or exchange your funds into Canadian currency upon arrival. MasterCard and Visa are almost universally accepted, and American Express is gaining acceptance. *Note:* Travelers who rely on credit cards should be warned that some companies are starting to impose a foreign-exchange fee for out-of-country transactions; be sure to check with your credit card company before you start ringing up bills.

If you do spend American money at Canadian establishments, you should understand how the conversion is calculated. Many times, especially in downtown Toronto, there will be a sign at the cash register that reads "U.S. Currency 50%." This 50% is the "premium," which means that for every U.S. greenback you hand over, the cashier will consider it $1.50 Canadian. For example, for a $15 tab you need pay only $10 in U.S. currency.

The Canadian Dollar, the U.S. Dollar & the British Pound

The prices quoted in this guide are in Canadian dollars, with the U.S. equivalent in parentheses. The exchange rate we've used is $1.40 Canadian to $1 American. The conversion rate for the British pound is $2.30 Canadian.

Here's a quick table of equivalents:

Canada $	U.S. $	British £	Canada $	U.S. $	British £
1	0.70	.40	50	34.00	20.50
5	3.40	2.10	80	54.40	32.90
10	6.80	4.10	100	68.00	41.10
20	13.60	8.20			

It used to be that you were well advised to purchase traveler's checks and arrange to carry some ready cash (usually about $200) before leaving home. Now that **ATMs** are almost everywhere—and often deliver a better exchange rate—I suggest obtaining money from them. Do try to limit your transactions because you will pay a fee for each ATM withdrawal. You can find ATMs at most banks. For the location of the nearest ATM that services the **Cirrus** network, dial ☎ **800/424-7787** (a global access number); for **Plus,** call ☎ **800/843-7587** (U.S. only). On the Web, try **www.visa.com** or **www.mastercard.com** for the location of the nearest Plus ATM. Most ATMs will make cash advances against MasterCard and Visa, but make sure you have your personal identification number with you.

For those who prefer the extra security of **traveler's checks,** almost all hotels, restaurants, shops, and attractions accept U.S. dollar traveler's checks. Traveler's checks can be exchanged for cash at banks, and you're best off doing so there. As in the United States, most small businesses will not cash traveler's checks in denominations greater than $50.

American Express (☎ **800/221-7282** in the U.S. and Canada) is the most widely recognized traveler's check; depending on where you purchase them, expect to pay a 1% to 4% commission. Checks are free to members of the **American Automobile Association (AAA).**

Citicorp (☎ **800/645-6556** in the U.S., or 813/623-1709 collect in Canada) issues checks in U.S. dollars or British pounds.

MasterCard International (☎ **800/223-9920** in the U.S.) issues checks in about a dozen currencies.

Thomas Cook (☎ **800/223-7373** in the U.S.) issues checks in a variety of currencies.

3 When to Go

THE CLIMATE

Spring runs from late March to mid-May (though occasionally there's snow in mid-April); **summer,** mid-May to mid-September; **fall,** mid-September to mid-November; **winter,** mid-November to late March. The highest recorded temperature is 105°F; the lowest, -27°F. The average date of first frost is October 29; the average date of last frost is April 20. The wind blasts from Lake Ontario can be fierce, even in June. Bring a light jacket or cardigan.

Toronto's Average Temperatures (°F)

	Jan	Feb	Mar	Apr	May	June	July	Aug	Sept	Oct	Nov	Dec
High	30	31	39	53	64	75	80	79	71	59	46	34
Low	18	19	27	38	48	57	62	61	54	45	35	23

HOLIDAYS

Toronto celebrates the following holidays: New Year's Day (January 1), Good Friday and/or Easter Monday (March or April), Victoria Day (Monday following the third weekend in May), Canada Day (July 1), Civic Holiday (first Monday in August), Labour Day (first Monday in September), Thanksgiving (second Monday in October), Remembrance Day (November 11), Christmas Day (December 25), and Boxing Day (December 26).

On Good Friday and Easter Monday, schools and government offices are closed; most corporations close on one or the other, and a few close on both. Only banks and government offices close on Remembrance Day (November 11).

Toronto Calendar of Events

January, February, March, and April are dominated by trade shows, such as the **International Boat and Automobile shows, Metro Home Show, Outdoor Adventure Sport Show,** and more. For information, call **Tourism Toronto** (☎ **800/363-1990** or 416/203-2600).

January

- **Chinese New Year Celebrations,** downtown. The year 2001 is the year of the snake. It is ushered in with traditional and contemporary performances of Chinese opera, dancing, music, and more. For **Harbourfront** celebration information, call ☎ **416/973-3000;** for **SkyDome,** call ☎ **877/666-3838.** The new year starts on January 24.

February

- **Winterfest,** Nathan Phillips Square, Yonge and Eglinton, and Mel Lastman Square. This 3-day celebration spreads over three neighborhoods. It features ice-skating shows, snow play, midway rides, performances, ice sculpting, arts-and-crafts shows, and more. For information, call ☎ **416/338-0338.** Usually around Valentine's Day.
- **Toronto Festival of Storytelling,** Harbourfront. Now in its 23rd year, this event celebrates international folklore, with 60 storytellers imparting legends and fables from around the world. For information, call ☎ **416/973-3000.** Last weekend of February.

March

- **Canada Blooms,** Metro Toronto Convention Centre. At this time of year, any glimpse of greenery is welcome. There are 6 acres of indoor garden and flower displays, seminars with green-thumb experts, and competitions. For information, call ☎ **416/593-0223.** Usually the second week of March.
- **St. Patrick's Day Parade,** downtown. Toronto's own version of the classic Irish celebration. For information, call ☎ **416/487-1566.** March 17.

April

- **Blue Jays' Season Opener,** SkyDome. Turn out to root for your home-away-from-home team. For information, call ☎ **416/341-1000;** for tickets, which aren't too hard to get, call ☎ **888/654-6529.** Mid-April.

Don't Forget the Sunscreen

Because of Canada's image of a land of harsh winters, many travelers don't realize that summer in Toronto can be scorching. "The UV index goes quite high, between 7 and 10, in Toronto," says Dr. Patricia Agin of the Coppertone Solar Research Center in Memphis. "It's the same as in New York, Boston, Chicago, or Detroit." All you need is a UV index reading of 7 to get a sunburn, so don't forget to pack your sunscreen and a hat, especially if you're planning to enjoy Toronto's many parks and outdoor attractions.

✪ **The Shaw Festival,** Niagara-on-the-Lake, Ontario. Starting in mid-April and running through the fall, this festival presents the plays of George Bernard Shaw and his contemporaries. (For more information, see chapter 10.) Call ☎ **416/690-7301** or 905/468-2172. Mid-April through October.

• **Sante—The Bloor-Yorkville Wine Festival,** Yorkville. This 4-day gourmet festival brings together award-winning Ontario vintages, food from the city's top-rated chefs, and live jazz. For information, call ☎ **416/504-3977.** Last weekend in April.

May

• **Milk International Children's Festival,** Harbourfront. This is a 9-day celebration of the arts for kids—from theater and music to dance, comedy, and storytelling. For information, call ☎ **416/973-3000.** Usually starts on Mother's Day.

✪ **The Stratford Festival,** Stratford, Ontario. Featuring a wide range of contemporary and classic plays, this festival always includes several works by Shakespeare. (For more information, see chapter 10.) Call ☎ **800/567-1600** or 416/364-8355. Early May through October.

• **North American Cycle Courier Championships,** downtown. Part of Toronto's Bike Week, this unique race is really an obstacle course filled with all the things that can ruin a bike courier's day: traffic lights, road problems, and pedestrians. For information, call ☎ **416/539-7007.** Last week in May.

June

✪ **Harbourfront Reading Series,** Harbourfront. Now in its 27th year, this festival celebrates the best of Canadian literature. Top writers such as Timothy Findley, Anne Michaels, and Barbara Gowdy flock here to read from their latest works. For information, call Harbourfront at ☎ **416/973-3000;** for tickets, call ☎ **416/973-4000.** Readings go on through most of June.

• **North by Northeast Festival,** citywide. Known in the music biz as NXNE, the 3-day event features rock and indie bands at 28 venues around Toronto. For information, call ☎ **416/469-0986.** Second weekend in June.

✪ **Toronto International Festival Caravan,** citywide. This popular 9-day event is North America's largest international festival. It features more than 40 themed pavilions, craft demonstrations, opportunities to sample authentic dishes, and traditional dance performances by 100 cultural groups. For information, call ☎ **416/977-0466.** Usually third and fourth weekends of June.

- **Benson & Hedges Symphony of Fire,** Ontario Place. This international fireworks competition is set to music and draws 2 million people to the waterfront. Six shows take place, on several Saturdays and Wednesdays. For information, call ☎ 416/442-3667; for tickets for waterfront seating, call ☎ 416/870-8000. Mid-June to July.
- **Taste of Little Italy,** along College Street between Euclid and Shaw streets. Restaurants, craftspeople, musicians, and other performers put on displays during this 2-day festival for the whole family. For information, call ☎ 416/531-9991. Mid-June.
- **International Dragon Boat Festival,** Centre Island. More than 160 teams of dragon-boaters compete in the 2-day event, which commemorates the death of the Chinese philosopher and poet Qu Yuan. For information, call ☎ 416/598-8945. Third weekend in June.
- **Gay & Lesbian Pride Celebration,** citywide. A week of events, performances, symposiums, and parties culminates in an extravagant Sunday parade. For information, call ☎ 416/92PRIDE or 416/927-7433. Late June.
- **Du Maurier Downtown Jazz Festival,** citywide. Going strong since 1987, this 10-day festival showcases more than 2,000 international artists playing every jazz style conceivable—blues, gospel, Latin, African, traditional—at 60 venues around town. For information, call ☎ 416/363-8717. Late June.

July

- **Canada Day Celebrations,** citywide. July 1, 2001, marks the nation's 134th birthday. Street parties, fireworks, and other special events across town mark the day. For information, call Tourism Toronto (☎ 800/363-1990 or 416/203-2600). Weekend of July 1.
- **The Fringe—Toronto's Theatre Festival,** citywide. More than 90 thespian troupes participate in this 10-day festival of contemporary and experimental theater. Shows last no more than an hour. For information, call ☎ 416/534-5919 (e-mail: fringe@interlog.com). First week of July.
- **Great Canadian Blues Festival,** Harbourfront Centre. Toronto shows that it's got soul in this 3-day festival of Canada's best blues musicians. In case the rhythm isn't enough to catch you, the Blues Festival coincides with a lip-smacking BBQ fest also at Harbourfront. For information, call Harbourfront (☎ 416/973-3000); for tickets, call ☎ 416/973-4000. Second weekend in July.
- **Molson Indy,** the Exhibition Place Street circuit. One of Canada's major races on the IndyCar circuit. Away from the track, there's live music and beer gardens. For information, call ☎ 416/922-7477. Third weekend in July.
- ✪ **Caribana,** citywide. Toronto's version of Carnival transforms the city. It's complete with traditional foods from the Caribbean and Latin America, ferry cruises, island picnics, children's events, concerts, and arts-and-crafts exhibits. This festival draws more than 1 million people from across North America and Britain. Call ☎ 416/465-4884 for more information. Late July to early August.

August

- **Festival of Beer,** Fort York. More than 70 major Ontario breweries and microbreweries turn out for this celebration of suds. There's also a wide selection of food from local restaurants, and live music of the blues, swing, and jazz persuasions. For information, call ☎ 416/698-7206. First weekend in August.

- ○ **Canadian National Exhibition,** Exhibition Place. One of the world's largest exhibitions, this 18-day extravaganza features midway rides, display buildings, free shows, and grandstand performers. The 3-day Canadian International Air Show (first staged in 1878) is an added bonus. Call ☎ **416/393-6000** for information. Mid-August to Labour Day.
- **Du Maurier Ltd. Open,** National Tennis Centre at York University. Canada's international tennis championship is an important stop on the pro tennis tour. It attracts players such as Sampras, Agassi, Seles, and Sanchez-Vicario. The Open runs in conjunction with a tournament in Montreal during the middle of August. In 2001, the women play in Toronto and the men in Montreal. In 2002, they'll alternate. For information, call ☎ **416/665-9777.** Mid- to late August.

September

- ○ **Toronto International Film Festival,** citywide. The stars come out for the second-largest film festival in the world. More than 250 films from 70 countries are shown over 10 days. For information, call ☎ **416/967-FILM.** Early September.
- **PGA Tour Canadian Open,** Glen Abbey Golf Club, Oakville. Canada's national golf tournament (☎ **905/844-1800**) has featured the likes of Greg Norman and Tiger Woods in recent years. It's almost always held at Glen Abbey, though Montreal played host in 1997. First or second weekend of September.
- **Word on the Street,** Queen Street West between Simcoe Street and Spadina Avenue. This street fair celebrates the written word with author readings, discounted books and magazines, and children's events. Other major Canadian cities hold similar events on the same weekend. For information, call ☎ **416/504-7241.** Last weekend in September.

October

- **Oktoberfest,** Kitchener–Waterloo, about 1 hour (60 miles) from Toronto. This famed 9-day drinkfest features cultural events plus a pageant and parade. For information, call ☎ **519/570-4267.** Mid-October.
- ○ **International Festival of Authors,** Harbourfront. This renowned 11-day literary festival is the most prestigious in Canada. It draws more than 100 authors from 25 countries to perform readings and on-stage interviews. Among the literary luminaries who have appeared are Salman Rushdie, Margaret Drabble, Thomas Kenneally, Joyce Carol Oates, A. S. Byatt, and Margaret Atwood. For information, call Harbourfront (☎ **416/973-3000**); for tickets, call ☎ **416/973-4000.** Third weekend of October.
- ○ **Toronto Maple Leafs Opening Night,** Air Canada Centre. Torontonians love their team, so securing a ticket will be a challenge. The Air Canada Centre seats 18,700 hockey fans. For information, call ☎ **416/216-1700;** for tickets, call ☎ **416/872-5000.** Mid-October.
- **The Old Clothing Show & Sale,** Exhibition Place. Everything from Jazz Age flapper frocks to Austin Powers–like '60s suits, all under one roof. For information, call ☎ **416/410-1310.** Third weekend of October.

November

- **Royal Agricultural Winter Fair and Royal Horse Show,** Exhibition Place. The 12-day show is the largest indoor agricultural and equestrian competition in the world. Vegetables and fruits are on display, along with crafts, farm machinery, livestock, and more. A member of the British royal family traditionally attends the horse show. Call ☎ **416/393-6400** for information. Mid-November.

- **Santa Claus Parade,** downtown. A favorite with kids since 1905, it features marching bands, magical floats, clowns, and jolly St. Nick himself. American visitors are usually surprised that the parade's in November, but really, it's better than watching Santa try to slide through slush. For information, call ☎ **416/249-7833.** Third Sunday of November.
- **One-of-a-Kind Craft Show & Sale,** Exhibition Place. More than 400 craft artists from across Canada display their unique wares at this 11-day show—just in time for the holidays. For information, call ☎ **416/960-3680.** Last weekend in November through early December.
- **Cavalcade of Lights.** During this holiday celebration, the trees in and around Nathan Phillips Square are lit up, parties and performances take over the skating rink, and ice sculptures decorate the square. Late November through December 31.
- **Canadian Aboriginal Festival,** SkyDome. More than 1,500 Native American dancers, drummers, and singers attend this weekend celebration. There are also literary readings, an arts-and-crafts marketplace, and traditional foods. Call ☎ **519/751-0040.** Last weekend in November.

December

- **First Night Toronto and New Year's Eve at City Hall.** First Night is a nonalcoholic family New Year's Eve celebration. A C$8 (US$5.45) button admits you to a variety of musical, theatrical, and dance performances at downtown venues. To celebrate New Year's Eve, Torontonians gather in Nathan Phillips Square and in Mel Lastman Square in North York, where concerts begin at around 10pm to usher in the countdown to the New Year. December 31.

4 Travel Insurance

Before you decide to purchase travel insurance, check your existing policies to see whether they'll cover you while you're traveling. Check with your **health insurance** company to make sure that your coverage extends to Canada. Some credit cards offer automatic **flight insurance** when you buy an airline ticket with the card. These policies insure against death or dismemberment in the event of a plane crash.

If you plan to rent a car, check your credit cards to see if any of them picks up the **collision damage waiver (CDW)** in Canada. The CDW can run as much as C$16 a day and add as much as 50% to the cost of renting a car. Check your automobile insurance policy, too; it might cover the CDW. If you own a home or have renter's insurance, see if that policy covers off-premises **theft and loss** wherever it occurs. Find out what procedures you need to follow to make a claim. If you're traveling on a tour or package deal and have prepaid a large chunk of your travel expenses, you might want to ask a travel agent about buying **trip-cancellation insurance** from an independent agency.

If, after checking all your existing insurance policies, you decide that you need additional insurance, a good travel agent can give you information on a variety of options. Or contact **Wallach & Company,** 107 W. Federal St., P.O. Box 480, Middleburg, VA 20118 (☎ **800/237-6615** or 540/687-3166). It provides a comprehensive travel policy that covers all contingencies—cancellation, health, emergency assistance, and loss.

5 Tips for Travelers with Special Needs

FOR TRAVELERS WITH DISABILITIES

Toronto is a very accessible city. Curb cuts are well made and common throughout the downtown area; special parking privileges are extended to people with disabilities who have special plates or a pass that allows parking in "No Parking" zones. The subway and trolleys are, unfortunately, not accessible; but the city operates a special service for those with disabilities, **Wheel-Trans.** Visitors can register for this service. For information, call ☎ **416/393-4111.**

The **Community Information Centre of Metropolitan Toronto,** 425 Adelaide St. W., at Spadina Avenue, Toronto, ON M5V 3C1 (☎ **416/ 392-0505**), may be able to provide limited information and assistance about social-service organizations in the city. It does not have specific accessibility information on tourism or hotels. It's available weekdays 8am to 10pm, weekends 10am to 10pm.

FOR SENIORS

Many city attractions grant senior discounts, and some hotels offer special rates. Bring a form of photo ID.

If you haven't already done so, think about joining the **American Association of Retired Persons (AARP),** 601 E St. NW, Washington, DC 20049 (☎ **202/434-2277;** www.aarp.org).

Also look into the fun courses offered in the Toronto region at incredibly low prices by **Elderhostel,** 75 Federal St., Boston, MA 02110 (☎ **617/ 426-7788;** www. elderhostel.org). For a catalog, write Elderhostel, P.O. Box 1959, Wakefield, MA 01880-5959.

FOR STUDENTS

The key to securing discounts and other special benefits is the **International Student Identity Card (ISIC),** available to any high school or university student. Contact the **Council on International Educational Exchange (CIEE),** 205 E. 42nd St., New York, NY 10017 (☎ **212/822-2600** or 212/822-2700; www.ciee.com). The card is available at all Council Travel offices and at many U.S. college campuses. To find the office nearest you, call ☎ **888/COUNCIL** (888/268-6245) or ☎ **800/GETANID** (800/438-2643).

If you'd like to meet other students, you've come to the right place. Toronto has several major colleges in addition to the sprawling **University of Toronto.** The largest university in Canada, with more than 50,000 students (41,000 full-time), the University of Toronto offers many year-round activities and events that any visitor can attend—lectures, seminars, concerts, and more. U of T Day is usually celebrated in the middle of October. The university holds an open house for the community and celebrates with a children's fair and the annual homecoming football game and parade. Call ☎ **416/ 978-8342** for more information, or 416/978-5000 for campus tours.

FOR GAY & LESBIAN TRAVELERS

Toronto has a large gay population, estimated at about 250,000. Community life is centered north and south of the intersection of Church and Wellesley streets. Gay and lesbian travelers can pick up a copy of the biweekly *Xtra!* It's available free at many bookstores, including the **Glad Day Bookshop,** 598A Yonge St., 2nd floor (☎ **416/961-4161**). It's open Monday to Wednesday 10am to 6:30pm, Thursday and Friday 10am to 9pm, Saturday 10am to 6pm,

Sunday noon to 6pm. To receive a copy of *Xtra!* ahead of time, write to 491 Church St., Suite 200, Toronto, ON M4Y 2C6 (☎ 416/925-6665).

For information on upcoming events, call **Tel-Xtra** (☎ 416/925-9872).

6 Getting There

BY PLANE

Wherever you're traveling from, always shop the airlines and ask for the lowest fare. You'll have a better chance of landing a deal if you're willing to be flexible about when you arrive and leave.

You may be able to fly for less than the standard advance (APEX) fare by contacting a ticket broker or consolidator. These companies, which buy tickets in bulk and sell them at a discount, advertise in the Sunday travel sections of major city newspapers. You may not be able to get the lowest price they advertise, but you're likely to pay less than the price quoted by the major airlines. Bear in mind that tickets purchased through a consolidator are often nonrefundable. If you change your itinerary after purchase, chances are you'll pay a stiff penalty.

FROM THE U.S. **Air Canada** (☎ 800/776-3000) operates direct flights to Toronto from most major American cities and many smaller ones. It also flies from major cities around the world and operates connecting flights from other U.S. cities. In 2000, Air Canada took over Canadian Airlines International, making the former Canada's only national airline.

Among U.S. airlines, **US Airways** (☎ 800/428-4322) operates directly into Toronto from a number of U.S. cities, notably Baltimore, Indianapolis, Philadelphia, and Pittsburgh. **American** (☎ 800/433-7300) has daily direct flights from Chicago, Dallas, Miami, and New York. **United** (☎ 800/241-6522) has direct flights from Chicago, San Francisco, and Washington (Dulles). **Northwest** (☎ 800/225-2525) flies directly from Detroit and Minneapolis. **Delta** (☎ 800/221-1212) flies direct from Atlanta and Cincinnati.

FROM ABROAD There's frequent service (direct or indirect) to Toronto from around the world.

Several airlines operate from the **United Kingdom. British Airways** (☎ 0345/222-111), **Air Canada** (☎ 0990/247-226), and **Air India** (☎ 800/442-4455) fly direct from London's Heathrow. Air Canada also flies direct from Glasgow and Manchester.

In **Australia, Canadian International** (☎ 1300/655-767) has an agreement with Qantas and flies from Sydney to Toronto, stopping in Honolulu. From **New Zealand, Canadian International** (☎ 0800/802-245) cooperates with Air New Zealand, scheduling on average three flights a week from Auckland to Toronto, stopping in Honolulu, Fiji, or both. Air Canada has taken over Canadian International, but these arrangements are still in place; Canadian's offices are open and bookings can be made through them.

From Cape Town, **South Africa, Delta** (☎ 800/221-1212, or 011/482-4582 in South Africa) operates via New York; **Air Canada** (call Cardinal Associates in Johannesburg at ☎ 011/880-8931) via Frankfurt; **Swissair** (☎ 021/214-938) via Zurich; and **South African Airways** (☎ 021/254-610) via Miami or New York. Several airlines fly from Johannesburg, including **British Airways** (☎ 011/441-8600) via Heathrow, **South African Airways** (☎ 011/333-6504) via Miami or New York, and Swissair (☎ 011/484-1980) via Zurich.

CYBERDEALS FOR NET SURFERS

It's possible to get some great deals on airfare, hotels, and car rentals on the Internet. Grab your mouse and start surfing before you head to Toronto—you could save a bundle on your trip. The Web site I've highlighted below is worth checking out; see "Planning Your Trip: An Online Directory" in this guide for additional Internet resources to help you plan your trip.

- **Air Canada** (www.aircanada.ca)   On Wednesdays, the airlines' Web sites offer deeply discounted flights to Canada for that weekend. You need to reserve the flight on Wednesday or Thursday to fly on Friday (after 7pm only) or Saturday (all day) and return on Monday or Tuesday (all day). Once you register with Air Canada's Web Specials page, you'll receive an e-mail every Wednesday about available discounts.

BY TRAIN

Amtrak's *Maple Leaf* links New York City and Toronto via Albany, Buffalo, and Niagara Falls. It departs daily from Penn Station. The journey takes 11¾ hours. From Chicago, the *International* carries passengers to Toronto via Port Huron, Michigan, a 12½-hour trip. Note that these lengthy schedules allow for extended stops at customs and immigration checkpoints at the border. Both trains arrive in Toronto at Union Station on Front Street, 1 block west of Yonge Street, opposite the Royal York Hotel. The station has direct access to the subway, so you can easily reach any Toronto destination from there.

To secure the lowest round-trip fares, book as far in advance as possible, and try to travel midweek. Seat availability determines price levels; the earlier you book, the more likely you are to land a lower fare. Sample one-way fares (for use as guidelines only), depending on seat availability: from New York, US$65 to $99 one-way or US$130 to $198 round-trip; from Chicago, US$98 one-way, US$108 to $196 round-trip. Prices do not include meals. Always ask about the availability of discounted fares, companion fares, and any other special tickets. Call **Amtrak** at ☎ **800/USA-RAIL or 800/872-7245.**

From **Buffalo's** Exchange Street Station, you can make the trip to Toronto's Union Station on the **Toronto/Hamilton/Buffalo Railway (THB).** Connecting service is also available from other major cities along the border.

BY BUS

Greyhound/Trailways (☎ **800/231-2222**) is the only bus company that crosses the U.S. border. You can travel from almost anywhere in the United States, changing buses along the way. You'll arrive at the Metro Coach Terminal downtown at 610 Bay St., near the corner of Dundas Street.

The bus may be faster and cheaper than the train, and its routes may be more flexible if you want to stop along the way. Bear in mind that it's also more cramped, toilet facilities are meager, and meals are taken at somewhat depressing rest stops along the way.

Depending on where you are coming from, check into Greyhound/Trailways' special unlimited-travel passes and any discount fares that might be offered. It's hard to provide sample fares because bus companies, like airlines, are adopting yield-management strategies, causing prices to change from one day to the next depending on demand.

BY CAR

Hopping across the border by car is no problem—the U.S. highway system leads directly into Canada at 13 points. If you're driving from Michigan, you'll enter at Detroit–Windsor (via I-75 and the Ambassador Bridge) or Port

Huron–Sarnia (via I-94 and the Bluewater Bridge). If you're coming from New York, you have more options. On I-190, you can enter at Buffalo–Fort Erie; Niagara Falls, N.Y.–Niagara Falls, ON; or Niagara Falls, N.Y.–Lewiston. On I-81, you'll cross the Canadian border at Hill Island; on Rte. 37, you'll enter at either Ogdensburg–Johnstown or Rooseveltown–Cornwall.

From the United States you are most likely to enter Toronto from the west on Hwy. 401 or Hwy. 2 and the Queen Elizabeth Way. If you come from the east via Montreal, you'll also use 401 and 2.

Here are approximate driving distances in miles to Toronto: from Boston, 566; Buffalo, 96; Chicago, 534; Cincinnati, 501; Detroit, 236; Minneapolis, 972; New York, 495.

Be sure you are carrying your driver's license and car registration if you plan to drive your own vehicle into Canada. It isn't a bad idea to carry proof of automobile liability insurance, either.

If you are a member of the American Automobile Association (AAA), the **Canadian Automobile Association (CAA)** Central Ontario Branch in Toronto (☎ **416/221-4300**), provides emergency road service.

Planning Your Trip: An Online Directory

by Lynne Bairstow

Lynne Bairstow is the co-author of *Frommer's Mexico 2001*
and the editorial director of *e-com* magazine.

Day by day, the Internet becomes more integrated into our lives—
including the way we plan and book our travel. By early 2000, one
in every ten trips was being booked online, a trend that's sure to
accelerate.

The Internet not only provides a wealth of destination information,
but also gives you the chance to compare experiences with fellow travelers, ask experts for pre-trip advice, seek out discounted fares once
accessible only to travel-industry insiders, and stay in touch via e-mail
while you're away. The instant communication and storehouse of
information have revolutionized the way travel is researched, reserved,
and realized.

This Online Directory will help you take better advantage of the
planning information available online, and it's best used in conjunction with this book. Part 1 lists general Internet resources that can
make any trip easier, such as sites for obtaining the best possible prices
on airline tickets. In Part 2, you'll find some top online guides for
Toronto, including city guides, visitor information, and activities.

Please keep in mind that this is not a comprehensive list, but rather
a discriminating selection to get you started. Recognition is given to
sites based on their content value and ease of use, and are not paid
for—unlike some Web-site rankings, which are based on payment.
Finally, remember this is a press-time snapshot of leading Web sites—
some undoubtedly will have evolved, changed, or moved by the time
you read this.

1 Top Travel-Planning Web Sites

While the Internet was once a conglomerate of sites for researching
places to visit, several key companies have emerged that offer comprehensive travel planning and booking. In addition to Frommer's
Online, we list the other top online travel agencies below, along with
some more specialized services.

WHY BOOK ONLINE?

Online agencies have come a long way over the past few years, now
providing tips for finding the best fare as well as giving you suggested
dates or times to travel that yield the lowest price if your plans are at
all flexible. Other sites even allow you to establish the price you're
willing to pay, and then check the airlines' willingness to accept it.

Editor's Note: What You'll Find at the Frommer's Site

We highly recommend **Arthur Frommer's Budget Travel Online (www. frommers.com)** as an excellent travel planning resource. Of course, we're a little biased, but you'll find indispensable travel tips, reviews, monthly vacation giveaways, and online booking. Among the most popular features of this site is the regular "Ask the Expert" bulletin boards, which feature one of the Frommer's authors answering your questions via online postings.

Subscribe to Arthur Frommer's Daily Newsletter (**www.frommers.com/ newsletters**) to receive the latest travel bargains and insider travel secrets in your e-mailbox every day. You'll read daily headlines and articles from the dean of travel himself, highlighting last-minute deals on airfares, accommodations, cruises, and package vacations. You'll also find great travel advice by checking our "Tip of the Day" or "Hot Spot of the Month."

Search our Destinations archive (**www.frommers.com/destinations**) of more than 200 domestic and international destinations for great places to stay, tips for traveling there, and what to do while you're there. Once you've researched your trip, the online reservations system (**www. frommers.com/booktravelnow**) takes you to Frommer's favorite sites for booking your vacation at affordable prices.

However, in some cases, these sites may not always yield the best price. Unlike a travel agent, for example, they may not have access to charter flights offered by wholesalers.

Online booking sites aren't the only places to reserve airline tickets—all major airlines have their own Web sites and often offer incentives, like bonus frequent flyer miles or Net-only discounts, when you buy online or buy an e-ticket.

The best of the travel-planning sites are now highly personalized; they store your seating preferences, meal preferences, tentative itineraries, and credit-card information, allowing you to quickly plan trips or check agendas.

In many cases, booking your trip online can be better than working with a travel agent. It gives you the widest variety of choices, control, and the 24-hour convenience of planning your trip when you choose. All you need is some time—and often a little patience—and you're likely to find the fun of online travel research will greatly enhance your trip.

WHO SHOULD BOOK ONLINE?

Online booking is best for travelers who want to know as much as possible about their travel options, for those who have flexibility in their travel dates and are looking for the best price, and for bargain hunters driven by a good value, who are open-minded about where they travel.

One of the biggest successes in online travel for both passengers and airlines is the offer of last-minute specials, such as American Airlines' weekend deals or other Internet-only fares that must be purchased online. Another advantage is that you can cash in on incentives for booking online, such as rebates or bonus frequent flyer miles.

Business and other frequent travelers also have found numerous benefits in online booking, as the advances in mobile technology provide them with the

More people still look online than book online, partly due to fear of putting their credit-card numbers out on the Net. Secure encryption has removed this fear for most travelers. In some cases, however, it's simply easier to buy from a local travel agent who can deliver your tickets to your door (especially if your travel is last-minute or if you have special requests). You can find a flight online and then book it by calling a toll-free number or contacting your travel agent, though this is somewhat less efficient. To be sure you're in secure mode when you book online, look for a little icon of a key or a closed padlock at the bottom of your Web browser.

ability to check flight status, change plans, or get specific directions from handheld computing devices, mobile phones, and pagers. Some sites will even e-mail or page passengers if their flights are delayed.

Online booking is increasingly able to accommodate complex itineraries, even for international travel. The pace of evolution on the Net is rapid, so you'll probably find additional features and advancements by the time you visit these sites. What the future holds for online travelers is ever-increasing personalization and customization.

TRAVEL-PLANNING & BOOKING SITES

Below are listings for the top sites for planning and booking travel. The following sites offer domestic and international flight, hotel, and rental-car bookings, plus news, destination information, and deals on cruises and vacation packages. Free (one-time) registration is required for booking.

Travelocity (incorporates Preview Travel). www.travelocity.com; www. previewtravel.com; www.frommers.travelocity.com

Travelocity is Frommer's online travel-planning and booking partner. Travelocity uses the SABRE system to offer reservations and tickets for more than 400 airlines, plus reservations and purchase capabilities for more than 45,000 hotels and 50 car-rental companies. An exclusive feature of the SABRE system is its **Low Fare Search Engine,** which automatically searches for the three lowest-priced itineraries based on a traveler's criteria. Last-minute deals and consolidator fares are included in the search. If you book with Travelocity, you can select specific seats for your flights with online seat maps, and also view diagrams of the most popular commercial aircraft. Its hotel finder provides street-level location maps and photos of selected hotels. With the **Fare Watcher** e-mail feature, you can select up to five routes and receive e-mail notices when the fare changes by $25 or more.

Travelocity's **Destination Guide** includes updated information on some 260 destinations worldwide—supplied by Frommer's.

Note to AOL Users: You can book flights, hotels, rental cars, and cruises on AOL at keyword: Travel. The booking software is provided by Travelocity/Preview Travel and is similar to the Internet site. Use the AOL "Travelers Advantage" program to earn a 5% rebate on flights, hotel rooms, and car rentals.

Expedia. expedia.com

Expedia is Travelocity's major competitor. It offers several ways of obtaining the best possible fares: **Flight Price Matcher** service allows your preferred airline to match an available fare with a competitor; a comprehensive **Fare**

Airline Web Sites

Below are the Web sites for the major airlines serving Toronto. These sites offer schedules, flight booking and most have pages where you can sign up for e-mail alerts for weekend deals and other late-breaking bargains.

Air Canada   **www.aircanada.ca**
Air India   **www.airindia.com**
American Airlines   **www.americanair.com**
British Airways   **www.british-airways.com**
Canadian Airlines International   **www.cdnair.ca**
Delta   **www.delta-air.com**
Northwest Airlines   **www.nwa.com**
South African Airways   **www.saa.co.za**
Swissair   **www.swissair.com**
US Airways   **www.usair.com**

Compare area shows the differences in fare categories and airlines; and **Fare Calendar** helps you plan your trip around the best possible fares. Its main limitation is that like many online databases, Expedia focuses on the major airlines and hotel chains, so don't expect to find too many budget airlines or one-of-a-kind B&Bs here.

TRIP.com. www.trip.com

TRIP.com began as a site geared toward business travelers, but its innovative features and highly personalized approach have broadened its appeal to leisure travelers as well. It is the leading travel site for those using mobile devices to access Internet travel information.

TRIP.com includes a trip-planning function that provides the average and lowest fares for the route requested, in addition to the current available fare. An on-site "newsstand" features breaking news on airfare sales and other travel specials. Among its most popular features are **Flight TRACKER** and **intelliTRIP.** Flight TRACKER allows users to track any commercial flight en route to its destination anywhere in the United States, while accessing real-time FAA-based flight monitoring data. intelliTRIP is a travel search tool that allows users to identify the best airline, hotel, and rental-car rates in less than 90 seconds.

In addition, the site offers e-mail notification of flight delays, plus city resource guides, currency converters, and a weekly e-mail newsletter of fare updates, travel tips, and traveler forums.

Yahoo! Travel. www.travel.yahoo.com

Yahoo! is currently the most popular of the Internet information portals, and its travel site is a comprehensive mix of online booking, daily travel news, and destination information. The **Best Fares** area offers what it promises, plus provides feedback on refining your search if you have flexibility in travel dates or times. There is also an active section of Message Boards for discussions on travel in general and specific destinations.

TOP VACATION-PACKAGE SITES

Both **Expedia** and **Travelocity** (see above) offer excellent selections and searches for complete vacation packages. Travelers can search by destination and desired dates coupled with how much they are willing to spend. Travelocity has a

Online Directory

valuable "Cruise Critic" function, to help would-be cruisers obtain first-hand accounts of the quality and details of a cruise from recent passengers.

Travel wholesalers, like **Apple Vacations** (**www.applevacations.com**) and **Funjet** (**www.funjet.com**), are also good starting points, but still require that the final booking be handled through a travel agent.

As travel agents tend to be more expert at sorting through the values in vacation packages, you might find **Vacation.com** (**www.vacation.com**) helpful in previewing packages and finding an appropriate agent to help you book the deal. This site represents a nationwide network of 9,800 local travel agencies that specialize in finding the best values in cruises, vacation packages, tours, and other leisure travel services.

LAST-MINUTE DEALS & OTHER ONLINE BARGAINS

There's nothing airlines hate more than flying with lots of empty seats. The Net has enabled airlines to offer last-minute bargains to entice travelers to fill those seats. Most of these are announced on Tuesday or Wednesday and are valid for travel the following weekend, but some can be booked weeks or months in advance. You can sign up for weekly e-mail alerts at the airlines' sites (see "Airline Web Sites," above) or check sites that compile lists of these bargains, such as **Smarter Living** or **WebFlyer** (see below). To make it easier, visit a site that will round up all the deals and send them in one convenient weekly e-mail. But last-minute deals aren't the only online bargains; other sites can help you find value even if you haven't waited until the eleventh hour. Increasingly popular are travel auction sites and services that let you name the price you're willing to pay for an air seat or vacation package.

Cheap Tickets. **www.cheaptickets.com**

Cheap Tickets has exclusive deals that aren't available through more mainstream channels. One caveat about the Cheap Tickets site is that it will offer fare quotes for a route, then later show this fare is not valid for your dates of travel—most other Web sites, such as Expedia, consider your dates of travel before showing what fares are available. Despite its problems, Cheap Tickets can be worth the effort because its fares can be lower than those offered by its competitors.

✪ 1travel.com. **www.1travel.com**

Here you'll find deals on domestic and international flights, cruises, hotels, and all-inclusive resorts such as Club Med. 1travel.com's **Saving Alert** compiles last-minute air deals so you don't have to scroll through multiple e-mail alerts. A feature called "Drive a little using low-fare airlines" helps map out strategies for using alternate airports to find lower fares. And **Farebeater** searches a database that includes published fares, consolidator bargains, and special deals exclusive to 1travel.com. *Note:* The travel agencies listed by 1travel.com have paid for placement.

Bid for Travel. **www.bidfortravel.com**

Bid for Travel is another of the travel auction sites, similar to Priceline (see below), which are growing in popularity. In addition to airfares, Internet users bid on vacation packages and hotels.

Go4less.com. **www.go4less.com**

Specializing in last-minute cruise and package deals, Go4less has some excellent offers. The Hot Deals section gives an alphabetical listing by destination of super discounted packages.

LastMinuteTravel.com. **www.lastminutetravel.com**

Suppliers with excess inventory come to this online agency to distribute unsold airline seats, hotel rooms, cruises, and vacation packages. It's got great deals, but you have to put up with an excess of advertisements and slow-loading graphics.

Moment's Notice. **www.moments-notice.com**

As the name suggests, Moment's Notice specializes in last-minute vacation and cruise deals. You can browse for free, but if you want to purchase a trip, you have to join Moment's Notice, which costs $25. Go to World Wide Hot Deals for a complete list of special deals on international destinations.

✪ Priceline.com. **travel.priceline.com**

Even people who aren't familiar with many Web sites have heard about Priceline.com. Launched in 1998 with a $10-million ad campaign featuring William Shatner, Priceline lets you "name your price" for domestic and international airline tickets and hotel rooms. In other words, you select a route and dates, guarantee with a credit card, and make a bid for what you're willing to pay. If one of the airlines in Priceline's database has a fare lower than your bid, your credit card will automatically be charged for a ticket.

But you can't say when you want to fly—you have to accept any flight leaving between 6am and 10pm on the dates you selected, and you may have to make a stopover. No frequent flyer miles are awarded, and tickets are non-refundable and can't be exchanged for another flight. So if your plans change, you're out of luck. Priceline can be good for travelers who have to take off on short notice (and who are thus unable to qualify for advance-purchase discounts). But be sure to shop around first, because if you overbid, you'll be required to purchase the ticket—and Priceline will pocket the difference between what it paid for the ticket and what you bid.

Priceline says that over 35% of all reasonable offers for domestic flights are being filled on the first try, with much higher fill rates on popular routes (New York to San Francisco, for example). It defines "reasonable" as not more than 30% below the lowest generally available advance-purchase fare for the same route.

Smarter Living. **www.smarterliving.com**

Best known for its e-mail dispatch of weekend deals on 20 airlines, Smarter Living also keeps you posted about last-minute bargains on everything from Windjammer Cruises to flights to Iceland.

SkyAuction.com. **www.skyauction.com**

An auction site with categories for airfare, travel deals, hotels, and much more.

Travelzoo.com. **www.travelzoo.com**

At this Internet portal, over 150 travel companies post special deals. It features a Top 20 list of the best deals on the site, selected by its editorial staff each Wednesday night. This list is also available via an e-mail list, free to those who sign up.

Know When the Sales Start

While most people learn about last-minute weekend deals from e-mail dispatches, it can pay to check the airline sites to find out precisely when they post their special fares. Because deals are limited, they can vanish within hours, sometimes minutes—often before you even read your e-mail. An example: Southwest's specials are posted at 12:01am Tuesdays (Central time). So if you're looking for a cheap flight, stay up late and check Southwest's site to grab the best new deals.

Travel Discussion Sites

One of the best sources of travel information is word-of-mouth, from someone who has just been there. Internet discussion groups are offering an unprecedented way for travelers around the globe to connect and share experiences. **Frommer's Online (www.frommers.com)** offers these message boards, as well as areas where you can pose questions to the guidebook writers themselves, in its section "Ask the Expert." **Yahoo! Travel, Expedia,** and **Travelocity** are other good sources of online travel discussion groups.

The granddaddy of specialized discussions on particular topics is **Usenet,** a collection of over 50,000 newsgroups. You'll find a comprehensive listing at **Deja News (www.dejanews.com/usenet)** or at **www.liszt.com**.

WebFlyer. www.webflyer.com
WebFlyer is a comprehensive online resource for frequent flyers and also has an excellent listing of last-minute air deals. Click on "Deal Watch" for a round-up of weekend deals on flights, hotels, and rental cars from domestic and international suppliers.

ONLINE TRAVELER'S TOOLBOX

Veteran travelers usually carry some essential items to make their trips easier. Following is a selection of online tools to smooth your journey.

Visa ATM Locator. www.visa.com/pd/atm/
MasterCard ATM Locator. www.mastercard.com/atm
Find ATMs in hundreds of cities in the United States and around the world. Both include maps for some locations and both list airport ATM locations. *Tip:* You'll usually get a better exchange rate using ATMs than exchanging traveler's checks at banks, but check in advance to see what kind of fees your bank will assess for using an overseas ATM.

Intellicast. www.intellicast.com
Weather forecasts for all 50 states and cities around the world. Note that temperatures are in Celsius for many international destinations, so don't think you'll need that winter coat for your next trip to Athens.

✪ **Mapquest. www.mapquest.com**
The best of the mapping sites that lets you choose a specific address or destination; in seconds, it will return back a map and detailed directions. It really is easier than calling, asking, and writing down directions. The site also links to special travel deals and helpful sites.

Universal Currency Converter. www.xe.net/currency
See what your dollar or pound is worth in more than a hundred other countries.

U.S. Customs Traveler Alerts. www.customs.gov/travel/travel.htm
Wondering what you're allowed to bring in to the United Sates? Check at this thorough site, which includes maximum allowance and duty fees.

2 Top Sites for Toronto
CITY GUIDES

✪ **About Toronto. toronto.about.com/aboutcanada/toronto**
This comprehensive site includes sections about Toronto's history, attractions, and events. Some of its best features are its interactive options: There are message boards about everything from sports to dining, and live chats.

Check E-Mail at Internet Cafes While Traveling

Until a few years ago, most travelers who checked their e-mail while traveling carried a laptop—an expensive and often technologically problematic option. Thankfully, Web-based free e-mail programs have made it much easier to check your mail.

Just open an account at any one of the numerous "freemail" providers—the original leaders continue to be **Hotmail** (hotmail.com), **Excite** (www.excite.com), and **Yahoo! Mail** (mail.yahoo.com), though many are available. AOL users should check out **AOL Netmail,** and **USA.NET** (www.usa.net) comes highly recommended for functionality and security. You can find hints, tips, and a mile-long list of freemail providers at **www.emailaddresses.com**.

Then, all you'll need to check your mail is a Web connection, easily available at Net cafes and copy shops around the world. After logging on, just call up your freemail's Internet address, enter your username and password, and you'll have access to your mail. From these sites, you can download all of your e-mail—even from office accounts—or your local or national Internet service provider address. There will be a section generally called "check other mail" that allows you to add the names of other e-mail servers.

The downside is that most Web-based e-mail sites allow only a maximum of 3MB capacity per mail account, which can fill up quickly. Also, message sending and receiving is not immediate; some messages may be delayed by several hours, or even days.

Internet cafes have become ubiquitous, so for a few dollars an hour you'll be able to check your mail and send messages from virtually anywhere in the world. Interestingly, Internet cafes tend to be more common in very remote areas, where they may offer the best form of access for an entire community, especially if phone lines are difficult to obtain. Surf the excellent **Net Café Guide** before leaving home (www.netcafeguide.com) for listings across the U.K. divided up by town.

Online Directory

Bizlook. www.bizlook.com
If you're a serious shopper en route to Toronto, check this site first for coupons issued by local businesses. Bizlook provides directories of retailers (clothes, books, toys, and so on) and services (like child care or dry cleaners) as well as entertainment venues and tourist attractions.

City of Toronto. www.city.toronto.on.ca
A slide show of lovely city views introduces the official municipal guide to Toronto, a straightforward source of practical information peppered with profiles of fun places to visit and announcements of festivals, free concerts, kids' events, and more.

FYI Toronto. www.fyitoronto.com
This city guide features everything you ever wanted to know about Toronto events, attractions, and activities. There's also a large database of restaurants.

Gay Toronto. www.gaytoronto.com
This site provides one-stop shopping with its gay-friendly restaurants, bars, nightclubs, guest houses, travel agencies, and other businesses and organizations.

**✪ Girl Talk Toronto: A Mini City Guide. www.journeywoman.com/
girltalk/toronto.html**
Journeywoman runs the gamut from the serious (assessing transit safety) to the
frivolously fun (such as the best places to shop for shoes). This user-friendly
site also highlights arty spots, off-the-beaten-path attractions, and the best
places for brunch, all from a female perspective.

Green Tourism Association. www.greentourism.on.ca
This is an excellent resource for eco-friendly travelers. There's information
about car-free transportation, outdoor activities and sports, and healthy dining.

Outside Toronto. www.outsidetoronto.com
Each week Outside Toronto suggests new things to see and do within a 2-hour
drive of the city: antiques shows, farmers' markets, recreational events. The
Places to Go section directs you to ongoing museums, festivals, and charming
little towns. The site provides maps, too.

Show Me Toronto. www.showmetoronto.com
Show Me will show you a large but standard directory of sites for Toronto's
arts and entertainment, restaurants, shops and services, sports, and travel
information—all divided into more than 70 subcategories.

Torinfo. www.torinfo.com
Search this site for any Toronto topic. Or visit the link-filled tourism section
(lodging, dining, attractions, events) and entertainment pages (comedy, film,
music, arts, nightlife).

Toronto.com. www.toronto.com
This site boasts articles on arts and culture as well as a hotel directory, restaurant reviews, community news, and events listings. One of its best features is
its extensive use of photographs.

**Toronto Hotel Discounts and City Guide. www.worldexecutive.com/
cityguides/toronto**
Find out how to get to and from the airport, how much to tip, what to
wear, and where to get an Internet connection in Toronto. The site also provides photographs, maps, an attractions guide, and an online hotel reservation
service.

Toronto Online. www.toronto-online.com
It's always nice to put a city in historical and cultural context before traveling
there, and this is a great tool for that purpose. A condensed history lesson
covers the 1600s through the present. A neighborhood guide describes the
character of each district. Fact sheets cover statistics, currency rates, laws, customs, and so forth. Other sections lead to attractions, restaurants, and shops.

**Toronto Seniors Community Guide. www.ageofreason.com/
projontoronto.htm**
Travelers aged 50 and over will appreciate this guide, which lists accommodations, tours, and events geared toward mature visitors. Best of all is the
discounts section, which lists special savings and deals.

✪ Tourism Toronto. www.tourism-toronto.com
If you're a journalist—or just like to travel like one—don't miss this site's
Media Room: press releases, promotional materials, and background info
about the city's neighborhoods. The rest of the much-lauded guide tells you
what's new, where to eat and sleep, what to see, and how to get great deals on
lodging, food, and entertainment. Searchable directories abound.

Where Toronto. www.wheremags.com/wheremag.nsf/Cities
Scroll down, click on "Toronto," and you'll find a featured event for the month (accessible a month or two in advance). You can also peruse select arts and entertainment listings, neighborhood profiles, restaurant reviews, and shopping tips. Links lead to lodging sites.

NEWS & MAGAZINES

The Globe and Mail. www.globeandmail.com
Based in Toronto, this national newspaper boasts arts-oriented reviews along with local and national news. One caveat: Articles are archived on this site for only 7 days, so you can't delve too far back, though you can be sure that the information posted is always fresh.

The National Post. www.nationalpost.com
Canada's new national newspaper is headquartered in Toronto, and it's site features a wealth of local theater, arts and restaurant reviews. Articles are permanently archived in a searchable database.

Toronto Life Online. www.torontolife.com
Look to this magazine's Best of T.O. section to learn where to find the city's best bets for gelato, falafel, or panini. The site also offers a restaurant section filled with short reviews, fashion articles, shopping guides, an events calendar, and golf course reviews.

The Toronto Star. www.thestar.com
There's no need to try to dig up a copy at your nearby newsstand—just get online to find weather, sports, movie listings, concert previews, and local news.

DINING GUIDES

Send Me Food. www.sendmefood.com
If you're tired from a day of sightseeing and want dinner to come to you, a visit to this site is essential. Simply select your favorite food and your Toronto neighborhood or suburb, and the guide will cook up a list of names and numbers of nearby eateries that deliver, cater, or offer takeout.

✪ **Smoke Free Dining. www.city.toronto.on.ca/health/smokefree.htm**
For those who've dined in a restaurant's non-smoking section only to discover that smoke is wafting over from the bar, here's an excellent resource. This long list of Smoke Free eateries ban smoking anywhere on their premises. This ban is voluntary, but seems to be gathering steam, and the list is frequently updated.

Taste Toronto. www.tastetoronto.com
Along with more than 200 menus for local restaurants, this site sponsors forums where gourmands and gourmets discuss fine dining, pub grub, and wine. Taste Toronto also serves up restaurant reviews and local recipes.

✪ **TorDine. www.tordine.com**
This award-winning site purports to be the best Toronto dining guide. You'll find restaurant reviews penned by average, food-loving folks, as well as coupons and special deals. You can search the directory by name, food type, or price, and you can make reservations online. Each entry gives descriptive details, from dress codes to wheelchair access.

TOP ATTRACTIONS

Canadian National Exhibition. www.theex.com
Known simply as The Ex, this annual extravaganza is a veritable circus of interactive events, live music, international dance performances, and ethnic

Online Directory

fairs combined with air shows, agricultural exhibits, laser shows, live animals, kids' activities, sports, stand-up comedy, and everything else under the Toronto sun.

CN Tower. www.cntower.ca

Toronto's best-known landmark, also the world's tallest building, now sponsors concerts, dances, holiday celebrations, and other fun stuff. Check the tower's site to learn about permanent attractions in its base and observation levels, to read the restaurant's menu, or to absorb bits of tower history and trivia.

Ontario Place. www.OntarioPlace.com

Set the kids loose among bumper boats, mazes, and adventure rides at this Toronto family fun center. The site lets you know what's showing at the IMAX theater and when to catch events like fireworks, boat shows, or a Chinese lantern festival.

Ontario Science Center. www.osc.on.ca

Sample a few of the center's 800-plus exhibits online: Omnimax films, technological exhibits, educational science games. The site keeps you up-to-date on special programs, new exhibits, show times, and prices.

SkyDome. www.skydome.com

Though this ostentatious site would suggest something more grand, SkyDome is essentially a large arena attached to a hotel and fitness club, where you can see rock concerts or professional baseball games. Check the events calendar online or take a virtual-reality tour of the facilities.

Slate Art Gallery Guide. www.slateartguide.com

Are you up for a little gallery hopping? This site will tell you where to go to see some of the best art in the greater Toronto area. Find out whose work is on display in local venues, and stay abreast of upcoming opening receptions.

Surf the Beaches, Toronto. www.wineva-oak.com

Take a photo tour of both sandy and snowy beaches lining Toronto's shoulder of Lake Ontario. Also look at this site's beach neighborhood map and guides to tourist resources, water sports, an annual jazz festival, nightlife, and specialty food and clothing shops.

Toronto Zoo. www.torontozoo.com

See elephants and white lions at the Toronto Zoo's Kesho Park, an area designed to replicate the African savanna. The zoo's site profiles other exhibits, such as the Canada beaver and the Tasmanian devil, as well as education and conservation programs. A map and basic info are included.

MUSEUMS

The McMichael Canadian Art Collection. www.mcmichael.com

Collections range from traditional Inuit art to modern multimedia design at this Toronto cultural center. Get details on exhibits, events, and hours online.

The Museum for Textiles. www.museumfortextiles.on.ca

Log cabin quilts, Japanese wedding kimonos, Burmese temple hangings, and African indigo cottons make up just part of this Toronto museum's collection. This site provides a sneak preview of select pieces along with facts about the museum's history, hours, special events, and gallery shows.

Museum of Television. www.mztv.com

As you might expect, this site features video clips showing highlights from television history. There are virtual galleries of Philco TV models, the mechanical TV era, and the 1939 World's Fair. The Exhibits page tells viewers what's showing at the physical museum in Toronto.

✪ **Royal Ontario Museum. www.rom.on.ca**
Along with a slew of science, culture, and history exhibitions, the Toronto museum hosts courses and kids' events. The site is an enticing sampler of photos, interactive games and quizzes, QuickTime movies, virtual-reality tours, and other marvels.

TAKE ME OUT TO THE BALL GAME

Toronto Maple Leafs (pro hockey)   **www.torontomapleleafs.com**
Toronto Blue Jays (pro baseball)   **www.bluejays.ca**
Toronto Argonauts (Canadian football)   **www.argonauts.on.ca**
Toronto Raptors (pro basketball)   **www.nba.com/raptors**
One of the great pleasures of visiting a major city can be enjoying a sports event. Toronto today boasts pro teams in four major sports. Consult the sites above for schedules, ticket and arena information, and player profiles.

GETTING AROUND

Toronto Transit Commission. www.city.toronto.on.ca/ttc
Toronto's public transit system is a safe and affordable way to get around town. The site provides route maps and schedules, fares, safety and security information, and an overview of special services.

Go Transit. www.gotransit.com
If you need to get from one part of the greater Toronto area to another, this site can help. Get facts about train stations and terminals in all the region's towns. Find out how to get to special events and venues, and look at schedules and fare information online.

Lester B. Pearson International Airport. www.gtaa.com
Guidelines for going through customs are included in this guide to the Toronto airport, which also lists airlines and destinations, offers tips for travelers, and provides a thorough overview of services at each of its three terminals.

3

Getting to Know Toronto

Toronto is a wonderful city in which to get lost. Start anywhere in the downtown core and walk in any direction for no more than 15 minutes. You'll see eclectic modern buildings side by side with neo-Gothic and art-deco architecture, catch a fair glimpse of the city's ethnic spectrum, and walk right into a pleasing patch of greenery.

This is a happy coincidence because the layout and organization of the city mean you *will* get lost at least once during your stay. Streets are named, not numbered, and they have a crazy-making habit of changing their monikers as they go along. Midtown must-see Avenue Road, for example, turns into Queen's Park Crescent and then into University Avenue as you head south, and Oriole Parkway if you go north. My best advice: Relax and enjoy the ride. In this chapter, you'll find information on the highways and byways and services that make Toronto tick.

1 Orientation

ARRIVING IN TORONTO
BY PLANE

Most flights arrive at **Pearson International Airport,** in the northwest corner of Metro Toronto, approximately 30 minutes from downtown. The trip may take longer during the morning rush (7 to 9am). A few (mostly commuter) flights land at the **Toronto Island Airport,** a short ferry ride from downtown.

Pearson has three terminals, served by more than 50 airlines. The most spectacular is the **Trillium Terminal 3** (☎ **905/612-5100**). This supermodern facility has moving walkways, a huge food court, and many retail stores. There is a new, equally grand terminal currently under construction, which will one day replace the existing terminals 1 and 2.

To get from the airport to downtown, take Highway 427 south to the Gardiner Expressway East. A **taxi** costs about C$36 (US$24.50). A slightly sleeker way to go is by flat-rate **limousine,** which costs around C$38–$40 (US$25.85–$27.20). Two limo services are **Aaroport** (☎ **416/745-1555**) and **AirLine** (☎ **905/676-3210**). You don't need a reservation. Most first-class hotels run their own **hotel limousine** services; check when you make your reservation.

The convenient **Airport Express bus** (☎ **905/564-6333**) travels between the airport, the bus terminal, and all major downtown hotels—Harbour Castle Westin, the Royal York, Crowne Plaza Toronto Centre, the Sheraton Centre, and the Delta

Chelsea Inn—every 20 minutes all day. The adult fare is C$12.50 (US$9) one-way, C$21.50 (US$15) round-trip; children under 11 accompanied by an adult ride free. **PW Transportation** (☎ **905/564-6333**) operates bus service between the airport and York Mills and Yorkdale subway stations every 40 minutes. The fare is C$8.30 (US$5.60) each way.

The cheapest way to go is by **subway and bus,** which takes about an hour. The **TTC** airport bus (no. 58A) travels between the Lawrence West subway station and Pearson Airport Terminal 2. The total fare of C$4 (US$2.85) includes a C$2 (US$1.35) supplement due at the airport. For more information, call ☎ **416/393-4636.**

BY TRAIN

Trains arrive at Union Station on Front Street, 1 block west of Yonge Street, opposite the Royal York Hotel. The station has direct access to the subway, so you can easily reach any Toronto destination.

VISITOR INFORMATION

For hotel, dining, and other tourist information, head to (or write to) **Tourism Toronto,** 207 Queens Quay W., Suite 590 (P.O. Box 126), Toronto, ON M5J 1A7 (☎ **800/ 363-1990** or 416/203-2600; www.tourism-toronto.com). It's in the Queens Quay Terminal at Harbourfront, and is open Monday to Friday 9am to 5pm. Take the LRT (light rapid transit system) from Union Station to the York Street stop. The Web site has up-to-the-minute city calendar and events information.

More conveniently located is the drop-in **Ontario Visitor Information Centre,** in the Eaton Centre, on Yonge Street at Dundas Street. It's on Level 1 (1 floor below street level) and is open Monday to Friday 10am to 9pm, Saturday 9:30am to 6pm, Sunday noon to 5pm.

If you're in the neighborhood, the **Community Information Centre,** 425 Adelaide St. W. (☎ **416/392-0505**), specializes in social, government, and health-service information for residents or potential residents, but staff members will try to answer questions. And if they can't, they will direct you to someone who can.

To pick up brochures and a map before you leave **Pearson International Airport,** stop by the **Transport Canada Information Centre** (☎ **905/676-3506** or 416/ 247-7678). There's one in each terminal. A staff fluent in a dozen languages can answer questions about tourist attractions, ground transportation, and more.

PUBLICATIONS & WEB SITES

Toronto has four daily newspapers: the *Globe and Mail,* the *National Post,* the *Toronto Star,* and the *Toronto Sun.* All have some local listings, but the best are in the *Star,* which lists events, concerts, theater performances, first-run films, and the like.

An even better bet are the free weeklies *Now* and *Eye,* both published on Thursday and available in news boxes and at cafes and shops around town. *Xtra!* is another weekly freebie; it lists events, seminars, and performances, particularly those of interest to the gay and lesbian community. A free annual directory called *The Pink Pages* is targeted at Torontonians, but out-of-towners will find the information about gay- and lesbian-friendly restaurants, bars, and other businesses around town quite useful. It's available at shops, restaurants, and bars along Church Street.

Where Toronto is a glossy monthly magazine that lists events, attractions, restaurants and shops; it's available free at most hotels in the city and at some restaurants in the Theater District. *Toronto Life* is an award-winning lifestyle magazine that has excellent listings of kids' events, theater, speeches, and art exhibitions; its April issue

Underground Toronto

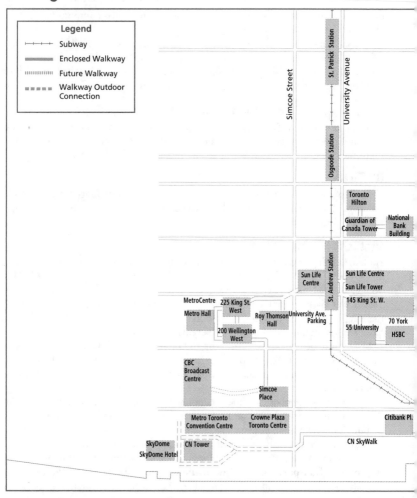

always contains a dining guide. *Toronto Life Fashion* magazine will be of interest to serious shoppers.

If you have Internet access, log on to the **MyToronto** Web site (www.myto.net) for its extensive restaurant reviews, events listings and feature articles. *Toronto Life's* Web site (www.torontolife.com) is another popular choice, particularly for its restaurant reviews and contests. **Toronto.com** (www.toronto.com), operated by the *Toronto Star*, has events, shopping, and services listings.

CITY LAYOUT

Toronto is laid out in a grid system . . . with a few interesting exceptions. **Yonge Street** (pronounced *Young*) is the main north-south street, stretching from Lake Ontario in the south well beyond Highway 401 in the north. Yonge Street divides western cross streets from eastern cross streets. The main east-west artery is **Bloor Street,** which cuts through the heart of downtown.

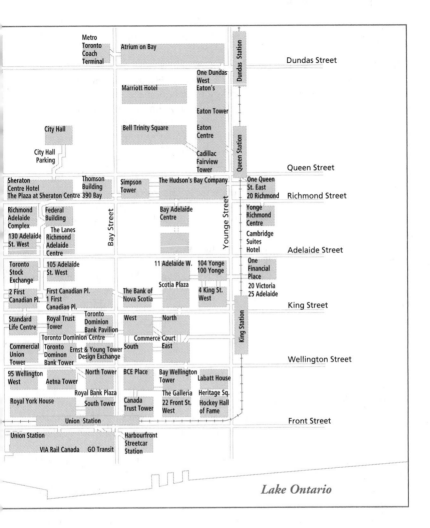

Downtown Toronto map showing:

Metro Toronto Coach Terminal • Atrium on Bay • Dundas Station • Dundas Street

Marriott Hotel • One Dundas West • Eaton's • Eaton Tower

City Hall • Bell Trinity Square • Eaton Centre

City Hall Parking • Cadillac Fairview Tower • Queen Station

Sheraton Centre Hotel • Thomson Building • Simpson Tower • The Hudson's Bay Company • One Queen St. East • Queen Street

The Plaza at Sheraton Centre • 390 Bay • 20 Richmond • Richmond Street

Richmond Adelaide Complex • Federal Building • Bay Adelaide Centre • Yonge Richmond Centre

130 Adelaide St. West • The Lanes • Richmond Adelaide Centre • Cambridge Suites Hotel

Bay Street • Adelaide Street

Toronto Stock Exchange • 105 Adelaide St. West • 11 Adelaide W. • 104 Yonge 100 Yonge • One Financial Place

2 First Canadian Pl. • First Canadian Pl. 1 First Canadian Pl. • Scotia Plaza • The Bank of Nova Scotia • 4 King St. West • 20 Victoria 25 Adelaide • King Street

Standard Life Centre • Royal Trust Tower • Toronto Dominion Bank Pavilion • West • North • King Station

Commercial Union Tower • Toronto Dominion Bank Tower • Ernst & Young Tower Design Exchange • Commerce Court South • East • Wellington Street

Toronto Dominion Centre • Commerce Court

95 Wellington West • North Tower • BCE Place • Bay Wellington Tower • Labatt House

Aetna Tower • Royal Bank Plaza • The Galleria • Heritage Sq.

Royal York House • South Tower • Canada Trust Tower • 22 Front St. West • Hockey Hall of Fame • Front Street

Union Station

Union Station • VIA Rail Canada • GO Transit • Harbourfront Streetcar Station

Yonge Street

Lake Ontario

"Downtown" usually refers to the area from Eglinton Avenue south to the lake, between Spadina Avenue in the west and Jarvis Street in the east. Because this is such a large area, I have divided it into **downtown** (from the lake north to College/Carlton St.), **midtown** (College/Carlton St. north to Davenport Rd.), and **uptown** (north of Davenport Rd.). In the first area, you'll find the lakeshore attractions—Harbourfront, Ontario Place, Fort York, Exhibition Place, and the Toronto Islands. It also holds the CN Tower, City Hall, SkyDome, Chinatown, the Art Gallery, and the Eaton Centre. Midtown includes the Royal Ontario Museum, the Gardiner Museum, the University of Toronto, Markham Village, and chic Yorkville, a prime area for browsing and dining alfresco. Uptown is a fast-growing residential and entertainment area for the young, hip, and well heeled. North Toronto is another burgeoning area, with new theaters and galleries and some excellent dining; it's not yet a prime tourist destination, but it gets a few mentions throughout this guide.

Toronto sprawls so widely that quite a few of its primary attractions lie outside the downtown core. They include the Ontario Science Centre, the Toronto Zoo,

Canada's Wonderland, and the McMichael art collection. Be prepared to journey somewhat.

UNDERGROUND TORONTO It is not enough to know the streets of Toronto; you also need to navigate the labyrinth of walkways beneath the pavement. If the weather's bad, you can eat, sleep, dance, shop, and go to the theater without even donning a coat. Consult our map, "Underground Toronto," on p. 38, or look for the large, clear underground PATH maps throughout the concourse.

You can walk from the Dundas subway station south through the Eaton Centre until you hit Queen Street, turn west to the Sheraton Centre, then head south. You'll pass through the Richmond-Adelaide Centre, First Canadian Place, and Toronto Dominion Centre, and go all the way (through the dramatic Royal Bank Plaza) to Union Station. En route, branches lead off to the stock exchange, Sun Life Centre, and Metro Hall. Additional walkways link Simcoe Plaza to 200 Wellington West and to the CBC Broadcast Centre. Other walkways run around Bloor Street and Yonge Street and elsewhere in the city.

While its wide-ranging network makes this an excellent way to get around the downtown core when the weather is grim, the underground city has its own attractions too. First Canadian Place in particular is known for hosting free lunch-hour lectures, opera and dance performances, and art exhibits.

FINDING AN ADDRESS This isn't as easy as it should be. Your best bet is to call ahead and ask for directions, including landmarks and subway stations. Even the locals need to do this.

Neighborhoods in Brief

Most of the following neighborhoods are in the downtown city center.

The Toronto Islands These three islands in Lake Ontario—Ward's, Algonquin, and Centre—are home to a handful of residents—and no cars. They're a welcome spring and summer haven where Torontonians can go to in-line skate, bicycle, boat, and picnic. Centre Island, the most visited, holds the children's theme park Centreville. Catch the ferry at the foot of Bay Street by the Westin Hotel.

Harbourfront/Lakefront The landfill where the railroad yards and dock facilities once stood is now a glorious playground opening onto the lake. This is home to Queen's Quay, to a major antiques market, and to the Harbourfront Centre, one of the most important literary, artistic, and cultural venues in Canada.

Financial District Toronto's major banks and insurance companies have their head-quarters here, from Front Street north to Queen Street, between Yonge and York streets. It's the location of Toronto's first skyscrapers; fortunately, some of the older structures have been preserved. Ultramodern BCE Place incorporated the façade of a historic bank building into its design.

Old Town/St. Lawrence Market During the 19th century, this area, east of Yonge Street between the Esplanade and Adelaide Street, was the focal point of the community. Today the market's still going strong, and attractions like the glorious St. James Cathedral draw visitors.

Theater District An area of dense cultural development, this area stretches from Front Street north to Queen Street, and from Bay Street west to Bathurst Street. King Street West is home to most of the important sights, including the Royal Alexandra Theatre, Princess of Wales Theatre, Roy Thomson Hall, and Metro Hall. Farther south are the Convention Centre and the CN Tower.

Chinatown   Dundas Street West from University Avenue to Spadina Avenue, and north to College Street are the boundaries of Chinatown. As the Chinese community has grown, it has extended along Dundas Street and north along Spadina Avenue. Here you'll see a fascinating mixture of old and new. Hole-in-the-wall restaurants that have been in business for years share the sidewalks with glitzy shopping centers built with Hong Kong money.

Yonge Street   Toronto's main commercial drag, Yonge Street is lined with stores and restaurants of all sorts. It sometimes segues into the seedy, particularly just outside the Eaton Centre at Dundas, but a massive restoration and cleanup project is under way.

Queen Street West   This stretch of Queen Street from University Avenue to Bathurst Street is youngish, hip, and home to many of the city's up-and-coming fashion designers. It offers an eclectic mix—antiques stores, secondhand bookshops, fashion boutiques, and antique clothing emporiums. It's also home to Toronto's gourmet ghetto, with bistro after trattoria after cafe lining the street. There's excellent food along this strip, but it's too frequently served with heaps of attitude. Despite the intrusion of such mega-retailers as Club Monaco and the GAP, many independently owned boutiques flourish.

Queen's Park and the University   Home to the Ontario Legislature and many of the colleges and buildings that make up the University of Toronto, this neighborhood extends from College Street to Bloor Street between Spadina Avenue and Bay Street.

Church Street   Between Gerrard Street and Bloor Street East along Church Street lies the heart of Toronto's gay and lesbian community. Restaurants, cafes, and bars fill this relaxed, casual neighborhood. Church Street is where 19th-century Toronto's grandest cathedrals stood.

Cabbagetown   Once described by writer Hugh Garner as the largest Anglo-Saxon slum in North America, this gentrified neighborhood of Victorian and Edwardian homes stretches east of Parliament Street to the Don Valley between Gerrard Street and Bloor Street. The sought-after residential district got its name because the front lawns of the homes occupied by Irish immigrants (who settled here in the late 1800s) were, it is said, covered with row upon row of cabbages. Toronto's only inner-city farm, Riverdale, is at the southeastern end of this district.

Yorkville   Originally a village outside the city, this area north and west of Bloor and Yonge streets became Toronto's Haight-Ashbury in the 1960s. Now, it's a haute, haute, haute district filled with designer boutiques, galleries, cafes, and restaurants.

The Annex   Like Cabbagetown, this area fell from grace for many years; today much of it has been lovingly restored. It stretches from Bedford Road to Bathurst Street, and from Harbord Street to Dupont Avenue. Many of the tremendous turn-of-the-century homes are still single-family dwellings, though as you walk west it segues into the U of T student ghetto. Revered urban-planning guru Jane Jacobs has long called this area home.

Rosedale   Meandering tree-lined streets with elegant homes and manicured lawns are the hallmarks of this residential community, from Yonge and Bloor streets northeast to Castle Frank and the Moore Park Ravine. Named after Sheriff Jarvis's residence, its name is synonymous with Toronto's wealthy elite.

Koreatown   The bustling blocks along Bloor Street West between Bathurst and Christie streets are filled with Korean restaurants, alternative-medicine practitioners such as herbalists and acupuncturists, and shops filled with made-in-Korea merchandise. This neighborhood was one of the first Korean settlements in Toronto, though now it is primarily a business district.

Forest Hill   Second to Rosedale as the city's prime residential area, Forest Hill is home to Upper Canada College and Bishop Strachan School for girls. It stretches west of Avenue Road between St. Clair Avenue and Eglinton Avenue.

Little Italy   A thriving, lively neighborhood filled with open-air cafes, trattorias, and shops serving the Italian community along College Street between Euclid and Shaw. The trendies can't seem to stay away, which has driven up prices in this once inexpensive neighborhood.

The Beaches   Communal, youthful, safe, and comfortable. These adjectives best describe the Beaches, just 15 minutes from downtown at the end of the Queen Street East streetcar line. It was a summer resort in the mid-1800s, and its boardwalk and beach continue to make it a casual, family-oriented neighborhood.

The East End—the Danforth   This continuation of Bloor Street across the Don Valley Viaduct is widely known as **Greektown.** Its main drag, Danforth Avenue, is lined with old-style Greek tavernas and hip Mediterranean bars and restaurants that are crowded from early evening until early morning. The densest wining-and-dining area starts at Broadview Avenue and runs 4 blocks east.

Eglinton Avenue   The neighborhood surrounding the intersection of Yonge Street and Eglinton Avenue is jokingly known as "Young and Eligible." It's a bustling area filled with restaurants, including some of the town's top-rated, and nightclubs. To the east it intersects with the 600-acre Sunnybrook park system and with the Ontario Science Centre.

North York   Times are booming in this area, which was a separate political entity from Toronto until 1997. Many companies have relocated their offices from downtown to the Yonge and Sheppard areas, fueling the growth. There's still not too much for sightseers except the Ford Centre for the Performing Arts, though there are a few superb restaurants just a bit north. The area is set to become more popular: A tunnel is currently been excavated under Sheppard Avenue to make way for a new subway line.

2 Getting Around

BY PUBLIC TRANSPORTATION

The **Toronto Transit Commission,** or TTC (☎ **416/393-4636** daily from 7am to 10pm for information), operates the subway, bus, streetcar, and light rapid transit (LRT) system.

    Fares (including transfers to buses or streetcars) are C$2/US$1.35 (or 10 tickets for C$17/US$11.60) for adults. Students under 20 and seniors pay C$1.40/US$1 (8 tickets for C$7/US$4.75), and children under 12 pay C50¢/US35¢ (10 tickets for C$4/US$2.85). You can buy a special day pass C$7 (US$4.75) that's good for unlimited travel for one person after 9:30am on weekdays, and good for up to six people (a maximum of two adults) anytime on Sunday and holidays. There's no Saturday pass, and no multiple-day deals.

    For surface transportation, you need a ticket, a token, or exact change. You can buy tickets and tokens at subway entrances and at authorized stores that display the sign TTC TICKETS MAY BE PURCHASED HERE. Bus drivers do not sell tickets, nor will they make change. Always obtain a free transfer *where you board the train or bus,* in case you need it. In the subways, use the push-button machine just inside the entrance. On streetcars and buses, ask the driver for a transfer.

THE SUBWAY   It's a joy to ride—fast, quiet, and clean—and very simple to use. There are two lines—Bloor-Danforth and Yonge-University-Spadina—that basically

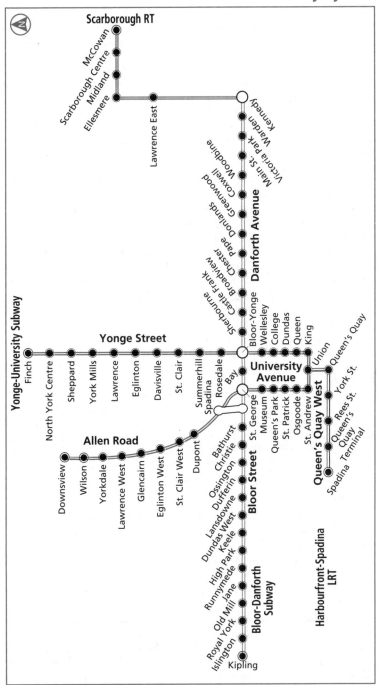

The TTC Subway System

Scarborough RT

McCowan
Scarborough Centre
Midland
Ellesmere

Lawrence East

Kennedy
Warden
Victoria Park
Main St.
Woodbine
Coxwell
Greenwood
Donlands
Pape
Chester
Broadview
Castle Frank
Sherbourne

Danforth Avenue

Yonge-University Subway

Yonge Street

Finch
North York Centre
Sheppard
York Mills
Lawrence
Eglinton
Davisville
St. Clair
Summerhill
Rosedale
Bay
Bloor-Yonge
Wellesley
College
Dundas
Queen
King
Union

University Avenue

St. George
Museum
Queen's Park
St. Patrick
Osgoode
St. Andrew

Queen's Quay
York St.
Rees St.
Queen's Quay
Spadina

Queen's Quay West

Queen's Quay Terminal

Spadina

Allen Road

Downsview
Wilson
Yorkdale
Lawrence West
Glencairn
Eglinton West
St. Clair West
Dupont
Bathurst
Christie
Ossington
Dufferin
Lansdowne
Dundas West
Keele
High Park
Runnymede
Jane
Old Mill
Royal York
Islington
Kipling

Bloor Street

Bloor-Danforth Subway

Harbourfront-Spadina LRT

form a cross. The Bloor Street east-west line runs from Kipling Avenue in the west to Kennedy Road in the east (where it connects with Scarborough Rapid Transit to Scarborough Centre and McCowan Rd.). The Yonge Street north-south line runs from Finch Avenue in the north to Union Station (Front St.) in the south. From there, it loops north along University Avenue and connects with the Bloor line at the St. George station. A Spadina extension runs north from St. George to Downsview station at Sheppard Avenue.

The light rapid transit (LRT) system connects downtown to Harbourfront. The fare is one ticket or token. It runs from Union Station along Queen's Quay to Spadina, with stops at Queen's Quay ferry docks, York Street, Simcoe Street, and Rees Street, then continues up Spadina to the Spadina subway station. The transfer from the subway to the LRT (and vice versa) at Union Station is free.

The subway operates Monday to Saturday 6am to 1:30am, Sunday 9am to 1:30am. From 1am to 5:30am, the Blue Night Network operates on basic surface routes. It runs about every 30 minutes. For route information, pick up a "Ride Guide" at subway entrances or call ☎ **416/393-4636.** Multilingual information is available. You can also use the automated information service at ☎ **416/393-8663.**

Smart commuters park their cars at subway terminal stations at Kipling, Islington, Finch, Wilson, Warden, Kennedy, York Mills, Victoria Park, and Keele. Certain conditions apply. Call ☎ **416/393-8663** for details. You'll have to get there very early.

BUSES & STREETCARS   Where the subway leaves off, buses and streetcars take over. They run east-west and north-south along the city's arteries. When you pay your fare (on bus, streetcar, or subway), always pick up a transfer, so that if you want to transfer to another mode of transportation, you won't have to pay another fare. For complete TTC information, call ☎ **416/393-4636.**

BY TAXI

As usual, this is an expensive mode of transportation. It's C$2.50 (US$1.80) the minute you step in, and C25¢ (US20¢) for each additional 0.235 kilometer (.145 mile). Cab fares can quickly mount up, especially during rush hours. You can hail a cab on the street, find one in line in front of a big hotel, or call one of the major companies—**Diamond** (☎ **416/366-6868**), **Royal** (☎ **416/777-9222**), or **Metro** (☎ **416/504-8294**). If you experience problems with cab service, call the Metro Licensing Commission (☎ **416/392-3082**).

BY CAR

Toronto is a rambling city, but that doesn't mean that a car is the best way to get around. Toronto has the dubious distinction of being recognized as the worst city in Canada in which to drive. It's gotten so bad that there are government proposals to monitor certain intersections with cameras. Driving can be a frustrating experience because of the high volume of traffic, drivers' disregard for red lights, and meager but pricey parking options. This is particularly true downtown, where traffic inches along and parking lots are scarce.

RENTAL CARS   If you decide to rent a car, try to make arrangements in advance during the high season. Companies with outlets at Pearson International Airport include **Thrifty** (☎ **800/367-2277**), **Budget** (☎ **800/527-0700**), **Avis** (☎ **800/ 331-1084**), **Hertz** (☎ **800/654-3001**), **National** (☎ **800/227-7368**), and **Enterprise** (☎ **800/736-8222**). Keep in mind that there's usually a steep fee when you rent a vehicle in one city and drop it off it in another. The rental fee depends on the type of car you want, but the starting point is around C$45 (US$32.50) a day—not including the 14% tax. This does not include insurance, though if you pay with a particular credit card, you might get automatic coverage (check with your credit card issuer before you go). Be sure to read the fine print of the rental agreement—some companies add conditions that will boost your bill if you don't fulfill certain obligations, like filling the gas tank before returning the car.

Note: If you're under 25, check with the company—many will rent on a cash-only basis, some only if you have a credit card, and others will not rent to you at all.

PARKING   Parking lots downtown run about C$4 to $6 (US$2.85) per half hour, with a C$16 to $20 (US$10.90 to $13.60) maximum between 7am and 6pm. After 6pm and on Sunday, rates drop to around C$8 (US$5.45). Generally the city-owned lots, marked with a big green "P," are slightly cheaper than private facilities. Observe the parking restrictions—otherwise the city will tow your car away, and it'll cost more than C$100 (US$68) to get it back.

DRIVING RULES   A right turn at a red light is permitted after coming to a full stop, unless posted otherwise. The driver and front-seat passengers must wear seat belts; if you're caught not wearing one, you'll incur a substantial fine. The speed limit in the city is 50kmph (30 m.p.h.). You must stop at pedestrian crosswalks. If you are following a streetcar and it stops, you must stop well back from the rear doors so passengers can exit easily and safely. (Where there are concrete safety islands in the middle of the street for streetcar stops, this rule does not apply, but exercise care nonetheless.) Radar detectors are illegal.

BY FERRY

Metro Parks operates ferries that travel to the Toronto Islands. Call ☎ **416/392-8193** for schedules and information. Round-trip fares are C$4 (US$2.85) adults, C$2 (US$1.35) seniors and students 15 to 19, C$1 (US70¢) for children under 15.

BY BICYCLE

Toronto is one of the best biking cities in North America. Getting around on two wheels is safe, and many major streets have bike lanes. See "Cycling," in chapter 6, for more details. Tourism Toronto distributes a pamphlet that outlines biking routes. The Toronto Islands, the Beaches, Harbourfront/Lakefront, High Park, and Sunnyside (just south of High Park) are all great biking areas.

You can **rent bicycles** at Harbourfront (☎ **416/973-3000**), across from Queen's Quay, year-round; on Centre Island from **Toronto Island Bicycle Rental** (☎ **416/ 203-0009**) May to September; and year-round at **High Park Cycle and Sports,** 24 Ronson Dr. (☎ **416/614-6689**). Prices range from C$12 to $24 (US$8.15 to $16.30) per day.

Fast Facts: Toronto

Airport   See "Getting There," in chapter 2.

Area Code   Toronto's area code is **416;** outside the city, the code is **905.**

Baby-Sitting   Hotel concierges can suggest reliable sitters if there aren't child-care facilities on-site. In a pinch, call **Care-on-Call** (☎ **416/975-1313**), a 24-hour service.

Business Hours   Banks are generally open Monday to Thursday 10am to 3pm, Friday 10am to 6pm. Most stores are open Monday to Wednesday 10am to 6pm and Saturday and Sunday 10am to 5pm, with extended hours (until 8 to 9:30pm) on Thursday and usually Friday.

Car Rentals See "Getting Around," earlier in this chapter.

Climate See "When to Go," in chapter 2.

Currency Exchange Generally, the best place to exchange your currency is at an ATM or bank. You can also change money at the airport, but at a less favorable rate.

Dentist For emergency services from 8am till midnight, call the **Dental Emergency Service** (☎ **416/485-7121**). After midnight, your best bet is the **Toronto Hospital,** 200 Elizabeth St. (☎ **416/340-3948**). Otherwise, ask the front-desk staff or concierge at your hotel.

Doctor The staff or concierge at your hotel should be able to help you locate a doctor. You can also call the **College of Physicians and Surgeons,** 80 College St. (☎ **416/967-2600,** ext. 626), for a referral between 9am to 5pm. See also "Emergencies," below.

Documents See "Visitor Information & Entry Requirements," in chapter 2.

Driving Rules See "Getting Around," earlier in this chapter.

Electricity It's the same as in the United States—110 volts, 50 cycles, AC.

Embassies/Consulates All embassies are in Ottawa, the national capital. They include the **Australian High Commission,** 50 O'Connor St., Suite 710, Ottawa, ON K1P 6L2 (☎ **613/236-0841**); the **British High Commission,** 80 Elgin St., Ottawa, ON K1P 5K7 (☎ **613/237-1530**); the **Irish Embassy,** 130 Albert St., Ottawa, ON K1P 5G4 (☎ **613/ 233-6281**); the **New Zealand High Commission,** 727–99 Bank St., Ottawa, ON K1P 6G3 (☎ **613/238-5991**); the **South African High Commission,** 15 Sussex Dr., Ottawa, ON K1M 1M8 (☎ **613/744-0330**); and the **U.S. Embassy,** 100 Wellington St., Ottawa, ON K1P 5T1 (☎ **613/238-4470**). Consulates in Toronto include **Australian Consulate-General,** 175 Bloor St. E., Suite 314, at Church Street (☎ **416/323-1155**); **British Consulate-General,** 777 Bay St., Suite 2800, at College (☎ **416/593-1290**); and the **U.S. Consulate,** 360 University Ave. (☎ **416/595-1700**).

Emergencies Call ☎ **911** for fire, police, or ambulance. The **Toronto General Hospital,** 200 Elizabeth St., provides 24-hour emergency service (☎ **416/ 340-3946** for emergency or 416/340-4611 for information). Also see "Hospitals," below.

Hospitals In the downtown core, go to **Toronto General,** 200 Elizabeth St. (☎ **416/340-4611,** or 416/340-3946 for emergency); **St. Michael's,** 30 Bond St. (☎ **416/360-4000,** or 416/864-5094 for emergency); or **Mount Sinai,** 600 University Ave. (☎ **416/596-4200,** or 416/586-5054 for emergency). Also downtown is the **Hospital for Sick Children,** 555 University Ave. (☎ **416/ 813-1500**). Uptown there's **Sunnybrook Hospital,** 2075 Bayview Ave., north of Eglinton (☎ **416/480-6100,** or 416/480-4207 for emergency). In the eastern part of the city, go to **Toronto East General Hospital,** 825 Coxwell Ave. (☎ **416/ 461-8272,** or 416/469-6435 for emergency).

Hot Lines **Poison Information Centre** (☎ 416/813-5900). **Distress Centre** suicide prevention line (☎ 416/598-1121). **Rape Crisis Line** (☎ 416/ 597-8808). **Assaulted Women's Help Line** (☎ 416/863-0511). **AIDS & Sexual Health InfoLine** (☎ 800/668-2437). **Toronto Prayer Line** (☎ 416/ 929-1500). For kids or teens in distress, there's **Kids Help Phone** (☎ 800/ 668-6868).

Laundry/Dry Cleaning   Bloor Laundromat, 598 Bloor St. W., at Bathurst Street (☎ **416/588-6600**), is conveniently located. At the **Laundry Lounge,** 531 Yonge St., at Wellesley Street (☎ **416/975-4747**), you can do your wash while sipping a cappuccino and watching TV in the lounge. It's open daily 7am to 11pm. **Careful Hand Laundry & Dry Cleaners Ltd.** has outlets at 195 Davenport Rd. (☎ **416/923-1200**), 1415 Bathurst St. (☎ **416/ 530-1116**), and 1844 Avenue Rd. (☎ **416/787-6006**); for pickup and delivery, call ☎ **416/787-6006.**

Liquor Laws   The minimum drinking age is 19. Drinking hours are daily 11am to 2am. The government is the only retail vendor. **Liquor Control Board of Ontario** (LCBO) stores sell liquor, wine, and some beers. They're open Monday to Saturday. Most are open from 10am to 6pm; some stay open evenings, and a few are open Sunday from noon to 5pm.

Wine lovers will want to check out **Vintages** stores (also operated by the LCBO), which carry a more extensive, specialized selection of wines. The most convenient downtown locations are in the lower-level concourse of **Hazelton Lanes** (☎ **416/924-9463**) and at Queen's Quay (☎ **416/864-6777**). The **Wine Rack,** 560 Queen St. W. (☎ **416/504-3647**), and 77 Wellesley St. E., at Church (☎ **416/923-9393**), sells only Ontario wines.

Most branches of the **Beer Store** (also part of the LCBO) are open Monday to Friday 10am to 10pm, Saturday 10am to 8pm. There's a downtown location at 614 Queen St. W. (☎ **416/504-4665**).

Lost Property   If you leave something on a bus, a streetcar, or the subway, call the **TTC Lost Articles Office** (☎ **416/393-4100**) at the Bay Street subway station. It's open Monday to Friday 8am to 5pm.

Luggage Storage/Lockers   Lockers are available at Union Station and at the Eaton Centre.

Mail   Postage for letters and postcards to the United States costs C55¢ (US40¢); overseas, C90¢ (US65¢). Mailing letters and postcards within Canada costs C45¢ (US30¢).

Maps   Free maps of Toronto are available in every terminal at **Pearson International Airport** (look for the Transport Canada Information Centre signs), the Metropolitan Toronto Convention & Visitors Association at **Harbourfront,** and the Visitor Information Centre in the **Eaton Centre,** on Yonge Street at Dundas Street. Convenience stores and bookstores sell a greater variety of maps. Or try **Canada Map Company,** 63 Adelaide E., between Yonge and Church streets (☎ **416/362-9297**), or **Open Air Books and Maps,** 25 Toronto St., near Yonge and Adelaide streets (☎ **416/363-0719**).

Newspapers/Magazines   The four daily newspapers are the *Globe and Mail,* the *National Post,* the *Toronto Star,* and the *Toronto Sun. Eye* and *Now* are free arts-and-entertainment weeklies. *Xtra!* is a free weekly targeted at the gay and lesbian community. In addition, many English-language ethnic newspapers serve Toronto's Portuguese, Hungarian, Italian, East Indian, Korean, Chinese, and Caribbean communities. *Toronto Life* is the major monthly city magazine; its sister publication is *Toronto Life Fashion. Where Toronto* is usually free at hotels and some Theater District restaurants.

Pharmacies   One big chain is **Pharma Plus,** which has a store at 68 Wellesley St., at Church Street (☎ **416/924-7760**). It's open daily 8am to midnight. Other Pharma Plus branches are in College Park, Manulife Centre, Commerce

Court, and First Canadian Place. The only 24-hour drugstore near downtown is **Shopper's Drug Mart,** 700 Bay St., at Gerrard Street West (☎ **416/979-2424**).

Police   In a life-threatening emergency, call ☎ **911.** For all other matters, contact the Metro police, 40 College St. (☎ **416/808-2222**).

Post Office   Postal services are available at convenience and drug stores. Almost all sell stamps, and many have a separate counter where you can ship packages from 8:30am to 5pm. Look for the sign in the window indicating such services. There are also post-office windows in **Atrium on Bay** (☎ **416/506-0911**), in **Commerce Court** (☎ **416/956-7452**), and at the **TD Centre** (☎ **416/ 360-7105**).

Radio   The Canadian Broadcasting Corporation offers a great mix of intelligent discussion and commentary as well as drama and music. In Toronto, the **CBC** broadcasts on 740AM and 94.1FM. **CHIN** (1540AM and 100.7FM) will get you in touch with the ethnic and multicultural scene in the city; it broadcasts in more than 30 languages.

Rest Rooms   Finding a public rest room is usually not difficult. Most tourist attractions have them, as do hotels, department stores, and public buildings. There are rest rooms at major subway stations such as Yonge/Bloor, but they are best avoided.

Safety   As large cities go, Toronto is generally safe, but be alert and use common sense, particularly at night. The Yonge/Bloor, Dundas, and Union subway stations are favorites with pickpockets. In the downtown area, Moss Park is considered one of the toughest areas to police. Avoid Allan Gardens and other parks at night.

Taxes   The provincial retail sales tax is 8%; on accommodations it's 5%. There is an additional 7% national goods-and-services tax (GST).

In general, nonresidents may apply for a tax refund. They can recover the accommodations tax, the sales tax, and the GST for nondisposable merchandise that will be exported for use, provided it is removed from Canada within 60 days of purchase. The following do not qualify for rebate: meals and restaurant charges, alcohol, tobacco, gas, car rentals, and such services as dry cleaning and shoe repair.

The quickest and easiest way to secure the refund is to stop at a duty-free shop at the border. You must have proper receipts with GST registration numbers. Or you can apply through the mail, but it will take about 4 weeks to receive your refund. For an application form and information, write or call **Visitor Rebate Program, Revenue Canada,** Summerside Tax Center, Summerside, PEI C1N 6C6 (☎ **902/432-5608**), *well in advance* of your trip. You can also contact **Ontario Travel,** Queen's Park, Toronto, ON M7A 2R9 (☎ **800/668-2746** or 416/314-0944).

Taxis   See "Getting Around," earlier in this chapter.

Telephone   A local call from a telephone booth costs C25¢ (US20¢). Watch out for hotel surcharges on local and long-distance calls; often a local call will cost at least C$1 (US70¢) from a hotel room. The United States and Canada are on the same long-distance system. To make a long-distance call between the United States and Canada, use the area codes as you would at home. Canada's international prefix is **1.**

Time   Toronto is on eastern time. Daylight saving time is in effect from April to October.

Tipping   Basically it's the same as in major U.S. cities: 15% in restaurants, 10% to 15% for taxis, C$1 (US70¢) per bag for porters, C$2 (US$1.35) per day for hotel housekeepers.

Transit Information   For information on the subway, bus, streetcar, and light rapid transit (LRT) system, call ☎ **416/393-4636.**

Weather   Call the **talking yellow pages** (☎ **416/292-1010**) for a current weather report and lots of other information.

4 Accommodations

Toronto has no shortage of hotels. Whether you're seeking old-world elegance in a historic building or looking for all the conveniences of the office in your home away from home, you'll find it here. But there is one catch: Bargains are hard to come by, particularly in the downtown core.

The city has become increasingly popular with both business and leisure travelers, and demand has driven prices skyward. In exchange for proximity to top attractions like the Harbourfront Centre, SkyDome, and the Eaton Centre, even budget hotels charge more than C$100 (US$68) a night in the high season, which runs from April through October. Factor in the 5% accommodations tax and the 7% GST (which are refundable to nonresidents), and you're looking at spending a sizable sum of money.

There are some ways around the problem. First, always ask for a discount when you book your accommodations. Even the most expensive luxury hotel will reduce its rates during the low season and on weekends, and sometimes simply because the hotel isn't full. This reduction can be anywhere from 20% to 50%—after all, having a guest pay a reduced rate is much preferred to having an empty room that generates no revenue.

Do not be shy—always ask for a deal. If you belong to a group (such as the military, seniors, students, or an auto club), so much the better. You'll qualify for an instant discount as long as you have appropriate ID. Members of frequent flyer clubs may qualify for discounts, room upgrades, or other perks—if they ask for them. A hotel may offer special packages, which might include theater tickets, meals, or museum passes with the cost of your accommodations. At the risk of sounding like a broken record, I will say it again: Always ask for a deal.

When you make your reservations, it's important to keep in mind what you're planning to see and do. Toronto is a vast metropolis with attractions, dining districts, and ethnic communities scattered throughout. If you're spending money and time to reach the areas that interest you, even a great deal is no bargain.

I have grouped accommodations by price and location. Most are in the neighborhoods defined in chapter 3 as **downtown, midtown,** and **uptown.** I've also included a few hotels to the east of the city and close to Pearson International Airport.

AN IMPORTANT NOTE ON PRICES The prices quoted in this chapter are rack rates; discounts can knock the price down as much as

50%. The 5% accommodations tax and the 7% GST are refunded to nonresidents upon application (see "Taxes" under "Fast Facts: Toronto," in chapter 3).

A NOTE TO NONSMOKERS   Hotels that reserve floors for nonsmokers are now commonplace, so we don't single them out in this guide. However, people who want a smoke-free room should make that clear when making a reservation. Rooms for smokers are concentrated on particular floors, and the rooms and even the hallways in those areas tend to smell strongly of smoke, even in the cleanest hotels. Never assume that you'll get a smoke-free room if you don't specifically request one.

BED & BREAKFASTS   A B&B can be an excellent—and inexpensive—alternative to standard hotel accommodations. **Toronto Bed & Breakfast,** 253 College St., P.O. Box 269, Toronto, ON M5T 1R5 (☎ 416/588-8800; www.torontobandb.com), has a lengthy list of accommodations in the city. Doubles cost roughly C$65 to $95 (US$44 to $65). The organization will make your reservation and send you a confirmation. The phones are staffed Monday to Friday 9am to noon and 2pm to 7pm. The **Downtown Association of Bed-and-Breakfast Guesthouses,** P.O. Box 190, Station B, Toronto, ON M5T 2W1 (☎ 416/368-1420; www.bnbinfo.com), lists only nonsmoking B&Bs. Doubles range from C$60 to $130 (US$41 to $88.40). **Bed and Breakfast Homes of Toronto,** P.O. Box 46093, College Park Post Office, 44 Yonge St., Toronto, ON M5B 2L8 (☎ 416/363-6362; www.bbcanada.com), is a cooperative of about 20 independent B&B operators. Doubles run C$60 to $100 (US$41 to $68).

ACCOMMODATIONS SERVICES   If you're having trouble finding a hotel, call **Accommodations Toronto** (☎ 800/363-1990 or 416/203-2500), which represents more than 100 member properties throughout Toronto.

FOR TRAVELERS IN NEED   If you run into trouble once you arrive in Toronto, call the **Travelers Aid Society** (☎ 416/366-7788); the organization provides shelter for people in crisis situations.

1 Downtown

Downtown runs from the lakeshore to College/Carlton Street, bordered on the west by Spadina Avenue and on the east by Jarvis Street. This area encompasses the Financial District, CN Tower, Air Canada Centre, the Theater District, Chinatown, the Eaton Centre, and the Art Gallery of Ontario.

VERY EXPENSIVE

Cambridge Suites Hotel. 15 Richmond St. E. (near Yonge St.), Toronto, ON M5C 1N2. ☎ 800/463-1990 or 416/368-1990. Fax 416/601-3751. www.cambridgesuiteshotel.com. 231 units. A/C MINIBAR TV TEL. C$330–$380 (US$224–$258) double. Rates include continental breakfast. AE, DC, DISC, ER, MC, V. Parking C$16 (US$10.90). Subway: Queen.

This hotel has three main selling points: location, location, location. In the heart of the Financial District, the all-suite hotel caters to a corporate crowd that never wants to be more than a few steps from the office. Units start at 550 square feet and move up to deluxe duplexes. The amenities for business travelers are solid. If you can drag yourself away from the comfy desk area, which has two two-line telephones and a fax, you can enjoy some of the comforts of home: refrigerator, microwave, and dining ware, plus coffee, tea, and snacks. (Hand over your shopping list, and the staff will stock the fridge, too.) And of course, the luxury penthouse suites are something else, with Jacuzzis and breathtaking views. The rooms were fully refurbished in spring 2000.

   Dining: The cozy bar is a treat at the end of the day—servers ply guests with nonstop nibbles. The dining room serves competent standard fare, though given the wealth of wonderful food in this neighborhood, it's hard to imagine choosing to dine in.

Downtown Toronto Accommodations

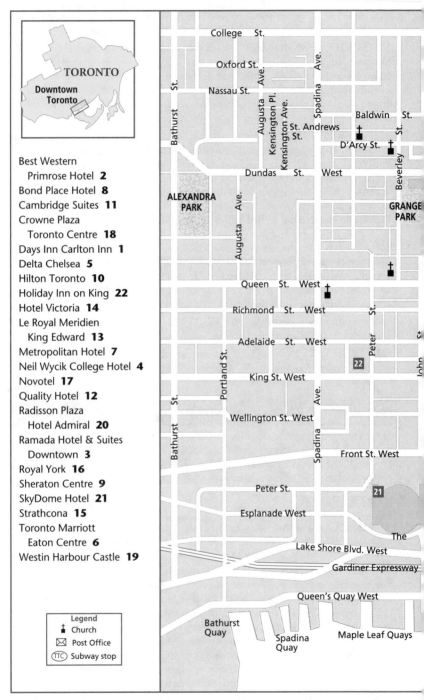

TORONTO

Downtown
Toronto

Best Western
  Primrose Hotel **2**
Bond Place Hotel **8**
Cambridge Suites **11**
Crowne Plaza
  Toronto Centre **18**
Days Inn Carlton Inn **1**
Delta Chelsea **5**
Hilton Toronto **10**
Holiday Inn on King **22**
Hotel Victoria **14**
Le Royal Meridien
  King Edward **13**
Metropolitan Hotel **7**
Neil Wycik College Hotel **4**
Novotel **17**
Quality Hotel **12**
Radisson Plaza
  Hotel Admiral **20**
Ramada Hotel & Suites
  Downtown **3**
Royal York **16**
Sheraton Centre **9**
SkyDome Hotel **21**
Strathcona **15**
Toronto Marriott
  Eaton Centre **6**
Westin Harbour Castle **19**

Legend
✝ Church
⊠ Post Office
Ⓣ Subway stop

College St.
Oxford St.
Nassau St.
Bathurst St.
Augusta Ave.
Kensington Pl.
Kensington Ave.
Spadina Ave.
Baldwin St.
St. Andrews St.
D'Arcy St.
Beverley St.
Dundas St. West
ALEXANDRA PARK
GRANGE PARK
Augusta Ave.
Queen St. West
Richmond St. West
Adelaide St. West
Peter St.
Portland St.
King St. West
Bathurst St.
Wellington St. West
Spadina Ave.
Front St. West
Peter St.
John
Esplanade West
The
Lake Shore Blvd. West
Gardiner Expressway
Queen's Quay West
Bathurst Quay
Spadina Quay
Maple Leaf Quays

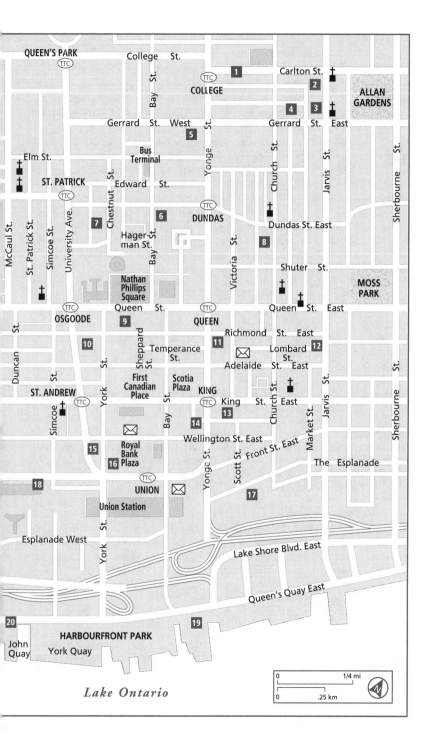

Amenities: Business center, room service (11am to 11pm), laundry and valet, concierge. In-room massage, twice-daily maid service, convenience store. Fitness center with exercise equipment, whirlpool, and sauna.

Le Royal Meridien King Edward. 37 King St. E., Toronto, ON M5C 2E9. ☎ **416/ 863-3131.** Fax 416/367-5515. www.lemeridien-hotels.com. 294 units. A/C MINIBAR TV TEL. C$239-$383 (US$163–$260) double; from C$445 (US$303) suite. AE, DC, MC, V. Parking C$25 (US$17). Pets accepted. Subway: King.

At one time the only place in Toronto that Hollywood royalty like Liz Taylor and Richard Burton would consider staying at, the King Eddy fell into neglect for many years. In the 1980s, a group of local investors spent C$40 million (US$27 million) to rescue it. The result recalls its former glory, with rosy marble columns and a glass-domed rotunda dominating the lobby. The sense of grandeur carries into the guest rooms and suites. Not every room is spacious, but they are all charmingly appointed; unlike those at many uptown competitors, the King Eddy's rooms feel personally designed. The bathrooms are particularly nice, with generously proportioned marble tubs. Top-of-the-line features include plush bathrobes and fluffy towels, makeup mirrors, hair dryers, and daily newspaper delivery.

Dining: The formal dining room, Chiaro's, wins solid reviews for its seafood starters. But with goldfish swimming in bowls on many tables, you might wish to stick to the decadent desserts. Chiaro's also has one of the best wine lists in the city, but the markup on most bottles will startle those not traveling on expense accounts. Just off the lobby is a mirrored lounge that serves traditional English afternoon tea; it's a favorite haunt of would-be literary types. The wood-paneled Consort Bar is wonderfully clubby, and its 8-foot-high windows afford fun people watching. The Café Victoria offers light, casual fare all day.

Amenities: 24-hour room service, laundry and valet, concierge, complimentary newspaper and shoeshine, nightly turndown, fitness center.

EXPENSIVE

Crowne Plaza Toronto Centre. 225 Front St. W., Toronto, ON M5V 2X3. ☎ **800/ 422-7969** or 416/597-1400. Fax 416/597-8128. www.crowneplazatoronto.com. 587 units. A/C MINIBAR TV TEL. C$209–$329 (US$142–$224) double. Extra person C$20 (US$14). Weekend packages available. AE, DC, DISC, MC, V. Valet parking C$25 (US$17). Subway: Union.

Here's a choice for sightseers who want to be at the center of it all. The Crowne Plaza is cheek-by-jowl with the CN Tower, SkyDome, Roy Thomson Hall, and the Theater District. It's also a hub for business from the attached Convention Centre. Rooms are pleasantly decorated with a minimum of fuss. Business amenities include two phone lines and a fax-modem hookup. All rooms are equipped with a coffeemaker.

Dining: The formal Accolade dining room is a good pre-theater choice. The Trellis Bistro and Lounge is open late and serves weekend brunch.

Amenities: Room service (6am to 2am), laundry and valet, concierge. Fitness center with indoor pool, whirlpool, saunas, exercise room, squash courts, and sundeck.

✪ **Hilton Toronto.** 145 Richmond St. W., Toronto, ON M5H 2L2. ☎ **800/445-8667** or 416/869-3456. Fax 416/869-1478. www.hilton.com. 601 units. A/C MINIBAR TV TEL. C$210–$300 (US$143–$204) double. Extra person C$20 (US$14). Weekend packages available. AE, MC, V. Parking C$22 (US$15). Subway: Osgoode.

The Hilton Toronto isn't what it used to be: With a gorgeous C$25 million (US$17 million) renovation completed in spring 2000, the Hilton has become one of the most attractive hotels in the city. On the western edge of the Financial District, the 32-story Hilton boasts good-sized rooms decorated with streamlined luxury in mind; because of the hotel's excellent location, many have superb vistas (another fine view can be experienced in the glass elevators). Executive rooms include perks such as a terry bathrobe, a trouser press, and access to a private lounge that serves complimentary breakfast and evening snacks.

Dining: As part of its renovation, the Hilton unveiled Tundra, which serves top-notch Canadian cuisine (see review on page 75). For casual meals there's Ovo, an egg-shaped restaurant that serves lighter fare. There's also an intimate wood-paneled bar, Barristers.

Amenities: 24-hour room service; indoor/outdoor lap pool; sundeck; fitness center with exercise room, whirlpool, and sauna; massage rooms. Business center; laundry and valet; concierge; twice-daily housekeeping; baby-sitting.

◐ **The Metropolitan Hotel.** 108 Chestnut St., Toronto, ON M5G 1R3. ☎ **416/ 977-5000.** Fax 416/977-9513. www.metropolitan.com. 495 units. A/C MINIBAR TV TEL. C$220–$260 double. Children under 16 stay free in parents' room. AE, DC, DISC, EC, ER, JCB, MC, V. Parking C$20 (US$14). Subway: St. Patrick.

One of the few major hotels in Toronto that isn't part of a large chain, the Metropolitan caters to a business-oriented clientele. Just off Dundas Street West, the hotel is a 5-minute stroll north of the business district and west of the Eaton Centre. But why walk when you can take advantage of the complimentary limo service (to any downtown core address, during business hours)?

That perk is just one of the ways in which the Metropolitan attempts to compete with its pricier competitors. Rooms are furnished with comfort in mind, but are work-ready. Standard features include telephones with jacks for computer and fax use, and in-closet safes. The luxury and executive suites boast Jacuzzis, Dolby Surround Sound televisions, CD players, and cordless phones.

Dining: The modern-themed Hemispheres boasts a continental menu filled with Asian-inspired flourishes. Lai Wah Heen (see chapter 5) serves classic Cantonese cuisine; it is a top choice for business entertaining. The Mezzanine Café turns into a candlelit piano bar come evening.

Amenities: 24-hour room service; 24-hour business center (with PCs and Macs); indoor swimming pool; fitness center with sauna, whirlpool, and massage treatments. Laundry and valet; Gold Key concierge; complimentary limousine transportation (in downtown core).

Novotel. 45 The Esplanade, Toronto, ON M5E 1W2. ☎ **800/668-6835** or 416/367-8900. Fax 416/360-8285. www.novotel.com. 270 units. A/C TV TEL. From C$119 (US$80.90) double. AE, DC, ER, MC, V. Parking C$13.50 (US$9.20). Subway: Union.

A short stroll from the St. Lawrence Centre and the Hummingbird Centre, a longer walk from Harbourfront, this hotel feels out of the way. It's actually at the heart of downtown, with office buildings to the north and warehouses to the south. Relatively new to Toronto, having opened in 1990, it tempers its modernity with allusions to neoclassical French architecture and hints of chinoiserie. Rooms are pleasant though lacking in character. Standard amenities include two telephones, hair dryers, and radio and TV speakers in the bathrooms.

Dining: The casual Café Nicole is open all day.

Amenities: Room service (6am to midnight); fitness center with indoor pool, exercise room, whirlpool, and sauna; laundry and valet; concierge; airport shuttle bus.

Radisson Plaza Hotel Admiral. 249 Queen's Quay W., Toronto, ON M5J 2N5. ☎ **800/ 333-3333** or 416/203-3333. Fax 416/203-3100. 157 units. A/C MINIBAR TV TEL. C$185–$230 (US$126–$156) double. Extra person C$20 (US$14). Weekend packages available. AE, DC, ER, MC, V. Parking C$18 (US$12.25). Subway: Union, then LRT to Rees St.

This intimate hotel overlooks Lake Ontario and is steps from the Harbourfront Centre. Its nautical-theme decor includes lacquered wood and gleaming brass in the lobby, with oil paintings of marine scenes littering the walls. The rooms are nicely appointed, with heavy chests of drawers, imposing desks, and standard amenities like two telephones, hair dryers, and clotheslines in the bathroom. Lakefront rooms offer superb views, though all guests can enjoy the sights (and a dip in the outdoor pool) on the roof deck.

Dining: The Commodore's Dining Room affords lovely views and serves predictable continental cuisine for dinner. The Galley Café serves lighter lunch and dinner fare. Bosun's Bar is unremarkable, but does serve snack-type food until the wee hours.

Amenities: Expansive roof deck with outdoor pool, lounging chairs, cabana-style bar, whirlpool, and squash court; 24-hour room service; concierge; complimentary newspaper delivery.

Royal York. 100 Front St. W., Toronto, ON M5J 1E3. ☎ **800/441-1414** or 416/863-6333. 1,365 units. A/C MINIBAR TV TEL. C$175–$270 (US$119–$184) double. Packages available. AE, DC, DISC, MC, V. Parking C$22 (US$15). Subway: Union.

Looming across from Union Station, Toronto's hub for cross-country trains, is the Royal York, which was built by the Canadian-Pacific Railroad in 1929. The CP hotels across the country tend to the monolithic, and this one is no exception. Because it has 35 meeting and banquet rooms, most Torontonians have been through its hallowed halls at some point (my first time there was for a prom). The lobby is magnificent in an old-fashioned, old-world way, and just sitting on a plush couch and watching the crowd is an event. Still, you have to decide whether you want to stay under the same roof with more than 1,000 others. Service is remarkably efficient, but necessarily impersonal.

Guest rooms, though furnished with charming antique reproductions, are a mixed bag. Some are reasonably airy, but there's generally not much spare space. And while some have excellent views, a common complaint from guests is that the windows are dirty—though the rooms themselves, it should be noted, are spotless. The well-equipped rooms for travelers with disabilities are designed for wheelchair users, as well as hearing-impaired and visually-impaired travelers. "Entrée Gold" perks include a private floor with superior rooms and separate check-in, a private lounge, complimentary breakfast and newspaper, and nightly turndown service.

Dining: The 10 eateries and lounges include the Acadian Room, a solid, traditional choice; the worthwhile wine list offers more than 100 Ontario vintages. Other restaurants include Benihana (Japanese), the Gazebo (lunch), and Piper's Bar & Eatz (pub grub). The posh Library Bar is renowned for its martinis.

Amenities: Skylit indoor lap pool; 24-hour room service; fitness center with exercise equipment, saunas, steam rooms and whirlpool; business center. Laundry and valet; concierge; barbershop and salon; shopping arcade with American Express travel center.

The Sheraton Centre. 123 Queen St. W., Toronto, ON M5H 2M9. ☎ **800/325-3535** or 416/361-1000. Fax 416/947-4854. www.sheratoncentretoronto.com. 1,377 units. A/C TV TEL. C$260–$295 (US$177–$200) double. Extra person C$20 (US$14). 2 children under 18 stay free in parents' room. Packages available. AE, CB, DC, EC, ER, JCB, MC, V. Parking C$25 (US$17). Subway: Osgoode.

A convention favorite, the Sheraton is across the street from New City Hall, a block from the Eaton Centre, and a short stroll from the trendy restaurant and boutique area of Queen Street West. It's entirely possible to stay here and never venture outside— the Sheraton complex includes half a dozen restaurants and bars and a cinema, and the building connects to Toronto's fabled underground city. If you long for a patch of green, the hotel provides that, too: The south side of the lobby contains a manicured garden with a waterfall.

A C$50 million (US$34 million) renovation in the early 1990s completely refurbished the good-sized guest rooms. Most lack a serious view, though as you near the top of the 46-story complex the sights are inspiring. The decor is uninspiring. Club Level rooms have mini business centers that include a fax/printer/copier and two-line speakerphone.

Dining: Good Queen Bess, in the shopping concourse, is a true English pub that pours excellent dark ales. The Long Bar and Lounge has gorgeous City Hall views to go with its chi-chi drink menu. The Reunion is a basic sports bar, complete with pool tables. Postcards Café and Grill serves a good breakfast if you're in a hurry.

Amenities: Gigantic indoor/outdoor pool, sundeck; 24-hour room service; fitness center with exercise rooms, sauna, and hot tub; business center. Laundry and valet, concierge, supervised play center, and baby-sitting services available.

Renaissance Toronto Hotel at SkyDome. 1 Blue Jays Way, Toronto, ON M5V 1J4. ☎ **800/237-1512** or 416/341-7100. Fax 416/341-5091. www.renaissancehotels.com/yyzbr. 346 units. A/C MINIBAR TV TEL. City view from C$189 (US$129) double; field side from C$305 (US$207) double. AE, DC, DISC, ER, JCB, MC, V. Parking C$25 (US$17). Subway: Union.

This is a dream come true for diehard baseball fans—70 rooms overlook the diamond's verdant Astroturf. Those who enjoy the view should remember that it goes both ways: Just after it opened, the hotel enjoyed a moment of notoriety when the amorous antics of a pair of guests ended up on the JumboTron. All rooms have shades—remember to use them.

The rooms with a city view are the least expensive (and the view isn't one of the best, either), but all units have standard amenities such as a hair dryer and coffeemaker. There are nine wheelchair-accessible guestrooms.

Dining: The view is the main thing at Café on the Green. Other options include Sightlines and the Hard Rock Cafe, which are adjacent to the hotel and also overlook the field.

Amenities: 24-hour room service; laundry and valet; concierge; fitness center with pool, squash courts, sauna, and exercise room.

Toronto Marriott Eaton Centre. 525 Bay St. (at Dundas St.), Toronto, ON M5G 2L2. ☎ **800/228-9290** or 416/597-9200. Fax 416/597-9211. www.marriott.com/marriott/yyzec. 459 units. A/C MINIBAR TV TEL. C$189–$239 (US$129–$163) double. AE, DC, MC, V. Subway: Dundas.

Attention, shoppers: Those who want proximity to Toronto's central shrine to commerce should check in here. Connected to the Eaton Centre, the Marriott is just a few minutes' walk from the Financial and Theater districts, Chinatown, and SkyDome. Most rooms are spacious (the better to store your loot?). Amenities include hair dryers, irons, and ironing boards. The hotel offers rooms for travelers with disabilities.

Dining: The Parkside restaurant specializes in unfussy fare. JW's is the fancy dining room. Characters is mainly a sports bar.

Amenities: 24-hour room service, indoor rooftop swimming pool, whirlpool, sauna, fitness center, laundry and valet, concierge, baby-sitting.

Westin Harbour Castle. 1 Harbour Sq., Toronto, ON M5J 1A6. ☎ **800/228-3000** or 416/869-1600. Fax 416/361-7448. 980 units. A/C MINIBAR TV TEL. C$180–$300 (US$122–$204) double; from C$335 (US$228) suite. Extra person C$20 (US$14). Children stay free in parents' room. Weekend packages and long-term rates available. AE, DC, ER, MC, V. Parking C$25 (US$17). Subway: Union, then LRT to Queen's Quay.

ⓘ Family-Friendly Hotels

Delta Chelsea *(see p. 59)*   This is a perennial family favorite—with good cause. To ease the burden on frazzled parents, a children's creative center and baby-sitting services are available between 9:30am and 10pm. Kids will enjoy the in-room family movies, Super Nintendo, cookie jar (replenished daily), and the nightly turndown gift. Further reducing the strain on the family purse, kids have a half-price menu at the Delta Chelsea's restaurants.

Four Seasons Hotel Toronto *(see p. 61)*   A hop and a skip away from the Children's Own Museum and the Royal Ontario Museum, this hotel has its own attractions. There are free bicycles and video games for borrowing, and an indoor-outdoor pool. Upon arrival, room service delivers complimentary cookies and milk to the kids. The concierge and housekeeping staff work magic, including conjuring up excellent baby-sitting services.

The Sheraton Centre *(see p. 56)*   The endless attractions of this complex— including a half-dozen restaurants (some with a special menu for tykes) and a cinema—mean there's a lot to keep the kiddies entertained. There's a supervised play center as well as on-call baby-sitting services. Kids also enjoy in-room video games and a welcome gift.

A popular spot for conventions, the Westin is on the lakefront, just across from the Toronto Islands ferry docks and down the road from the Harbourfront Centre and Queen's Quay. Not surprisingly, the views are among the best in the city. The trade-off is that it's somewhat out of the way, but a shuttle bus to Union Station and LRT access mean it's not too far from civilization. Accommodations are in two towers, linked only at their base. The rooms are modern in decor and amenities; about half of them are designated nonsmoking.

Dining: Grand Yatt Dynasty restaurant offers menus in English and Chinese. The all-you-can-eat dim sum lunch (C$12.50/US$8.50) attracts mobs weekends. The Lighthouse revolving restaurant on the 38th floor depends on its view more than its kitchen to satisfy customers. The Chartroom is a comfy piano bar. The Lobby Lounge serves afternoon tea and evening cocktails.

Amenities: 24-hour room service; fitness center with indoor pool, whirlpool, sauna, and steam room; two squash courts; two outdoor tennis courts; massage clinic. Concierge; laundry and valet; guest-room voice mail; shopping arcade; beauty shop.

MODERATE

Best Western Primrose Hotel. 111 Carlton St. (between Church and Jarvis sts.), Toronto, ON M5B 2G3. ☎ **800/268-8082** or 416/977-8000. Fax 416/977-6323. 342 units. A/C TV TEL. C$129–$199 (US$88–$135) double; C$229–$260 (US$156–$177) suite. Extra person C$15 (US$10). Weekend packages available Oct–June. AE, DC, MC, V. Parking C$18 (US$12.25). Subway: College.

Comfort is key in this hotel. Guest rooms aren't particularly large, but they don't feel cramped. Furnishings and decor aim for the inoffensive. All rooms have wall-to-wall carpeting and individual climate control. Room service is available from 7am to 10pm, and there is laundry and valet service. Guests have the use of a sauna and decent-sized outdoor pool. The surprisingly charming coffee shop is downstairs.

Bond Place Hotel. 65 Dundas St. E., Toronto, ON M5B 2G8. ☎ **416/362-6061.** Fax 416/360-6406. 287 units. A/C TV TEL. High season C$140 (US$95.20) single or double; low season C$79 (US$54) single or double. Extra person C$15 (US$10). Weekend packages available. AE, DC, DISC, ER, MC, V. Parking C$12. Subway: Dundas.

The location is right—a block from the Eaton Centre, around the corner from the Pantages and Elgin theaters—and so is the price. The rooms at the Bond Place are on the small side, and can best be described as quaint. There's a concierge, and laundry and valet service is available.

The recently spruced-up Freddy's restaurant serves lunch and dinner, as well as complimentary hors d'oeuvres during happy hour.

Days Inn Carlton Inn. 30 Carlton St., Toronto, ON M5B 2E9. ☎ **800/329-7466** or 416/977-6655. Fax 416/977-0502. 536 units. A/C TV TEL. C$129–$169 (US$88–$115) double. Extra person C$15 (US$10). Children under 18 stay free in parents' room. Summer discounts available. AE, DC, DISC, MC, V. Parking C$16 (US$10.90). Subway: College.

Now that Maple Leaf Gardens is semi-retired (hockey has moved to the Air Canada Centre), the Carlton Inn's location isn't what it used to be. Still, this hotel isn't far from the downtown core, and its reasonable rates continue to draw business. The unremarkable rooms tend to be small, but do have coffeemakers and hair dryers; refrigerators are available on request. There is an on-site restaurant, a lounge, and a sports bar. Laundry and valet service is available, and there are an indoor pool, sauna, and salon.

✪ Delta Chelsea. 33 Gerrard St. W., Toronto, ON M5G 1Z4. ☎ **800/243-5732** or 416/595-1975. Fax 416/585-4362. www.deltahotels.com. 1,591 units. A/C TV TEL. C$129–$340 (US$88–$231) double with signature service; C$149–$360 (US$101–$245) deluxe double; C$195–$380 (US$133–$258) Signature Club double (on business floor); from C$475 (US$323) suite. Extra person C$20 (US$14). Children under 18 stay free in parents' room. Weekend packages available. AE, DC, DISC, MC, V. Valet parking C$26 (US$17.70); self-parking C$20 (US$13.60; parking available only to 575 cars). Subway: College.

While not a budget hotel, the Delta Chelsea offers bang for the buck. Its downtown location draws heaps of tour groups and a smattering of business travelers, its family-friendly facilities lure those with tykes, and its weekend packages capture the cost-conscious. Rooms are bright and cheery; a few have kitchenettes. On the special floor for business travelers, rooms have cordless speakerphones, faxes, well-stocked desks, and ergonomic chairs, and rates include free local calls and newspaper delivery. Many rooms have been designed for travelers with disabilities. There's 24-hour room service, and laundry and valet service. Baby-sitting for children aged 3 to 8 is available (for an extra charge) between 9:30am and 10pm.

Dining options include Wittles and the Market Garden cafeteria, which sells soups, salads, and sandwiches. The Chelsea Bun offers daily live entertainment (usually jazz or R&B), and Deck 27 has a view of the skyline. There are two pools (one for adults only); a fitness center with an exercise room, whirlpool, and sauna; a billiards room; a beauty salon; a children's center; and a business center.

Holiday Inn on King. 370 King St. W. (at Peter St.), Toronto, ON M5V 1J9. ☎ **800/263-6364** or 416/599-4000. Fax 416/599-7394. www.hiok.com. 431 units. A/C TV TEL. C$179–$319 (US$122–$217) double. Extra person C$15 (US$10). AE, DISC, ER, MC, V. Parking C$22 (US$15). Subway: St. Andrew.

The blinding-white facade of this building suggests that some architect mistook Toronto for the tropics. No matter, its location is hot, with the Theater District, Gourmet Ghetto, Chinatown, and SkyDome nearby. Half the floors are office space; guest rooms start at the 9th floor and go up to the 20th. The pastel rooms are vintage Holiday Inn, and all have hair dryers.

Great food is just steps away, and for those who want to stick close to the hotel, there's a Japanese restaurant, a jazzy lounge, and a deli. The hotel has a small outdoor pool, and a fitness center with exercise room, whirlpool, and sauna.

Ramada Hotel & Suites Downtown. 300 Jarvis St. (just south of Carlton St.), Toronto, ON M5B 2C5. ☎ **800/567-2233** or 416/977-4823. Fax 416/977-4830. 102 units. A/C TV TEL. C$159–$279 (US$108–$190) double. AE, DISC, ER, JCB. Parking C$18 (US$12.25). Subway: College.

Popular with tour groups because of its proximity to the Eaton Centre and other downtown attractions, the Ramada is on a rather seedy (though not unsafe) strip of real estate. For years this has been a comfortable, moderately priced hotel, but with its 1999 renovations it started reaching for boutique status. The attractive guest rooms, which boast either a queen- or a king-size bed, emphasize comfort. Standard furnishings include a sofa, a desk, and a coffee table. Rooms have refrigerators, coffeemakers, hair dryers, and complimentary newspaper delivery.

The ground-floor restaurant is open all day. Room service is available from 7am to 9pm. The hotel has an indoor pool, exercise room, whirlpool, sauna, squash courts, and sundeck.

INEXPENSIVE

Hotel Victoria. 56 Yonge St. (at Wellington St.), Toronto, ON M5E 1G5. ☎ **416/363-1666.** Fax 416/363-7327. www.toronto.com/hotelvictoria. 48 units. A/C TV TEL. C$125–$169 (US$85–$115) double. Extra person C$15 (US$10). AE, DC, MC, V. Parking C$20 (US$14). Subway: King.

This hotel underwent a complete renovation in 1999. In a landmark downtown building near the Hummingbird Centre and the Hockey Hall of Fame, the Victoria boasts the glamorous touches of an earlier age, such as crown moldings and marble columns in the lobby. Standard rooms are small and simply decorated; select rooms are larger. All rooms have hair dryers, coffeemakers, and (on request) complimentary newspapers. There is a restaurant and lobby bar. Laundry and valet service is available. Guests receive passes to a nearby health club.

Neil Wycik College Hotel. 96 Gerrard St. E. (between Church and Jarvis sts.), Toronto, ON M5B 1G7. ☎ **800/268-4358** or 416/977-2320. Fax 416/977-2809. 304 units (none with bathroom). TEL C$41–$51 (US$28–$35) double; C$45–$58 (US$31–$39) family (2 adults plus children). MC, V. Closed Sept to mid-May. Parking nearby C$10 (US$7). Subway: College.

During the school year, this is a residence for nearby Ryerson Polytechnic University. Some students work here in the summer, when the Neil Wycik morphs into a guest house. Travelers on tight budgets won't mind the minimalist approach—rooms have beds, chairs, desks, and phones, but no air-conditioning or TVs. Groups of five bedrooms share two bathrooms and one kitchen with a refrigerator and stove. There are two roof decks (on the 5th and 23rd floors), a TV lounge, sauna, and 24-hour laundry room. The cafe serves breakfast from 7 to 11am.

Quality Hotel. 111 Lombard St. (between Adelaide and Richmond sts.), Toronto, ON M5C 2T9. ☎ **800/228-5151** or 416/367-5555. Fax 416/367-3470. www.choicehotels.ca. 196 units. A/C TV TEL. C$109–$189 (US$74–$129) double. AE, DC, MC, V. Parking C$13 (US$8.85). Subway: King or Queen.

Close by the Financial District and the Eaton Centre, this hotel always seems to be running a special promotion, so be sure to ask for a deal. Rooms aren't large, but they do have many amenities, including voice mail, coffeemakers, irons and ironing boards, hair dryers, and individual climate control. There is a cafe on the ground floor, and a modest exercise room.

The Strathcona. 60 York St., Toronto, ON M5J 1S8. ☎ **416/363-3321.** Fax 416/363-4679. 193 units. A/C TV TEL. May–Oct C$90–$159 (US$61–$108) double; Nov–Apr C$75–$129 (US$51–$88) double. AE, DC, MC, V. Parking nearby C$15 (US$10.20). Subway: Union.

Completely renovated in 1999, the Strathcona remains one of the best buys in the city. In the shadow of the Royal York, the hotel is a short walk from all major downtown attractions. Rooms are small, but efficiently designed. The ground-floor cafe is open all day. There's laundry and valet service, and a concierge. Room service is available from 6am to 8pm.

2 Midtown

Midtown starts above College/Carlton Street and runs north to Davenport Road, between Spadina Avenue and Jarvis Street. In this area, you'll find the Royal Ontario Museum, the Yorkville shopping district, the University of Toronto, and the Bata Shoe Museum.

VERY EXPENSIVE

✪ **Four Seasons Hotel Toronto.** 21 Avenue Rd., Toronto, ON M5R 2G1. ☎ **800/ 268-6282** or 416/964-0411. Fax 416/964-2301. www.fourseasons.com. 380 units. A/C MINI-BAR TV TEL. C$305–$410 (US$207–$279) double; from C$435 (US$296) suite. Weekend discounts and packages available. AE, CB, DC, ER, JCB, MC, V. Parking C$25 (US$17). Subway: Bay.

The Four Seasons is famous as the favored haunt of visiting celebrities. The hotel, in the ritzy Yorkville district, has earned a reputation for offering fine service and complete comfort. While not even close to being the largest hotel in the city, the building—with its myriad ballrooms, meeting rooms, and restaurants—is monolithic. It's easy to get lost inside (I've done it myself).

Even if you do get lost, it's an interesting place. The public areas are decorated like a French parlor, with marble floors and dramatic floral arrangements. Once you make it to your room, you'll find that while it may not be the largest in the city (a standard model is about 325 square feet), it's well designed and easy on the eye. Corner rooms have balconies. Amenities include two-line phones, fax-modem hookups, and windows that open. The marble bathrooms are outfitted with hair dryers, makeup mirrors, and plush robes. There are specially designed rooms for travelers with disabilities.

Dining: The formal dining room, Truffles, is a Toronto institution (see chapter 5). The second-floor Studio Cafe is open for breakfast, lunch, and dinner, and is a favorite with the business crowd; its menu features many health-conscious, low-fat dishes. La Serre is a perfect perch for people watching—it overlooks Yorkville Avenue. It's a piano bar in the evening and serves brunch on weekends. The ground-floor Lobby Bar serves the best afternoon tea in the city.

Amenities: 24-hour concierge, room service, and valet pickup; 1-hour pressing; complimentary shoeshine; business center; health club with indoor/outdoor pool, whirlpool, and treadmills; weekday courtesy limo to downtown. Twice-daily maid service; in-room massage; complimentary coffee and newspaper; baby-sitting; free bicycles, and video-game units for children.

Inter-Continental. 220 Bloor St. W., Toronto, ON M5S 1T8. ☎ **416/960-5200.** Fax 416/960-8269. 209 units. A/C MINIBAR TV TEL. C$275–$345 (US$187–$235) double. AE, DC, JCB, MC, V. Parking C$25 (US$17). Subway: St. George.

On the edge of Yorkville, the Inter-Continental is less than a 5-minute walk from the Royal Ontario Museum, the Bata Shoe Museum, and one of the best shopping districts in the city. It's a favorite with business travelers, who appreciate its attentive, personalized service. The building looks rather nondescript, but it is filled with European and art-deco details that give it character. The spacious guest rooms come equipped with stylish love seats and roomy desks. They have two-line phones, fax-modem hookups, windows that open, and luxe bathrobes.

Midtown Toronto Accommodations

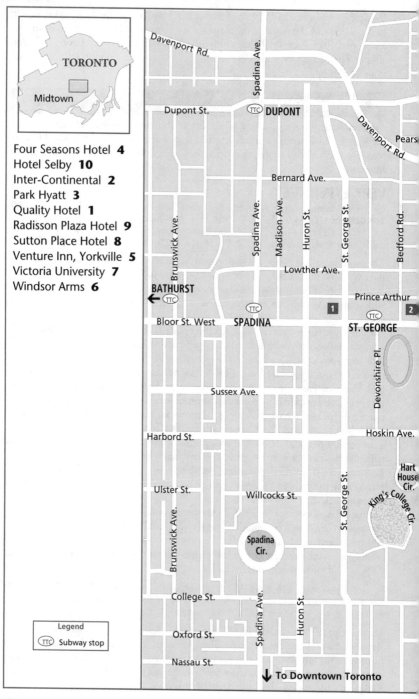

Four Seasons Hotel **4**
Hotel Selby **10**
Inter-Continental **2**
Park Hyatt **3**
Quality Hotel **1**
Radisson Plaza Hotel **9**
Sutton Place Hotel **8**
Venture Inn, Yorkville **5**
Victoria University **7**
Windsor Arms **6**

TORONTO

Midtown

Legend
TTC Subway stop

Davenport Rd.
Spadina Ave.
Dupont St. TTC DUPONT
Davenport Rd.
Pears
Bernard Ave.
Spadina Ave.
Madison Ave.
Huron St.
St. George St.
Brunswick Ave.
Bedford Rd.
Lowther Ave.
BATHURST
TTC
Prince Arthur
Bloor St. West   SPADINA   TTC
ST. GEORGE
Devonshire Pl.
Sussex Ave.
Harbord St.
Hoskin Ave.
Hart House Cir.
Ulster St.
Willcocks St.
St. George St.
King's College Cir.
Brunswick Ave.
Spadina Cir.
College St.
Spadina Ave.
Huron St.
Oxford St.
Nassau St.
↓ To Downtown Toronto

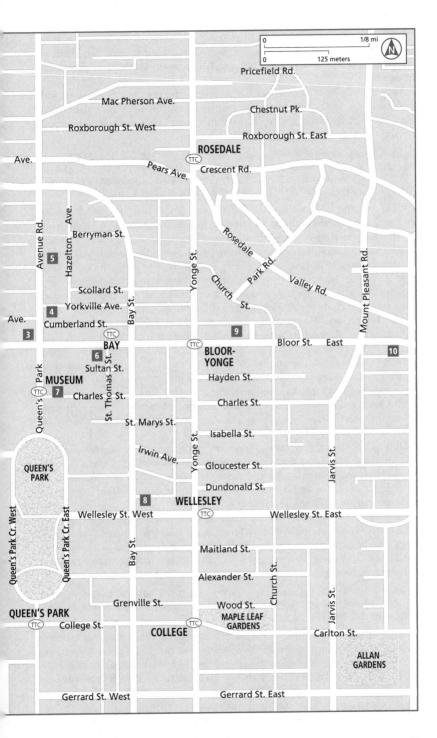

Dining: Signatures overlooks a small courtyard, where there's dining in warm weather; the globe-trotting menu boasts many imported ingredients. The Harmony Lounge is for afternoon tea by day and cocktails by night; it has a piano player until the wee hours.

Amenities: 24-hour room service; lap pool with adjacent patio; fitness room with treadmill, bikes, StairMaster; sauna and massage room. Business center; laundry and valet; twice-daily maid service; nightly turndown; concierge; complimentary shoeshine and newspaper.

✪ **Park Hyatt Toronto.** 4 Avenue Rd., Toronto, ON M5R 2E8. ☎ **800/233-1234** or 416/925-1234. Fax 416/924-6693. 346 units. A/C MINIBAR TV TEL. C$225-$499 (US$153-$339) double; from C$299 (US$203) suite. Weekend packages available. AE, DC, DISC, MC, V. Parking C$25 (US$17). Subway: Museum or Bay. Pets accepted.

With its ongoing C$60 million (US$41 million) renovations, the Park Hyatt has cemented its reputation for being the last word in luxe. Its new owner, Chicago-based Hyatt, renovated every corner of the 65-year-old art-deco building, but just as they finished working on all of the guestrooms and public areas, they launched new plans to create an on-site spa (work should be completed by early 2001). It's in the posh Yorkville district, steps from the Royal Ontario Museum and the Children's Own Museum. Its neighbor, the Four Seasons, is home away from home to the glitterati, while the Park Hyatt prides itself on luring the literati. The official hotel of the Toronto International Film Festival, it's the venue of choice for the literary in-crowd.

A glamorous lobby dotted with Eastern-inspired objets d'art links the north and south towers. In the evening, soft piano music drifts down from the Mezzanine Bar. Guest rooms and suites have oak and cherry appointments, and glass walls now cover the terraces, increasing floor space so that even the smallest room boasts a generous 500 square feet. Every unit has two-line phones, a fax machine, Internet hookup, and ironing board and iron. The bathrooms have their own phones, plush terry robes, and full-size hair dryers. One more thing: The Park Hyatt calls itself "dog-friendly," so there's no need to leave your best friend at home.

Dining: The ground-floor restaurant Annona (see chapter 5) is a treat for gourmets. The 18th-floor Roof Lounge is a favorite meeting spot for journalists, who congregate on couches in front of the fireplace. Morton's of Chicago, an upscale steak house that serves dinner only, is in the North Tower. The Mezzanine Bar just off the lobby serves afternoon tea, evening drinks, and canapés.

Amenities: 24-hour room service featuring many spa-inspired dishes; 24-hour business center with secretarial services; fitness center with indoor lap pool, treadmills, sauna, whirlpool, and treatment rooms for massage and other spa-like pampering. Twice-daily maid service, laundry and valet, baby-sitting, complimentary newspaper and shoeshine, concierge.

Windsor Arms. 118 St. Thomas St., Toronto, ON M5S 3E7. ☎ **416/971-9666.** Fax 416/971-3303. 28 units. A/C MINIBAR TV TEL. From C$375 (US$255) double. Weekend discounts available. AE, DC, DISC, MC, V. Subway: Bay.

Take one exquisite neo-Gothic building, tear it down, and replace it with an identical structure that incorporates some of the original's elements. That's the recipe the new owner of the Windsor Arms followed in re-creating the hotel, which was built in 1927 and closed in 1991. The result is a stunning mix of new and old, with state-of-the-art technology behind leaded-glass windows. Only 4 of the 15 stories offer hotel rooms; the rest consists of million-dollar condominiums.

The guest rooms and suites are exquisite confections of ivory, celadon, and silver. All feature a "butler's cupboard," with a door from the hallway and another in the room (in case you want room service but don't feel like answering the door). Amenities include two-line phones, fax-modem hookups, large closets with built-in dressers, and CD players. The generously proportioned bathrooms have Jacuzzi jets in the tubs, plush robes, and phones.

Dining: The ground-floor Courtyard Café serves lunch and dinner. The lounge, Club 22, includes both a caviar-and-champagne bar and a 9-by-9-foot humidor.

Amenities: 24-hour room service; lap pool; sauna; spa with massage, aromatherapy, and aquatherapy treatments; laundry and valet; twice-daily maid service; nightly turn-down; concierge.

EXPENSIVE

Radisson Plaza Hotel. 90 Bloor St. E., Toronto, ON M4W 1A7. ☎ **800/333-3333** or 416/961-8000. Fax 416/961-4635. 246 units. A/C MINIBAR TV TEL. From C$195 (US$133) double; from C$290 (US$197) suite. Extra person C$15 (US$10). Children under 18 stay free in parents' room. Weekend packages available. AE, DC, DISC, JCB, MC, V. Parking C$20 (US$14). Subway: Yonge/Bloor.

In a great location at Yonge and Bloor, the Radisson Plaza is easy to miss—it takes up only six floors of a towering multiuse building. The lobby is on the ground floor, alongside Matisse, the hotel's only eatery. The rooms, which start on the seventh floor, are decorated with antique-reproduction wooden furniture. All have two-line phones with voice mail, fax-modem hookups, coffeemakers, hair dryers, and individual climate control.

Dining: Matisse is the not-so-formal dining room. There is also a private lounge for Plaza Club members.

Amenities: Room service (6:30am to 11pm); laundry and valet; concierge. Guests have access to the Bloor Park Club, in the building; it offers exercise classes and equipment, squash courts, whirlpools, and saunas.

The Sutton Place Hotel. 955 Bay St., Toronto, ON M5S 2A2. ☎ **800/268-3790** or 416/924-9221. Fax 416/924-1778. www.suttonplace.com. 292 units. A/C MINIBAR TV TEL. C$235–$325 (US$160–$221) double; from C$400 (US$272) suite. Extra person C$20 (US$14). Children under 18 stay free in parents' room. Weekend discounts available. AE, DC, JCB, MC, V. Valet parking C$25 (US$17); self-parking C$20 (US$14). Subway: Museum or Wellesley. Pets accepted.

Although it towers over the intersection of Bay and Wellesley, the Sutton Place boasts the advantages of a small hotel. In addition to more than its share of celebrities, the hotel draws sophisticated business and leisure travelers with personalized service and serious pampering. The Sutton aims for European panache, littering the public spaces with antiques and tapestries. The spacious guest rooms are decorated in a similar, though scaled-down, style. All rooms boast a substantial desk, two-line phone with voice mail, fax-modem hookup, complimentary weekday newspaper, bathrobes, and hair dryers. A few suites have full kitchens.

Dining: The elegant Accents is open all day; it's a popular spot for locals as well as guests. The adjoining Accents Bar boasts live music and a multitude of wines by the glass.

Amenities: 24-hour room service; indoor pool with spacious sundeck; sauna; massage; fully equipped fitness center. Business center; laundry and valet; complimentary newspaper and shoeshine; twice-daily maid service; concierge; limo to the Financial District (weekdays during business hours).

MODERATE

Quality Hotel. 280 Bloor St. W. (at St. George St.), Toronto, ON M5S 1V8. ☎ **416/968-0010.** www.choicehotels.ca. 210 units. A/C TV TEL. C$139–$209 (US$95–$142) double.

Weekend and other packages available. AE, DC, DISC, MC, V. Parking C$12 (US$8). Subway: St. George.

Considering this hotel's tony location—steps from Yorkville and several museums, including the Royal Ontario Museum—the price is hard to beat. The rooms are small but comfortable, and outfitted with well-lit worktables. Choice Club members receive a complimentary daily newspaper and have access to in-house secretarial services; executive rooms have fax-modem hookups. There is a restaurant and coffee shop, and room service is available from 7am to 11am and 5pm to 8pm. Laundry and valet service is available. Guests have access to the facilities of a nearby health club.

Venture Inn. Yorkville. 89 Avenue Rd., Toronto, ON M5R 2G3. ☎ **800/387-3933** or 416/964-1220. Fax 416/964-8692. 71 units. A/C TV TEL. C$120–$170 (US$82–$116) double. Rates include continental breakfast. AE, DC, DISC, ER, MC, V. Parking C$14 (US$9.55). Subway: Bay.

Unlike its pricey neighbors, the Venture Inn is a no-frills place. The location is excellent, which is the trade-off for small rooms with few amenities. The well-kept hotel does offer a few services, such as laundry and dry-cleaning.

INEXPENSIVE

Hotel Selby. 592 Sherbourne St., Toronto, ON M4X 1L4. ☎ **800/387-4788** or 416/921-3142. Fax 416/923-3177. 67 units (8 with shared bathroom). A/C TV TEL. C$95–$110 (US$65–$75) double; C$120–$145 (US$82–$99) suite. Rates include continental breakfast. Senior and student discounts available. AE, MC, V. Limited free parking; otherwise C$12 (US$8). Subway: Sherbourne.

This hotel is one of Toronto's better-kept secrets. Ornate chandeliers, stucco moldings, and high ceilings enhance the 1890s Victorian building. In a predominantly gay neighborhood, the Selby attracts gay and straight couples, as well as students and seniors. Most of the rooms with private bath have a good-sized claw-footed tub. There is an on-site coin laundry; for a small fee, guests can use a nearby fitness center.

Victoria University. 140 Charles St. W., Toronto, ON M5S 1K9. ☎ **416/585-4524.** Fax 416/585-4530. 700 units (none with bathroom). C$65 (US$44.20) double. Rates include breakfast. Senior and student discounts available. MC, V. Closed Sept–April. Nearby parking C$12 (US$8). Subway: Museum.

This is a summer steal. From early May to late August, Victoria University (which is federated with the University of Toronto) makes its student accommodations available to travelers. Furnishings are simple—a bed, desk, and chair are standard—but the surroundings are splendid. Many of the rooms are in Burwash Hall, which overlooks a peaceful, leafy quad; all rooms are down the street from the Royal Ontario Museum, and up the street from Queen's Park. Guests receive linens, towels, and soap; a self-service laundry is on-site. Athletic facilities, including tennis courts, are nearby.

3 Uptown

MODERATE

Best Western Roehampton Hotel. 808 Mount Pleasant Rd., Toronto, ON M4P 2L2. ☎ **800/387-8899** or 416/487-5101. Fax 416/487-5390. www.bestwestern.com. 110 units. A/C TV TEL. C$145–$160 (US$99–$109) double. Packages available. AE, DC, DISC, ER, JCB, MC, V. Valet parking C$8 (US$5). Subway: Eglinton.

The Roehampton is removed from downtown attractions, but still well located. It is a short walk from one of the best dining districts in the city, and a short bus ride from the Ontario Science Centre and 600 acres of parkland (including hiking and cross-country skiing trails, and the Sunnybrook stables). The large, nicely furnished rooms boast big windows and peaceful views. Each has a coffeemaker, individual climate control, and a window that opens; many have mini-refrigerators and heavy-duty desks. The Champs restaurant and lounge is open all day. There is room service between 10am and 11pm; laundry and valet service is also available. The hotel has a fitness center, an outdoor rooftop pool, and a sundeck.

4 East Toronto

Although it's not at all close to the downtown attractions, this area has many sights that are worth noting. They include the Ontario Science Centre, the Toronto Zoo, the Scarborough Bluffs (which homesick English settlers compared to the white cliffs of Dover), and the Scarborough Town Centre, a vast shopping complex.

There are a number of moderately priced chain hotels in this area. They include **Embassy Suites**, 8500 Warden Ave., Markham, ON L6G 1A5 (☎ **905/470-8500**); **Howard Johnson**, 940 Progress Ave., Scarborough, ON M1G 3T5 (☎ **800/ 446-4656**); **Radisson**, 1250 Eglinton Ave. E., Don Mills, ON M3C 1J3 (☎ **416/ 449-4111**); **Ramada**, 185 Yorkland Blvd., Don Mills, ON M2J 4R2 (☎ **800/ 2-RAMADA**); and **Sheraton**, 2035 Kennedy Rd., Scarborough, ON M1T 3G2 (☎ **416/299-1500**).

EXPENSIVE

Westin Prince Hotel. 900 York Mills Rd., Don Mills, ON M3B 3H2. ☎ **800/WESTIN-1** or 416/444-2511. Fax 416/444-9597. www.westin.com. 381 units. A/C TV TEL. C$240–$320 (US$163–$218) double. Extra person C$20 (US$14). Children under 18 stay free in parents' room. Weekend packages available. AE, DC, MC, V. Free parking. Subway: York Mills.

This hotel is less than half an hour from downtown, but its location and 16 acres of parkland make it feel like a secluded resort. The generously proportioned rooms are designed for comfort. Many have a bay window or balcony, and the view makes Toronto look like one big forest. Standard features include a refrigerator, two phones, and a marble bathroom outfitted with a hair dryer.

Dining: The menu at Le Continental offers an impressive array of meat, fowl, and seafood dishes, and vegetarian platters. Pan-Asian Katsura specializes in sushi and tempura. The Coffee Garden offers light fare. The Brandy Tree is an upscale piano bar.

Amenities: 24-hour room service; business center; outdoor heated pool; sauna; tennis court; fitness center. Laundry and valet; concierge; children's center; complimentary newspaper delivery; twice-daily maid service; beauty salon. Game room; putting green; nature trails; jogging track.

INEXPENSIVE

University of Toronto at Scarborough. Student Village. Scarborough Campus, University of Toronto, 1265 Military Trail, Scarborough, ON M1C 1A4. ☎ **416/287-7356.** Fax 416/287-7323. C$180 (US$122) double for 2-night minimum; each additional night C$90 (US$61). Family rates available. MC. V. Closed Sept to mid-May. Free parking. Subway: Kennedy, then Scarborough Rapid Transit to Ellesmere, then bus no. 95 or 95B to college entrance. By car: take exit 387 north from Hwy. 401.

Like the downtown U of T campus, this student residence opens to travelers from mid-May to late August. The greenery-surrounded student village consists of townhouses that sleep a maximum of six. Each has a complete kitchen, but none has air-conditioning, a telephone, or a TV. There is a fitness center with squash and tennis courts and exercise rooms, as well as a cafeteria and pub.

A RURAL RETREAT

The Guild Inn. 201 Guildwood Pkwy., Scarborough, ON M1E 1P6. ☎ **416/261-3331.**
Fax 416/261-5675. 85 units. A/C TV TEL. From C$95 (US$65) double. Extra person C$10
(US$7). Children under 12 stay free in parents' room. Packages available. AE, ER, MC, V. Free
parking. Subway: Kennedy.

The Guild Inn, which overlooks the scenic Scarborough Bluffs, is on 95 acres of
parkland—it's as close to a country manor house as you'll find this close to a big city.
The grounds are littered with historical debris, including several Ionic stone columns
from a long-gone building in the Financial District. The interior is pure Brideshead
Revisited, with a sweeping staircase, wrought-iron chandeliers, and pastoral paintings.
In its heyday, the inn entertained such luminaries as Queen Juliana of the Nether-
lands, Lillian Gish, Rex Harrison, and Sir John Gielgud. Today the quiet setting
attracts mainly vacationing couples and families. Rooms vary in size, but all boast
balconies and clock radios.

Dining: The formal dining room serves a traditional menu of grilled meats and
seafood. It is a popular spot for Sunday brunch. In good weather, the verandah transforms into the perfect spot to sip a mint julep.

Amenities: Outdoor swimming pool, tennis court, fitness center, nature trails.

5 At the Airport

Don't be fooled by anyone who tells you that the airport isn't far from the city. It's at
least a 30-minute drive to downtown, and public transit doesn't come this far. A taxi
downtown costs roughly C$36 (US$24.50). Many of the hotels along the airport strip
cater to business travelers. Others may wish to stay in this area if they're planning to
divide their time between Toronto and its outlying areas, such as the Niagara region.
Serious golfers come here for the area's many golf courses, including the 18-hole championship layout at the Royal Woodbine Golf Club.

EXPENSIVE

Hilton Toronto Airport. 5875 Airport Rd., Mississauga, ON L4V 1N1. ☎ **800/567-9999**
or 905/677-9900. Fax 905/677-7782. www.hilton.com. 413 units. A/C MINIBAR TV TEL.
C$205 (US$139) double; from C$235 (US$160) minisuite. Extra person C$20 (US$14).
Children stay free in parents' room. Weekend packages available. AE, DC, DISC, ER, MC, V.
Parking C$9 (US$6.10). Downtown shuttle C$11 (US$7.50) one-way. Take the Gardiner Expwy.
west to Hwy. 427 north, to Airport Expwy. (Dixon Rd. exit).

One of the Hilton's main attractions is its 152 minisuites—all have a king-size bed in
the bedroom, a sofa bed in the living room, a color TV in both rooms, and three
phones. Standard guest rooms have one TV and telephone apiece, and all units have
hair dryers and coffeemakers. The building underwent a C$9 million (US$6 million)
face-lift in 1999; in the fall of 2001, there will be further renovations to the hotel's suites.

Dining: The menu at the Harvest Restaurant has many meaty mains and a few
dishes for vegetarians. The Coffee Bar in the lobby dispenses gourmet java and snacks.
Misty's Club offers live music, drinks, and light fare.

Amenities: Business center; 24-hour room service; outdoor heated pool with poolside
deck; laundry and valet; concierge; squash courts; exercise room; beauty salon.

Sheraton Gateway at Terminal Three. Toronto AMF, Box 3000, Toronto, ON L5P 1C4.
☎ **800/325-3535** or 905/672-7000. Fax 905/672-7100. www.sheraton.com. 480 units.
A/C MINIBAR TV TEL. C$190–$280 (US$129–$190) double. AE, DC, DISC, ER, JCB, MC, V.
Parking C$9 (US$6.10).

You don't even need to go outdoors to get here—just take the skywalk from Terminal 3.
Rooms are comfortable, spacious, and, more to the point, fully soundproofed. The

standard Sheraton features include in-room coffeemakers, two phones, fax-modem hookups, hair dryers, and complimentary newspaper delivery. Club rooms have extra inducements, such as ergonomic chairs, a fax/printer/copier, and access to a private lounge that serves complimentary breakfast and snacks.

Dining: The formal Mahogany Grill serves meat, pasta, and Asian-inspired dishes. The Café Suisse serves buffet breakfast, lunch, and dinner. There is also a lobby bar.

Amenities: 24-hour room service and fitness center; business center; indoor pool; whirlpool; sauna; laundry and valet; baby-sitting; in-room massage; hair salon; shopping arcade.

✪ **Wyndham Bristol Place.** 950 Dixon Rd., Rexdale, ON M9W 5N4. ☎ **416/675-9444.** Fax 416/675-4426. 287 units. A/C TV TEL. C$175–$295 (US$119–$201) double; from C$400 (US$272) suite. Extra person C$15 (US$10). Children under 18 stay free in parents' room. Packages available. AE, DC, DISC, JCB, MC, V. Parking C$8 (US$5.45).

The Wyndham's claim to fame is personalized service. This is undoubtedly the most glamorous hotel for miles around—and the only one with a waterfall in its lobby. Guest rooms are attractively furnished in mahogany, and all have two phones, a fax-modem hookup, and an iron and ironing board.

Dining: Zachary's aims high, with a seasonal menu and glamorously appointed dining room. Le Café is an upscale coffee shop.

Amenities: 24-hour room service; business center; indoor/outdoor pool with skylight dome and sundeck; fitness center with exercise room and sauna; laundry and valet; concierge.

MODERATE

Regal Constellation Hotel. 900 Dixon Rd., Etobicoke, ON M9W 1J7. ☎ **416/675-1500.** Fax 905/675-4611. www.regal-hotels.com/toronto. 710 units. A/C TV TEL. C$115–$195 (US$78.20–$133). Extra person C$15 (US$10). Children under 16 stay free in parents' room. Weekend and honeymoon packages available. AE, DC, DISC, MC, V. Parking C$8 (US$5.45).

This hotel started small almost four decades ago, but it has steadily grown into one of the best bets in the airport region. Its excellent meeting space makes it a favorite for trade shows and conventions. Because the hotel was constructed piece by piece, the rooms vary greatly from floor to floor. Every unit is a minisuite that houses a king or two double beds, a sturdy desk, and an L-shaped sofa.

Not surprisingly, the hotel is a self-contained entertainment complex. There are four restaurants, including the Mitaka (Japanese), the Grill (steak), and the Atrium (all-day buffet). The lounge, the Banyan Tree, offers live evening entertainment.

In addition to 24-hour room service, there's a concierge desk, and laundry and valet service. The hotel has an indoor/outdoor pool, a bank, a beauty salon, and a recreation complex that contains an exercise room and a sauna.

Toronto Airport Marriott Hotel. 901 Dixon Rd, Toronto, ON M9W 1J5. ☎ **800/228-9290** or 416/674-9400. Fax 416/674-8292. 424 units. A/C MINIBAR TV TEL. C$110–$199 (US$74.80–$135) double. Extra person C$15 (US$10). Weekend packages available. AE, DC, DISC, ER, MC, V. Parking C$8 (US$5.45).

One of the newest airport hotels, the Marriott is popular with business travelers. The hotel is trying to attract leisure travelers, too, so expect a weekend discount of up to 50%. Rooms are comfortable and spacious; pastel shades are the norm. The amenities are in keeping with the Marriott name. The hotel has 24-hour room service, an indoor pool with a skylight, volleyball and basketball courts, and a fitness center with exercise room and sauna. There's laundry and valet service, and a concierge.

There are two restaurants off the lobby. The Terrace serves international fare all day. The Mikado is a Japanese restaurant where your meal can be cooked right at your table.

INEXPENSIVE

Comfort Inn—Airport. 240 Belfield Rd., Rexdale, ON M9W 1H3. ☎ **416/241-8513.** Fax 416/249-4203. www.choicehotels.com. 122 units. A/C TV TEL. From C$90 (US$61) double. Extra person C$10 (US$7). Children under 18 stay free in parents' or grandparents' room. Rates include continental breakfast. AE, DC, MC, V. Free parking for 1 night, then C$5 (US$3) per day. Take Hwy. 27 north to Belfield Rd.

Recently refurbished with new carpets, beds, and draperies, the Comfort Inn offers simple rooms at reasonable rates. Rooms are decorated in pine, and just big enough to hold a queen-size bed, dresser, desk and chair, and plush armchair or loveseat. The hotel offers free local calls and complimentary newspapers; hair dryers, irons, and ironing boards are available on request. KD's Restaurant and Lounge is open all day.

Days Inn—Toronto Airport. 6257 Airport Rd., Mississauga, ON L4V 1N1. ☎ **800/387-6891** or 905/678-1400. Fax 905/678-9130. 201 units. A/C TV TEL. C$90–$169 (US$61–$115) double. Extra person C$10 (US$7). Children under 17 stay free in parents' room. Weekend packages available. AE, DC, DISC, ER, JCB, MC, V. Parking C$6 (US$4) per day, C$18 (US$12) per week.

For the price, this is one of the best bets on the airport strip; the facilities are similar to those at pricier hotels. The guest rooms were renovated in 1998, and the results are bright and cheery. All rooms are equipped with coffeemakers and hair dryers. Upgraded rooms have bathrobes, irons and ironing boards, and fax-modem hookups. The Garden Café Restaurant is open all day. Room service is available from 6:30am until midnight, and there is a small laundry room for guests. The hotel has an indoor pool, sauna, and exercise room.

Delta Meadowvale Resort & Conference Centre. 6750 Mississauga Rd. (at Hwy. 401), Mississauga, ON L5N 2L3. ☎ **800/422-8238** or 905/821-1981. Fax 905/542-4036. www.deltahotels.com. 382 units. A/C TV TEL. C$110–$240 (US$74.80–$163) double. Weekend discounts available. AE, DC, DISC, MC, V. Free parking. Downtown shuttle C$11 (US$7.50) one-way.

Set on 23 acres of greenery, the Delta has all the attributes of a restful resort. There are hiking and biking trails, tennis and squash courts, and indoor and outdoor swimming pools. The cozy rooms have modern wooden furniture, and each boasts a small balcony—all the better for relaxing. Each room also has a coffeemaker, refrigerator, hair dryer, and two phones. The Regatta Bar & Grille serves a variety of dishes throughout the day; there is also a lounge for evening drinks. Twenty-four-hour room service and laundry and valet service are available. The resort also has a business center and a beauty salon. Of special interest to young families are the children's creative center and the baby-sitting services.

Four Points Hotel. 5444 Dixie Rd. (at Hwy. 401), Mississauga, ON L4W 2L2. ☎ **800/737-3211** or 905/624-1144. Fax 416/624-9477. www.fourpoints.com/torontoairport. 287 units. A/C TV TEL. C$119–$230 (US$81–$156) double. Extra person C$15 (US$10). Weekend discounts available. AE, CB, DC, DISC, ER, MC, V. Free parking.

On a 6-acre woodland site, the Four Points offers a relaxing setting. Guest rooms were renovated in 1999, with bathrooms, carpets, and draperies singled out for attention. Rooms are decorated in light colors and natural woods, and equipped with coffeemakers and hair dryers. There is 24-hour room service, laundry and valet service, a concierge, and baby-sitting available. In the hotel are a business center, a children's activity center, and a beauty salon. The fitness center has an indoor pool, sundeck, sauna, and exercise room. The Chardonnay Grill & Lounge features daily buffets as well as an à la carte menu.

Dining 5

"**Y**ou are so *spoiled.*" So said an old friend who had returned to Toronto for a visit after more than a decade away. What had I done to incur her wrath? Well, first I took her out to one of my favorite French bistros for dinner; the next night I recommended a gem of a Japanese restaurant; after that, I think I suggested an Ethiopian eatery. And so it went for the length of her stay.

With more than 5,000 eateries, and cooking styles from any country or nationality you can name, Toronto's culinary scene is eclectic, palate teasing, and affordable. Citizens and visitors are indeed spoiled. But it wasn't always so. Until about two decades ago, dining out in the city meant either steak house or pub grub. Now the sheer wealth of choices is dizzying.

Mediterranean cuisine still dominates the scene, but fusion is on the rise. Many restaurants that started out as, say, Italian, have incorporated ingredients and cooking styles from Southeast Asia and north Africa, among other *haute* spots. Each wave of immigration has brought new ideas and flavors. You'll find restaurants of all types and price ranges, but some neighborhoods are renowned for their specialties: Little Italy for its trattorias, Chinatown for its Chinese and Vietnamese eateries, and the Danforth for its Greek tavernas.

DINING NOTES   Dining out in Toronto does not have to be an expensive venture, but the tax level is high. Meals are subject to the 8% provincial sales tax and to the 7% GST. In other words, tax and tip together can add 30% to your bill. Tips are normally left to the diners' discretion, unless there are six or more people at the table; 15% is the usual amount for good service. The price of a bottle of wine is generally quite high because of the tax on imports; get around it by ordering an Ontario vintage—local wines enjoy a rising international reputation. Remember that there is a 10% tax on alcohol, whatever you're sipping.

1 Restaurants by Cuisine

AMERICAN
Far Niente (Downtown West, *E*)
Jump Café and Bar (Downtown West, *E*)

ASIAN
Kubo (Downtown East, *I*)
SpringRolls (Midtown West, *I*)
Youki (Midtown West, *M*)

BELGIAN
Café Brussel (Midtown East/ The East End, *E*)

BISTRO
Cities (Downtown West, *M*)
Lakes (Uptown, *E*)
Pony (Downtown West, *M*)
Roxborough's (Uptown, *E*)
Stork on the Roof (Uptown, *M*)

BURGERS
Fran's (Uptown, *I*)

CAJUN
Southern Accent (Midtown West, *E*)

CANADIAN
Canoe Restaurant & Bar (Downtown West, *VE*)
Tundra (Downtown West, *VE*)

CHINESE
Grand Yatt (North of the City, *M*)
Happy Seven (Downtown West, *I*)
Lai Wah Heen (Downtown West, *E*)
Lee Garden (Downtown West, *I*)
Sang Ho (Downtown West, *M*)

CONTINENTAL
Café Societa (Downtown West, *E*)
Centro (Uptown, *VE*)
Jamie Kennedy at the Museum (Midtown West, *E*)
Opus (Midtown West, *VE*)
Oro (Downtown West, *E*)
Senses (Midtown West, *E*)

360 Revolving Restaurant (Downtown West, *VE*)
Truffles (Midtown West, *VE*)

CREPES
Le Papillon (Downtown East, *I*)

DELI
Lox, Stock & Bagel (Midtown West, *I*)
Shopsy's (Downtown East, *I*)

ECLECTIC
Avalon (Downtown West, *VE*)
Citron (Downtown West, *M*)
The Fifth (Downtown West, *E*)
Goldfish (Midtown West, *M*)
Messis (Midtown West, *M*)
Mildred Pierce (Downtown West, *M*)
Octavia (Midtown East/East End, *M*)
Swan (Downtown West, *M*)
Taro Grill (Downtown West, *M*)

ETHIOPIAN
Lalibela (Midtown West, *I*)

FRENCH
Auberge du Pommier (Uptown, *E*)
Bistro 990 (Midtown West, *VE*)
Jacques Bistro du Parc (Midtown West, *M*)
La Bodega (Downtown West, *M*)
Le Select (Downtown West, *M*)
Matignon (Midtown West, *M*)
Zola (Midtown West, *VE*)

FUSION
Agora (Downtown West, *E*)
Boba (Midtown West, *E*)
Mercer Street Grill (Downtown West, *E*)
Monsoon (Downtown West, *VE*)
Pangaea (Midtown West, *E*)
Queen Mother Café (Downtown West, *I*)
The Rivoli (Downtown West, *I*)
Veni Vidi Vici (Downtown West, *M*)

Key to Abbreviations: *VE* = Very Expensive   *E* = Expensive   *M* = Moderate   *I* = Inexpensive

GREEK

Astoria (Midtown East/East End, *I*)
Avli (Midtown East/East End, *I*)
Christina's (Midtown East/
    East End, *M*)
Mezes (Midtown East/East End, *I*)
Ouzeri (Midtown East/East End, *I*)
Pan on the Danforth (Midtown
    East/East End, *M*)
Penelope (Downtown West, *I*)

INDIAN

Indian Rice Factory (Midtown
    West, *I*)
Nataraj (Midtown West, *I*)
Shala-Mar (Downtown West, *I*)

INTERNATIONAL

Annona (Midtown West, *E*)
Courthouse Market Grille (Down-
    town East, *E*)
North 44 (Uptown, *VE*)
Rosewater Supper Club (Downtown
    East, *E*)
Scaramouche (Uptown, *VE*)
Splendido Bar and Grill (Midtown
    West, *E*)
Terra Restaurant Oyster & Martini
    Bar (North of the City, *E*)
ZooM Caffe & Bar (Downtown
    East, *E*)

ITALIAN

Amore Trattoria (Uptown, *M*)
Café Nervosa (Midtown West, *M*)
Dante's (North of the City, *I*)
Ecco La (Downtown West, *M*)
Florentine Court (Downtown
    East, *M*)
Gio's (Uptown, *M*)
Il Posto Nuovo (Midtown West, *E*)
La Bruschetta (Uptown, *E*)
Mediterraneo (Uptown, *M*)
Mistura (Midtown West, *E*)
Serra (Midtown West, *I*)
Sotto Sotto (Midtown West, *M*)
Trattoria Giancarlo (Downtown
    West, *E*)

Tuscany Café (Downtown West, *M*)
Veni Vidi Vici (Downtown West, *M*)

JAPANESE

Hiro Sushi (Downtown East, *E*)
Japan Deli (Midtown West, *I*)

LAOTIAN

Vanipha Lanna (Uptown, *M*)

LATIN AMERICAN

Xango (Downtown West, *E*)

LIGHT FARE

Bloor Street Diner (Midtown West, *I*)
Hannah's Kitchen (Uptown, *I*)
Hello Toast (Downtown East, *I*)
Kalendar (Downtown West, *I*)
Peter Pan (Downtown West, *M*)
Rebel House (Uptown, *I*)
Sottovoce (Downtown West, *I*)

MEDITERRANEAN

Kensington Kitchen (Midtown
    West, *I*)
Lolita's Lust (Midtown East/East
    End, *M*)
Millie's Bistro (Uptown, *E*)
Myth (Midtown East/East End, *M*)
Octavia (Midtown East/East End, *M*)
Quartier (Uptown, *E*)

MIDDLE EASTERN

Cedar's (Midtown West, *I*)
Free Times Café (Downtown West, *I*)
Mezzetta (Uptown, *M*)

PORTUGUESE

Chiado (Downtown West, *E*)

QUEBECOIS

Montreal Bistro and Jazz Club
    (Downtown East, *M*)

SEAFOOD

Joso's (Midtown West, *M*)
Rodney's Oyster House (Downtown
    East, *M*)

STEAK

Barberian's (Downtown West, *VE*)
The Senator (Downtown East, *E*)

TEX-MEX

Tortilla Flats (Downtown West, *I*)

THAI

Thai Magic (Uptown, *E*)
Vanipha Lanna (Uptown, *M*)

Young Thailand (Downtown East, *I*)

VEGETARIAN

Annapurna Vegetarian Restaurant (Midtown West, *I*)
Juice for Life (Midtown West, *I*)

VIETNAMESE

Pho Hung (Midtown West, *I*)

2 Downtown West

This is where you will find Toronto's greatest concentration of great restaurants. You'll see a lot of high-price, low-quality eateries in the area, too. There also tends to be more attitude from wait staffs, particularly along the Gourmet Ghetto of **Queen Street West.** I'm a firm believer that even the best food can't make up for shoddy service, so the restaurants I've selected generally get high marks in both categories. **Little Italy,** which runs along **College Street,** and **Chinatown,** which radiates from **Spadina Avenue,** have more restaurants than any other parts of the city.

VERY EXPENSIVE

Avalon. 270 Adelaide St. W. (at John St.). ☎ **416/979-9918.** Reservations required. Main courses C$21–$36 (US$14.30–$24.50). AE, DC, MC, V. Thurs noon–2:30pm; Mon–Thurs 5:30–10pm, Fri–Sat 5:30–11pm. Subway: St. Andrew. ECLECTIC.

Follow the slim marble staircase into the elegant, compact dining room. Careful attention to detail is clear, whether in the spray of fresh flowers on each table or the daily chef's menu. (The regular menu changes with the seasons.) Avalon has one of the most inventive kitchens in the city, and the chef's creativity is expressed through creative pairing of flavors rather than a showy multiplicity of ingredients. Main courses favor fish and fowl, such as potato-crusted halibut fillet with buttery Savoy cabbage and parsley sauce, or a seared rare Muscovy duck breast with dauphinoise potatoes and pomegranate glaze. Desserts follow suit, with treats like pear-and-elderflower sorbet. The globe-trotting wine list represents New World and Old.

✪ **Barberian's.** 7 Elm St. ☎ **416/597-0335.** Reservations required. Main courses C$22–$37 (US$15–$25.15). AE, DC, MC, V. Mon–Fri noon–2:30pm; daily 5pm–midnight. Subway: Dundas. STEAK.

Not getting enough protein in your diet? Get thee to Harry Barberian's upscale steak house, which has been going strong since 1959 (his son, Arron, has since taken over). The room is cozy in a clubby way, with dark woods, framed newspapers, and a host of pre-Confederation doodads. The menu rarely changes, but you won't hear any grousing about it—the crowd is too busy slurping pre-dinner martinis. The highlights are the eight steaks, from the 9-ounce sirloin to the 23-ounce porterhouse, all served with rice and spuds. The less traditional can partake of dishes like cheese or beef fondue for two, which is on the late-night menu (10pm to midnight). For all intents and purposes, there is only one dessert: the Grand Marnier soufflé for two. Yes, there are other sweets, including a fine baked Alaska, but if it's your first time here, get the soufflé. The wine list is about 1,000 strong, so bring your reading specs. Celebrity sightings aren't uncommon, but autograph-seeking is frowned upon.

Canoe Restaurant & Bar. 54th floor, Toronto Dominion Tower, 66 Wellington St. W. ☎ **416/364-0054.** Reservations required. Main courses C$25–$35 (US$17–$23.80). AE, DC, ER, MC, V. Mon–Fri 11:45am–2:30pm and 5–10:30pm. Subway: King. CANADIAN.

The inspiring view makes this the place to see Toronto lit up at night. The restaurant's interior isn't so shabby, either, with its polished wooden floors and furnishings. Corporate types predominate, not only because Canoe is in the Financial District but also because the prices are best suited to expense accounts. The meat-heavy menu showcases modern Canadian cuisine. Grilled veal tenderloin served with acorn squash and warm sage-infused goat cheese vies for attention with herb-stuffed pheasant served atop maple-poached dates and cremini mushrooms. A few dishes, deemed "spa inspired," are lower in fat. The wine list only scratches the surface—roughly two-thirds of the bottles in stock aren't included—so if you're craving a particular grape of a certain vintage, be sure to ask.

✪ **Monsoon.** 100 Simcoe St. ☎ **416/979-7172.** Reservations required. Main courses C$21–$37 (US$14.30–$25.15). AE, DC, MC, V. Mon–Fri noon–2:30pm; Mon–Sat 5:30–11pm. Subway: Osgoode. FUSION.

Monsoon is more famous for its award-winning interior design than for its food. That's a pity, because while the brown-on-black Zen-like setting is easy on the eye (especially with that fabulously flattering lighting), the cooking is subtly sensual. Sophisticated palates are familiar with Thai, Chinese, Japanese, and Indian flavors, but it's unusual to find them so seductively intertwined with North American staples. Veal goes vindaloo, accompanied by a mango glaze, curried cauliflower, and grilled okra. Beef and prawns meet up in a Cabernet-teriyaki reduction with wasabi mashed potatoes. The wine list runs the gamut from French Bordeaux to Australian shiraz.

360 Revolving Restaurant. CN Tower, 301 Front St. W. ☎ **416/362-5411.** Reservations required. Main courses C$25–$40 (US$17–$27.20). AE, DC, MC, V. May–Sept daily 10:30am–2:30pm; year-round daily 4:30–10:30pm. Subway: Union. CONTINENTAL.

Let's be frank: Most people do not come here for the food. The view's the thing, a breathtaking, awe-inspiring panorama that will make you see the city in a new light. Unfortunately, the kitchen doesn't keep pace, as it offers up uninspiring fare like cold crab and shrimp salad on Bibb lettuce. The highlight of the dessert list is a chocolate rendition of the CN Tower. The wine list makes for interesting viewing, with its collection of three-figure vintages, though there are a few choices by the glass. When the charm of the view starts to wane, be sure to check out the art on the walls.

✪ **Tundra.** Hilton Toronto, 145 Richmond St. W. ☎ **416/860-6800.** Reservations strongly recommended. Main courses C$28–$40 (US$19.05–$27.20). AE, DC, ER, MC, V. Mon–Fri 11:30am–2:00pm, daily 6:30am–10:30am and 5:30pm–11:00pm. Subway: Osgoode. CANADIAN.

A key element of the Hilton's $25 million renovation was the creation of this luxurious restaurant just off its foyer. Sophisticated and opulent, the restaurant is designed to bring to mind elements of the Canadian landscape. How does one suggest the majesty of, say, a giant redwood? With thunderous columns wrapped in semi-transparent fabric and lit from within, of course! (The result is like a gargantuan Naguchi lamp, and is visually stunning.) Every detail, from the one-armed wing chairs to the Frette linens, is beautifully executed.

The sense of theater doesn't stop with the design. Tundra's Canadian cuisine has been artfully designed by chef Andre Walker, a New Zealander. Arctic char (a fish that's often called a hybrid of salmon and trout) is paired up with Malapeque oysters

Downtown Toronto Dining

360° Revolving Restaurant **21**
Agora **12**
Avalon **17**
Barberian's **29**
Canoe Restaurant & Bar **38**
Cities **1**
Citron **3**
Courthouse Market Grille **35**
Ecco La **6**
Far Niente **39**
The Fifth **25**
Florentine Court **32**
Free Times Café **7**
Happy Seven **8**
Hiro Sushi **43**
Jump Café and Bar **40**
Kubo **30**
La Bodega **10**
Lai Wah Heen **27**
Le Papillon **42**
Le Select **14**
Lee Garden **9**
Left Bank **5**
Mercer Street Grill **20**
Monsoon **23**
Montréal Bistro and Jazz Club **44**
Oro **28**
Penelope **22**
Peter Pan **16**
Queen Mother Café **26**
The Rivoli **13**
Rodney's Oyster House **36**
Rosewater Supper Club **34**
Sang Ho **11**
The Senator **31**
Shopsy's **41**
Swan **4**
Taro Grill **2**
Tortilla Flats **15**
Tundra **24**
Tuscany Café **19**
Xango **18**
Young Thailand **33**
Zoom Caffe & Bar **37**

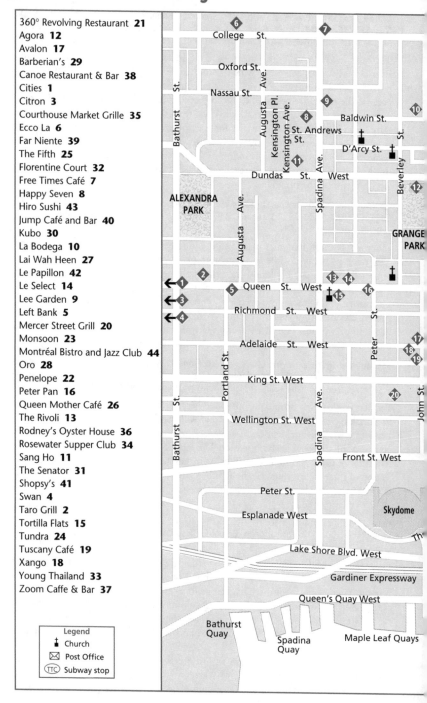

Legend
† Church
✉ Post Office
Ⓣ Subway stop

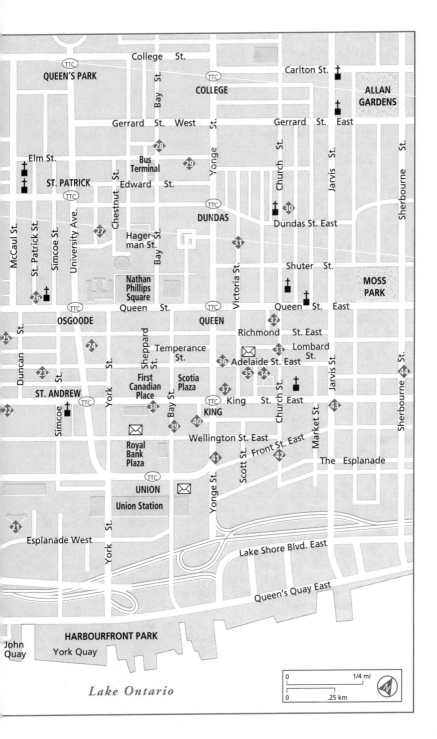

and fried leeks; Nova Scotia lobster mates with a tomato-avocado-bean salad and Yukon Gold potatoes. The results are elegantly complex. While the wine list is exhaustive, don't hesitate to ask for recommendations—service here is well-informed and helpful.

EXPENSIVE

✪ **Agora.** At the Art Gallery of Ontario, 317 Dundas St. W. ☎ 416/977-0414. Reservations recommended for lunch. Main courses C$12–$18 (US$8.20–$12.25). AE, DC, MC, V. Tues–Fri noon–3pm, Sat–Sun 11am–3pm. Subway: St. Patrick. FUSION.

I'm biased—restaurants attached to larger institutions (say, museums) usually scare me off. Agora is an exception. Located in the Tannenbaum sculpture gallery of the AGO, and open only for lunch and brunch, Agora serves food that's inventive without being artsy. The menu does have its precious moments, like the "Still life with pear, pancetta, and fig," but the food is uniformly delightful. Some dishes play it straight with a continental flair, like the spicy Italian sausage with creamy polenta, bell peppers, and fennel. The more playful pairings are fine examples of fusion (think scallops with caramelized pineapple served atop lime-scented black beans). The weekend brunch glams up scrambled eggs with smoked salmon and fresh asparagus, and the *torta rustica*, with its layers of ricotta, mozzarella, leeks, peas, and smoked trout, is a treat.

Café Societa. 796 College St. ☎ **416/588-7490.** Reservations recommended. Main courses C$12–$21 (US$8.20–$14.30). MC, V. Sat–Sun 11am–3pm; daily 6–11pm. Subway: Queen's Park, then any streetcar west to Ossington Ave. CONTINENTAL.

The Lilliputian dining room is cramped, the menu is the shortest in the city, and yet the crowds can't stay away. Why? Simply because the food is seductive. The trick is in the unusual marriages of fruits and vegetables flavoring many of the dishes. Rosti and rhubarb compote enliven a veal chop, and it turns out that grilled calamari tastes better with citrus fruit. Who knew? The highlight of the triad of desserts is chocolate mousse with heavy cream and paper-thin pear shavings.

✪ **Chiado.** 484 College St. (at Concorde Ave.). ☎ **416/538-1910.** Reservations required. Main courses C$17–$30 (US$11.60–$20.40). AE, DC, ER, MC, V. Mon–Sat noon–3pm; Mon–Thurs 5–10pm, Fri–Sat 5pm–midnight. Subway: Queen's Park, then any streetcar west to Bathurst St. PORTUGUESE.

Alone in this Mediterranean-obsessed part of town, Chiado serves modern Portuguese cuisine. Designed to evoke opulence, with marble floors, oil paintings, and fresh orchids, it draws a sophisticated, luxury-loving crowd. Servers are models of Euro professionalism, attentive without hovering. The menu favors seafood, from starters—such as grilled squid with roasted peppers—to entrees, such as poached or grilled salted cod. Fresh fish is flown in daily. There is also a choice of braised rabbit or capon, among fowl and game dishes. Don't skimp on the lovingly prepared sweets. The wine list is a treat. It includes many unfamiliar but rich and complex wines, most priced in the bargain-basement range.

Far Niente Napa Grill. 187 Bay St. (at Wellington St.). ☎ **416/214-9922.** Reservations recommended. Main courses C$17–$35 (US$11.60–$23.80). AE, DC, ER, JCB, MC, V. Mon–Fri 11:30am–midnight, Sat–Sun 5pm–midnight. Subway: King. AMERICAN.

A hangout favored by the suited set, this restaurant offers fine cuisine in a casual setting. The setting is intended to invoke sunnier climes, with an earthy palette, mounds of greenery, walls of wine racks, and simple wooden tables and chairs. The kitchen uses plenty of garden-fresh ingredients and a light touch. Many menu staples—including tuna steak, teriyaki chicken, and even a Caesar salad—are designated as "living well" dishes, which have reduced fat, cholesterol, and calories. Almost every dish is available in small and whole portions. You might try Sonoma salad of tomato, goat cheese, and avocado; a pumpkin ravioli with cranberries and pecans in an apple cider butter sauce; or New Zealand lamb chops with rosemary-garlic mashed potatoes and veggie ragout. Steaks are a specialty, with filet mignon and New York strip loin available in 6- to 14-ounce cuts.

Downstairs is Soul of the Vine, a wine bar that looks as if it was built in the middle of a wine cellar. It has its own menu, which features mainly appetizers and pasta. The room can get loud and smoky, so serious eaters should stay upstairs.

The Fifth. 225 Richmond St. W. ☎ **416/979-3005.** Reservations required. Prix-fixe menu C\$75 (US\$51). Thurs–Sat 6pm–midnight. Subway: Osgoode. ECLECTIC.

Je pense que Le Cinquième n'est pas comme des autres. Ah, *pardon,* was I just speaking French? I must have been confused by the menu at The Fifth, which insists on listing all its plates *en français* and *en anglais. Soufflé au Grand Marnier* is helpfully translated (Grand Marnier soufflé)—*ça va?* This is a restaurant that is in danger of becoming a victim of its own success. Since *Toronto Life* magazine named The Fifth as the best restaurant in the city last year, it has become all but impossible to get a reservation without a couple of months' lead time. And while the kitchen serves up consistently stellar fare, the level of service fails to impress.

✪ Jump Café and Bar. 1 Wellington St. W. ☎ **416/363-3400.** Reservations required. Main courses C\$19–\$32. AE, DC, ER, JCB, MC, V. Mon–Fri 11:30am–11pm, Sat 4:30–11pm. Subway: King. AMERICAN.

Jump is, appropriately enough, always hopping. A sprawling space in Commerce Court, one of the Financial District's towering monoliths, it can be tricky to find. Just follow the buzz—as the decibel level rises, you'll know you're on the right track. Power brokers drop by for lunch or after-work drinks. The dinner scene is a mix of celebratory couples and suits in deal-making mode. The restaurant—one big room strategically sectioned off with wooden screens and greenery—is such a see-and-be-seen spot that you might suspect it's all show and no substance. Actually, the food is anything but an afterthought. The menus feature "suit-able" dishes like grilled 10-ounce New York black Angus steak with Yukon Gold fries, salsa, and mushroom gravy. The more gastronomically adventurous have other choices, such as roasted sea bass with fragrant coconut basmati rice and green curry, or osso bucco with spinach-and-lemon risotto. To start, consider steamed mussels in ginger-and-coconut-milk broth, or grilled tiger shrimps on top of Thai mango-peanut salad. The wine list favors the New World, and there are a fair number of selections by the glass. Luxe desserts will put your diet back by about a month. Service is smooth, and the only complaint I could possibly make is that Jump never seems to settle down.

✪ Lai Wah Heen. In the Metropolitan Hotel, 110 Chestnut St. ☎ **416/977-9899.** Reservations recommended. Main courses C\$16–\$30 (US\$10.90–\$20.40). AE, DC, MC, V. Daily 11:30am–3pm; Sun–Thurs 5:30–10:30pm, Fri–Sat 5:30–11pm. Subway: St. Patrick. CHINESE.

This is one hotel dining room where you'll find more locals than visitors. The interior is vintage art deco; spare pictograms dominate the walls of the two-level space. A suited-up crowd dominates at lunch, though by dinner a few dolled-up couples manage to sneak in. The massive menu is mainly Cantonese, with some Szechwan specialties mixed in. There are more than a dozen shark's fin soups, from a thick broth with bamboo fungi to an Alaska king crab bisque. Abalone gets similar attention, shredded and stir-fried with bean sprouts or braised with fresh vegetables and oyster sauce. Those with tamer tastes (or restricted budgets) can choose from a variety of meat or noodle dishes; the dim sum list alone goes on for several pages. There are several prix-fixe specials at lunch and dinner, which offer five or six dishes for C$38 (US$25.85) and up.

Mercer Street Grill. 36 Mercer St. ☎ **416/599-3399.** Reservations recommended. Main courses C$25–$30 (US$17–$20.40). AE, ER, MC, V. Sun–Wed 5:15–10pm, Thurs 5:15–10:30pm, Fri–Sat 5:15–11pm. Subway: St. Andrew. FUSION.

From the street, the Mercer Street Grill looks like a corrugated tin hut out of a postmodern fairy tale. But open the door and you'll find rare beauty within. The crowd changes with the hour. Early in the evening the 40-seat room is packed with noisy suits; after the nearby theaters empty out, this becomes the late-night dining venue of choice among equally raucous thespians. In temperate weather, a canopied Japanese-themed patio opens, complete with bamboo fencing and a waterfall. (It's heated, so it can remain open for much of the year.)

The menu leans heavily to Asia, too. Beef tenderloin with a gorgonzola sauce, shitake mushrooms, and leek dumplings is presented Japanese-style in a refined bento box, and Chilean sea bass meets up with black beans, Shanghai noodles, and garlic yar choy greens. The recent trend toward simplifying food presentation hasn't caught on here—the plates are constructed with skyscraper-like detail, and they soar. The highlight of the imaginative dessert list is the chocolate sushi—four hand-rolled confections filled with raspberry coulis, hazelnut praline, and white chocolate; it's superb, but it's not always on the menu.

Oro. 45 Elm St. ☎ **416/597-0155.** Reservations recommended. Main courses C$16–$31 (US$10.90–$21). AE, DC, MC, V. Mon–Sat 6–10:30pm. CONTINENTAL.

The trappings of modern luxury set the scene, with blond wood, a tile floor, and a substantial fireplace that warms that room (figuratively if not always literally). Softly lit tables are spaced far apart, allowing intimate conversation to rise above a whisper. The menu ventures further and further from its Italianate roots. Pasta figures in half a dozen main courses, but the showstoppers are West-meets-East offerings like hoisin-tamarind glazed pork tenderloin accompanied by braised Asian greens. Most dishes, like Cornish hen with a cheddar corn cake and foie gras, don't veer too far from the Continent, though. The lengthy wine list leans toward Italy and America, with only a select few by the glass. The oft-praised service is relaxed yet attentive.

Trattoria Giancarlo. 41–43 Clinton St. (at College St.). ☎ **416/533-9619.** Reservations required. Main courses C$16–$30. AE, DC, MC, V. Mon–Sat 6–11pm. Subway: Queen's Park, then any streetcar west to Clinton St. ITALIAN.

It's always disappointing to report that what was once a wonderful restaurant is no longer quite so appetizing, but that's the position I'm in with Trattoria Giancarlo. It's a tremendously popular spot, but the nonstop stream of diners has not convinced the owners to hire more staff; instead, harried servers get to run from kitchen to dining room to patio all evening. They manage as best they can, but the result is that service is poor. It's a shame, because the food is still lovely: Antipasti runs the gamut from *luna di Camembert,* cheese baked and wrapped in Parma prosciutto paired with fresh fruit, to *polpi grigliati,* a tender octopus awash in braised onion and balsamic vinegar. Then there are the pasta plates, like linguine with shrimp, roasted tomatoes, and sweet onions, or meat dishes, like quail flavored with Marsala and sage, served with creamy polenta. Traditional Italian sweets like tiramisu and tartufo round out the meal. But no matter how charming the meal, the inadequate service might leave a bad taste in your mouth.

Xango. 106 John St. ☎ **416/593-4407.** Reservations recommended. Main courses C$16–$24 (US$10.90–$16.30). AE, DC, MC, V. Tues–Sat 5–11pm. Subway: St. Andrew. LATIN AMERICAN.

The lust for all things Latin rages on, but curiously enough Xango is one of the few restaurants in Toronto where you can indulge the passion. Are would-be imitators intimidated by the bold bright yellow space or the inventive menu? The cooking borrows from the traditions of countries as diverse as Cuba, Honduras, and Ecuador. To start, oysters are introduced to plantains, spinach, bacon, and manchego cheese. As a main course, grilled salmon meets up with blue and gold potatoes drizzled with sweet yellow pepper vinaigrette. A hit of rum or brandy warms up the uniformly rich desserts. Chilean and Argentinean vintages dominate the wine list, with a few Spanish picks thrown in. Do try one of the Latin cocktails—the tart Brazilian caiiprinhia is a specialty.

MODERATE

Cities. 859 Queen St. W. ☎ **416/599-7720.** Main courses C$12–$20 (US$8.20–$13.60). AE, MC, V. Daily noon–2:30pm and 5–10:30pm. Subway: Osgoode, then any streetcar west to Bathurst St. BISTRO.

This charming bistro, where a rococo Elvis presides over the bar, personifies the pleasures and problems of metropolitan life. First there's overcrowding. Nineteen tables for two cram the narrow room, forcing neighbors to rub elbows. And pollution—in such a minute space, there's little practical difference between the smoking and nonsmoking sections. The food, however, makes it all worthwhile. The menu is deliberately short, allowing the kitchen to focus hothouse-flower care on its featured selections: rack of lamb, Atlantic salmon, veal tenderloin. Starters, like three-mushroom salad, get equal attention.

Citron. 813 Queen St. W. ☎ **416/504-2647.** Reservations not accepted. Main courses C$12–$20 (US$8.20–$13.60). AE, MC, V. Mon–Thurs 5–10:30pm, Fri–Sat 5–11pm. Subway: Osgoode, then any streetcar west to Bathurst St. ECLECTIC.

At once chic and attitude-free, Citron draws casual but hip twenty-somethings. The menu borrows heavily from every corner of the globe, favoring seafood and vegetarian offerings. North African couscous stew, Tex-Mex lasagne, and Thai-spiced salmon compete for attention. For dessert, the white chocolate cheesecake is highly recommended.

Ecco La. 356 College St. ☎ **416/926-9899.** Reservations recommended. Main courses C$10–$21 (US$6.80–$14.30). AE, MC, V. Mon–Fri 11am–1am, Sat–Sun 4pm–1am. Subway: Queen's Park, then any streetcar west to Brunswick Ave. ITALIAN.

Tiny trattorias litter Little Italy, but Ecco La stands out. The rustic dining room is all red brick and ochre walls, with a wood-burning pizza oven as the centerpiece. The results speak for themselves. Arugula and smoked salmon make a good match for robust tomatoes and Parmesan. There's also pasta (rigatoni goes nicely with wild mushrooms, sage cream, and truffle essence), and tender, meaty main dishes, which include capon and salmon. The menu always offers a vegetarian risotto, too. Desserts are strictly for chocolate lovers.

La Bodega. 30 Baldwin St. ☎ **416/977-1287.** Reservations recommended. Main courses C$15–$26 (US$10.20–$17.70). AE, DC, ER, MC, V. Mon–Fri noon–2:30pm; Mon–Sat 5–10:30pm. Subway: St. Patrick. FRENCH.

This is a quiet spot infused with Gallic charm. In a turn-of-the-century town house, La Bodega is a short walk from the Art Gallery of Ontario. The two dining rooms have fireplaces, and tapestries and gilt-framed mirrors line the walls. The menu is traditional French, with much made of meats. Veal medallions soak up a wild mushroom and port sauce, and duck breast mixes well with wild blueberries. The daily specials feature market-fresh finds. The wine list boasts some Bordeaux *grandes dames,* and there's a nice mix of Ontario vintages, too.

Le Select. 328 Queen St. W. ☎ **416/596-6405.** Reservations recommended. Main courses C$13–$21 (US$8.85–$14.30). AE, DC, MC, V. Mon–Thurs 11:30am–11:30pm, Fri 11:30am–midnight, Sun noon–10:30pm. Subway: Osgoode. FRENCH.

What says Paris bistro to you? Le Select sets the tone with posters, decorative objects straight from *grand-mère*'s attic, and sultry jazz in the background. Breadbaskets hang from the ceiling above each table, and require gentle coaxing to reach the diners. The menu emphasizes traditional rib-sticking fare such as steak frites and cassoulet, all nicely done. The service can be a trifle slow, but the casually dressed professionals who come here don't seem to mind.

✪ **Mildred Pierce.** 99 Sudbury St. ☎ **416/588-5695.** Reservations not accepted. Main courses C$14–$22 (US$9.55–$15). AE, DC, ER, MC, V. Mon–Fri noon–2pm, Sun 10am–3pm; Sun–Thurs 6–10pm, Fri–Sat 6–11pm. Subway: Osgoode, then any streetcar west to Dovercourt; walk south on Dovercourt and turn right at Sudbury. ECLECTIC.

Named after a Joan Crawford film, this restaurant is appropriately theatrical, with organza drapes tumbling down from the high ceiling. Murals of a Roman feast cover the walls (a local in-joke, they depict characters including the restaurant's owner and a few food critics). The menu fits right in, rich in inspiration and dramatic flourishes borrowed from different countries. Grilled salmon accompanies saffron risotto and a ragout of fennel, baby beets, and bok choy, while a Thai hot pot boasts tiger shrimp, scallops, mussels, and clams brewing in a coconut-lime-cilantro sauce. The wine list is short but includes options from Italy, Spain, South Africa, and California. Lush desserts include maple crème brûlée, and a rustic cranberry and walnut tart.

  Because Mildred Pierce does not accept reservations, getting in on Friday or Saturday night is a challenge, even if you arrive early; on other nights, there's rarely much of a wait. The dining room is entirely smoke-free; smokers can lay claim to the small outdoor patio and enjoy the view of the city's skyline.

Peter Pan. 373 Queen St. W. ☎ **416/593-0917.** Reservations recommended. Main courses C$10–$18 (US$6.80–$12.25). AE, MC, V. Mon–Wed noon–midnight, Thurs–Sat noon–1am, Sun noon–11pm. Subway: Osgoode. LIGHT FARE.

When I was in high school, Peter Pan was the classy restaurant you went to for pre-prom dinner or a big date. The crowd at this fun, relaxed place is forever young, easily impressed by the old-fashioned bar, ever-changing art exhibits, and friendly service. The menu is awash in Eurasian food-speak, but the important thing to keep in mind is that simpler dishes are best. The Peter Pan burger is always a top choice. Desserts are strictly for sweet tooths.

Pony. 488 College St. ☎ **416/923-7665.** Reservations recommended. Main courses C$14–$18 (US$9.55–$12.25). AE, MC, V. Mon–Sat 5–11pm. Subway: Queen's Park, then any streetcar west to Euclid Ave. BISTRO.

While it is on the periphery of hyper-trendy Little Italy, Pony is still the kind of place where you can relax. The candlelit dining room is charming, the upholstered chairs are comfy, and the service is smooth. The menu sticks mainly to bistro classics, such as roasted chicken stuffed with prosciutto, smoked mozzarella, and apple slices. The Caesar salad has the creamiest dressing in town—even a devoted calorie-counter won't be able to resist.

⊕ Family-Friendly Restaurants

Fran's (*see p. 107*). In addition to being open round the clock, Fran's caters to kiddies, who get their own menu. Crayons and paper are provided for budding artistes, too.

Kensington Kitchen (*see p. 97*). Whimsically decorated, with colorful toys and model airplanes amid the Oriental rugs. It seems to be easier to get kids to eat their greens when veggies are tucked into pita sandwiches, like the ones here.

Millie's Bistro (*see p. 105*). This is a perennially popular spot with families. There's a special menu for tykes, and most of the Mediterranean food can be eaten without cutlery. The entire restaurant is smoke-free.

Shopsy's (*see p. 89*). When the kids are sick of eating out and craving comfort food, this is where to take them. Home-style chili and macaroni and cheese hit the spot, and a whole section of the menu is devoted to ice cream.

Sang Ho. 536 Dundas St. W. ☎ **416/596-1685.** Reservations not accepted. Main courses C$8–$18 (US$5.45–$12.25). MC, V. Sun–Thurs noon–10pm, Fri–Sat noon–11pm. Subway: St. Patrick. CHINESE.

There's no end of eateries in the eastern end of Chinatown, but Sang Ho will be the one with the longest queue out front. This restaurant boasts not only a top-notch kitchen, but also a lovely dining room filled with several teeming aquariums. The regular menu of 100-plus dishes never changes, but many specials of the day are listed on wall-mounted boards. Seafood—shrimp, clams, or red snapper—is the obvious choice. Service is speedy and responsive. Try to go on a weeknight, when there's no more than a short wait for a table.

Swan. 892 Queen St. W. ☎ **416/532-0452.** Reservations recommended. Main courses C$15–$20 (US$10.20–$13.60). AE, DC, MC, V. Mon–Fri noon–4:30pm and 5–10:30pm, Sat 5–11pm, Sun 5–10:30pm. Subway: Osgoode, then any streetcar west to Euclid Ave. ECLECTIC.

The room brings to mind a retro soda fountain, with a counter and swirly stools on one side, and booths with Formica tables on the other. Just don't expect to find a strawberry-banana float on the menu. The youngish hipsters who congregate here slurp up martinis and oysters. Happily, the menu avoids the too-trendy trap, managing both roasted capon with bourbon gravy and corn fritters, and braised beef short ribs marinated in beer and marmalade and served with mashed root vegetables. There's a nice selection of wines, with almost all available by the glass. The popular weekend brunch features the usual eggy plates as well as some surprises: spicy Moroccan olives or smoked arctic char salad, anyone?

✪ Taro Grill. 492 Queen St. W. ☎ **416/504-1320.** Reservations recommended. Main courses C$13–$20 (US$8.85–$13.60). AE, MC, V. Daily noon–4pm and 6–10pm. Subway: Osgoode, then any streetcar west to Bathurst St. ECLECTIC.

Pass through the curtain hanging at the door, and enter a hip new world. Actually, it's not that new, but the Taro Grill has something that most hot spots of the moment can't claim—staying power. Its secret? A mix of clever cooking, helpful service, and a glamorous high-ceilinged space. The menu refuses to be easily characterized. Just when you think you've pegged the Cal-Ital pizza-pasta-salad triad, out of the blue comes tempura veggies or Asian-influenced New Zealand lamb. Affordable bottles, mainly from Australia and South Africa, fill the wine list.

Tuscany Café. 113 John St. (at King St.). ☎ **416/971-4432.** Reservations recommended. Main courses C$12–$17 (US$8.20–$11.60). AE, MC, V. Mon–Sat 5:30–10:30pm. Subway: St. Andrew. ITALIAN.

Unique among Toronto's Italian eateries, the Tuscany Café has a chef who used to be a doctor in the Chinese navy. Not that one could discern it from the menu, which is filled with veal piccata and tarragon chicken. Still, subtle twists suggest an Eastern disposition, with ginger and chilies used to good effect. The setting is unusual, too. The restaurant takes up the basement and ground floor of a late-19th-century row house. The generally speedy service and proximity to venues such as Roy Thomson Hall and the Royal Alexandra Theatre make this a good pre-show pick.

✪ **Veni Vidi Vici.** 650 College St. (at Grace St.). ☎ **416/536-8550.** Reservations recommended. Main courses C$12–$25 (US$8.20–$17). AE, MC, V. Tues–Sun 11am–3pm and 5pm–midnight. ITALIAN/FUSION.

This is Little Italy's brightest new addition, a little gem of a restaurant that serves up delicious food in a swanky setting—but, unlike many of its neighborhood cousins, it does so without attitude. There's no sign outside, just a gilt-covered fresco of a mustachioed deity looming over the doorway (quite adequate as an attention-getter, really). Inside, the staff is quick to greet and usher diners to high-backed velvet banquettes (perfect for romance but less so for people watching). At the back there's a private dining room for 12, smashingly decked out in midnight blue and gold.

The menu can be divided into two parts. On the Italian side, there are pasta dishes such as linguine with mixed seafood, or risotto with portobello, cremini, and porcini mushrooms. But the Asian-inspired Fusion plates are the showstoppers: Think cashew-studded sea bass with fennel, or phyllo-wrapped salmon with basmati rice. Desserts return to the classics, like crème brûlée with fresh berries. The wine list is particularly strong in Italian reds.

✪ **Youki.** 4 Dundonald St. (at Yonge St.). ☎ **416/924-2925.** Reservations strongly recommended. Main courses C$14–$19 (US$9.55–$12.90). AE, DC, MC, V. Tue–Wed 5:30pm–10:00pm, Thu–Sat 5:30pm–11:00pm, Sun 11:30am–3:00pm. Subway: Wellesley. ASIAN.

A stone's throw from the hectic pace of Yonge Street, Youki seems impossibly serene. Maybe it's the earthy palette, or the rice paper lanterns that hang from the ceiling, but there's something positively cozy about the place. A long wooden counter stretches along one wall, making this a popular spot for solo diners; the tables get the best view though, set as they are by the windows. The pan-Asian menu serves up a delicious Korean-style tuna sashimi salad with pears and pine nuts as a starter, and an equally attractive Vietnamese-inspired lemongrass-marinated poussin. For dessert, try the oolong tea ice cream.

INEXPENSIVE

Free Times Café. 320 College St. ☎ **416/967-1078.** Main courses C$7–$15 (US$4.80–$10.20). AE, MC, V. Mon–Sat 11:30am–2am, Sun 11am–midnight. Subway: Queen's Park, then any streetcar west to Robert St. MIDDLE EASTERN.

The name isn't false advertising: This is a rollicking scene at all hours. Students and grown-up hippies come for the folk and acoustic music, which is featured nightly and at the Sunday brunch. The reasonably priced menu features salads, pita sandwiches, and platters filled with falafel and couscous. The Sunday buffet brunch is better known as "Bella! Did ya eat?" and features blintzes, salmon patties, and latkes, among other dishes, for C$13 (US$8.85).

Happy Seven. 358 Spadina Ave. ☎ **416/971-9820.** Reservations not accepted. Main courses C$7–$15 (US$4.80–$10.20). MC, V. Daily 4pm–4am. Subway: Spadina, then LRT south to Baldwin St. CHINESE.

This eatery boasts kitschy touches like plastic Buddhas and a tank full of fish and crawly critters. They may not be everybody's cup of (green) tea, but the kitchen is widely acknowledged as one of the best in Chinatown. The menu is classic Cantonese, with a few Szechwan choices. Seafood dishes are a favorite, though there are many plates for vegetarians; portions are extremely generous. This is one of those rare restaurants that keeps cooking until the wee hours.

Kalendar. 546 College St. (just west of Bathurst St.). ☎ **416/923-4138.** Main courses C$10–$13 (US$6.80–$8.85). MC, V. Mon–Fri 11am–4pm. Subway: Queen's Park, then any streetcar west to Bathurst St. LIGHT FARE.

I can't go to this restaurant without snickering at the menu—pizzas are called "nannettes," for example—but the food inspires satisfied sighs. There are sandwiches stuffed with portobello mushrooms, havarti, and roasted red peppers, and five "scrolls"—phyllo pastries filled with delights like artichoke hearts, eggplant, and hummus. The "nannettes" are baked nan breads topped with ingredients like smoked salmon, capers, and red onions. The restaurant consists of two mirrored rooms. The ambiance is very like that of a French bistro. In summer the sidewalk patio is just the place to sit and watch the world go by.

Lee Garden. 331 Spadina Ave. ☎ **416/593-9524.** Reservations not accepted. Main courses C$7–$18 (US$4.80–$12.25). AE, MC, V. Daily 4pm–midnight. Subway: Spadina, then LRT south to Baldwin St. CHINESE.

If lines are a measure of the success of a restaurant, then Lee Garden is the hands-down Toronto champ. The draw is a Cantonese menu weighted heavily toward seafood. While there's no shark fin, there's no shortage of shrimp, lobster, or cod. The signature dish, however, is fork-tender grandfather smoked chicken with honey and sesame seeds. The kitchen works wonders with tofu, too.

Penelope. 225 King St. W. ☎ **416/351-9393.** Main courses C$8–$16 (US$5.45–$10.90). AE, MC, V. Daily 5–10:30pm. Subway: St. Andrew. GREEK.

If you're in a rush to see a show at the Royal Alex or Roy Thomson Hall, this is one of your best bets. Give the friendly staff an hour or less, and they will stuff you with spanakopita, moussaka, or souvlaki. This is the home of hearty food in a hurry.

Queen Mother Café. 208 Queen St. W. ☎ **416/598-4719.** Reservations not accepted. Main courses C$11–$15 (US$7.50–$10.20). AE, MC, V. Daily 11:30am–1am. Subway: Osgoode. FUSION.

Fussy dowager this is not. Beloved by vegetarians, trend-hoppers, and reformed hippies, the Queen Mum is a Queen Street West institution with old-fashioned wooden furnishings and an underlit interior. The menu's lengthy descriptions are required reading. "Ping Gai" turns out to be chicken breast marinated in garlic, coriander, and peppercorns, served with lime sauce atop steamed rice. "Salmon Sottha" is served with hotter-than-hot Cambodian chili sauce and black rice. The menu is anything but pricey, so the wine list is a surprise, with few bargains in sight.

✪ **The Rivoli.** 332 Queen St. W. ☎ **416/597-0794.** Reservations not accepted. Main courses C$9–$15 (US$6.10–$10.20). AE, MC, V. Daily 11:30am–2am. Subway: Osgoode. FUSION.

The Riv is better known as a club than as a restaurant—the 125-seat back room plays host to live music, stand-up comics, and poetry readings. What most people don't know is that the kitchen is just as creative. Chicken marinated in jerk spices comes with sautéed spinach and a slaw of Asian veggies; mussels are steamed in red curry jazzed up with tarragon pesto, and served on a bed of glass noodles. The less adventurous can partake of the heaping Caesar salad or the house burger (beef on a challah bun with caramelized onions). The low prices draw a mixed crowd of starving artists, budget-conscious boomers, and Gen-Xers. In summer the sidewalk patio is in high demand. *One caveat:* If you're planning to talk over dinner, get there before the back room starts filling up.

Shala-Mar. 391 Roncesvalles Ave. ☎ **416/588-9877.** Main courses C$10–$13 (US$6.80–$8.85). MC, V. Tues–Thurs and Sun noon–10pm, Fri noon–11pm, Sat 5–11pm. Subway: Dundas West. INDIAN.

Swathed in burgundy and gold, this abbreviated space could almost pass for a den of iniquity. As it turns out, it's a family business, where papá Khalid Bukhari cooks up a storm while his progeny wait tables. The menu highlights traditional Punjabi meat dishes such as beef *karahi* and chicken *biryani.* Medium spice here would be considered hot anywhere else, so only the fearless should consider ordering anything vindaloo. Portions are generous, but be warned that Bukhari leaves his kitchen just long enough to chide customers with weak appetites.

Sottovoce. 595 College St. ☎ **416/536-4564.** Reservations not accepted. Main courses C$6–$12 (US$4.10–$8.20). AE, MC, V. Mon–Sat 5:30–11pm. Subway: Queen's Park, then any streetcar west to Clinton St. LIGHT FARE.

The name of this tiny eatery is more than a little misleading. *Sotto* (soft) it isn't. Forget trying to have a conversation and instead try to score one of the window seats, which will afford a full view of College Street and its habitués. The youngish crowd that mills in after 7pm enjoys the pumped-up music that refuses to stay in the background. In the middle of this frenetic scene you will find the most lovingly prepared, and least expensive, salads and focaccia sandwiches in town. There are daily pasta specials, and many wines by the glass. Do be aware that Sottovoce fills with cigarette smoke after about 8pm—and in such a small space, it's impossible not to notice.

Tortilla Flats. 429 Queen St. W. ☎ **416/593-9870.** Reservations accepted only for groups of 5 or more. Main courses C$8–$20 (US$5.45–$13.60). MC, V. Sun–Wed noon–10pm, Thurs–Sat noon–11pm. Subway: Osgoode, then any streetcar west to Spadina Ave. TEX-MEX.

It's best to park your fear of sour cream and oil at the door because it will spoil the fun. The dining room is all riotous color and southwestern knickknacks; think Georgia O'Keefe meets Salvador Dalí. The crowd is mainly 20- to 30-something, though a number of boomers come for the weekend brunch and the best frozen margaritas in town. The menu never changes, though there are some daily specials. The potato skins piled high with bacon and sharp cheddar are at the top of my list, though the enchilada and chimichurri platters, which include rice, salad, and refried beans, are pretty satisfying, too.

3 Downtown East

EXPENSIVE

✪ **Courthouse Market Grille.** 57 Adelaide St. E. ☎ **416/214-9379.** Reservations required. Main courses C$13–$30 (US$8.85–$20.40). AE, DC, MC, V. Mon–Fri 11:30am–10:30pm. Subway: King. INTERNATIONAL.

This hangout for the suited set boasts gargantuan fluted columns, sky-high ceilings, swinging chandeliers, and miles of marble. Pretty good for an 1850 building that used to be a jail. Financial District types lap it up, along with the generous martinis. The menu features grilled and rotisserie meats of excellent quality, though daring palates will not be pleased by timid seasoning. Appetizers are uniformly fine, with simple but well-executed numbers like steamed Prince Edward Island mussels in creamy white wine sauce. There are some impressive vintages on the wine list, though most of the prices are equally grand.

✪ **Hiro Sushi.** 171 King St. E. ☎ **416/304-0550.** Reservations recommended. Main courses C$20–$30 (US$13.60–$20.40). AE, DC, MC, V. Mon–Fri noon–2:30pm; Mon–Sat 6–10:30pm. Subway: King. JAPANESE.

Widely regarded as the best sushi chef in the city, Hiro Yoshida draws a horde of Financial District types at lunch, though dinner patrons are mainly couples. The monochromatic setting is comfortably minimalist, and diners are encouraged to relax and leave their meal in Hiro's capable hands. The sushi varieties range from the expected to the inventive, and you can also choose sashimi, tempura, and bento box combinations. Service can be rather slow. Forget the few wines listed in favor of sake or beer.

Rosewater Supper Club. 19 Toronto St. (at Adelaide). ☎ **416/214-5888.** Reservations required. Main courses C$20–$32 (US$13.60–$21.75). AE, DC, ER, MC, V. Mon–Fri 11:30am–2:30pm and 5:30–10:30pm, Sat 5:30–11:30pm. Subway: King. INTERNATIONAL.

This triple-decked pleasure dome is packed almost every night with dressed-up diners who pass the time checking each other out. Personally, I'm still caught on the scenery: Marble, moldings, and a waterfall make quite the impression. So does the menu, which casually tours the globe. First up are delectables like sweetbread tarte Tatin in an apple reduction. Main courses include a potato-zucchini mille-feuille with truffle oil and asparagus salad, and pan-baked pork with honey and cloves. The can't-miss desserts include ganache-topped chocolate-caramel cake, and baked mascarpone pear with caraway ice cream. The serious wine list focuses mainly on France and California, with some excellent Ontario vintages.

The Senator. 249 and 253 Victoria St. ☎ **416/364-7517.** Reservations required for dinner in steak house. Main courses C$20–$37 (US$13.60–$25.15). AE, DC, MC, V. Diner Mon–Fri 7:30am–8:30pm, Sat 8am–8:30pm, Sun 8am–3pm. Steak house Tues–Fri 11:30am–2:30pm; Tues–Thurs 5–11:30pm, Fri 5pm–midnight, Sat 5pm–12:30am, Sun 5–10pm. Subway: Dundas. STEAK.

The retro-leaning Senator recalls the days when red meat, rich food, and cigar smoking weren't considered a threat to one's health. The diner looks like the set of a Humphrey Bogart movie, with dark leatherette booths and dim lighting. It serves hearty bacon-and-egg breakfasts, old-fashioned comfort foods like liver and onions, and hefty burgers. The adjoining dining room is swankier, with etched-glass doors and heavy wood paneling. Beef in all its strip loin, prime rib, and rib-eye glory is the specialty. Decadent desserts like chocolate bourbon cake round out the meal. Upstairs, there's jazz at the glamorous Top O' the Senator, and the Victory Lounge for cigar aficionados.

✪ **ZooM Caffe & Bar.** 18 King St. E. ☎ **416/861-9872.** Reservations recommended. Main courses C$18–$36 (US$12.25–$24.50). AE, DC, ER, MC, V. Mon–Fri noon–3pm; Mon–Tues 5–11pm, Wed–Sat 5pm–midnight. Subway: King. INTERNATIONAL.

Perhaps because its design is so striking, ZooM has had some trouble being taken seriously as a restaurant. Located in the space of a long-gone bank, it has a vaulted ceiling, velvet lounges, and halogen lighting. It's about as lovely as can be, all the better to serve as a setting for the Beautiful People who frequent it. Its oft-overlooked menu is short but to the point. It features creations like taro root–encrusted foie gras as a starter, and a main course of "wonder spiced" lamb loin with smoked corn polenta and plantains. Desserts are less esoteric, though no less satisfying (I can't resist the chocolate mud pie). The wine list has about five bottles under C$40 (US$27.20), so bargain vintages are in short supply. And this is *the* spot for private parties, so be sure to call ahead.

MODERATE

Florentine Court. 97 Church St. ☎ **416/364-3687.** Reservations recommended. Main courses C$10–$20 (US$6.80–$13.60). AE, MC, V. Tues–Fri noon–2:30pm; Tues–Sat 5:30–10:30pm. Subway: Queen. ITALIAN.

The granddaddy of Toronto's many Italian restaurants, the Florentine Court is going on its 35th birthday. The kitchen hasn't changed much over the years, because its saucy Northern Italian specialties have never gone out of vogue. Veal scaloppine appears in various guises, served straight up with white-wine sauce or lightly breaded and paired with herbed tomato sauce. Homemade pastas come with creamy sauces, and there's a selection of surf 'n' turf dishes, too. The list of Italian vintages—all personally selected by the restaurant's owner—is a delight.

Montreal Bistro and Jazz Club. 65 Sherbourne St. (at Adelaide). ☎ **416/363-0179.** Reservations recommended. Main courses C$10–$18 (US$6.80–$12.25). AE, MC, V. Mon–Fri 11:30am–3pm; Mon–Thurs 6–11pm, Fri–Sat 6pm–midnight. Subway: King, then any streetcar east to Sherbourne St. QUEBECOIS.

Ontario and Quebec share a border, but it's no mean feat to find top-notch *tourtière* (traditional beef, veal, and pork pie) in Toronto. Anyone who craves Quebecois staples like pea soup and smoked-meat sandwiches can return their train ticket and stop at this bistro. Besides being a restaurant, this is one of the city's premier jazz clubs, so you can *écouter* while you *manger*.

Rodney's Oyster House. 9 Adelaide St. E. ☎ **416/363-8105.** Main courses C$13–$19 (US$8.85–$12.90). AE, DC, MC, V. Mon–Sat 11:30am–midnight. Subway: King. SEAFOOD.

You could pass this restaurant a half-dozen times before you'd see it from the street. The tiny sign points, Alice-in-Wonderland style, to a flight of stairs down to the basement. Follow them into a series of aquarium-cluttered rooms with fishing nets cast around the walls. Another favorite with the Bay Street set, Rodney's is rowdy at all times of day. The main draw is oysters, of course, though the lobster and salmon dishes are worth more than a look. The drinks list is a mile long, though there are only about a dozen wines, none of them vintages.

INEXPENSIVE

Hello Toast. 993 Queen St. E. ☎ **416/778-7299.** Main courses C$7–$15 (US$4.80–$10.20). MC, V. Tues–Sun noon–10pm. Subway: Queen, then any streetcar east to Pape Ave. LIGHT FARE.

Humorist Fran Leibowitz once asked why there were places called Bonjour Croissant but not Hello Toast. Well, now there is. The kitschy dining room is bedecked with gleaming toasters and retro furniture. The menu is a mix of pizza and pasta specials, with a few salads, soups, and rich desserts mixed in. If you're springing for the toast, choose the inspired challah.

Kubo. 155 Dalhousie St. (at Dundas St. W.). ☎ **416/366-5826.** Main courses C$10–$14 (US$6.80–$9.55). AE, MC, V. Mon–Sat 6–10:30pm, Sun 11am–3pm. Subway: Dundas. ASIAN.

From its perch just east of the Eaton Centre, Kubo beckons. The scene is all swanky minimalism, with loft-like ceilings, Mondrian glass, and manicured plants. Pretty cool for an old Sears warehouse (no joke). The short menu bestows goofy names to its Asian-inspired offerings ("To Fumanchu With Love" is a tofu stir-fry with broccoli, shiitake mushrooms, and oyster sauce). The real attraction for the so-hip-it-hurts twenty-something crowd? Divine drinks, like the sake martini.

Le Papillon. 16 Church St. (between Front St. E. and Esplanade). ☎ **416/363-0838.** Reservations required. Crepes C$6–$10 (US$4.10–$6.80). AE, DC, MC, V. Tues–Fri noon–2:30pm; Tues–Wed 5–10pm, Thurs 5–11pm, Fri 5pm–midnight; Sat 11:30am–midnight; Sun noon–10pm. Subway: Union. CREPES.

If you thought crepes were simply for breakfast, stop by Le Papillon for re-education. While there are many fruit-filled numbers, the best are savory crepes, which combine, for example, bacon, apples, and cheddar. Made from a mixture of white and buckwheat flour, the crepes make a satisfying lunch. For dinner, add some onion soup and a green salad, or go for *tourtière*, a rich pie that includes beef, veal, and pork.

Shopsy's. 33 Yonge St. ☎ **416/365-3333.** Sandwiches and main courses C$7–$14 (US$4.80–$9.55). AE, DC, MC, V. Mon–Wed 6:30am–11pm, Thurs–Fri 6:30am–midnight, Sat–Sun 8am–midnight. Subway: Union. DELI.

This Toronto institution has been in business for more than three-quarters of a century. Its large patio, festooned with giant yellow umbrellas, draws crowds for breakfast, lunch, and dinner and in between. This is where you go for heaping corned beef or smoked-meat sandwiches served on fresh rye. There's also a slew of comfort foods, like macaroni and cheese and chicken pot pie. Shopsy's also boasts one of the largest walk-in humidors in the city.

✪ **Young Thailand.** 81 Church St. (south of Lombard St.). ☎ **416/368-1368.** Reservations recommended. Lunch buffet C$9.95 (US$6.75); main courses C$8–$16 (US$5.45–$10.90). AE, DC, MC, V. Mon–Fri 11:30am–2pm; daily 4:30–11pm. Subway: Queen or King. THAI.

Wandee Young was one of the first chefs to awake Toronto's taste buds to the joys of Thai cuisine. That was more than two decades ago, and Young Thailand is still going strong, with several locations around the city. The large dining room contains a few Southeast Asian decorative elements, but it's the low-priced, high-quality cuisine that attracts the hip-but-broke and boomers alike. The bargain buffet at lunch is always a mob scene. The dinner menu is à la carte, with popular picks like spiced chicken and bamboo shoots in coconut milk, satays with fiery peanut sauce, and the ever-present pad Thai. Soups tend to be sinus-clearing, though mango salads offer a sweet antidote.

4 Midtown West

VERY EXPENSIVE

✪ **Bistro 990.** 990 Bay St. (at St. Joseph). ☎ **416/921-9990.** Reservations required. Main courses C$19–$33 (US$12.90–$22.45). AE, ER, MC, V. Mon–Fri noon–3pm; Mon–Sat 5–11pm. Subway: Museum or Wellesley. FRENCH.

Because Hollywood types frequent Toronto, it's no surprise to see the stars out for a night on the town. Bistro 990 is just across the street from the tony Sutton Place hotel, so it drags in more than its fair share of big names. (One friend has had a couple of Whoopi Goldberg sightings here. Why do these things never happen when I'm around?) In any case, the Gallic dining room is charming, and the service is all-around attentive. The menu offers updated hors d'oeuvres, such as octopus and veggies in citrus marinade. Main dishes stick to grand-mère's recipes, like the satisfying roasted half chicken with garlicky mashed potatoes, and calf's liver in white-wine sauce. Sweets, such as fruit tarts and sorbets, are made daily.

Opus. 37 Prince Arthur Ave. ☎ **416/921-3105.** Reservations recommended. Main courses C$20–$34 (US$13.60–$23.10). AE, MC, V. Daily 5:30–11:30pm; bar until 2am. Subway: St. George. CONTINENTAL.

Popular with the price-is-no-object set, Opus is nonetheless low-key. Smooth, personable servers make you feel at home in the elegant renovated town house, which is divided into several small dining areas. The look is casually chic, and there's no shortage of suits. The menu changes every other month, and always features classic French as well as lightened-up dishes. Tuna tartare meets its match with black sesame seeds and lotus chips, and beef tenderloin with dauphinoise potatoes and rosemary-shallot *jus* is memorable. Desserts are easy on the eye *and* easy on the palate. The wine list runs to volumes, with highlights of new and old worlds; the knowledgeable staff can set you straight.

✪ **Truffles.** In the Four Seasons Hotel, 21 Avenue Rd. ☎ **416/964-0411.** Reservations required. Main courses C$29–$44 (US$19.70–$29.90). AE, DC, MC, V. Mon–Sat 6–11pm. Subway: Bay. CONTINENTAL.

On the second floor of the Four Seasons Hotel, this formal dining room is a study in elegance. Every last detail has been attended to, from the exotic sculptures to the stunning marquetry floor. Winner of numerous hotelier awards, Truffles has a reputation for inventive cooking. Appetizers boast exquisite ingredients, with results such as pan-seared foie gras atop pineapple and mango chutney. Main courses, such as bacon-wrapped veal tenderloin served side-by-side with morel mushroom ravioli, are more down-to-earth. Desserts like peach Napoleon and lemon soufflé are uniformly delightful. The mile-long wine list frequently veers into the stratosphere.

Zola. 162 Cumberland St. ☎ **416/515-1222.** Reservations required. Main courses C$25–$38 (US$17–$25.85). AE, DC, MC, V. Daily noon–midnight. Subway: Bay. FRENCH.

You're in Toronto, but your heart is set on, say, Paris. Dinner at Zola could give you the French fix you need. This ambitious bistro re-creates a train station with its steel beams and girders. Along one wall, glassed like a window, is the skyline of Gay Paree with the Eiffel Tower rising triumphant. Tear your eyes away to consider the menu, and you'll find it brimming with Left Bank fare. The ingredients are rich—most first courses contain foie gras, caviar, lobster, or some combination thereof. Main courses are a mix of seafood, like fillet of grouper in a red-wine sauce with Swiss chard, and meat, such as Angus tenderloin in truffle *jus* with green beans and, yes, more foie gras. Waistline watchers had best skip to the next stop. One hint that you're still in Toronto: The waiters aren't snobby at all.

EXPENSIVE

Annona. Park Hyatt Toronto, 4 Avenue Rd. ☎ **416/924-5471.** Reservations recommended for dinner. Main courses C$16–$30 (US$10.90–$20.40). AE, DC, ER, MC, V. Mon–Fri 6:30am–11pm, Sat–Sun 7am–11pm. Subway: Museum or Bay. INTERNATIONAL.

Why is it that so many of the fascinating new restaurants in Toronto are owned by hotels? Annona, at the Park Hyatt, is the latest case in point. Newly opened in April 2000, the ground-level dining room is an exercise in elegance, with dusky blue draperies and banquettes, gold accents, and floor-to-ceiling windows (all the better to people-watch, my dears). Professional kitchen staff trot out plates all day long: scrambled eggs with smoked salmon and capers for breakfast, seafood risotto with morel mushrooms and asparagus at lunch, and pan-seared Black Angus medallions in a red wine sauce for dinner. The desserts are to die for, especially the caramelized pineapple tart with rum ice cream.

Boba. 90 Avenue Rd. ☎ **416/961-2622.** Reservations recommended. Main courses C$20–$29 (US$13.60–$19.70). AE, DC, ER, MC, V. Mon–Sat 5:30–10pm. Subway: Bay. FUSION.

There is no shortage of stunning turn-of-the-century houses in this part of town, and Boba happens to be in one of the most charming. Set back from the street, it has a front patio for summer dining. Inside, the pastel-hued walls and tasseled lampshades exude warmth, Provençal style. Boba is a scene every night, with a mix of dressed-up and dressed-down professionals table-hopping with abandon. What draws them in is the inventive cuisine, which has turned co-chefs Barbara Gordon and Bob Bermann into local celebrities. One highlight is Gordon's wonderful Muscovy duck two ways, with the breast cooked rare and the leg braised. Grilled salmon is also just so, nicely mated with curried vegetable risotto. Desserts are overwhelming, particularly the Valrhona chocolate triangle with crème fraîche ice cream, raspberries, and berry coulis (don't try to eat this alone!). There are several award-winning Ontario ice wines. The entire restaurant is smoke-free.

✪ **Il Posto Nuovo.** 148 Yorkville Ave. (at Avenue Rd.). ☎ **416/968-0469.** Reservations required. Main courses C$14–$25 (US$9.55–$17). AE, DC, ER, MC, V. Mon–Sat 12– 2:30pm and 6–11pm. Subway: Bay or Museum. ITALIAN.

All of those ladies who lunch can't be wrong. Now celebrating its twentieth year, Il Posto Nuovo (formerly known simply as Il Posto) has new management and a new direction — and business is booming. Still, some things don't change: white-linened tables still sit cheek-by-jowl, making this an eavesdropper's Eden. The service here is among the best in the city, considerate and efficient and well-versed in the intricacies of the menu. And what a menu it is, rich with classic dishes like the bresaola salad (thinly sliced air-cured beef and Asiago cheese atop a bed of arugula) and ravioli stuffed with veal and spinach. The wine cellar favors Italy, France, and California; it's constantly updated, so do ask for recommendations.

✪ **Jamie Kennedy at the Museum.** Royal Ontario Museum, 100 Queen's Park Crescent. ☎ **416/586-5578.** Reservations required. Main courses C$12–$17 (US$8.20–$11.60). AE, DC, MC, V. Mon–Sat 11:30am–2:30pm. Subway: Museum. CONTINENTAL.

Most people who visit the ROM never suspect that there's a top-rated restaurant on the fifth floor. Accessible by one elevator, the secluded spot is open only for lunch. It draws a power crowd enamored with the serenity that's hard to find at downtown eateries of equal caliber. Jamie Kennedy is one of the city's top chefs and an aficionado of organic produce. The menu staple is steak frites served with lemon mayo; other delightful choices include herbed goat cheese and tomato tart, and terrine of foie gras with walnuts and marinated veggies. Desserts work wonders with phyllo and cream. Most dishes are paired up with wine suggestions, making the lengthy list easier to navigate.

Mistura. 265 Davenport Rd. ☎ **416/515-0009.** Reservations recommended. Main courses C$20–$28 (US$13.60–$19.05). AE, DC, MC, V. Mon–Sat 5–11pm. Subway: Bay. ITALIAN.

While the curvy bar up front is still the place to meet, the modern Italian menu is the real draw at Mistura. The food is satisfying without being overly heavy—think spinach and ricotta gnocchi with light but creamy Gorgonzola sauce and toasted walnuts. The meaty entrees might include a tender veal chop with rosemary roasted potatoes and portobello mushrooms, or sweetbreads with chickpea polenta and caramelized root veggies. The well-organized wine list is heavy with Italian and California vintages.

Midtown Toronto Dining

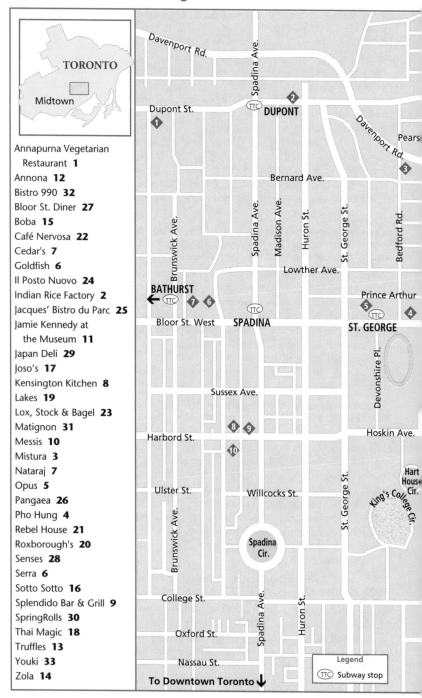

Annapurna Vegetarian
  Restaurant **1**
Annona **12**
Bistro 990 **32**
Bloor St. Diner **27**
Boba **15**
Café Nervosa **22**
Cedar's **7**
Goldfish **6**
Il Posto Nuovo **24**
Indian Rice Factory **2**
Jacques' Bistro du Parc **25**
Jamie Kennedy at
  the Museum **11**
Japan Deli **29**
Joso's **17**
Kensington Kitchen **8**
Lakes **19**
Lox, Stock & Bagel **23**
Matignon **31**
Messis **10**
Mistura **3**
Nataraj **7**
Opus **5**
Pangaea **26**
Pho Hung **4**
Rebel House **21**
Roxborough's **20**
Senses **28**
Serra **6**
Sotto Sotto **16**
Splendido Bar & Grill **9**
SpringRolls **30**
Thai Magic **18**
Truffles **13**
Youki **33**
Zola **14**

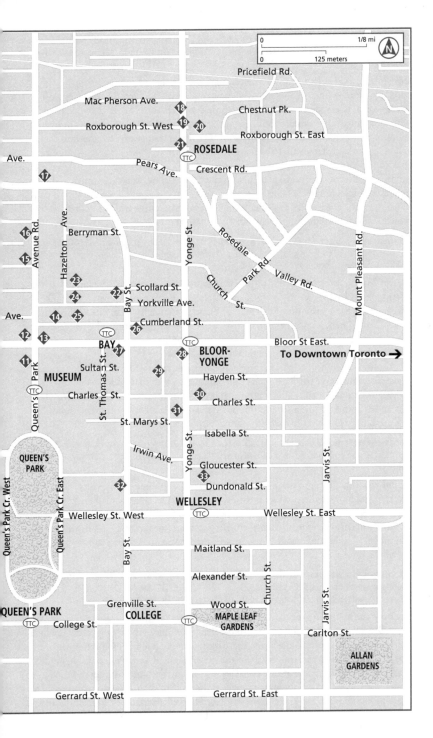

Pricefield Rd.

Mac Pherson Ave.

Chestnut Pk.

Roxborough St. West

Roxborough St. East

ROSEDALE

Ave.

Pears Ave.

Crescent Rd.

Berryman St.

Hazelton Ave.

Avenue Rd.

Yonge St.

Rosedale

Park Rd.

Valley Rd.

Mount Pleasant Rd.

Scollard St.

Bay St.

Church St.

Yorkville Ave.

Ave.

Cumberland St.

BAY

BLOOR-
YONGE

Bloor St East.

To Downtown Toronto →

MUSEUM

Queen's Park

Sultan St.

St. Thomas St.

Hayden St.

Charles St.

Charles St.

St. Marys St.

Yonge St.

Isabella St.

Irwin Ave.

QUEEN'S
PARK

Gloucester St.

Dundonald St.

WELLESLEY

Queen's Park Cr. West

Queen's Park Cr. East

Wellesley St. West

Wellesley St. East

Bay St.

Maitland St.

Alexander St.

Church St.

Jarvis St.

QUEEN'S PARK

Grenville St.

COLLEGE

Wood St.

MAPLE LEAF
GARDENS

College St.

Carlton St.

Jarvis St.

ALLAN
GARDENS

Gerrard St. West

Gerrard St. East

0   1/8 mi

0   125 meters

N

Pangaea. 1221 Bay St. ☎ **416/920-2323.** Reservations recommended. Main courses C$22–$28 (US$15–$19.05). AE, DC, ER, MC, V. Mon–Sat 11:30am–11:30pm. Subway: Bay. FUSION.

I used to think this location was cursed. For years, I watched restaurants open with a bang and fold with a whimper. Well, Pangaea seems to have broken that losing streak—and deservedly so. The massive dining room is as dramatic as ever, complete with an undulating aluminum ceiling and coral walls. Perhaps to compete with its surroundings, the chic crowd likes to dress up. The menu changes every month so that it can stick with in-season ingredients. Appetizers such as white asparagus soup with roasted shallots and morel mushrooms are classically French. The main dishes strike boldly in different directions: glazed salmon with bok choy, water chestnuts, and ginger, for example, or rack of lamb roasted in sunflower seeds and honey and served with whiskey sauce. The professional staff knows its way around the wide-ranging wine list, which favors the Western Hemisphere.

✪ **Senses.** 15 Bloor St. W. ☎ **416/935-0400.** Reservations required. Main C$18–$36 (US$12.25–$24.50). AE, DC, MC, V. Mon–Fri 11:30am–2:30pm, Sat 11:30am–3pm; Mon–Sat 5–10pm. Subway: Yonge/Bloor. CONTINENTAL.

Harry Wu, not content to rest on his laurels with two successful restaurants at the Metropolitan Hotel, recently opened this latest venture. Senses is a combination bakery, gourmet food emporium (see chapter 8), and restaurant, all in one sophisticated space. Dining here is an experience for—what else?—all the senses. The serene sandy tones are serious eye candy, the background music soothes, and velvety banquettes rub you the right way. Smell and taste get revved up for starters like delicately rich asparagus risotto or crabmeat salad with apple, scallions, and mustard sprouts. Main courses make for some clever pairings, such as grilled salmon with roasted fennel and spinach atop couscous and lemon-ginger cream, and duck breast spiked with sun-dried cherries and star anise *jus*. Do save room for dessert—the seven choices are all solid, but my personal favorite is the elegantly simple raspberry tart.

Southern Accent. 595 Markham St. ☎ **416/536-3211.** Reservations recommended. Main courses C$13–$26 (US$8.85–$17.70). AE, ER, MC, V. Daily 5:30–10:30pm. Subway: Bathurst. CAJUN.

Cajun food isn't Toronto's claim to fame, so this down-home Annex eatery is a find. Background blues and zydeco set the tone, and the menu attracts casual neighborhood boomers. Anyone who has admired the work of New Orleans celebrity chef Paul Prudhomme will cotton to the blackened entrees—chicken, steak, lamb, and fish all get the treatment. Gumbo and crawfish make occasional appearances, too. *Warning:* The corn bread is a mite addictive.

✪ **Splendido Bar and Grill.** 88 Harbord St. ☎ **416/929-7788.** Reservations recommended. Main courses C$20–$30 (US$13.60–$20.40). AE, DC, ER, MC, V. Mon–Sat 5–11pm. Subway: Spadina, then LRT south to Harbord St. INTERNATIONAL.

Let's say you're looking for a quiet spot for an intimate dinner, somewhere where you can talk. Stay as far away as you can from Splendido. This over-the-top eatery is where suits come to cut loose, so the atmosphere is rollicking, table-hopping is rampant, and the overall atmosphere is frenetic. On the other hand, if you're looking for modern Italian cooking with a few exotic twists in a strikingly decorated dining room, you've come to the right place. The menu ranges from venison with apricot-cranberry *jus* to scallops with a pistachio crust. There are several excellent pasta selections. The international wine list is pricey, but some nice vintages are available by the glass.

MODERATE

Café Nervosa. 75 Yorkville Ave. ☎ **416/961-4642.** Reservations recommended. Main courses C$10–$18 (US$6.80–$12.25). AE, MC, V. Mon–Sat 6–11pm. Subway: Bay. ITALIAN.

There are reed-thin models playing with their food at the next table, leopard skin decking the room, and limos parked out front. Where are you? One possible answer is Café Nervosa, a casually hip Yorkville hangout. The name is borrowed from the coffee shop on TV's "Frasier," though its wacky ambiance is all its own. The menu boasts nicely constructed panini, pizzas, and salads, and the portions tend to be generous (curious, given the you-can-never-be-too-rich-or-too-thin crowd). Upstairs there's a cigar lounge where young trendoids get their stogie fix.

✪ **Goldfish.** 372 Bloor St. W. ☎ **416/513-0077.** Reservations required. Main courses C$12–$20 (US$8.20–$13.60). AE, DC, ER, MC, V. Mon–Fri noon–10:30pm, Sat noon–11pm. Subway: Spadina. ECLECTIC.

Behind the floor-to-ceiling front window that reveals all to passersby, dining at this new hot spot is rather like being in a fishbowl. The cool, crisp lines of Scandinavian design mix with miniature Japanese plants for an upscale Zen ambiance. While the look may be trendier-than-thou, the staff's attitude is consistently considerate. The menu is far less austere than the surroundings. Main dishes run the gamut from ostrich tenderloin with orange-peppercorn sauce and beet salad to grilled salmon with an okra cake and coconut vinaigrette. Even the simplest green salad is refreshed with dollops of pumpkin seeds and a light dressing that contains a hint of lavender emulsion. The short dessert list includes some inventive pairings, such as delicious apple tart with rosemary ice cream. The wine list is short but contains 10 selections by the glass.

Jacques Bistro du Parc. 126A Cumberland St. ☎ **416/961-1893.** Main courses C$8–$22 (US$5.45–$15). AE, MC, V. Mon–Sat 11:30am–3pm; daily 5–10:30pm. Subway: Bay. FRENCH.

There are about three ladies who lunch for every lad who happens by Jacques Bistro du Parc around noontime. In the evening, the ratio evens out as the ladies return on the arms of their escorts. The menu is that of a genuine French brasserie, with omelets, quiches, and Niçoise salads galore. There are meatier main courses, too, like green peppercorn steak and Dijon-coated rack of lamb. Many wines are available by the glass, and bottles tend to be reasonably priced. Service can be considered relaxed or slow, depending on your mood.

Joso's. 202 Davenport Rd. (just east of Avenue Rd.). ☎ **416/925-1903.** Reservations recommended. Main courses C$14–$44 (US$9.55–$29.90); pasta dishes C$10–$16 (US$6.80–$10.90). AE, MC, V. Mon–Fri 11:30am–2:30pm; Mon–Sat 5:30–11pm. Subway: Bay. SEAFOOD.

This Annex mainstay keeps packing 'em in, drawing a crowd of regulars and a sprinkling of celebrities. The Spralja family has a show-biz history (chef Joso was half of the folk-singing duo of Malka and Joso, who appeared on *The Tonight Show*), which may explain the theatricality of the surroundings. The two-story house is crammed with art depicting the female form in all its naked glory (or buxom female forms, at least). Tables are inches apart, foiling intimate conversation but letting you get to know your neighbors. Fresh seafood is carted out directly to your table for inspection, then returned to the kitchen for cooking. There is also a selection of pastas, such as delightful spaghettini al Leonardo, which combines shrimp, octopus, and capers. Desserts range from jam-filled crepes to sorbets.

Matignon. 51 St. Nicholas St. ☎ **416/921-9226.** Reservations recommended. Main courses C$14–$18 (US$9.55–$12.25). AE, MC, V. Mon–Fri 11:30am–2:30pm; Mon–Thurs 5–10pm, Fri–Sat 5–11pm. Subway: Wellesley. FRENCH.

A little bit off the beaten track, this small restaurant offers the thrill of discovery. Spread over two floors, the intimate rooms are festooned with all things French. The crowd includes many regulars, and the ambiance is that of a low-key bistro. The short menu is filled with classics from the old county, including Angus steak rolled in crushed pepper and flambéed with cognac, and rack of lamb with mustard and herbs of Provence. Desserts stay on the same track, like vanilla ice cream under hot chocolate sauce. Bon appétit!

✪ **Messis.** 97 Harbord St. ☎ **416/920-2186.** Main courses C$10–$18 (US$6.80–$12.25). AE, DC, MC, V. Tues–Fri noon–2pm; Sun–Thurs 5:30–10pm, Fri–Sat 5:30–11pm. Subway: Spadina, then LRT south to Harbord St. ECLECTIC.

This is one of Toronto's prime training grounds for up-and-coming young chefs. The food is for serious gourmets, though the prices are comparatively low. That explains the presence of earnest artsy types and casual boomers in the small, saffron-walled dining room. The menu changes frequently, keeping as its mainstay Italian pastas and Mediterranean meat dishes, though there are forays into Asia, too. For a starter, the roasted Vidalia onion filled with goat cheese and walnuts is hard to beat. Main courses, like duck breast in Grand Marnier sauce, follow up nicely. Service is well intentioned though occasionally clunky. The California-dominated wine list is as reasonably priced as the food.

Sotto Sotto. 116A Avenue Rd. (north of Bloor St.). ☎ **416/962-0011.** Reservations required. Main courses C$14–$24 (US$9.55–$16.30). AE, MC, V. Mon–Thurs 6–10pm, Fri–Sat 6–11pm. Subway: Bay or Museum. ITALIAN.

Imagine the Bat Cave decorated by a Florentine, with aged frescoes, wall-mounted stonework, and wax-dripping gilt candelabra. A few steps down from street level, this restaurant transports diners a world away. Tables are cheek-by-jowl, but the jovial suits and couples who make the scene don't seem to mind. Efficient service lacks warmth, though the kitchen makes up for it. The Northern Italian menu leans to the light-weight, with a few irresistible creamy-sauced pastas. Main courses of meat or fish, like Cornish hen and swordfish, are nicely grilled. The risotto is fine—though, annoyingly, at least two people at the table must order it. There's a nice wine list, with many selections available by the glass.

INEXPENSIVE

✪ **Annapurna Vegetarian Restaurant.** 1085 Bathurst St. (just south of Dupont St.). ☎ **416/537-8513.** All menu items less than C$7 (US$4.80). No credit cards. Mon–Tues and Thurs–Sat 11:30am–9pm, Wed noon–6:30pm. Subway: Bathurst. VEGETARIAN.

While the number of herbivores is steadily rising, Toronto still has few vegetarian restaurants. The long-established Annapurna—it's been around for more than 20 years—serves Indian vegetable dishes, hearty tofu burgers, and a variety of fruit and vegetable juices to a crowd of students and boomers. This is one place carnivores and their vegan friends can enjoy together. (I speak from experience, having originally been dragged here by a veggie-loving pal.) In keeping with the aura of health, Annapurna hosts free meditation classes every week, and the entire restaurant is smoke-free.

Bloor Street Diner. In the Manulife Centre, 55 Bloor St. W. ☎ **416/928-3105.** Main courses C$10–$18 (US$6.80–$12.25). MC, V. Daily 7am–1am. Subway: Bay. Light Fare.

If you've shopped until you've dropped along Bloor Street West, this is just the place to grab a bite to eat and let your feet and your Visa card recover. It's two restaurants in one. Le Café/Terrasse is an informal bistro that serves decent soups, salads, and sandwiches all day long, and La Rotisserie is a slightly more upscale dining room with heartier Provençal-style fare. The basics are what they do best. Try to snag a seat on the umbrella-covered patio overlooking Bay Street (all the better for people watching).

Cedar's. 394 Bloor St. W. ☎ **416/923-3277.** Reservations not accepted. Main courses C$11–$14 (US$7.50–$9.55). MC, V. Mon–Thurs noon–10pm, Fri–Sat noon–11pm. Subway: Spadina or Bathurst. MIDDLE EASTERN.

As the evening goes on, the decibel level rises, and throngs of diners and Middle Eastern music vie for attention. The menu is mainly Lebanese, with plates of meze-like nibbles such as grilled zucchini and *moujarardara* (rice and lentils with onions). Main courses include a variety of meaty shish kebobs. Servers are pleasant but prone to vanishing for extended periods.

✪ **Indian Rice Factory.** 414 Dupont St. ☎ **416/961-3472.** Reservations recommended. Main courses C$8–$16 (US$5.45–$10.90). AE, DC, MC, V. Mon–Sat noon–11pm, Sun 5–10pm. Subway: Dupont. INDIAN.

A Toronto institution since it opened in the late 1970s, the Indian Rice Factory is in a league of its own. The corduroy banquettes and macramé wall hangings still draw boomers who started coming here 20 years ago. The Punjabi-influenced menu features heaping helpings of beef *dhansak* (braised beef with lentil-eggplant-tomato curry) and chicken *khashabad,* a chicken breast stuffed with almonds, cashews, and raisins in coconut-milk cream. There are many beers from local microbreweries, and a small but well-chosen wine list.

Japan Deli. 11 Balmuto St. ☎ **416/920-2051.** Reservations not accepted. Complete dinners $7–$9 (US$4.80–$6.10). MC, V. Mon–Sat noon–10pm. Subway: Yonge/Bloor. JAPANESE.

Tucked into a cubbyhole on a side street just off Bloor Street West, Japan Deli succeeds at bringing tempura and teriyaki to the masses. Fine Japanese cuisine takes hours to prepare, but this is more like what time-pressed Tokyo residents are used to—a friend who used to live in Japan swears that this is as close as you can get to the experience without boarding a plane. Complete dinners include miso soup, salad, a meat dish, side vegetables, and fresh fruit for dessert—all nicely prepared, and all for under C$10 (US$6.80).

Juice for Life. 521 Bloor St. W. ☎ **416/531-2635.** Reservations not accepted. Main courses C$7–$13 (US$4.80–$8.85). MC, V. Daily noon–10:30pm. Subway: Bathurst. VEGETARIAN.

If there's such a thing as an elixir of life, one of the bartenders at this Annex favorite is sure to find it one day. They've already developed a Bionic Brain Tonic (peach, strawberry, and orange juices revved up with gotu kola and three types of ginseng) and about 40 other blends intended to boost your immune system, sex drive, or mood. The noodle and rice dishes have equally esoteric names (Buddha, Green Goddess), though their contents are down-to-earth. The high-protein almond grain burgers and hemp-seed bread get top marks.

✪ **Kensington Kitchen.** 124 Harbord St. ☎ **416/961-3404.** Reservations recommended. Main courses C$10–$14 (US$6.80–$9.55). AE, CB, DC, ER, MC, V. Mon–Sat 11:30am–11pm, Sun 11:30am–10pm. Subway: Spadina, then LRT south to Harbord St. MEDITERRANEAN.

Drawing a crowd of regulars—students and profs—from the nearby University of Toronto, Kensington Kitchen is a perennial gem. The decor hasn't changed in years, with the same Oriental carpets covering the walls, painted wood floor, and decorative objects scattered about. The tradition of big portions at small cost stays constant, too. The menu ventures between the ports of the Mediterranean. There's angel-hair pasta with heaps of shrimp, scallops, and mussels in tomato-coriander sauce; saffron paella with chicken and sausage; and Turkish-style braised lamb stuffed with raisins, eggplant, apricots, and figs. In clement weather, head to the rooftop patio, which is shaded by a mighty Manitoba maple.

Lalibela. 869 Bloor St. W. ☎ **416/535-6615.** Main courses C$5–$9 (US$3.40–$6.10). MC, V. Mon–Thurs 6–10pm, Sat 6–11pm. Subway: Christie. ETHIOPIAN.

Perhaps it's the fact that you don't need cutlery to dine in Ethiopian style that makes it so much fun. A flatbread called *injera* takes the place of flatware as you scoop up spicy hot meats and thick lentil stews. Lalibela has numerous choices for vegetarians and meat-lovers, and the helpful staff will arrange mixed plates with three different dishes for tasting.

Lox, Stock & Bagel. Hazelton Lanes, 55 Avenue Rd. ☎ **416/968-8850.** Reservations only for groups. Main courses C$8–$12 (US$5.45–$8.20). AE, DC, MC, V. Daily 7:30am-9pm. Subway: Bay or Museum. DELI.

If you're tuckered out while shopping in Yorkville—and not feeling up to facing the chic scene at the neighborhood's many bistros—head to the sanctuary of Lox, Stock & Bagel. Located in a courtyard of the Hazelton Lanes shopping complex, this deli serves up snacks, salads, and sandwiches. The menu isn't sophisticated, but it's hard to resist comfort foods like cheese blintzes, matzo ball soup, and a classic Reuben sandwich. There are a few hot dishes too, such as vegetarian lasagna. Of course, you could always just grab a bagel—but why pass up the chance to have it with lox, cream cheese, tomato, and cucumber?

Nataraj. 394 Bloor St. W. ☎ **416/928-2925.** Reservations not accepted. Main courses C$7–$12 (US$4.80–$8.20). MC, V. Mon–Sat 5:30–10:30pm. Subway: Spadina. INDIAN.

There's usually a bit of a wait for a table—Nataraj's upscale cuisine is popular with Annex residents, and its downscale prices are affordable to U of T students. But the service is swift, so tables do open up rather quickly. The cooking is from the northern part of the subcontinent, so there are lots of fish and seafood dishes. A number of plates will appeal to vegetarians. The tandoor-baked breads are simply sublime.

Pho Hung. 200 Bloor St. W. ☎ **416/963-5080.** Main courses C$7–$13 (US$4.80–$8.85). MC, V. Daily noon–10pm. Subway: St. George. VIETNAMESE.

Pho is usually translated as "soup," but that's a bit of a misnomer—it's more like a meal in a bowl. There are 15 to choose from here, and the lemongrass- or coriander-scented broths are chock-full of meat, noodles, and vegetables. There's also a range of chicken, pork, and seafood dishes, and a tangy beef fondue. The wine list is longer and better than you might expect.

✪ Serra. 378 Bloor St. W. ☎ **416/922-6999.** Main courses C$8–$14 (US$5.45–$9.55). AE, MC, V. Mon–Sat noon–2:30 and 6–10:30pm. Subway: Spadina. ITALIAN.

This diminutive eatery would fit in nicely in Little Italy. The diners are casually chic, and the look is sleek, with a wood-paneled bar in one corner and mahogany tables for two. The trattoria-worthy fare includes thin-crust pizza topped with olives, prosciutto, and goat cheese; light-sauced pasta dishes teeming with shrimp; and grilled focaccia sandwiches.

SpringRolls. 687 Yonge St. ☎ **416/972-7655.** Reservations recommended. Main courses C$5–$10 (US$3.40–$6.80). Mon–Sat 5:30–10:30pm. Subway: Yonge/Bloor. ASIAN.

What to have for dinner tonight: Chinese, Vietnamese, Thai, Singaporean? If you can't decide, your best bet is SpringRolls. The name may make you think its offerings are meager, but the multi-page menu will set you straight. There is no end in sight of

Great Greasy Spoons

While I'm enchanted by Toronto's top-notch dining spots, I just can't resist the lure of the greasy spoon. You know the kind of place I mean: fluorescent lighting, a bottle of ketchup on every Formica tabletop, vinyl-upholstered booths, and mingled aromas of strong coffee and frying bacon. This combination spells heaven for those of us who don't count calories or cholesterol   and the health nuts can enjoy the laid-back atmosphere while they sip a (diet) fountain soda. Some suggestions:

Mars, 432 College St. at Bathurst St. (☎ **416/921-6332**), sports a neon sign that claims the diner is "Just out of this world." It is perhaps Toronto's best-known greasy spoon, and in addition to the standard all-day breakfast menu, it boasts cheese blintzes, grilled burgers, and a great turkey club sandwich. There's another location at 2363 Yonge St., just north of Eglinton Ave. (☎ 416/322-7111), but its kitschy mock-diner decor doesn't hold a candle to the real McCoy.

Flo's Diner, 10 Bellair St. (☎ **416/961-4333**), lurks just behind the shiny facade of Yorkville. This is a family favorite, as much for the warm welcome kids get (crayons and coloring paper readily available) as for the homey comfort food. One trendy touch: Flo's has its own rooftop patio, the perfect perch from which to watch chic Yorkville denizens stroll by.

Avenue Coffee Shop, 222 Davenport Rd. at Avenue Rd. (☎ **416/924-5191**), is just up the street from the Park Hyatt and the Four Seasons hotels, which explains the frequent celebrity sightings here (signed and framed photos stand as a permanent record of such visits). In business since 1946, the Avenue serves up a steady supply of omelets, French toast, and hamburgers.

The Goof, 2379 Queen St. E. (☎ **416/694-3605**), is officially named the Garden Gate Restaurant. But ever since certain letters burned out of the neon "Good Food" sign, this Beaches neighborhood mainstay has been known as The Goof. In addition to the usual diner grub, this spot has got star power, as evidenced by recent Jennifer Lopez sightings.

---

barbecued pork or fried shrimp dishes, which are tenderly executed. Vegetarians don't have as many choices as you might expect, though there are a few top-notch vermicelli-and-veggie plates.

5 Midtown East/The East End

Just about everything *will* be Greek to you in the East End along Danforth Avenue. Known appropriately enough as Greektown, this is where to come for low-cost, delicious dining, or for a midnight meal—the tavernas along this strip generally stay open until the wee hours, even on weeknights.

EXPENSIVE

Café Brussel. 786 Broadview Ave. ☎ **416/465-7363.** Reservations recommended. Main courses C$15–$28 (US$10.20–$19.05). AE, MC, V. Mon–Sat 5:30–11pm, Sun 11:30–11pm. Subway: Broadview. BELGIAN.

Perhaps this was to be a challenge to the supremacy of Greek food in this neighborhood. The Café Brussel is defiantly . . . Belgian? It's the only such eatery in the city.

The menu could pass for French in most regards, with staples like onion soup and duck confit. This is food you could get drunk on—try beef simmered in dark ale (*carbonnades flamandes*), or seafood with shots of hard stuff (*moules au bourbon*). There's also a great selection of European lagers and wines. On Sunday, the Brie omelets make this a popular spot for brunch.

MODERATE

Christina's. 492 Danforth Ave. ☎ **416/463-4418.** Reservations recommended. Main courses C$10–$24 (US$6.80–$16.30). AE, DC, MC, V. Daily 11am–4am. Subway: Chester. GREEK.

This restaurant takes itself a little more seriously than its nearby cousins. The walls are plastered with photographs of celebrities caught in the act of dining here. (There's one infamous old snapshot of "Friends" star Matt LeBlanc dining out with angst diva Alanis Morissette.) The menu offers reliable souvlaki and eggplant pies, but it veers into pasta and burger territory, too. The hearty all-day breakfast of feta-spiked omelets and herbed taters is a popular choice.

Lolita's Lust. 513 Danforth Ave. ☎ **416/465-1751.** Main courses C$10–$25 (US$6.80–$17). AE, MC, V. Sun–Thurs 6–11pm, Fri–Sat 6pm–midnight. Subway: Pape. MEDITERRANEAN.

Lolita's is a bit of a tease. The front window is painted acid green, leaving the smallest hint of glass to peer through. Perhaps this hush-hush air is a draw because the restaurant has been packed since it first opened; it's a favorite port of call for casually dressed boomers. The menu travels around the Mediterranean, from Greece to Morocco to Italy. Pan-seared tuna goes well with green lentil sauce, though there are more than a few odd-couple pairings, like roasted beets with Gorgonzola. The wait staff occasionally suffers memory lapses.

✪ **Myth.** 417 Danforth Ave. (between Logan and Chester). ☎ **416/461-8383.** Reservations not accepted. Main courses C$9–$22 (US$6.10–$15). AE, MC, V. Mon–Wed 5pm–2am, Thurs–Sat noon–4am, Sun noon–2am. Subway: Chester. MEDITERRANEAN.

Part trendy bar, part restaurant, this generous space is large enough to encompass both. The ambiance is classical Greece meets MTV. Ornate oversized shields share space with a series of TVs running an endless loop of mythic movies. Who can pay attention to what's on the plate with so much going on? Fortunately, the food calls attention to itself. Starters, ranging from traditional spanakopita (spinach pie) to herb-crusted goat cheese with saffron poached pears, are impossible to ignore. Main courses, such as lamb brochette atop basmati rice and chicken-mushroom-bacon-shallot pizza, are just as demanding. As the night goes on, the crowd gets younger, and would-be sharks line the pool tables.

Octavia. 414 Danforth Ave. ☎ **416/461-3562.** Reservations not accepted. Main courses C$14–$22 (US$9.55–$15). AE, MC, V. Sun–Thurs 5pm–midnight, Fri–Sat 5pm–2pm. Subway: Chester. ECLECTIC/MEDITERRANEAN.

Who brought Thai satays onto the Danforth? This swanky new addition to the Greektown strip may have a name that fits right in, but its sensibility is decidedly different. The look is highly polished, with velvety banquettes against one wall and French doors that open to the sidewalk for an impromptu patio. Most of the main courses, such as grilled seafood and squid-ink pastas, come from the Mediterranean, but there's room on the menu for California salads and satays, too.

✪ **Pan on the Danforth.** 516 Danforth Ave. ☎ **416/466-8158.** Reservations accepted only for parties of 6 or more. Main courses C$13–$19 (US$8.85–$12.90). AE, MC, V. Sun–Thurs 5pm–midnight, Fri–Sat 5pm–1am. Subway: Chester or Pape. GREEK.

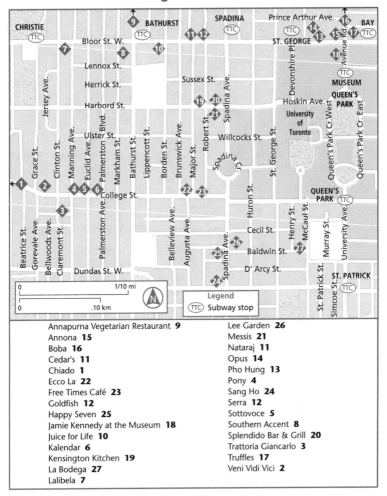

Annapurna Vegetarian Restaurant **9**
Annona **15**
Boba **16**
Cedar's **11**
Chiado **1**
Ecco La **22**
Free Times Café **23**
Goldfish **12**
Happy Seven **25**
Jamie Kennedy at the Museum **18**
Juice for Life **10**
Kalendar **6**
Kensington Kitchen **19**
La Bodega **27**
Lalibela **7**

Lee Garden **26**
Messis **21**
Nataraj **11**
Opus **14**
Pho Hung **13**
Pony **4**
Sang Ho **24**
Serra **12**
Sottovoce **5**
Southern Accent **8**
Splendido Bar & Grill **20**
Trattoria Giancarlo **3**
Truffles **17**
Veni Vidi Vici **2**

To the best of my knowledge, Pan was a god of music, not of food. I must have mixed it up because if he's the inspiration for this restaurant, he certainly knows his way around a kitchen. This long-established eatery takes classic Greek dishes and updates them with panache. Grilled swordfish is wrapped in vine leaf and served with spinach orzo, and a smoked and baked pork chop comes with feta scalloped potatoes and zucchini relish. The well-chosen wine list favors the New World. The crowd is fairly sophisticated, which may explain the cryptic message over the bar: "You've done it already."

INEXPENSIVE

Astoria. 390 Danforth Ave. ☎ **416/463-2838.** Reservations recommended; accepted on weekdays only. Main courses C$9–$15 (US$6.10–$10.20). AE, MC, V. Mon–Wed and Fri–Sat 11am–1am, Thurs and Sun 11am–midnight. Subway: Chester. GREEK.

The restaurant subtitles itself a shish-kebab house, but its offerings are much broader. And it's more upscale than the name would suggest, with a patio fountain

Sleepless in Toronto: What to Do When the Midnight Munchies Attack

There are cities that never sleep. Well, Toronto isn't one of them. The city starts to doze off around 11:30pm, even on weekends. Sure, there are 24-hour dough-nut shops, but if you're looking for something more substantial, try one of the following late-night options:

- **Caribbean Roti Corner,** 607 Queen St. W. (☎ **416/504-9558**), provides take-out dishes of jerk chicken, rice and peas, and meaty stews until 4am on weekends. Subway: Osgoode, then streetcar west to Spadina Ave.

- **Fran's** (*see page 107*) is the original 24/7 lifesaver. With three locations around the city, you can always find burgers, pastas, and salads.

- **Free Times Café** (*see page 84*) is open until 2am Monday through Saturday, until midnight on Sunday. It serves light Middle Eastern food, with many choices for vegetarians.

- **Happy Seven** (*see page 85*) serves reliable Chinese food in a kitschy setting until 5am.

- **7 West Café,** 7 Charles St. W. (☎ **416/928-9041**), is open 24 hours a day. Delish sandwiches and pasta platters hit the spot. Those with severe sugar cravings can indulge in cakes and pies from several of the city's best bakers. Subway: Yonge/Bloor.

- If you're on the Danforth, you're in luck: Many of the terrific Greek tavernas and restaurants there, like **Myth, Octavia,** and **Christina's,** stay open until the wee hours even on weeknights (see "Midtown East/The East End," *page 99*).

and colorful decor. Whatever the meat, it seems to respond well to broiling—beef, lamb, chicken, and seafood all get similar treatment. There are several choices for vegetarians, including souvlaki and moussaka. Expect a wait if you arrive after 8:30 or so on weekends.

✪ Avli. 401 Danforth Ave. ☎ **416/461-9577.** Main courses C$9–$16 (US$6.10–$10.90). MC, V. Mon–Thurs 11:30am–midnight, Fri–Sat 11:30am–3am, Sun 4pm–midnight. Subway: Chester. GREEK.

The white stucco archway at the front contributes to the cave-like feel of the narrow room. Always noisy, occasionally raucous, this taverna serves up some of the most delicate food on the Danforth. Meze starters are standard: *kopanisti* (spicy feta with peppers) and hummus for those who want cold food, grilled octopus and steamed mussels for those who like it hot. Main courses are standouts. The half chicken stuffed with cashews, dates, apples, and rice is exquisite, and the meat moussaka is the best around. The charming service is on a par with the food.

Mezes. 456 Danforth Ave. ☎ **416/778-5150.** Reservations not accepted. Appetizers C$3–$8 (US$2.05–$5.45). MC, V. Mon–Thurs and Sun 5pm–midnight, Fri–Sat 5pm–3am. Subway: Chester. GREEK.

This sophisticated space doles out exactly what it promises. Mezes are the Greek equivalent of tapas—light snacks meant to keep you going until you have a real dinner in front of you. Still, it's worth spoiling your appetite to indulge in these appetizers.

Choices range from grilled calamari and octopus to spicy eggplant dip and leek pie. Do try to save room for the honey-sweet baklava.

Ouzeri. 500A Danforth Ave. ☎ **416/778-0500.** Reservations recommended. Main courses C$8–$18 (US$5.45–$12.25). AE, DISC, ER, MC, V. Sun–Mon and Wed–Thurs 11am–midnight, Tues and Fri–Sat 11am–2am. Subway: Chester. GREEK.

This is one of the longtime stars of the neighborhood. Ouzeri has been packing in the crowds for years and shows no sign of slowing down. Just inside the foyer it looks like a sports bar, with TV sets tuned in to the athletic event of the minute. Farther inside, colorful ceramic tiles and wrought iron surround the terrazzo tables and wicker chairs. Charming as the interior is, if you're lucky you'll be outside on the small patio. Portions of the main dishes, such as lamb pies and pork kebabs, tend to be quite generous. As the evening goes on the convivial atmosphere deepens into festival-like celebration; on Tuesday nights, there's live Greek music.

6 Uptown

This area is too large to be considered a neighborhood, stretching as it does from north of Davenport Road to Steeles Avenue. While it doesn't have the concentration of restaurants that the downtown area enjoys, it has a number of stellar options that make the trip north worthwhile.

VERY EXPENSIVE

✪ **Centro.** 2472 Yonge St. ☎ **416/483-2211.** Reservations required. Main courses C$24–$39 (US$16.30–$26.50). AE, DC, MC, V. Mon–Sat 5–11:30pm. Subway: Eglinton. CONTINENTAL.

The palace-grand main room, with its oxblood walls, is always bustling. The dressed-up all-ages crowd often starts out schmoozing at the wine bar downstairs, moves up to the main floor for dinner, then migrates back downstairs for R&B music and a nightcap (the wine bar stays open until 2am). French-born executive chef Marc Thuet, a motorcycle-riding local celebrity, takes his food seriously. The seasonal menu pays tribute to the restaurant's Northern Italian origins, with pasta dishes like pennette with Parma prosciutto and roasted sage. Many choices lean to contemporary Canadiana, like lean caribou chops with cloudberries and crabapple compote, or French modern, like rack of lamb in a Provençal honey mustard crust served with ratatouille. Delicious desserts run the gamut from traditional tiramisu to chocolate-vanilla baked Alaska. The stellar wine list is sure to thrill oenophiles.

✪ **North 44.** 2537 Yonge St. ☎ **416/487-4897.** Reservations required. Main courses C$27–$40 (US$18.35–$27.20). AE, DC, MC, V. Mon–Sat 5–11pm. Subway: Eglinton. INTERNATIONAL.

This is the one restaurant that even people who've never set foot in Toronto have heard about. It's profiled extensively in food and travel magazines, but can it possibly live up to its reputation? In a word, yes. The spare art-deco decor recently got a face-lift, and the results are stunning: sleek, adult glamour without a hint of trying too hard. The soft lighting and strategically situated mirrors wrap the dining room—and its occupants—in a gorgeous glow. People dress up to go here, though they don't have to, and if you scan the room you can pick out several couples obviously on a first date. The menu, which changes with the seasons, borrows from Mediterranean, American, and Asian sources. The results are inspiring to the palate and to the eye. On the list of main courses you might find grilled veal tenderloin with orange peppercorns, toasted barley, and root veggies, or roasted Muscovy duck breast with orange-soy marinade and foie gras. There are always a few pasta and pizza choices, such as caramelized squash ravioli with black truffle essence. It's impossible to come here without being seduced into a three-course meal. The desserts, like lemon meringue mille-feuille, are among the best in the city, and there's a wide selection of accompanying ice wines. The wine list is comprehensive, though most of the prices veer off into the stratosphere. What really sets North 44 apart is its seamless service. Those who don't like to be pampered should stay away.

Scaramouche. 1 Benvenuto Place (off Avenue Rd.). ☎ **416/961-8011.** Reservations required. Main courses C$25–$45 (US$17–$30.60); pasta dishes C$15–$25 (US$10.20–$17). AE, DC, MC, V. Main room Mon–Sat 6–10:30pm. Pasta bar Mon–Fri 6–10:30pm, Sat 6–11pm. Subway: St. Clair. INTERNATIONAL.

This is a contender for those who don't mind spending top dollar on splendid food. Tucked into an upscale apartment building, it isn't easy to find. That enhances its snob appeal—and the crowd here is more old money than at either of its uptown competitors, Centro and North 44. Scaramouche is blessed with one of the most romantic settings in the city. Floor-to-ceiling windows afford a panoramic view of the downtown skyline. (Securing a window seat is no mean feat, but fortunately most tables have decent sightlines.) The unobtrusive servers pay attention to the details. The menu is laden with caviar, foie gras, truffles, and oysters. The wine list has a broad reach, with many available by the glass. There is also a nice selection of cognacs.

EXPENSIVE

Auberge du Pommier. 4150 Yonge St. ☎ **416/222-2220.** Reservations recommended. Main courses C$23–$33 (US$15.65–$22.45). AE, DC, MC, V. Mon–Fri 11:30am–2:30pm; Mon–Sat 5–10:30pm. Subway: York Mills. FRENCH.

Don't have time to drop by your French country house this weekend? To the rescue comes Auberge du Pommier, a cozy chateau that exudes Provençal-style charm. Casually dressed diners relax in the care of expert servers. The menu doesn't offer many surprises, but what it does, it does well. Appetizers set a high standard, with dishes like Breton-style lobster bisque and warm goat cheese in Niagara vine leaf. Entrees, like sage-roasted pheasant breast with Jerusalem artichoke ragout and sweet-and-sour cranberry *jus,* keep up the pace. In the winter, fireplaces blaze; in summer, a canvas-covered terrace opens.

✪ **La Bruschetta.** 1317 St. Clair Ave. W. ☎ **416/656-8622.** Reservations recommended. Main courses C$14–$26 (US$9.55–$17.70). AE, DC, ER, MC, V. Mon–Fri 5–10:30pm. Subway: St. Clair West, then any streetcar west to Dufferin St. ITALIAN.

Star sightings are common in Toronto, but at La Bruschetta they're almost an everyday event. The entryway is covered from floor to ceiling with plates decorated by celebs such as Kelsey Grammer and Bette Midler. It's a surprise then to find the kitchen-like dining room, unrelieved in its homeliness but for vases of fresh-cut flowers. Owner Benito Piantoni, who charms patrons with tales of Italy and Hollywood gossip, provides local color. The menu lists a dozen pastas, with cream sauces ranging from brandy to Gorgonzola. Mouth-watering main courses include veal medallions simply presented in white-wine sauce with garlic and mushrooms. After a rich meal, you'll welcome the delicate lemon ice for dessert.

Lakes. 1112 Yonge St. ☎ **416/921-0995.** Reservations recommended. Main courses C$14–$33 (US$9.55–$22.45). AE, ER, MC, V. Mon–Fri noon–2:30pm and 5:30–10:30pm, Sat 6–10:30pm. Subway: Summerhill. BISTRO.

Plush banquettes and close-set tables heighten the sense of intimacy in the narrow dining room. A casually well-dressed crowd drops by during the week; on Saturday night, work-obsessed couples spend candlelit quality time. The menu changes every few months, but jazzed-up bistro classics such as duck confit with cranberry-shallot glaze and garlic mashed potatoes, grilled provimi veal liver, and Gruyère-and-Emmenthal fondue for two make frequent appearances. The banana crème brûlée on the short dessert menu is a perennial favorite.

❂ **Millie's Bistro.** 1980 Avenue Rd. (south of York Mills). ☎ **416/481-1247.** Reservations recommended. Main courses C$10–$22 (US$6.80–$15). AE, MC, V. Subway: York Mills, then walk west or take a taxi (about C$5/US$3.40). MEDITERRANEAN.

Subtle as its signage is, Millie's is hard to miss. The sole gastronomic draw in this neighborhood, it is splendid enough to lure even jaded downtown dwellers. Divided into two sunny, skinny rooms (both nonsmoking), it attracts an unusual mix of young-to-middle-age courting couples, families with tiny tykes, and groups gearing up for a night on the town. The sprawling menu includes dishes from Spain, southern France, Italy, Turkey, and Morocco (there is a shorter kids' menu, too). Start with tapas—perhaps Catalan-style goat cheese with basil and olive oil; Turkish flatbread with a topping of lamb, yogurt, and mint; or a *b'stilla* (aromatic chicken wrapped in herbed semolina). Better still, try them all—the cheery staff will arrange them on ceramic platters for sharing. Main dishes include a must-try chicken-and-shrimp paella; garlicky, spicy rib steak; and vegetarian lasagne with portobello mushrooms, sweet roasted peppers, and leeks. Sweets are seductive, though generous tapas and main portions make saving room for dessert almost impossible. On the wide-ranging wine list, Spanish selections are a particularly good value.

Quartier. 2112 Yonge St. ☎ **416/545-0505.** Reservations recommended. Main courses C$12–$24 (US$8.20–$16.30). AE, MC, V. Daily 11am–2:30pm and 5:30–10:30pm. Subway: Eglinton. MEDITERRANEAN.

The old-world elegance is palpable as you step into this refined bistro. Is it the languid sound of Edith Piaf's voice in the air? Perhaps the baroque mirrors and look-again prints that punctuate the walls? No matter. The French-born proprietor, Marcel Rethore, has created a romance-tinged atmosphere for a casually chic crowd. The menu boasts classic dishes such as grilled calf's liver in Provençal sauce with frites and asparagus, and duck à l'orange. Occasional experiments with more exotic fare, such as North African couscous in spicy sauce, are beautifully executed. Appetizers favor seafood, with simple soups and plates of salmon and mussels. Desserts, for those who have room, include a tender lemon-cream mille-feuille and a delicate crème brûlée. The short wine list is particularly well chosen—it's hard to go wrong.

Roxborough's. 1055 Yonge St. (at Roxborough Ave.). ☎ **416/323-0000.** Reservations strongly recommended. Main courses C$20-$26 (US$13.60–$17.70). AE, DC, MC, V. Mon–Sat 5:30pm–10:30pm. Subway: Rosedale. BISTRO.

This glamorous bistro boasts soft lighting, strategically placed privacy screens, and smooth service —the perfect setting for a grown-up night on the town. The crowd here is a mix of locals and visitors drawn from far-flung areas who made a special trip in for dinner. And Roxborough's makes it all worthwhile, with a stylish seasonal menu that features main plates like red snapper served atop cumin- and mint-scented couscous, or Atlantic salmon in a sauce of tomato, lemon and olive with leeks and baby potatoes. The desserts are classics, particularly the caramel-drenched bread pudding.

Thai Magic. 1118 Yonge St. ☎ **416/968-7366.** Reservations recommended. Main courses C$12–$20 (US$8.20–$13.60); complete dinners C$33–$34 (US$22.45–$23.10). AE, MC, V. Mon–Sat 5:30–11pm. Subway: Summerhill. THAI.

Arrangements of orchids, cascading vines, and Thai statuary grace the enchanting entry. The serene staff handles frenetic crowds with ease; this spot is filled with locals, especially on Thursday and Friday nights. The meal is served Western-style, rather than in the Thai fashion of bringing all courses to the table at once. Delicate appetizers like chicken-filled golden baskets vie for attention with not-too-spicy soups. Entrees range from chicken with cashews and whole dried chilies to fiery shrimp curry.

MODERATE

✪ **Amore Trattoria.** 2425 Yonge St. ☎ **416/322-6184.** Reservations recommended; accepted only for groups of 6 or more. Main courses C$10–$18 (US$6.80–12.25). AE, MC, V. Daily noon–3pm and 5:30–10:30pm. Subway: Eglinton. ITALIAN.

This double-decker restaurant is a neighborhood favorite with groups and families alike. Pandemonium reigns on the first floor; upstairs, the cognoscenti can gaze over a balcony at the tumult below. The cheerful staff takes it all in stride. Reading the menu takes much too long: With 22 pastas, 21 pizzas, 6 meat dishes, and daily specials, it can be an intimidating experience for the indecisive. Fortunately, the kitchen consistently produces top-notch dishes, from simple salads of mesclun and goat cheese to spaghetti in brandy-tomato sauce with sweet Bermuda onion. Wine is served in tumblers in classic rustic-Italian style. Weekend brunch always draws a crowd with hearty frittatas and fruit-laden waffles.

Gio's. 2070 Yonge St. ☎ **416/932-2306.** Reservations not accepted. Main courses C$8–$14 (US$5.45–$9.55). AE, MC, V. Mon–Thurs 5:30–10:30pm, Fri–Sat 5:30–11pm. Subway: Eglinton. ITALIAN.

Ask any local where you might find this tiny trattoria, and you'll be told to look for the nose. When you see it, you'll understand—in lieu of a sign, a schnozz of Durante-like proportions looms over Yonge Street. The sense of fun keeps up inside, where the 8-foot-wide dining room is covered with Italianate doodads like ceramic crockery, grappa bottles, and pastoral paintings. Waiters rush about, occasionally breaking into song. Prices look inexpensive, but portions aren't large, so ordering three or four courses is the norm. In true Italian style, pasta is not a main course but an appetizer; the list of entrees is mainly for meat-eaters, and you'll have to order veggies separately. This isn't the place for intimate conversation, but it's great fun with a group.

Mediterraneo. 2075 Yonge St. ☎ **416/322-0161.** Reservations recommended. Main courses C$8–$16 (US$5.45–$10.90). AE, MC, V. Mon–Sat 6–11pm. Subway: Eglinton. ITALIAN.

This trattoria underwent extensive renovations in 1999, and as a result it's difficult to decide whether to sit on the patio or in the airy interior. The kitchen has also spruced up its offerings—the list of pizzas and pastas has grown, though there are still only a handful of meat dishes. Dishes tend to the simple, like gnocchi in basil-Gorgonzola sauce, but are nicely executed. Service isn't always speedy, though the flip side is that the staff doesn't mind if you linger for ages over your espresso.

Mezzetta. 681 St. Clair Ave. W. ☎ **416/658-5687.** Reservations recommended. Appetizers C$3–$5.50 (US$2.05–$3.75). MC, V. Tues–Sat noon–10:30pm. Subway: St. Clair. MIDDLE EASTERN.

Tapas bars are a dime a dozen in Madrid, but in Toronto they're few and far between. Mezzetta is one such gem. Everything on the menu is served in appetizer-sized portions, from cold salads of feta, olives, and tomatoes, to steamy kofta, an Egyptian dish of beef, lamb, and potato in a spicy sauce. There are also pita sandwiches and barbecued items. Much of the menu will appeal to vegetarians. The wine list is short but priced for value, and there's a lengthy list of brews, too.

✪ **Stork on the Roof.** 2009 Yonge St. ☎ **416/483-3747.** Reservations required. Main courses C$15–$17 (US$10.20–$11.60). AE, ER, MC, V. Wed–Fri noon–2pm; Tues–Sat 6–10pm. Subway: Davisville. BISTRO.

The stork in question is a Dutch sign of good fortune. And luck it is to discover this charming bistro. The menu abounds with pan-European classics warmed up by exotic elements, such as grilled pork tenderloin with lemon curry sauce. Asian inspirations are in evidence, particularly with regard to seafood, like sautéed squid served with satay-worthy peanut sauce and pickled vegetables. For dessert, Dutch spiced apple pie is the standout. The restaurant is nonsmoking.

Vanipha Lanna. 471 Eglinton Ave. W. ☎ **416/484-0895.** Reservations recommended. Main courses C$7–$14 (US$4.80–$9.55). AE, MC, V. Mon–Sat 6–10:30pm. Subway: Eglinton. LAOTIAN/THAI.

There's no shortage of Thai eateries in Toronto, but this is one of the few that specializes in the cooking of Thailand's northwestern Lanna region. Strong, spicy Laotian influences permeate the cooking (many Laos natives have relocated to Lanna). One of the house specialties is grilled chicken and garlic served with lime-chili sauce. The busy dining room attracts casually dressed diners of all ages, all of whom are treated with care by the thoughtful staff.

INEXPENSIVE

✪ **Fran's.** 21 St. Clair Ave. W. ☎ **416/925-6337.** Reservations not accepted. Most items C$6–$12 (US$4.10–$8.20). Daily 24 hours. Subway: St. Clair. BURGERS.

One of three Fran's restaurants in the city, the St. Clair location was the first. It still has the feel of a 1940s diner, with chrome counter seats and faux-leather booths. While the menu has grown in recent years to include more sophisticated fare, there's nothing Fran's does better than a grilled burger with all the fixings, whether the classic beef-and-bacon combo or the vegetarian version. Fran's is also famous for its breakfast offerings (served all day)—there's nothing fancy, but a filling platter of eggs, sausage, toast, and hash browns will set you back a mere C$6 (US$4.10). The restaurant is a favorite with tiny tots, who have their own menu and are encouraged to express themselves with crayons; the resulting artworks are often put on display. Fran's is perpetually understaffed, so be prepared for a wait.

Hannah's Kitchen. 2221 Yonge St. ☎ **416/481-0185.** Reservations not accepted. Main courses C$7–$12 (US$4.80–$8.20). MC, V. Mon–Fri 10am–10pm. Subway: Eglinton. LIGHT FARE.

This cubbyhole-like eatery is easy to miss if you're not watching closely. National magazines and newspapers have published several of its recipes, but Hannah's remains defiantly low-key. Diners seat themselves at wooden banquettes or tiny tables. The menu is unchanging, but there are always three or four daily specials. It includes many pasta dishes, whether cold (pesto radiatore salad with chicken and pine nuts is the top pick) or hot (penne arrabiata has the spiciest sauce in town). Occasional forays into the exotic include a few Indonesian rice dishes and the ever-popular pad Thai. Desserts are a must, so check out the selection behind the counter on your way in. Service is usually quite speedy, and the kitchen will modify ingredients on request.

Rebel House. 1068 Yonge St. ☎ **416/927-0704.** Main courses C$8–$14 (US$5.45–$9.55). MC, V. Daily 5–11pm. Subway: Rosedale. LIGHT FARE.

This casual spot is beloved by locals, some of whom dine here almost every night. Is it the warm welcome, the better-than-average pub grub, or the impressive selection of microbrews that draws them in? The crowd is mainly 20- to 30-somethings decked out in designer casualwear, more intent on socializing than eating. The specialty of the house is hearty, simple fare, and grilled Atlantic salmon and seared Angus strip loin are top picks. Pastas and salads are worth a taste, too. In summer, the patio is the place to be.

7 North of the City

Toronto is a sprawling city, and as it has increased its reach, new and inspiring restaurants have cropped up in formerly out-of-the-way regions. The area north of Steeles Avenue is experiencing a remarkable boom, and the gastronomical scene there is just gaining its footing. These restaurants are beyond the reach of the Toronto subway system. If you've rented a car to go to the McMichael Gallery in Kleinburg or to the Canada's Wonderland theme park, you might want to stop on the way back downtown. (For driving directions, see chapter 6.)

EXPENSIVE

✪ **Terra Restaurant Oyster & Martini Bar.** 8199 Yonge St. (just south of Hwy. 407). ☎ **905/731-6161.** Reservations recommended. Main courses C$20–$33 (US$13.60–$22.45). AE, DC, ER, MC, V. Tues–Sun 6–11pm. INTERNATIONAL.

This restaurant feels as if it was airlifted out of the downtown core. Sleek and sophisticated, it is the sibling of uptown's North 44. Chef Mark McEwan believes in giving them equal attention, and so the cooking at Terra is appropriately splendid. The kitchen favors seafood, from appetizers like cherrywood-smoked salmon with peppercorn crust to entrees like grilled jumbo prawns with shiitake mushroom ravioli and garlic fried greens. There are several steak plates, and a few surprises, such as ostrich with scallion hashed potato and spinach. Desserts include a classic crème brûlée and a more unusual pecan and blueberry cheesecake. The lengthy wine list hits all the international high notes, though most bottles are quite pricey.

MODERATE

✪ **Grand Yatt.** 19019 Bayview Ave. ☎ **905/882-9388.** Main courses C$12–$18 (US$8.20–$12.25). AE, MC, V. Daily 9am–3pm and 6–10pm. CHINESE.

There's a Grand Yatt restaurant at the Westin Harbour Castle hotel, but this is the original. The large space is quite plain in comparison with its downtown offspring, but the cooking here is widely considered the better of the two. This is Cantonese cuisine at its finest. The seafood—black cod, geoduck (a rather large clam), or jumbo shrimp—is fresh as a daisy, and needs only light seasoning to bring out the intense natural flavors. Shark's fin soup is a perennial favorite. For those with tamer tastes, there are pork and poultry dishes. The swift servers are extremely helpful.

INEXPENSIVE

Dante's. 267 Baythorn Dr. (just off Yonge St.). ☎ **905/881-1070.** Main courses C$7–$14 (US$4.80–$9.55). AE, MC, V. Mon–Thurs noon–10pm, Fri–Sat noon–midnight. ITALIAN.

Predating the current boom in the area, Dante's has been the favorite local spot for down-home Italian cooking since 1976. It's not hard to figure out why. The menu has something for everyone, the food is consistently good, and the prices are entirely reasonable. Don't expect to find exotic risottos here—stick to heaping plates of pasta like rigatoni with black and green olives, or homemade cannelloni. One serving of chicken parmigiano can feed two adults.

What to See & Do in Toronto

First the good news: Toronto has amazing sights to see and places to be that appeal to travelers of all stripes. The bad news? No matter how long your stay, you won't be able to fit everything in. Toronto is a sprawling city, and while downtown and midtown boast a sizable collection of attractions, some truly wonderful sights are in less accessible areas.

Another difficulty is that many attractions could take up a day of your visit. Ontario Place, Harbourfront, the Ontario Science Centre, and Paramount Canada's Wonderland all come to mind. That's not even mentioning the expansive parks, the arts scene, or the shopping possibilities. My best advice is to relax and bring a good pair of walking shoes. There's no better way to appreciate the kaleidoscopic metropolis that is Toronto than on foot.

Suggested Itineraries

If You Have 1 Day

Start out early in the morning in **Kensington Market,** and pick up breakfast from one of the Middle Eastern, Asian, or North African cafes. Kensington adjoins Toronto's main **Chinatown,** so stroll down Spadina Avenue and head east along Dundas Street to enjoy it. Along Dundas you'll find the **Art Gallery of Ontario;** spend at least a couple of hours there, and be sure to take in the collection of sculptures by British artist Henry Moore. For lunch, head to the gallery's marvelous restaurant, Agora, or to nearby Baldwin Street for Chinese food. It's a short walk from here to **Queen's Park,** where the Ontario Legislature meets; the surrounding greenery affords a respite from the asphalt jungle. If you're a museum lover, the **Royal Ontario Museum** is just up the street, but I wouldn't recommend exploring two major institutions (like the AGO and the ROM) in 1 day. Instead, head up to trendy **Yorkville,** with its small galleries, boutiques, and cafes. If you have kids in tow, you might want to check out the **Children's Own Museum.** Before dinner, try to buy same-day tickets to a show in the adjoining **Theater District.** Then check out one of the fine restaurants in **Yorkville,** or head back downtown to **Queen Street West** (see chapter 5 for suggestions). If you didn't get theater tickets, Queen Street West has varied nightlife options.

If You Have 2 Days

On the first day, follow the itinerary for 1 day. On day 2, start out wandering the grounds of **Exhibition Place** and arrive at the gates of **Ontario Place** at 10am sharp; allow about half a day for Ontario Place. If it's a clear sunny day, go from there to the top of the **CN Tower** and drink in the matchless view. Glance over at **SkyDome** as you pass by. Head up to the architectural wonder that is **City Hall at Nathan Phillips Square,** then continue east to the **Eaton Centre.** After you've shopped until you drop, ride a streetcar to **Little Italy,** along College Street. There's no end of dining options; try to score a patio seat if the weather's fine. This is another prime neighborhood for nightlife, so unless you've scored tickets to a game at the **Air Canada Centre,** you can hang out here in style.

If You Have 3 Days

This is when I'd recommend going a little farther afield. (You could also just allot more time to the previously mentioned sights.) Start your day at the highly interactive **Ontario Science Centre.** If the weather's good, you could spend the rest of the day reveling in the 600 acres of **Sunnybrook Park,** which has hiking trails and a horseback riding center. If the weather isn't quite so clement, this could be your afternoon to explore the **Royal Ontario Museum** or the **Hockey Hall of Fame.** If another museum isn't your thing, head to the **Harbourfront Centre,** which offers restaurants, a daily antiques market, activities for kids, and varied events. At night, if you're up for something completely different, go to **Greektown** along the Danforth, where the many tavernas stay open until 3 or 4am most nights.

If You Have 4 Days or More

Now you can really start to explore Toronto. If you've followed the itinerary for the first 3 days, you might have some sights that you want to return to. Otherwise, you could head north of Toronto to see the **McMichael Collection in Kleinburg** or, if the kids outvote you, to spend the day at **Paramount Canada's Wonderland.** There's no better way to spend a day than picnicking on the lush **Toronto Islands,** where you can rent bicycles, take the kids to **Centreville** amusement park, and get a whole new view of the city. A less-traveled site is scenic **Cabbagetown,** with its Edwardian and Queen Anne–style architecture, **Riverdale Farm,** and Gothic **Necropolis.** With 4 days or more, you should also be able to sample the city's lively arts scene, taking in a **theater or dance performance.** Try to hit a **comedy club** while you're at it, and check out one of Toronto's **sports** teams, too.

1 The Top Attractions

ON THE LAKEFRONT

Ontario Place. 955 Lakeshore Blvd. W. ☎ **416/314-9811,** or 416/314-9900 for recorded info. www.ontarioplace.com. Free admission to grounds. Separate fee for some events. Admission to attractions C$12 (US$8.15); Play All Day pass C$22 (US$14.95) adults, C$11 (US$7.50) children 4–5, free for children 3 and under. IMAX movies after Labour Day (included in Play All Day pass) C$10 (US$6.80) adults, C$6 (US$4.10) seniors and children 13 and under. Mid-May to Labour Day, daily 10am–dusk; evening events end and dining spots close later. Parking C$9 (US$6.10). Subway: Bathurst or Dufferin, then Bathurst streetcar south.

When this 96-acre recreation complex on Lake Ontario opened in 1971, it seemed futuristic—and 29 years later, it still does. (The 1989 face-lift no doubt helped.) From a distance, you'll see five steel-and-glass pods suspended on columns 105 feet above the lake, three artificial islands, and a huge geodesic dome. The five pods contain a multimedia theater, a children's theater, a high-technology exhibit, and displays that tell the story of Ontario in vivid kaleidoscopic detail. The dome houses Cinesphere, where a 60-by-80-foot screen shows specially made IMAX movies year-round.

Under an enormous orange canopy, the Children's Village is the most creative playground you'll find anywhere. In a well-supervised area, children under 13 can scramble over rope bridges, bounce on an enormous trampoline, explore the foam forest, or slide down a twisting chute. The most popular activity allows them to squirt water pistols and garden hoses, swim, and generally drench one another in the water-play section. Afterward, parents can pop them into the convenient dryers before moving on to other amusements.

A stroll around the complex reveals two marinas full of yachts and other craft, the HMCS *Haida* (a destroyer, open for tours, that served in World War II and the Korean War), an 18-hole miniature golf course, and plenty of grassland for picnicking and romping. The restaurants and snack bars serve everything from Chinese, Irish, and German food to hot dogs and hamburgers. And don't miss the wildest rides in town—the Hydrofuge, a tube slide that allows you to reach speeds over 30 m.p.h.; the Rush River Raft Ride, which carries you along a lengthy flume in an inflatable raft; the pink twister and purple pipeline (water slides); plus bumper boats and go-karts. For something more peaceful, you can navigate pedal boats or remote-control boats between the artificial islands.

At night, the **Molson Amphitheatre** accommodates 16,000 under a copper canopy and outside on the grass. It features top-line entertainers such as Kenny G, James Taylor, the Who, and Hank Williams. For information, call ☎ **416/260-5600.** For tickets, call **Ticketmaster** (☎ **416/870-8000**).

○ **Harbourfront Centre.** Queen's Quay W. ☎ **416/973-3000** for information on special events, or 416/973-4000 (box office). www.harbourfront.on.ca. LRT: York Quay.

In 1972, the federal government took over a 96-acre strip of prime waterfront land to preserve the vista—and since then Torontonians have rediscovered their lakeshore. Abandoned warehouses, shabby depots, and crumbling factories have been refurbished, and a tremendous urban park now stretches on and around the old piers. Today it's one of the most popular hangouts for Torontonians and visitors—a great place to spend a day sunbathing, picnicking, biking, shopping, and sailing.

Queen's Quay, at the foot of York Street, is the closest quay to town, and it's the first one you'll encounter as you approach from the Westin Harbour Castle. From here, boats depart for tours of the harbor, and ferries leave for the Toronto Islands. In this renovated warehouse you'll find the Premiere Dance Theatre (which was specially designed for dance performances), and two floors of shops, restaurants, and waterfront cafes.

After exploring Queen's Quay, walk west along the glorious waterfront promenade to **York Quay.** You'll pass the **Power Plant,** a contemporary art gallery, and behind it, the **Du Maurier Theatre Centre.** At York Quay Centre, you can pick up information on Harbourfront programming. Galleries here include the **Craft Studio,** where you can watch artisans blow glass, throw pots, and make silk-screen prints. On the other side of the center, you can attend a free outdoor concert, held all summer long at Molson Place. Also on the quay is the Water's Edge Cafe, overlooking a small pond for electric model boats (there's skating here in the winter) and a children's play area.

Take the footbridge to John Quay, crossing over the sailboats moored below, to the stores and restaurants on **Pier 4**—Wallymagoo's Marine Bar and the Pier 4 Storehouse. Beyond, on Maple Leaf Quay, lies the Nautical Centre. At the **Harbourside**

Downtown Toronto Attractions

TORONTO

Downtown
Toronto

Air Canada Centre **26**
Allan Gardens **2**
Art Gallery of Toronto **4**
BCE Place **15**
Bus Station **3**
CBC Building **13**
Campbell House **6**
City Hall **7**
CN Tower **21**
Convention Centre **20**
Eaton Centre **9**
The Grange **5**
Harbourfront Antique
  Market **24**
Harbourfront Centre **25**
Hockey Hall of Fame **16**
Hummingbird Centre **17**
Maple Leaf Gardens **1**
Metro Hall **22**
Old City Hall **8**
Royal Alexandra Theatre **10**
Royal Bank Plaza **14**
Roy Thomson Hall **11**
St. Lawrence Market **18**
SkyDome **23**
Toronto Dominion Centre **12**
Union Station **19**

Legend
✝ Church
✉ Post Office
Ⓣ Subway stop

College St.
Oxford St.
Nassau St.
Bathurst St.
Augusta Ave.
Kensington Pl.
Kensington Ave.
Spadina Ave.
Baldwin St.
St. Andrews St.
D'Arcy St.
Beverley St.
④
Dundas St.West
ALEXANDRA PARK
Augusta Ave.
⑤
GRANGE PARK
Queen St. West
Richmond St. West
Spadina Ave.
Adelaide St. West
Portland St.
Peter St.
John St.
King St. West
Bathurst St.
Wellington St. West
Bathurst St.
Front St. West
Peter St.
Esplanade West
㉓
Lake Shore Blvd. West
Gardiner Expressway
㉔
Queen's Quay West
Bathurst Quay
Spadina Quay
Maple Leaf Quays

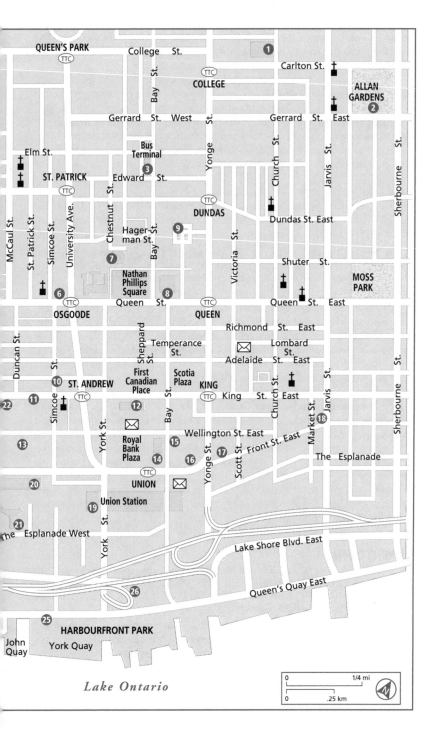

QUEEN'S PARK
College St.
(TTC)
Carlton St. †
COLLEGE
ALLAN
GARDENS
†
Gerrard St. West
Gerrard St. East
Bay St.
Yonge St.
Church St.
Jarvis St.
Sherbourne St.
Bus
Terminal
Elm St.
St. Patrick St.
McCaul St.
Simcoe St.
University Ave.
Chestnut St.
†
ST. PATRICK
†
Edward St.
(TTC)
DUNDAS
(TTC)
Dundas St. East
†
Hager-man St.
Bay St.
Victoria St.
Shuter St.
MOSS
PARK
Nathan
Phillips
Square
†
†
†
Queen St.
(TTC)
Queen St. East
OSGOODE
QUEEN
Richmond St. East
Duncan St.
Sheppard St.
Temperance St.
Lombard St.
Adelaide St. East
First
Canadian
Place
Scotia
Plaza
KING
†
ST. ANDREW
Simcoe St.
(TTC)
King St. East
Church St.
Jarvis St.
Sherbourne St.
York St.
Bay St.
Wellington St. East
Market St.
Royal
Bank
Plaza
Yonge St.
Scott St.
Front St. East
The Esplanade
(TTC)
UNION
Union Station
York St.
The Esplanade West
Lake Shore Blvd. East
Queen's Quay East
HARBOURFRONT PARK
John
Quay
York Quay

Lake Ontario

0 _____ 1/4 mi
0 _____ .25 km

Boating Centre (part of the Nautical Centre), 283 Queen's Quay W. (☎ **416/ 203-3000**), you can rent sailboats and powerboats or sign up for sailing lessons (see "Boating/Canoeing," below).

The **Harbourfront Antiques Market,** 390 Queen's Quay W., at the foot of Spadina Avenue (☎ **416/260-2626**), will keep antique-lovers busy browsing for hours. More than 100 antiques dealers spread out their wares—jewelry, china, furniture, toys, and books. Indoor parking is adjacent to the market, and a cafeteria serves fresh salads, sandwiches, and desserts. It's open Tuesday through Sunday from 10am to 6pm.

At the west end of the park stands **Bathurst Pier,** with a large sports field plus two adventure playgrounds, one for older kids and the other (supervised) for 3 to 7 year olds.

More than 4,000 events take place annually at Harbourfront, including the **Harbourfront Reading Series** in June, and the **International Festival of Authors** in October. Other happenings include films, dance, theater, music, children's events, multicultural festivals, and marine events.

✪ **The Toronto Islands.** Lake Ontario. ☎ **416/392-8193** for ferry schedules. Round-trip fare C$4 (US$2.70) adults, C$2 (US$1.35) seniors and youths 15–19, C$1 (US68¢) children under 15. Ferries leave from docks at the bottom of Bay St. Subway: Union Station, then LRT to Queen's Quay.

In only 7 minutes, an 800-passenger ferry takes you across to 612 acres of island parkland crisscrossed by shaded paths and quiet waterways—a glorious spot to walk, play tennis, bike, feed the ducks, putter around in boats, picnic, or lap up the sun. There are 14 islands, but the three major ones are **Centre, Ward's,** and **Algonquin.** The first is the busiest; the other two are home to about 600 people who live in modest cottages. Originally, the land was a peninsula, but in the mid-1800s a series of storms shattered the finger of land into islands.

On Centre Island, families enjoy **Centreville** (☎ **416/203-0405**), a 19-acre old-fashioned amusement park. You won't see the usual neon signs, shrill hawkers, and greasy hot-dog stands. Instead you'll find a turn-of-the-century village complete with a Main Street, tiny shops, a firehouse, and even a small working farm where the kids can pet lambs and chicks and enjoy pony rides. They'll also love trying out the antique cars, fire engines, old-fashioned train, authentic 1890s carousel, flume ride, and aerial cars. Individual rides (19 of them) cost C$1.50 to $3.50 (US$1 to $2.40). An all-day ride pass costs C$12 (US$8.20) under 49 inches tall, C$17.50 (US$11.90) for those over 4 feet. Centreville is open 10:30am to 6pm, daily from mid-May to Labour Day, and weekends in early May and September.

DOWNTOWN

CN Tower. 301 Front St. W. ☎ **416/360-8500.** www.cntower.ca. Admission C$17 (US$11.55) adults, C$14.50 (US$9.85) seniors, C$11 (US$7.50) children 5–12. Motion simulator rides C$7.50 (US$5.10). Combination tickets C$23 (US$15.65) and up. May–Sept daily 8am–11pm; Oct–Apr 9am–10pm. Subway: Union, then walk west on Front St.

As you approach the city, whether by plane, train, or automobile, the first thing you notice is this slender structure. Glass-walled elevators glide up the 1,815-foot tower, the tallest freestanding structure in the world. The elevators stop first at the 1,136-foot-high, 7-level sky pod (it takes just under a minute, so prepare for popping ears). From here, on a clear day you can't quite see forever, but the sweeping vista stretches to Niagara Falls, 100 miles south, and to Lake Simcoe, 120 miles north.

The tower attractions are often revamped. Among recent new draws are the IMAX theater, which shows a film of a cross-Canada journey, and two simulator airplane trips—one gentle and calm, the other a rocket ride through caves and over mountains. A series of interactive displays showcases the CN Tower along with such forerunners as the Eiffel Tower and the Empire State Building. The pod also contains broadcasting facilities, a nightclub, and **360 Revolving Restaurant** (☎ **416/362-5411;** see chapter 5).

Atop the tower sits a 335-foot antenna mast erected over 31 weeks with the aid of a giant Sikorsky helicopter. It took 55 lifts to complete the operation. Above the sky pod is the world's highest public observation gallery, the Space Deck, 1,465 feet above the ground (C$4/US$2.70 additional charge). The observation deck one floor below has a nervous-making glass floor (stand on it and look down—if you dare). But don't worry about the elements sweeping the tower into the lake—it's built of contoured reinforced concrete covered with thick glass-reinforced plastic and designed to keep ice accumulation to a minimum. The structure can withstand high winds, snow, ice, lightning, and earth tremors.

✪ **Art Gallery of Ontario.** 317 Dundas St. W. (between McCaul and Beverley sts.). ☎ **416/977-0414.** www.ago.on.ca. Pay what you can; suggested adult admission C$6 (US$4.10). Extra fee for special exhibits. Tues and Thurs–Fri 11am-6pm, Wed 11am–8:30pm, Sat–Sun 10am–5:30pm. Grange House Tues–Sun noon–4pm, Wed noon–9pm. Closed Jan 1, Dec 25. Subway: St. Patrick.

The exterior gives no hint of the light and openness inside this beautifully designed gallery. The space is dramatic, and the paintings imaginatively displayed. Throughout, audiovisual presentations and interactive computer presentations provide information on particular paintings or schools of painters.

The European collections are fine, but the Canadian galleries are the real treat. The paintings by the Group of Seven—which includes Tom Thomson, F. H. Varley, and Lawren Harris—are extraordinary. In addition, other galleries show the genesis of Canadian art from earlier to more modern artists. And don't miss the extensive collection of Inuit art.

The **Henry Moore Sculpture Centre,** with more than 800 pieces (original plasters, bronzes, maquettes, woodcuts, lithographs, etchings, and drawings), is the largest public collection of his works. The artist gave them to Toronto because he was so moved by the citizens' enthusiasm for his work—public donations bought his sculpture *The Archer* to decorate Nathan Phillips Square at City Hall after politicians refused to free up money for it. In one room, under a glass ceiling, 20 or so of his large works stand like silent prehistoric rock formations. Along the walls flanking a ramp are color photographs showing Moore's major sculptures in their natural locations, which reveal their magnificent dimensions.

The European collection ranges from the 14th century to the French impressionists and beyond. Works by Pissarro, Monet, Boudin, Sisley, and Renoir fill an octagonal room. De Kooning's *Two Women on a Wharf* and Karel Appel's *Black Landscape* are just two of the modern examples. There are several works of particular interest to admirers of the pre-Raphaelite painters, including one by Waterhouse. Among the sculptures, you'll find two beauties—Picasso's *Poupée* and Brancusi's *First Cry.*

Behind the gallery, connected by an arcade, stands the Grange (1817), Toronto's oldest surviving brick house, which was the gallery's first permanent space. Originally the home of the Boulton family, it was a gathering place for many of the city's social and political leaders and for such eminent guests as Matthew Arnold, Prince Kropotkin, and Winston Churchill. It has been meticulously restored and furnished to reflect the 1830s, and is a living museum of mid-19th-century Toronto life. Entrance is free with admission to the art gallery.

The gallery has an attractive restaurant, Agora, which is open for lunch, as well as a cafeteria and a gallery shop; there's also a full program of films, concerts, and lectures.

MIDTOWN

✪ **Royal Ontario Museum.** 100 Queen's Park Crescent. ☎ **416/586-8000.** www. rom.on.ca. Admission C$12 (US$8.20) adults; C$7 (US$4.80) seniors and students (with valid ID), C$6 (US$4.10) children 5–14; C$30 (US$20.40) families (2 adults and 2 children); free for children 4 and under. Pay what you can Fri 4:30–9:30pm. Mon–Thurs 10am–6pm, Fri 10am–9:30pm, Sat 10am–6pm, Sun 11am–6pm. Closed Jan 1, Dec 25. Subway: Museum.

The ROM (rhymes with "tom"), as it's affectionately called, is Canada's largest museum, with more than 6 million objects in its collections. Among the many highlights are the world-renowned **T. T. Tsui Galleries of Chinese Art,** which contain priceless Ming and Qing porcelains, embroidered silk robes, and objects made of jade and ivory. One of the collection's treasures is the procession of 100 earthenware figures, including ox-drawn carts, soldiers, musicians, officials, and attendants dating from the early 6th to the late 7th century. Another is the collection of 14 monumental Buddhist sculptures from the 12th to the 16th century. Visitors can also see outstanding examples of early weapons and tools, oracle bones, bronzes, ceramic vessels, human and animal figures, and jewelry.

The **Sigmund Samuel Canadiana galleries** display a premier collection of early Canadian decorative arts and historical paintings. More than 1,200 objects in elaborate period room settings reveal in a concrete way the French and English contributions to Canadian culture.

Other highlights include the **Ancient Egypt Gallery,** which features several mummies, the **Roman Gallery** (the most extensive collection in Canada), the excellent textile collection, and nine life-science galleries (devoted to evolution, mammals, reptiles, and botany). The **Gallery of Indigenous Peoples** features changing exhibitions that explore the past and present cultures of Canada's indigenous peoples. A recent addition is the **Gallery of Korean Art,** the largest exhibit of its kind in North America. It holds more than 200 works from the Bronze Age through modern times.

A favorite with kids is the **Bat Cave Gallery,** a miniature replica of the St. Clair bat cave in Jamaica. It's complete with more than 3,000 very lifelike bats roosting and flying through the air amid realistic spiders, crabs, a wildcat, and snakes. Kids also enjoy the spectacular **Dinosaur Gallery,** with 13 realistically displayed dinosaur skeletons, and the **Discovery Gallery,** a mini-museum where youngsters (and adults) can touch authentic artifacts from Egyptian scarabs to English military helmets.

The newest gallery is the **Joey and Toby Tanenbaum Gallery,** which is devoted to Byzantine art and has more than 300 objects—icons, frescoes, mosaics, gold jewelry, coins, and glassware.

The museum features several special exhibits every year (an extra admission charge usually applies). From February 17 through April 29, 2001, the ROM will host a rare exhibit entitled "Gold of the Nomads," which features Scythian artworks from the ancient Ukraine.

The ROM's light, airy dining lounge, **Jamie Kennedy at the Museum** (☎ **416/ 586-5578;** see chapter 5), has a small terrace for outdoor dining. It's under the expert supervision of Jamie Kennedy, one of Canada's top chefs. It's well worth stopping in for lunch.

George R. Gardiner Museum of Ceramic Art. 111 Queen's Park. ☎ **416/586-8080.** Suggested donation C$5 (US$3.40). Mon and Wed–Sat 10am–5pm, Tues 10am–8pm, Sun 11am–5pm. Closed Jan 1, Dec 25. Subway: Museum or St. George.

Across the street from the ROM, North America's only specialized ceramics museum houses a great collection of 15th- to 18th-century European pieces in four galleries. The pre-Columbian gallery contains fantastic Olmec and Maya figures, and objects from Ecuador, Colombia, and Peru. The majolica gallery displays spectacular 16th- and 17th-century salvers and other pieces from Florence, Faenza, and Venice, and a Delftware collection that includes fine 17th-century chargers.

Upstairs, the galleries are given over to 18th-century continental and English porcelain—Meissen, Sèvres, Worcester, Chelsea, Derby, and other great names. All are spectacular. Among the highlights are objects from the Swan Service—a 2,200-piece set that took 4 years (1737–41) to make—and an extraordinary collection of commedia dell'arte figures.

ON THE OUTSKIRTS

✪ **Ontario Science Centre.** 770 Don Mills Rd. (at Eglinton Ave. E.). ☎ **416/696-3127,** or 416/696-1000 for Omnimax tickets. www.osc.on.ca. Admission C$12 (US$8.20) adults, C$7 (US$4.80) seniors and youths 13–17, C$6 (US$4.10) children 5–12, free for children under 5. Omnimax admission C$10 (US$6.80) adults, C$6 (US$4.10) seniors and youths 13–17, C$5.50 (US$3.75) children 5–12. Combination discounts available. Daily 10am–5pm. Closed Dec 25. Parking C$7 (US$4.80). Yonge St. subway to Eglinton, then no. 34 Eglinton bus east to Don Mills Rd. By car from downtown, take Don Valley Pkwy. to Don Mills Rd. exit and follow signs.

Described as everything from the world's most technical fun fair to a hands-on museum for the 21st century, the Science Centre holds a series of wonders for adults and children—800 interactive exhibits in 10 cavernous exhibit halls. More than a million people visit every year, so it's best to arrive promptly at 10am—that way, you'll be able to get around with less hassle.

Wherever you look, there are things to touch, push, pull, or crank. Test your reflexes, balance, heart rate, and grip strength; surf the Internet; walk through a tropical rain forest; watch frozen-solid liquid nitrogen shatter into thousands of icy shards; study slides of butterfly wings, bedbugs, fish scales, or feathers under a microscope; tease your brain with a variety of optical illusions; land a spaceship on the moon; watch bees making honey; see how many lights you can light or how high you can elevate a balloon with your own pedal power. The fun goes on and on in 10 exhibit halls.

Throughout, small theaters show film and slide shows, and you can see regular 20-minute demonstrations of lasers, metal casting, and high-voltage electricity (watch your friend's hair stand on end). Another draw is the Omnimax Theatre, with a 24-meter domed screen that creates spectacular effects. The center has a restaurant and lounge (which serves alcohol), cafeteria, and science shop.

✪ **The Toronto Zoo.** Meadowvale Rd. (north of Hwy. 401 and Sheppard Ave.), Scarborough. ☎ **416/392-5900.** www.torontozoo.com. Admission C$13 (US$8.85) adults, C$10 (US$6.80) seniors, C$8 (US$5.45) children 4–14, free for children 3 and under. Summer daily 9am–7:30pm; spring and fall 9am–5pm; winter 9:30am–4:30pm. Last admission 1 hour before closing. Closed Dec 25. Parking C$6 (US$4.10). Subway: Bloor–Danforth line to Kennedy, then bus no. 86A north. By car: From downtown, take Don Valley Pkwy. to Hwy. 401 east, exit on Meadowvale Rd., and follow signs.

Covering 710 acres of parkland, this unique zoological garden contains some 5,000 animals, plus an extensive botanical collection. The plants and animals are housed in pavilions—including Africa, Indo-Malaya, Australasia, and the Americas—or in outdoor paddocks. It's a photographer's dream.

One popular zoo attraction is at the **African Savannah** project. It re-creates a market bazaar and safari through Kesho (Swahili for "tomorrow") National Park, past such

Midtown Toronto Attractions

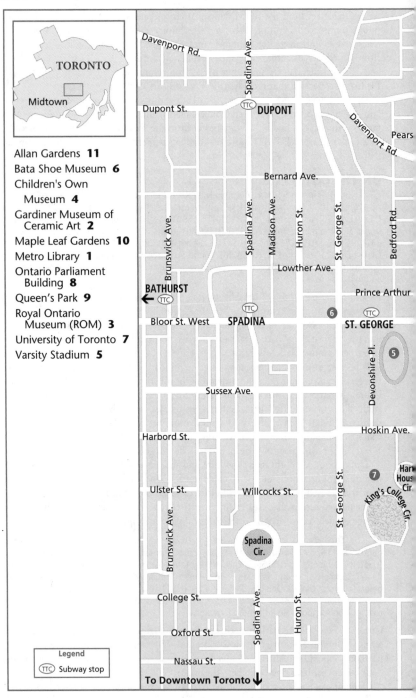

TORONTO

Midtown

Allan Gardens **11**
Bata Shoe Museum **6**
Children's Own
  Museum **4**
Gardiner Museum of
  Ceramic Art **2**
Maple Leaf Gardens **10**
Metro Library **1**
Ontario Parliament
  Building **8**
Queen's Park **9**
Royal Ontario
  Museum (ROM) **3**
University of Toronto **7**
Varsity Stadium **5**

Davenport Rd.

Spadina Ave.

Dupont St.   TTC **DUPONT**

Davenport Rd.

Pears

Bernard Ave.

Brunswick Ave.

Spadina Ave.

Madison Ave.

Huron St.

St. George St.

Bedford Rd.

Lowther Ave.

BATHURST
← TTC

Prince Arthur

Bloor St. West   TTC   **SPADINA**

6

TTC

ST. GEORGE

Devonshire Pl.

5

Sussex Ave.

Harbord St.

Hoskin Ave.

Ulster St.   Willcocks St.

St. George St.

7

Har
Hous
Cir

Brunswick Ave.

King's College Cir.

Spadina
Cir.

College St.

Spadina Ave.

Huron St.

Oxford St.

Nassau St.

Legend
TTC Subway stop

To Downtown Toronto ↓

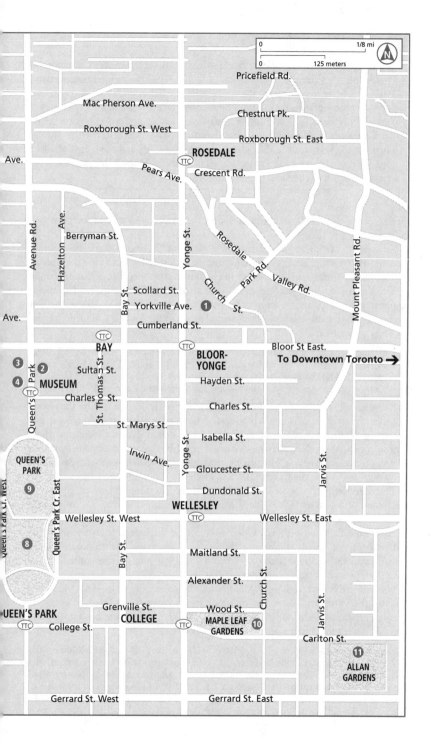

Pricefield Rd.

Mac Pherson Ave.

Roxborough St. West

Chestnut Pk.

Roxborough St. East

ROSEDALE

Ave.

Pears Ave.

(TTC)

Crescent Rd.

Avenue Rd.

Hazelton Ave.

Berryman St.

Yonge St.

Rosedale

Park Rd.

Valley Rd.

Mount Pleasant Rd.

Bay St.

Scollard St.

Yorkville Ave. ❶

Church

St.

Cumberland St.

Ave.

(TTC)

BAY

(TTC)

Bloor St East.

To Downtown Toronto →

❸

Queen's Park

❷

Sultan St.

BLOOR-YONGE

❹

(TTC)

MUSEUM

Charles St.

St. Thomas St.

Hayden St.

Charles St.

St. Marys St.

Isabella St.

Yonge St.

Irwin Ave.

Gloucester St.

Jarvis St.

QUEEN'S PARK

❾

Dundonald St.

WELLESLEY

Queen's Park Cr. East

Wellesley St. West

(TTC)

Wellesley St. East

❽

Maitland St.

Bay St.

Alexander St.

Church St.

Wood St.

Jarvis St.

UEEN'S PARK

Grenville St.

COLLEGE

MAPLE LEAF GARDENS ❿

(TTC)

College St.

(TTC)

Carlton St.

⓫

ALLAN GARDENS

Gerrard St. West

Gerrard St. East

0   1/8 mi

0   125 meters

N

119

Getting to the McMichael

The village of Kleinburg—home of the McMichael Canadian Art Collection—is 25 miles north of Toronto. Government of Ontario (GO) commuter transportation connects the city to the gallery. Buses run from the Bay and Dundas and the Yorkdale GO train stations. By car from downtown, take the Gardiner Expressway to Highway 427 north, follow it to Highway 7, and turn east. Turn left (north) at the first light onto Highway 27. Turn right (east) at Major Mackenzie Drive and left (north) at the first set of traffic lights to Islington Avenue and the village of Kleinburg. Or take Highway 401 to Highway 400 north. At Major Mackenzie Drive, go west to Islington Avenue and turn right.

special features as a bush camp, rhino midden, elephant highway, and several watering holes.

Six miles of walkways offer access to all areas of the zoo. During the warmer months, the Zoomobile takes visitors around the major walkways to view the animals in the outdoor paddocks. The zoo has restaurants, a gift shop, first aid, and a family center. Visitors can rent strollers and wagons, and borrow wheelchairs. The zoo is equipped with ramps and washrooms for those with disabilities. The African pavilion has an elevator for strollers and wheelchairs. There's ample parking and plenty of picnic areas with tables.

The McMichael Canadian Art Collection. 10365 Islington Ave., Kleinburg. ☎ **905/893-1121.** www.mcmichael.com. Admission C$9 (US$6.15) adults, C$7 (US$4.80) seniors and students, free for children 5 and under. May–Oct weekdays 10am–4pm, Sat 11am–4pm, Sun 11am–5pm; Nov–Apr Tues–Sat 10am–4pm, Sun 10am–5pm. Parking C$5 (US$3.40).

In Kleinburg, 25 miles north of the city, the McMichael is worth a visit for the setting as well as the art. The collection is in a log-and-stone gallery that sits amid quiet stands of trees on 100 acres of conservation land. Specially designed for the landscape paintings it houses, the gallery is a work of art. The lobby has a pitched roof that soars 27 feet on massive rafters of Douglas fir; throughout the gallery, panoramic windows look south over white pine, cedar, ash, and birch.

The collection includes the work of Canada's famous group of landscape painters, the Group of Seven, as well as David Milne, Emily Carr, and their contemporaries. These artists—inspired by the turn-of-the-century Canadian wilderness, particularly in Algonquin Park and northern Ontario—recorded the rugged landscape in highly individualistic styles. An impressive collection of Inuit and contemporary Native Canadian art and sculpture is also on display. In addition, four galleries contain changing exhibitions of works by contemporary artists.

Founded by Robert and Signe McMichael, the gallery began in 1965 when they donated their property, home, and collection to the Province of Ontario. The collection has expanded to include more than 6,000 works. The museum has a good book and gift store, and a fine restaurant that features Canadian cuisine.

Paramount Canada's Wonderland. 9580 Jane St., Vaughan. ☎ **905/832-7000** or 905/832-8131. www.canadaswonderland.com. Pay-One-Price Passport (includes unlimited rides and shows but not parking, special attractions, or Kingswood Music Theater) C$43 (US$29.20) adults and children age 4 and up, C$21.50 (US$14.65) seniors and children 3–6, free for children 2 and under. Admission only (no rides) C$25 (US$17). June 1–25 Mon–Fri 10am–8pm, Fri–Sat 10am–10pm; June 26–Labour Day daily 10am–10pm; late May and early Sept to early Oct Sat–Sun 10am–8pm. Closed mid-Oct to mid-May. Parking C$6.50 (US$4.45). Subway: Yorkdale or York Mills, then GO Express Bus to Wonderland. By car: Take

Will you have enough stories to tell your grandchildren

Yahoo! Travel

Yonge St. north to Hwy. 401 and go west to Hwy. 400. Go north on Hwy. 400 to Rutherford Rd. exit and follow signs. By car from the north, exit at Major Mackenzie.

Thirty minutes north of Toronto lies Canada's answer to Disney World. The 300-acre park features more than 140 attractions, including 50 rides, a 20-acre water park, a participatory play area (Kid's Kingdom), and live shows.

Adults and kids alike come for the thriller rides. Because the park relies on the local audience, it introduces new rides every year. The latest additions include Cliffhanger, a "super swing" that makes 360-degree turns and makers riders feel immune to gravity, and Scooby-Doo's Haunted Mansion, an updated take on the classic haunted house. One of the top attractions is the Fly, a roller coaster designed to make every seat feel as if it's in the front car—the faint of heart can't hide at the back of this one! Other stomach-churners include the Drop Zone, in which riders free-fall 230 feet in an open cockpit, and the Xtreme Skyflyer, a hang-gliding and skydiving hybrid that plunges riders 150 feet in a free fall. The most popular rides are the nine roller coasters, which range from a nostalgic, relatively tame wooden version to the looping, inverted Top Gun, the stand-up looping Sky Rider, and the suspended Vortex. The Splash Works water park offers a huge wave pool and 16 water rides, from speed slides and tube rides to special scaled-down slides and a kids' play area. To add to the thrills for Star Trek fans, Klingons, Vulcans, Romulans, and Bajorans (along with Hanna-Barbera characters) stroll around the park. Additional attractions include Speedcity Raceway, featuring two-seat go-karts, miniature golf, batting cages, restaurants, and shops. The Kingswood Theatre books top-name entertainers.

You'll probably need a full day to see everything. If you picnic on the grounds and forgo souvenirs, a family of four can "do" the park for about C$150 (US$102), depending on the age of the kids. Watch out, though, for the extra attractions not included in the admission pass, particularly the many carnival-type "games of skill," which the kids love, but your purse may not.

2 More Museums

The Bata Shoe Museum. 327 Bloor St. W. (at St. George St.). ☎ **416/979-7799.** www. batashoemuseum.ca. Admission C$6 (US$4.10) adults, C$4 (US$2.75) seniors and students, C$2 (US$1.35) children 5–14; C$12 (US$8.20) family admission (2 adults, 2 children). Free to all first Tues of the month. Tues–Wed and Fri–Sat 10am–5pm, Thurs 10am–8pm, Sun noon–5pm. Subway: St. George.

Imelda Marcos—or anyone else obsessed with shoes—will love this museum, which houses the Bata family's 10,000-item collection. The building, designed by Raymond Moriyama, is spectacular. The main gallery, "All About Shoes," traces the history of footwear. It begins with a plaster cast of some of the earliest known human footprints (discovered in Africa by anthropologist Mary Leakey), which date to 4 million B.C., then wanders through the fads and fashions of every era.

You'll come across such specialty shoes as spiked clogs used to crush chestnuts in 17th-century France, Elton John's 12-inch-plus platforms, and Pierre Trudeau's well-worn sandals. One display focuses on Canadian footwear fashioned by the Inuit, while another highlights 19th-century ladies' footwear. A smaller gallery houses changing exhibits; in 2001 there will be one about the Chinese tradition of foot binding.

Black Creek Pioneer Village. 1000 Murray Ross Pkwy. (at Steeles Ave. and Jane St.), Downsview. ☎ **416/736-1733.** Admission C$9 (US$6.15) adults, C$7 (US$4.80) seniors, C$5 (US$3.40) children 5–14, free for children 4 and under. May–June weekdays 9:30am–4:30pm, weekends and holidays 10am–5pm; July–Sept daily 10am–5pm; Oct–Dec weekdays 9:30am–4pm, weekends and holidays 10am–4:30pm. Closed Jan–Apr, Dec 25. Parking C$5 (US$3.40). Subway: Finch, then bus no. 60 to Jane St.

Life here moves at the gentle pace of rural Ontario as it was 100 years ago. You can watch the authentically dressed villagers going about their chores, spinning, sewing, rail splitting, sheep shearing, and threshing. Enjoy the villagers' cooking, wander through the cozily furnished homesteads, visit the working mill, shop at the general store, or rumble past the farm animals in a horse-drawn wagon. The beautifully landscaped village has more than 30 restored buildings to explore. Special events take place throughout the year, from a great Easter egg hunt to Christmas by lamplight.

The dining room (open May to Thanksgiving and December) serves lunch and afternoon tea.

Design Exchange. 234 Bay St. ☎ **416/363-6121.** Admission C$6 (US$4.10) adults, C$4.50 (US$3.10) students and seniors, free for children 13 and under. Mon–Fri 10am–6pm, Sat–Sun noon–5pm. Subway: King.

In the old Stock Exchange Building, this has become Toronto's design center. It showcases professionals' work, but the main purpose of the institution is to nurture designers of all types—graphic, industrial, interior, landscape, and urban. It also serves as a clearinghouse and resource center for the design community. Small free exhibitions on the first floor are open daily, while those in the upstairs Exhibition Hall are generally on view for 3 to 6 months and require admission. There's also a good bookstore and Cafe Deco, a relaxed eatery open Monday through Friday 7:30am to 5pm.

✪ **The Museum for Textiles.** 55 Centre Ave. ☎ **416/599-5321**. www.museumfortextiles. on.ca. Admission C$5 (US$3.40) adults, C$4 (US$2.70) students and seniors. Tues and Thurs–Fri 11am–5pm, Wed 11am–8pm, Sat–Sun noon–5pm. Subway: St. Patrick.

This fascinating museum is internationally recognized for its collection of more than 8,000 historic and ethnographic textiles and related artifacts. You'll find fine Oriental rugs, and cloth and tapestries from all over the world. One gallery presents the work of contemporary artists. The museum is small, so only a tiny portion of the collection is on display, but you'll always find a vibrant, interesting show. Through the first five months of 2001, you'll find a special exhibit entitled "Celebrating Virtue," which explores the role of textiles in the hierarchy of Late Imperial China.

Museum of Contemporary Canadian Art. Toronto Centre (formerly the Ford Centre for the Performing Arts), 5040 Yonge St., North York. ☎ **416/395-0067.** www.mocca.toronto. on.ca. Free admission. Tues–Sun noon–5pm. Subway: North York Centre.

This 6-year-old gallery is charged with collecting and exhibiting the best Canadian art created since 1985. Currently, the collection includes works by Stephen Andrews, Genevieve Cadieux, Ivan Eyre, Betty Goodwin, Micah Lexier, Arnaud Maggs, and Roland Poulin. Special shows are mounted approximately six times a year.

The Pier: Toronto's Waterfront Museum. 245 Queens Quay W. ☎ **416/338-PIER.** Admission C$5 (US$3.40) adults, C$4 (US$2.75) seniors, youths, and children; family admission C$15 (US$10.20). Open daily 10am–4pm from early Mar to June 30, daily 10am–6pm from July 1 through Labour Day, and daily 10am–4pm from day after Labour Day through Oct 31; closed Nov to early March. Subway: Union, then LRT to York Quay.

This is one of the city's newer museums, and it explores the history of nautical travel. Many exhibits are strictly hands-on, so it's popular with kids. You can explore a shipwreck, guide a vessel through a series of canals, or watch special exhibits about the ancient art of shipbuilding.

3 Exploring the Neighborhoods

Toronto is a patchwork of neighborhoods, and the best way to discover its soul and flavor is to meander along its streets. On foot you can best appreciate the sights, sounds, and smells—those elements that lend a particular area its unique character. These are some of the most interesting neighborhoods.

THE BEACHES   This is one of the neighborhoods that makes Toronto a unique city. Here, near the terminus of the Queen Street East streetcar line, you can stroll or cycle along the lakefront boardwalk. Because of its natural assets, it has become a popular residential neighborhood for young boomers and their families, and there are plenty of browsable stores along Queen Street. Just beyond Waverley Road, you can turn down through Kew Gardens to the boardwalk and walk all the way past the Olympic Pool to Ashbridge's Bay Park. To get to the Beaches, take any Queen Street East streetcar to Woodbine Avenue.

✪ CHINATOWN   Stretching along Dundas Street west from Bay Street to Spadina Avenue and north and south along Spadina Avenue, Chinatown is home to some of Toronto's 350,000 Chinese-Canadian residents. Packed with fascinating shops and restaurants, it even has bilingual street signs (in Chinese and English).

In **Dragon City,** a large shopping mall at Spadina and Dundas, you'll find all kinds of stores. Some sell Chinese preserves (like cuttlefish, lemon ginger, whole mango, ginseng, and antler), and others specialize in Asian books, tapes, records, fashion, and food. Downstairs, a fast-food court features Korean, Indonesian, Chinese, and Japanese cuisine.

As you stroll through Chinatown, stop at the **Kim Moon Bakery,** 438 Dundas St. W. (☎ **416/977-1933**) for Chinese pastries and a pork bun, or go to one of the tea stores. A walk through Chinatown at night is especially exciting—the sidewalks fill with people, and neon lights shimmer everywhere. You'll pass windows where ducks hang, gleaming noodle houses, record stores selling the Top 10 in Chinese, and trading companies filled with Asian produce. Another stop might be the **New Asia Supermarket,** 299 Spadina Ave. (☎ **416/591-9314**), around the corner from Dundas Street.

To get to Chinatown, take the subway to St. Patrick and walk west. For more details, see "Walking Tour 4: Chinatown & Kensington Market," in chapter 7.

THE DANFORTH—THE EAST END   This eclectic area along Danforth Street east of the Don River is hot, hot, hot. It swings until the early hours, when the restaurants and bars are still crowded and frenetic. During the day visitors can browse the traditional Greek stores—like **Akropol,** a Greek bakery at no. 458 (☎ **416/ 465-1232**) that displays stunning multi-tiered wedding cakes in the window. Along with the Greek food vendors and travel agents, you'll also find stores like **Blue Moon,** no. 375 (☎ **416/778-6991**), which sells beautiful crafts from the developing world (the store supports only producers that provide healthy working conditions and fair pay for their workers); **El Pipil,** no. 267 (☎ **416/465-9625**), which has colorful clothing, knapsacks, and jewelry; and some New Age and alternative stores. To get to the Danforth, ride the subway to Broadview and walk east.

LITTLE ITALY   Along College Street between Euclid and Shaw, Little Italy vies with Queen Street for the hottest spot in the city. The area hums at night, as people crowd the coffee bars, pool lounges, nightclubs, and trattorias. To reach the neighborhood, ride any College Street streetcar west to Euclid Avenue.

MIRVISH VILLAGE   One of the city's most illustrious characters is Honest Ed Mirvish, who started his career in the 1950s with a no-frills department store at the corner of Markham and Bloor streets (1 block west of Bathurst). Even from blocks away, neon signs race and advertisements touting bargains hit you from every direction. Among his other accomplishments, Mirvish saved the Royal Alexandra Theatre on King Street from demolition, established a row of adjacent restaurants for theater patrons, and developed this block-long area with art galleries, restaurants, and bookstores. He was responsible for saving and renovating London's Old Vic, too.

Stop by and browse, and don't forget to step into **Honest Ed's** (see "The Best Bargains" box in chapter 8) on the corner. To start your visit, take the subway to Bathurst.

QUEEN STREET WEST   This street has over the years been known as the heart of Toronto's avant-garde scene. It's home to several clubs—**BamBoo** and the **Rivoli,** in particular—where major Canadian artists and singers have launched their careers. The street is lined with an eclectic mix of stores and businesses. Although recent trends have brought mainstream stores to the street, it retains a certain edginess.

Here in the heart of the gourmet ghetto, there's a broad selection of bistros and restaurants, a number of fine antiquarian bookstores, and a lot of funky fashion stores. You'll also see outright junk shops, nostalgic record emporiums, kitchen supply stores, and discount fabric houses. East of Bathurst, the street is being slowly gentrified, but beyond Bathurst it retains its rough-and-ready energy.

To start exploring, take the subway to Osgoode and walk west along Queen Street West.

YORKVILLE   This area stretches north of Bloor Street, between Avenue Road and Bay Street. Since its founding in 1853 as a village outside the city proper, Yorkville has experienced many transformations. In the 1960s, it became Toronto's Haight-Ashbury, the countercultural mecca for young suburban runaways otherwise known as hippies. In the 1980s, it became the shopping ground of the chic, who dropped their money liberally at such boutiques as Hermès, Courrèges, Gianni Versace, Cartier, and Turnbull & Asser, and at the neighborhood's many fine art galleries. In the early 1990s, the recession left its mark—a fact that became glaringly obvious when Creeds, a Toronto institution, shut its doors. The restored town houses began to look a little forlorn, but today the energy is back. Bloor Street and Hazelton Lanes continue to attract high-style stores, including a branch of Tiffany's.

Stroll around and browse—or sit out and have an iced coffee in the sun at one of the cafes on Yorkville or Cumberland Avenue and watch the parade go by. Some good vantage points can be had at Hemingway's or at one of the many cafes along Yorkville Avenue. Most of the cafes have happy hours from 4 to 7 or 8pm.

Make sure you wander through the labyrinths of Hazelton Lanes between Avenue Road and Hazelton Avenue. You'll find a maze of shops and offices clustered around an outdoor court in the center of a building that is topped with apartments—one of the most sought-after addresses in the city. In summer, the courtyard is used for outdoor dining; in winter, for skating.

While you're in the neighborhood (especially if you're an architecture buff), take a look at the redbrick building on Bloor Street at the end of Yorkville Avenue that houses the **Toronto Reference Library.** Step inside and you'll find one of Toronto's most serene spots. To reach Yorkville, take the subway to Bay.

4 Architectural Highlights

○ **Casa Loma.** 1 Austin Terrace. ☎ **416/923-1171.** www.casaloma.org. Admission C$10 (US$6.80) adults, C$56.50 (US$38.45) seniors and youths 14–17, C$6 (US$4.10) children 4–13, free for children 3 and under. Daily 9:30am–5pm (last entry at 4pm). Closed Jan 1, Dec 25. Subway: Dupont, then walk 2 blocks north.

Every city has its folly, and Toronto has an unusually charming one. It's complete with Elizabethan-style chimneys, Rhineland turrets, secret passageways, an 800-foot underground tunnel, and a mellifluous name: Casa Loma.

Sir Henry Pellatt, who built it between 1911 and 1914, had a lifelong fascination with castles. He studied medieval palaces and gathered materials and furnishings from around the world, bringing marble, glass, and paneling from Europe, teak from Asia, and oak and walnut from North America. He imported Scottish stonemasons to build the massive walls that surround the 6-acre site.

It's a fascinating place to explore. Wander through the majestic Great Hall, with its 60-foot-high hammer-beam ceiling; the Oak Room, where three artisans took 3 years to fashion the paneling; and the Conservatory, with its elegant bronze doors, stained-glass dome, and pink-and-green marble. The castle has battlements and a tower; Peacock Alley, designed after Windsor Castle; Sir Henry's suite, containing a shower with an 18-inch-diameter shower head; and a 1,700-bottle wine cellar. The 800-foot tunnel runs to the stables, where horses were quartered amid the luxury of Spanish tile and mahogany. The tour is self-guided; you'll be given an audiocassette, available in eight languages, upon arrival. From May to October, the gardens are open, too. There are special events every March, July, and December.

○ **City Hall.** 100 Queen St. W. ☎ **416/338-0338.** www.city.toronto.on.ca. Free admission. Self-guided tours Mon–Fri 8:30am–4:30pm. Subway: Queen, then walk west to Bay.

An architectural spectacle, City Hall houses the mayor's office and the city's administrative offices. Daringly designed in the late 1950s by Finnish architect Viljo Revell, it consists of a low podium topped by the flying-saucer-shaped Council Chamber, enfolded between two curved towers. Its interior is as dramatic as its exterior. A cafeteria and dining room are in the basement.

In front stretches **Nathan Phillips Square** (named after the mayor who initiated the project). In summer you can sit and contemplate the flower gardens, fountains, and reflecting pool (which doubles as a skating rink in winter), as well as listen to concerts. Here you'll find Henry Moore's *The Archer* (formally, *Three-Way Piece No. 2*), purchased through a public subscription fund, and the Peace Garden, which commemorates Toronto's sesquicentennial in 1984. In contrast, to the east stands the **Old City Hall,** a green-copper-roofed Victorian Romanesque-style building.

Eaton Centre. Dundas and Yonge sts. ☎ **416/598-8700.** Mon–Fri 10am–9pm, Sat 9:30am–6pm, Sun noon–5pm. Subway: Dundas or Queen.

Buttressed at both ends by 30-story skyscrapers, this high-tech center, which cost over C$250 million (US$170 million) to build, stretches from Dundas Street south along Yonge Street to Queen Street, an area that encompasses 6 million square feet. **Eaton's** department store takes up 1 million square feet, and the rest is filled with more than 320 stores and restaurants and two garages. Some 20 million people shop here annually.

Inside, the structure opens into the impressive **Galleria,** an 866-foot-long glass-domed arcade dotted with benches, orchids, palm trees, and fountains; it's further adorned by Michael Snow's 60 soaring Canada geese, titled *Step Flight.* The birds are made from black-and-white photos mounted on cast fiberglass frames. Three tiers rise above, reached by escalator and glass elevators, which afford glorious views over this Crystal Palace and Milan–style masterpiece designed by Eb Zeidler (who also designed Ontario Place). Rain or shine, you can enjoy the sights, sounds, and aromas in comfort—don't be surprised by the twittering of the sparrows, some of whom have decided that this environment is as pleasant as the outdoors.

One more amazing fact about this construction: It was built around two of Toronto's oldest landmarks—**Trinity Church** (1847) and **Scadding House** (☎ **416/598-4521**), home of Trinity's rector, Dr. Scadding—because the public demanded that the developers allow the sun to continue to shine on the church's twin towers. It does!

✪ **Ontario Legislature.** 111 Wellesley St. W. (at University Ave.). ☎ **416/325-7500.** www.ontla.on.ca. Free admission. Mon–Fri and weekends Victoria Day–Labour Day. Weekend tours every ½ hour 9–11:30am and 1–4pm; call ahead at other times. Subway: Queen's Park.

At the northern end of University Avenue, with University of Toronto buildings to the east and west, lies Queen's Park. Embedded in its center is the rose-tinted sandstone-and-granite Ontario Legislature, with stately domes, arches, and porte cocheres. At any time of year other than summer, drop in around 2pm—when the legislature is in session—for some pithy comments during the question period, or take one of the regular tours. It's best to call ahead to check times.

Royal Bank Plaza. Front and Bay sts. Free admission. Subway: Union.

Shimmering in the sun, Royal Bank Plaza looks like a pillar of gold, and with good reason. During its construction, 2,500 ounces of gold were used as a coloring agent in the building's 14,000 windows. More important, it's a masterpiece of architectural design. Two triangular towers of bronze mirror glass flank a 130-foot-high glass-walled banking hall. The external walls of the towers are built in a serrated configuration so that they reflect a phenomenal mosaic of color from the skies and surrounding buildings.

In the banking hall, hundreds of aluminum cylinders hang from the ceiling, the work of Venezuelan sculptor Jésus Raphael Soto. Two levels below, there's a waterfall and pine-tree setting that's naturally illuminated from the hall above.

Toronto Reference Library. 789 Yonge St. ☎ **416/393-7000.** www.mtrl.toronto.on.ca. Free admission. Year-round Mon–Thurs 10am–8pm, Fri–Sat 10am–5pm; Thanksgiving–Apr Sun 1:30–5pm. Subway: Bloor.

Step inside—a pool and a waterfall gently screen out the street noise—and the space opens dramatically to the sky. Light and air flood every corner. This structure is another masterwork by Toronto architect Raymond Moriyama.

5 Historic Buildings

Campbell House. 160 Queen St. W. (at University Ave.). ☎ **416/597-0227.** Admission C$3.50 (US$2.40) adults; C$2.50 (US$1.70) seniors, students, and children; family C$8 (US$5.50). Mon–Fri 9:30am–4:30pm, Sat–Sun noon–4:30pm. Subway: Osgoode.

Just across from Osgoode Hall sits the 1822 mansion of Sir William Campbell, a Loyalist and sixth chief justice of Upper Canada. In 1829, he retired to this mansion, where he lived until his death in 1834. It was moved several blocks from its original location in 1972. The beautifully restored building features a collection of period furniture. Costumed interpreters conduct guided tours that provide insight into Toronto's early history.

Colborne Lodge. High Park. ☎ **416/392-6916.** Admission C$3.50 (US$2.40) adults, C$2.75 (US$1.90) seniors and youths 13–18, C$2.50 (US$1.70) children under 13. Tues–Sun noon–5pm. Call ahead; hours vary. Subway: High Park.

This charming, English-style Regency cottage with a three-sided verandah was built in 1836–37 to take advantage of the view of Lake Ontario and the Humber River. At the time, it was considered way out in the country, and a bother to travel to during the harsh winters. In 1873, the owner, a Toronto surveyor and architect named John Howard, donated the house and surrounding land to the city in return for an annual salary. That created High Park (see "Parks & Gardens," below), a great recreational area.

Fort York. Garrison Rd., off Fleet St., between Bathurst St. and Strachan Ave. ☎ **416/392-6907.** Admission C$5 (US$3.40) adults, C$3.25 (US$2.20) seniors and youths 13–18, C$3 (US$2.05) children 6–12, children 5 and under free. June–Oct Mon–Wed and Fri 10am–5pm, Thurs 10am–7pm, Sat–Sun noon–5pm; Nov–May Tues–Fri 10am–5pm, Sat–Sun noon–5pm. Subway: Bathurst, then streetcar no. 511 south.

Established by Lieutenant Governor Simcoe in 1793 to defend "little muddy York," as Toronto was then known, Fort York was sacked by Americans in 1813. You can tour the soldiers' and officers' quarters, clamber over the ramparts, and view demonstrations. The fort really comes to life in summer, with daily demonstrations of drill, music, and cooking. The fort is a few blocks west of the CN Tower and 2 blocks east of Exhibition Place.

Mackenzie House. 82 Bond St. ☎ **416/392-6915.** Admission C$3.50 (US$2.40) adults, C$2.75 (US$1.90) seniors and youths 13–18, C$2.50 (US$1.70) children 5–12. May–Sept 1 Tues–Sun noon–5pm, Sept 2–Dec Tues–Sun noon–4pm; Jan–Apr Sat–Sun noon–5pm. Subway: Dundas.

This typical mid-19th-century brick row house, 2 blocks east of Yonge and south of Dundas, gives some idea of what Toronto must have looked like then, when the streets were lined with similar buildings. Concerned friends and fund-raisers bought it for William Lyon Mackenzie, leader of the 1837 rebellion, and he lived here from 1859 to 1861. It's furnished in 1850s style, and in the back there's a print shop designed after Mackenzie's own.

Osgoode Hall. 130 Queen St. W. ☎ **416/947-3300.** Free admission. Mon–Fri 9am–6pm. Free tours July–Aug Mon–Fri 1:15pm. Subway: Osgoode.

West of City Hall, an impressive, elegant wrought-iron fence extends in front of an equally gracious public building, Osgoode Hall. Folklore has it that the fence was built to keep cows from trampling the flowerbeds. Tours of the interior reveal the splendor of the grand staircase, the rotunda, the Great Library, and the fine portrait and sculpture collection. Construction began in 1829, and troops were billeted here after the Rebellion of 1837. It's currently the home of the Law Society of Upper Canada, the headquarters of Ontario's legal profession. The Court of Appeal for Ontario has several magnificent courtrooms here—including one built with materials from London's Old Bailey. The courts are open to the public.

Spadina. 285 Spadina Rd. ☎ **416/392-6910.** Guided tour C$5 (US$3.40) adults, C$3.25 (US$2.20) seniors and youths, C$3 (US$2.05) children under 13. Tues–Fri noon–4pm, Sat–Sun noon–5pm. Subway: Dupont.

If you want to know how the leaders of the Family Compact (who ruled Toronto in the early 19th century) lived, visit the historic home of financier James Austin. The exterior is not imposing, but the house contains a remarkable collection of art, furniture, and decorative objects. The Austin family occupied the house from 1866 to

1980, which accounts for the richness of the collections. Tours (the only way to see the house) start on the quarter hour. In summer, you can also tour the gardens; during the Christmas season the house is decorated authentically. It's next door to Casa Loma.

6 For Sports Fans

✪ **Hockey Hall of Fame.** In BCE Place, 30 Yonge St. (at Front St.). ☎ **416/360-7765.** www.hhof.com. Admission C$12 (US$8.20) adults, C$7 (US$4.80) seniors and children/youths 4–18, free for children 3 and under; family rate (2 adults and 2 children/youths) C$32 (US$21.80). Late June through Labour Day Mon–Sat 9:30am–6pm, Sun 10am–6pm; Sept through mid-June Mon–Fri 10am–5pm, Sat 9:30am–6pm, Sun 10:30am–5pm. Closed Jan 1, Dec 25. Subway: Union.

Ice hockey fans will be thrilled by the artifacts collected here. They include the original Stanley Cup (donated in 1893 by Lord Stanley of Preston), a replica of the Montreal Canadiens' locker room, Terry Sawchuck's goalie gear, Newsy Lalonde's skates, and the stick Max Bentley used. You'll also see photographs of the personalities and great moments in hockey history. Most fun are the shooting and goalkeeping interactive displays, where you can take a whack at targets with a puck or don goalie gear and face down flying video pucks or sponge pucks.

SkyDome. 1 Blue Jays Way. ☎ **416/341-2770.** www.skydome.com. Tours C$10.50 (US$7.15) adults, C$8 (US$5.45) students 12–17 and seniors, C$7 (US$4.80) children 4–11, free for children 4 and under. Call ahead; tours usually begin on the hour daily 11am–3pm but are not given during events. Subway: Union.

In 1989, the opening of 53,000-seat SkyDome, home to the Toronto Blue Jays baseball team and the Toronto Argonauts football team, was a gala event. In 1992, SkyDome became the first Canadian stadium to play host to the World Series, and the Blue Jays won the championship for the first of two consecutive years. The stadium represents an engineering feat, featuring the world's first fully retractable roof, which spans more than 8 acres, and a gigantic video scoreboard. It is so large that a 31-story building would fit inside the complex when the roof is closed. The 11-story hotel has 70 rooms that face directly onto the field.

Air Canada Centre. 40 Bay St. (at Lakeshore Blvd.). ☎ **416/815-5500.** Tours C$10 (US$6.80) adults, C$8 (US$5.45) students and seniors, C$6.50 (US$4.45) children 13 and under. Tours on the hour Mon–Sat 10–3, Sun 11–3. Call ahead; no tours during events. Subway: Union, then LRT to Queen's Quay.

Toronto's newest sports and entertainment complex is home to the Maple Leafs (hockey) and the Raptors (basketball). While longtime fans were crushed when the Leafs moved here in 1999 from Maple Leaf Gardens—the arena that had housed the team since 1931—the Air Canada Centre has quickly become a fan favorite. Seating 18,700 for hockey games, 19,500 for basketball, and 20,000 for concerts, the center was designed with comfort in mind. Seating is on a steeper-than-usual grade so that even the "nosebleed" sections have decent sightlines, and the seats are wider . . . and upholstered.

Canada Sports Hall of Fame. Exhibition Place. ☎ **416/260-6789.** Free admission. Mon–Fri 10am–4:30pm. Subway: Bathurst, then streetcar no. 511 south to end of line.

In the center of Exhibition Place, this three-floor space is devoted to the country's greatest athletes in all major sports. It offers displays complemented by touch-screen computers that tell you everything you could want to know about particular sports personalities and Canada's athletic heritage.

7 Markets

✪ **Kensington Market.** Bounded by Dundas St., Spadina Ave., Baldwin St., and Augusta Ave. No central phone. Most stores open Mon–Sat. Subway: St. Patrick, then Dundas St. streetcar west to Kensington.

This colorful, lively area should not be missed. If you can struggle out of bed to get here around 5am, you'll see squawking chickens being carried from trucks to the stalls. You'll hear Caribbean, Portuguese, Italian, and other accents as merchants spread out their wares—squid and crabs in pails, chickens, pigeons, bread, cheese, apples, pears, peppers, ginger, and mangoes from the West Indies, salted fish from Portuguese dories, lace, fabrics, and other colorful remnants. There's no market on Sunday.

St. Lawrence Market. 92 Front St. E. ☎ **416/392-7219.** Tues–Thurs 9am–7pm, Fri 8am–8pm, Sat 5am–5pm. Subway: Union.

This handsome food market is in a vast building constructed around the façade of the second city hall, built in 1850. Vendors sell fresh meat, fish, fruit, vegetables, and dairy products as well as other foodstuffs. The best time to visit is early Saturday morning, shortly after the farmers arrive.

8 Parks & Gardens

Allan Gardens. Between Jarvis, Sherbourne, Dundas, and Gerrard sts. ☎ **416/392-7259.** Free admission. Daily dawn–dusk. Subway: Dundas.

George William Allan gave the city these gardens. He was born in 1822 to wealthy merchant and banker William Allan, who gave him a vast estate (it stretched from Carlton St. to Bloor St. between Jarvis and Sherbourne). George married into the ruling Family Compact when he wed John Beverley Robinson's daughter. A lawyer by training, he became a city councilor, mayor, senator, and philanthropist. The lovely old concert pavilion was demolished, but the glass-domed Palm House still stands in all its radiant Victorian glory. Today the park is rather seedy and certainly should be avoided at night.

Edwards Gardens. Lawrence Ave. E. and Leslie St. ☎ **416/397-1340.** Free admission. Daily dawn–dusk. Subway: Eglinton, then no. 51 (Leslie) or no. 54 (Lawrence) bus.

This quiet, formal 35-acre garden is part of a series of parks that stretch over 600 acres along the Don Valley. Gracious bridges arch over a creek, rock gardens abound, and rose and other seasonal flowerbeds add color and scent. The garden is famous for its rhododendrons. The Civic Garden Centre operates a gift shop and offers free walking tours on Tuesday and Thursday at 11am and 2pm. The Centre also boasts a fine horticultural library.

High Park. South of Bloor St. to the Gardiner Expwy., West End. Free admission. Daily dawn–dusk. Subway: High Park.

This 400-acre park was surveyor and architect John G. Howard's gift to the city. He lived in Colborne Lodge, which still stands in the park. The grounds contain a large lake called Grenadier Pond (great for ice-skating), a small zoo, a swimming pool, tennis courts, sports fields, bowling greens, and vast expanses of green for baseball, jogging, picnicking, bicycling, and more.

9 Cemeteries

✪ **Mount Pleasant Cemetery.** 375 Mount Pleasant Rd., north of St. Clair Ave. ☎ **416/ 485-9129.** Free admission. Daily 8am–dusk. Subway: St. Clair.

Home to one of the finest tree collections in North America, this cemetery is also the final resting place of many fascinating people. Of particular note are Glenn Gould, the celebrated classical pianist; Dr. Frederick Banting and Dr. Charles Best, the University of Toronto researchers who discovered insulin in 1922; golfer George Knudson; the Massey and Eaton families, whose mausoleums are impressive architectural monuments; Prime Minister William Lyon Mackenzie King; Canada's greatest war hero, Lieutenant Colonel William Barker; and Jim Cormier, one of Canada's top writers and editors.

Necropolis. 200 Winchester St. (at Sumach St.). ☎ **416/923-7911.** Free admission. Daily 8am–dusk. Subway: Parliament.

This is one of the city's oldest cemeteries, dating to 1850. Many of the remains were originally buried in Potters Field, where Yorkville stands today.

Before strolling through the cemetery, pick up a History Tour at the office. You'll find the graves of William Lyon Mackenzie, leader of the 1837 rebellion, as well as those of his followers, Samuel Lount and Peter Matthews, who were hanged for their part in the rebellion. Anderson Abbot, the first Canadian-born black surgeon; Joseph Tyrrell, who discovered dinosaurs in Alberta; world-champion oarsman Ned Hanlan; and many more notable Torontonians can be found in the 15-acre cemetery. The porte cochere and Gothic Revival chapel were designed by Henry Langley, who is also buried here.

10 Especially for Kids

The city puts on a fabulous array of special events for children at **Harbourfront.** In March, the **Children's Film Festival** screens 40 entries from 15 countries. In April, **Spring Fever** celebrates the season with egg decorating, puppet shows, and more; on Saturday mornings in April, **cushion concerts** are given for the 5 to 12 set. In May, the **Milk International Children's Festival** brings 100 international performers to the city for a week of great entertainment. For additional information, call ☎ **416/ 973-3000.**

For the last 30 years, the **Young Peoples Theatre,** 165 Front St. E., at Sherbourne Street (☎ 416/862-2222 for box office or 416/363-5131 for administration), has been entertaining youngsters. Its season runs from August to May.

Look in the sections above for the following Toronto-area attractions that have major appeal for kids of all ages. The first five on the list are tied for best venue, at least from a kid's point of view. The others address more specialized interests.

- **Ontario Science Centre** *(see p. 117)*   Kids race to be the first at this paradise of hands-on games, experiments, and push-button demonstrations—800 of them.
- **Paramount Canada's Wonderland** *(see p. 120)*   The kids can't wait to get on the theme park's roller coasters and daredevil rides. And don't forget to budget for video games.
- **Harbourfront** *(see p. 111)*   Kaleidoscope is an ongoing program of creative crafts, active games, and special events on weekends and holidays. There's also a pond, winter ice-skating, and a crafts studio.

- **Ontario Place** *(see p. 110)*   The Children's Village, water slides, a huge Cinesphere, a futuristic pod, and other entertainment are the big hits at this recreational and cultural park. In the Children's Village, kids under 13 can scramble over rope bridges, bounce on an enormous trampoline, or drench one another in the water-play section.
- **Toronto Zoo** *(see p. 117)*   One of the best in the world, modeled after San Diego's—the animals in this 710-acre park really do live in a natural environment.
- **Toronto Islands—Centreville** *(see p. 114)*   Riding a ferry to this turn-of-the-century amusement park is part of the fun.
- **CN Tower** *(see p. 114)*   Especially for the interactive simulator games and the terror of the glass floor.
- **Royal Ontario Museum** *(see p. 116)*   The top hits are the dinosaurs and the spooky bat cave.
- **Fort York** *(see p. 127)*   For its reenactments of battle drills, musket and cannon firing, and musical marches with fife and drum.
- **Hockey Hall of Fame** *(see p. 128)*   Who wouldn't want the chance to tend goal against Mark Messier and Wayne Gretzky (with a sponge puck), and to practice with the fun and challenging video pucks?
- **Black Creek Pioneer Village** *(see p. 121)*   For craft and other demonstrations.
- **Casa Loma** *(see p. 125)*   The stables, secret passageway, and fantasy rooms really capture children's imaginations.
- **The Pier: Toronto's Waterfront Museum** *(see p. 122)*   For any child fascinated by boats—and shipwrecks.
- **Art Gallery of Ontario** *(see p. 115)*   For its hands-on kids' exhibit.

Children's Own Museum. In the McLaughlin Planetarium Building, 90 Queen's Park. ☎ **416/542-1492.** Admission C$4.50 (US$3.10). Tues 10am–8pm, Wed–Sat 10am–5pm, Sun noon–5pm. Subway: Museum.

The ROM's next-door neighbor is another favorite with tykes. At the Children's Own Museum, everything is designed with kids aged 1 to 8 in mind. This interactive learn-while-you-play center includes a sensory tunnel, a construction site, a garden, an animal clinic, and a theater. Well-trained staff members are on hand to answer the inevitable endless questions.

Chudleigh's. 9528 Hwy. 25 (3km/1.8 miles north of Hwy. 401), Milton. ☎ **905/826-1252.** Orchard admission (applied to purchases) C$3 (US$2.05). July–Oct daily 9am–7pm; Nov–June Fri–Sun 10am–5pm.

A day here introduces kids to life on a farm. They'll enjoy hayrides, pony rides, and, in season, apple picking. There's a playground, straw maze, and more. The store sells pies, cider, and other produce.

Cullen Gardens & Miniature Village. Taunton Rd., Whitby. ☎ **905/686-1600.** www.cullengardens.com. Admission C$12 (US$8.15) adults, C$9 (US$6.10) seniors, C$5 (US$3.40) children 3–12. Summer daily 9am–8pm, spring and fall 10am–6pm. Closed early Jan to mid-Apr.

The half-scale miniature village has great appeal. The 27 acres of gardens, the playground (with two splash ponds), the shopping, and the live entertainment only add to the fun. There are special events year-round, including Halloween pumpkin carving in October and fireworks on New Year's Eve.

Playdium. 126 John St. ☎ **416/260-1400.** www.playdium.com. C$1–$6 (US68¢–$4.10) per game or attraction. Sun–Thurs 10am–midnight, Fri 10am–4am, Sat 10am–2am. Subway: St. Andrew.

The Playdium is an up-to-the-minute interactive pleasure palace, filled with more than 260 games and simulators like Speedzone (an IndyCar race). It also has rock-climbing walls, a go-kart track, an IMAX theater, batting cages, and mini golf. When you need a break, there's a lounge and restaurant. Beyond the sliding steel door activated by an infrared sensor, you'll discover a surreal scene of huge TV screens, circuit boards, and neon and strobe-lit "alien squid mushrooms."

✪ **Riverdale Farm.** 201 Winchester St., off Parliament, 1 block north of Carlton. ☎ **416/ 392-6794.** Free admission. Daily 9am–5pm.

Idyllically situated on the edge of the Don Valley Ravine, this working farm right in the city is a favorite with small tots. They enjoy watching the cows and pigs, and petting the other animals. There are farming demonstrations daily at 10:30am and 1:30pm.

Wild Water Kingdom. Finch Ave., 1 mile west of Hwy. 427, Brampton. ☎ **416/369-0774** or 905/794-0565. Admission C$20 (US$13.60) adults, C$16 (US$10.90) children 4–9, children 3 and under free. May 31 to mid-June weekends 10am–6pm; July–Labour Day daily 10am–8pm. Take Hwy. 401 to Hwy. 427 north; exit at Finch Ave. and drive 1 mile west. Or from downtown, take Queen Elizabeth Way (QEW) to Hwy. 427 north; exit at Finch Ave. and drive 1 mile west.

A huge water theme park, Wild Water Kingdom is complete with a 20,000-square-foot wave pool, tube slides, speed slides, giant hot tubs, and the super-thrilling Cyclone water ride. There are bumper boats, pedal boats, canoes, batting cages, and mini golf, too. Note that the park may not be open in inclement weather.

11 Guided Tours

INDUSTRIAL TOURS

✪ **Canadian Broadcasting Centre.** 250 Front St. W. ☎ **416/205-3700.** www.cbc.ca. Tour C$5 (US$3.40) adults, C$3 (US$2.05) students; by appointment only. Subway: Union.

The headquarters for the CBC's English Networks, this building was designed by Bregman and Hamann and Scott, with John Burgee and Philip Johnson as consultants. It's one of the most modern broadcasting facilities in North America. From the minute visitors enter, they know they're in a studio facility—there's even a lobby viewing studio. When you come for your tour, check out the **CBC Museum,** a series of interactive exhibits and film clips showcasing the CBC's broadcast history (open weekdays 9am to 5pm).

ChumCity. 299 Queen St. W. (at John St.). ☎ **416/591-5757.** Tours free; by appointment only. Subway: Osgoode.

This innovative television station contrasts dramatically with the CBC's formality. It's a television factory where cameras are not hard-wired to studios or control rooms, but can be plugged into any one of 35 hydrants that allow them to go on-air in minutes. Instead of formal shows confined to studios, programs can flow minute by minute from any working area in the building, including the hallways and rooftop. From this location, the cutting-edge company operates three channels. **Citytv** is a popular local TV station. **MuchMusic,** which is similar to MTV, and **Bravo,** a 24-hour arts channel, are available on many American cable systems. The staff is young and cutting-edge, with an impressive, fast-response news team. ChumCity has 100 permanently fixed remote-control cameras, 25 mobile news cruisers, plus remote terminals at key locations such as City Hall, Metro Hall, the TTC, and police headquarters. The results can be seen on CityPulse at noon, 6, and 11pm.

This futuristic, interactive TV station even invites casual visitors to air their opinions and grievances. Simply enter **Speakers Corner,** a video booth at the corner of John and Queen streets, and bare your soul before the camera. If you're compelling or bizarre enough, you'll get your 15 seconds of fame on a weekly half-hour show, or in short blurbs on Citytv and MuchMusic.

Stock Market Place at the Toronto Stock Exchange. Exchange Tower, 130 King St. W. (at York St.). ☎ **416/947-4670.** Admission C$5 (US$3.40) adults, $3 (US$2.05) students and seniors. Mon–Fri 10am–5pm. Subway: St. Andrew.

With C$1 billion (US$680 million) of stock being traded every business day, this is Canada's premier marketplace, and the second-largest stock exchange in North America. **Traders' Walk** traces the history of commerce from the days of bartering. There's even a **Learning Playground,** where kids get the chance to be pint-sized CEOs.

ORGANIZED TOURS

For summer weekends, it's always a good idea to make tour reservations in advance. At slower times, you can usually call the same day or simply show up.

BUS TOURS   If you enjoy hop-on, hop-off bus tours, try the one offered by **Olde Town Toronto Tours Ltd.,** 900 Dixon Rd., Etobicoke, ON M9W 1J7 (☎ **416/ 368-6877;** www.oldetown.toronto.on.ca). Tickets—C$29 (US$19.75) adults, C$27 (US$18.40) seniors and students 12 to 17, C$15 (US$10.20) children 4 to 11—are valid for 24 hours, allowing you to disembark from the double-decker bus whenever and wherever you wish. Tours operate daily year-round, 9am to 9pm in summer, 9am to 4pm in winter.

Grayline Tours, 184 Front St. E. (☎ **416/594-3310**), operates similar tours. They pass such major sights as the Eaton Centre, City Hall, the University of Toronto, Yorkville, Casa Loma, Chinatown, Harbourfront, and the CN Tower. These tours, which operate between early May and the end of October, cost C$29 (US$19.75) for adults, C$25 (US$17) seniors, C$19 (US$12.95) children 2 to 12.

HARBOR & ISLAND TOURS   Toronto Harbour Tours (☎ **416/869-1372**) operates 1-hour narrated tours of the port and the islands from May to the end of October. They leave every hour on the hour between 10am and 5pm (until 8pm in July and August) and cost C$18 (US$12.25) for adults, C$14 (US$9.55) seniors, C$11 (US$7.50) children 13 and under. Tours leave from 145 Queen's Quay W., at the foot of York Street.

For a real thrill, board the three-masted, 96-foot schooner *The Challenge* for a 1- or 2-hour cruise. They begin at 12:15, 1:15, 3:45, and 5pm on weekdays, and 11am, 1, 2, 4, and 5pm on weekends. Prices for the 1-hour cruise are C$14 (US$9.55) for adults, C$11 (US$7.50) seniors and students, C$9 (US$6.15) children 5 to 14. For more information, call the **Great Lakes Schooner Company,** 249 Queens Quay W., Suite 111 (☎ **416/260-6355**).

HELICOPTER TOURS   For an aerial view of the city, contact **National Helicopters,** Toronto City Centre Airport, Toronto ON M5V 1A1 (☎ **416/361-1100;** www.nationalhelicopters.com). Its helicopters take off from the Toronto Island Airport. The charge is C$50 (US$34) per person for 7 minutes of aerial sightseeing.

WALKING/BIKING TOURS   Toronto is a city made for walking, and there's no shortage of options for those willing to pound the pavement. **City Walk Civitas**

Cultural Resources (☎ 416/966-1550) offers downtown tours with guides who know their history—and a little local gossip, too. The charge is C$10 (US$6.80) for adults, free for children under 13.

A **Taste of the World Neighbourhood Bicycle Tours and Walks** (☎ 416/923-6813) leads visitors on tours of the nooks and crannies of places like Chinatown, Yorkville, and Rosedale. Walking tours cost C$15 (US$10.20) for adults, C$13 (US$8.85) seniors and students, C$9 (US$6.15) children under 13. Bike tours cost C$45, C$40, and C$30, respectively.

During the summer, the **Toronto Historical Board** (☎ 416/392-6827) offers free walking tours of several neighborhoods, including Cabbagetown and Rosedale. Call ahead for details. Also during the summer, the **Royal Ontario Museum** (☎ 416/586-5513) offers walking tours at 6pm Wednesday and 2pm Sunday in various neighborhoods across Toronto. Most of the walks are free, though a few cost C$5 (US$3.40) per person.

12 Outdoor Activities

Toronto residents love the great outdoors, whatever the time of year. In summer, you'll see people cycling, boating, and hiking; in winter, there's skating, skiing, and snow-boarding. So make like a native and enjoy the city's vast expanse of parkland.

For additional information on facilities in the parks, golf courses, tennis courts, swimming pools, beaches, and picnic areas, call **Metro Parks** (☎ 416/392-8186) or **City Parks** (☎ 416/392-1111). Also see "Parks & Gardens," earlier in this chapter.

BEACHES

Situated on Lake Ontario, Toronto boasts several beaches where you can lap up the sun. Just don't lap up the polluted water, even though you'll see many Torontonians doing just that. Lake Ontario has high counts of *escherichia coli*, a very nasty bacteria that can cause ear, nose, and throat infections, skin rashes, and diarrhea. Look, but don't touch.

The Beaches is the neighborhood running along Queen Street East from Coxwell Avenue to Victoria Park. It has a charming boardwalk that connects the beaches, starting at **Ashbridge's Bay Park,** which has a sizable marina. There's also **Woodbine Beach,** which connects to **Kew Gardens Park** and is a favorite with sunbathers and volleyball players. Woodbine also boasts the **Donald D. Summerville Olympic Pool.** Snack bars and trinket sellers line the length of the boardwalk.

The **Toronto Islands** are where you'll find the city's favorite beaches. The ones on **Centre Island,** always the busiest, are favored by families because of nearby attractions like **Centreville.** The beaches on **Wards Island** are much more secluded. They're connected by the loveliest boardwalk in the city, which is bordered by masses of fragrant flowers and raspberry bushes. **Hanlan's Point,** also in the Islands, is Toronto's only nude beach.

BOATING/CANOEING

At the **Harbourside Boating Centre,** 283 Queen's Quay W. (☎ 416/203-3000), you can rent sailboats or powerboats and take sailing lessons. Depending on the boat's size, a 3-hour sailboat rental costs at least C$60 (US$40.80). Powerboats cost C$95 (US$64.60) and up. Weeklong and weekend sailing courses are also offered.

The **Harbourfront Canoe and Kayak School,** 283A Queens Quay W. (☎ 416/203-2277), rents kayaks for C$40 to $50 (US$27 to $34) a day (the higher rates apply on weekends). Canoes go for C$35 to $45 (US$23.80 to $30.60). Open daily mid-June to Labour Day, weekdays only spring and fall, weather permitting.

You can also rent canoes, rowboats, and pedal boats on the **Toronto Islands** just south of Centreville.

CROSS-COUNTRY SKIING

Just about every park in Toronto becomes potential cross-country skiing territory as soon as snow falls. Best bets are Sunnybrook Park and Ross Lord Park, both in North York. For more information, call **Metro Parks** (☎ 416/392-8186). Serious skiers interested in day trips to excellent out-of-town sites like Horseshoe Valley can call **Trakkers Cross Country Ski Club** (☎ 416/763-0173), which also rents equipment.

CYCLING

With biking trails through most of the city's parks and more than 29 kilometers (18 miles) of street bike routes, it's not surprising that Toronto has been acclaimed as one of the best cycling cities in North America. Favorite pathways include the **Martin Goodman Trail** (from the Beaches to the Humber River along the waterfront); the **Lower Don Valley** bike trail (from the east end of the city north to Riverdale Park); **High Park** (with winding trails over 400 acres); and the **Toronto Islands,** where bikers roam free without fear of cars. For advice, call **Ontario Cycling** (☎ 416/426-7242) or **Toronto Parks and Recreation** (☎ 416/392-8186).

Official bike lanes are marked on College/Carlton streets, the Bloor Street Viaduct leading to the Danforth, Beverly/St. George streets, and Davenport Road. The Convention and Visitors Association can supply more detailed information.

There's no shortage of bike-rental options. Renting a bike usually runs about C$12 to $24 (US$8.15 to $16.30) a day. On Centre Island, try **Toronto Island Bicycle Rental** (☎ 416/203-0009). In the city, head for **Wheel Excitement,** 5 Rees St., near Harbourfront (☎ 416/260-9000); **McBride Cycle,** 180 Queens Quay W., at York Street, on the Harbourfront (☎ 416/203-5651); or **High Park Cycle and Sports,** 24 Ronson Dr. (☎ 416/614-6689). If you're interested in cycling with a group, call the **Toronto Bicycling Network** (☎ 416/766-1985) for information about daily excursions and weekend trips.

FITNESS CENTERS

The **Metro Central YMCA,** 20 Grosvenor St. (☎ 416/975-9622), has excellent facilities, including a 25-meter swimming pool, all kinds of cardiovascular machines, Nautilus equipment, an indoor track, squash and racquetball courts, and aerobics classes. A day pass costs C$15 (US$10.20).

For yoga aficionados, there's no better place to stretch than the **Yoga Studio,** 344 Bloor St. W. (☎ 416/923-9366). A 90-minute session costs C$10 (US$6.80). Incidentally, the ashtanga class draws visiting celebrities.

SPA

Maybe you've got a kink in your neck you just can't work out. Or perhaps you're just in the mood for some deluxe pampering. In Toronto, you won't have to look too far to get it. Several hotels, including the Park Hyatt, Le Royal Meridien King Edward, and the Royal York have their own on-site full-service spas for men and women. And then there are the independents:

Estée Lauder Spa. Holt Renfrew, 50 Bloor St. W. ☎ **416/960-2909.** Subway: Yonge/Bloor.

Located in one of Toronto's most luxurious shops is, appropriately enough, one of the city's most luxurious spas. Decorated in minimalist-chic blond wood and glass (and with a seemingly endless number of private treatment rooms), the spa delivers top-notch treatments. One of the most interesting is the Jet Lag facial, which rehydrates the skin; during the facial, one's legs are treated to a "lymphatic leg therapy" that reduces puffiness and swelling. While this unusual offering is priced at C$120 (US$81.60), most of the spa's services are priced between C$20–$90 (US$13.60–61.20).

HealthWinds. 2401 Yonge St., lower level. ☎ **416/488-4955.** Subway: Eglinton.

This is as serene a setting as you'll find anywhere in the city. Perhaps that's because the spa is set in a smaller space than some of its downtown cousins. The standards here are extremely high—owner Kaylee Kline is president of the Spas Ontario association. Some of the best treatments at HealthWinds take place in the tub—a hydrotherapy bath that is outfitted with 120 water and air jets, all the better to soothe your aching back (hydrotherapy treatments start at C$55/US$37.40).

The Spa at the Elmwood. 18 Elm St. ☎ **416/977-6751.** Subway: Dundas.

With its imposing entranceway, dark-wood paneling and old-fashioned glamour, the Elmwood looks more like a private club than a traditional spa. It's a stone's throw from the Financial District, so it attracts a sizable corporate clientele. Offerings include a range of massage therapies (take your pick from Swedish, Shiatsu, reflexology, or aromatherapy), whirlpool baths, and facials (prices start around C$35/US$23.80 and go up to C$115/US$78.20). There's also a hair salon and an elegant restaurant that specializes in heart-healthy cooking.

GOLF

Toronto is obsessed with golf, as evidenced by its more than 75 public courses within an hour's drive of the downtown core. Here's information on some of the best. **Don Valley,** Yonge Street south of Highway 401 (☎ **416/392-2465**). Designed by Howard Watson, this is a scenic par-71 scenic course with some challenging elevated tees. The par-3 13th hole is nicknamed the Hallelujah Corner (because it takes a miracle to make par). It's a good place to start your kids. Greens fees are C$30 (US$20.50) on weekdays, C$35 (US$23.80) on weekends.

Humber Valley (☎ **416/392-2488**), Albion Road at Beattie Avenue. The relatively flat par-70 course is easy to walk, and gets lots of shade from towering trees. The three final holes require major concentration (the 16th and 17th are both par-5s). Greens fees are C$26 to $30 (US$17.70 to 20.50).

The **Tam O'Shanter,** at Birchmount Avenue, north of Sheppard (☎ **416/392-2547**). Another par-70 course, it features links holes and water hazards among its challenges. Greens fees are C$29 to $33 (US$19.70 to $22.45).

The **Glen Abbey Golf Club,** Oakville (☎ **905/844-1800;** www.glenabbey.com). The championship course is one of the most famous in Canada. Designed by Jack Nicklaus, the par-73 layout often plays host to the Canadian Open. Greens fees are C$125 (US$85) in early spring and fall, C$235 (US$160) in summer.

Other championship courses of note include the **Lionhead Golf Club** in Brampton (☎ **905/455-8400**). It has two 18-hole par-72 courses; greens fees are C$120 (US$81.50) (for the tougher course) and C$110 (US$74.80). In Markham, the **Angus Glen Golf Club** (☎ **905/887-5157**) has a Doug Carrick–designed par-72 course and charges a C$130 (US$88.40) greens fee.

HORSEBACK RIDING

Believe it or not, you can go riding in parkland a mere 15 minutes from downtown. The **Central Don Riding Academy** (☎ **416/444-4044**), in Sunnybrook Park at Eglinton Avenue East and Leslie Street, has 12 miles of bridle trails. For beginners, there's an indoor ring and an outdoor ring. It's open Monday to Thursday 1 to 5pm, weekends noon to 5pm. Reservations are required. Rates vary depending on the level of instruction; a 1-hour trail ride costs C$25 (US$17). Happy trails!

ICE-SKATING

Nathan Phillips Square in front of City Hall becomes a free ice rink in winter, as does an area at Harbourfront Centre. Rentals are available. Artificial rinks (also free) are in more than 25 parks, including Grenadier Pond in High Park—a romantic spot, with a bonfire and vendors selling roasted chestnuts. They're open from November to March.

IN-LINE SKATING

In summer, in-line skaters pack Toronto's streets (and sidewalks). Go with the flow and rent some blades from **Planet Skate,** 2144 Queen St. E. (☎ 416/690-7588) or **Wheel Excitement** (see "Cycling," above). A 1-day rental runs C$18 to $22 (US$12.25 to $15). Popular sites include the Beaches, Harbourfront, and the Toronto Islands.

JOGGING

Downtown routes might include **Harbourfront** and along the lakefront, or through **Queen's Park** and the University. The **Martin Goodman Trail** runs 20 kilometers (12.4 miles) along the waterfront from the Beaches in the east to the Humber River in the west. It's ideal for jogging, walking, or cycling. It links to the **Tommy Thompson Trail,** which travels the parks from the lakefront along the Humber River. Near the Ontario Science Centre in the Central Don Valley, **Ernest Thompson Seton Park** is also good for jogging. Parking is available at the Thorncliffe Drive and Wilket Creek entrances.

PARACHUTING

Have you always wanted to jump out of a plane and trust a big piece of fabric to get you safely to the ground? You're in luck. The **Parachute School of Toronto** (☎ 800/361-5867), in Arthur, north of Toronto, will help you get a better understanding of gravity. Going for a dive costs C$200 (US$136) during the summer, C$100 ($68) the rest of the year. After morning instruction, you jump in the afternoon. Reservations (a day or two ahead) are recommended. Geronimo!

ROCK-CLIMBING

The dilemma: indoors or outdoors? Toronto has several climbing gyms, including **Joe Rockhead's,** 29 Fraser Ave. (☎ 416/538-7670), and the **Toronto Climbing Academy,** 100 Broadview Ave. (☎ 416/406-5900). You can pick up the finer points of knot-tying and belaying. Both gyms also rent equipment.

For the real thing, you need to head out of town. Weekend excursions to the Elora Gorge are organized through **Humber College** (☎ 416/675-5097).

SNOWBOARDING

The snowboard craze shows no sign of abating. Popular sites include High Park and Earl Bales Park. Call **Metro Parks** (☎ 416/392-8186) or **City Parks** (☎ 416/392-1111) for more information. Rentals (C$20/US$13.60 a day) are available from **Windward,** 5015 Yonge St. (☎ 416/512-8506).

SWIMMING

There are a dozen or so outdoor pools (open June to September) in the municipal parks, including High and Rosedale parks. Several community recreation centers have indoor pools. For **pool information,** call ☎ 416/392-1111.

The **University of Toronto Athletic Centre,** 55 Harbord St., at Spadina Avenue (☎ 416/978-4680), opens its swimming pool free to the public on Sunday from noon to 4pm. The pool at the **YMCA,** 20 Grosvenor St. (☎ **416/975-9622**), can be used on a day pass, which costs C$15 (US$10.20).

Anyone tempted by the waters of Lake Ontario, beware. It is unsafe and getting worse. People sometimes do swim in it, no matter how polluted it gets. A word of advice: Don't.

TENNIS

More than 30 municipal parks have free tennis facilities. The most convenient are the courts in High, Rosedale, and Jonathan Ashridge parks. They are open in summer only. At Eglinton Flats Park, west of Keele Street at Eglinton Avenue, six of the courts can be used in winter. Call the city (☎ **416/392-1111**) or Metro Parks (☎ **416/ 392-8186**) for additional information.

13 Spectator Sports

AUTO RACING   The Molson Indy (☎ **416/872-4639**) runs at the Exhibition Place Street circuit, usually on the third weekend in July.

BASEBALL   SkyDome, 1 Blue Jays Way, on Front Street beside the CN Tower, is the home of the **Toronto Blue Jays.** The team won the World Series in 1992 and 1993. For information, contact the Toronto Blue Jays, P.O. Box 7777, Adelaide St., Toronto, ON M5C 2K7 (☎ **416/341-1000**). For tickets, which cost C$15 to C$60 (US$10.20 to $40.50), call ☎ **888/654-6529** or 416/341-1234.

BASKETBALL   Toronto's basketball team, the **Raptors,** has generated urban fever. The team's home ground is the **Air Canada Centre,** 40 Bay St., at Lakeshore Boulevard. The NBA schedule runs from October to April. The arena seats 19,500 for basketball. For information, contact the **Raptors Basketball Club,** 40 Bay St. (☎ **416/ 815-5600**). For tickets, which cost C$25 to $125 (US$17 to $85), call **Ticketmaster** (☎ **416/870-8000**).

FOOTBALL   Remember Kramer on *Seinfeld*? He would only watch Canadian football. Here's your chance to catch a game. **SkyDome,** 1 Blue Jays Way, is home to the **Argonauts** of the Canadian Football League. They play between June and November. For information, contact the club at SkyDome, Gate 3, Suite 1300, Toronto, ON M5V 1J3 (☎ **416/341-5151**). Argos tickets cost C$10 to $40 (US$6.80 to $27.20); call ☎ **888/654-6529** or 416/341-1234.

GOLF TOURNAMENTS   Canada's national golf tournament, the **Bell Canadian Open,** is usually held at the **Glen Abbey Golf Club** in Oakville, about 40 minutes from the city (☎ **905/844-1800**). Most years, it's played over the Labour Day weekend.

HOCKEY   While basketball is still in its honeymoon phase in Toronto, hockey is a longtime love. The **Air Canada Centre,** 40 Bay St., at Lakeshore Boulevard, is the new home of the **Toronto Maple Leafs.** It replaced the revered Maple Leaf Gardens, which had housed the team since 1931. Though the arena seats 18,700 for hockey, tickets are not easy to come by, because many are sold by subscription. The rest are available through **Ticketmaster** (☎ **416/870-8000**); prices are C$25 to $100 (US$17 to $68).

HORSERACING   Thoroughbred racing takes place at **Woodbine Racetrack,** Rexdale Boulevard and Highway 427, Etobicoke (☎ **416/675-6110** or 416/675-7223).

It's famous for the Queen's Plate (usually contested on the third Sunday in June); the Canadian International, a classic turf race (September or October); and the North America Cup (mid-June). Woodbine also hosts harness racing in spring and fall.

Harness racing takes place at **Mohawk Raceway,** 30 miles west of the city at Highway 410, and **Guelph Line** (☎ **416/675-7223**) plays host to the Breeder's Crown in October.

TENNIS TOURNAMENTS   Canada's international tennis championship, the **Du Maurier Ltd. Open,** is an important stop on the pro tennis tour. It attracts stars like Pete Sampras, Andre Agassi, and Arantxa Sanchez-Vicario to the National Tennis Centre at York University in late August. The men's and women's championships alternate cities. In 2001, the men play in Montreal and the women in Toronto. For information, call ☎ **416/665-9777.**

7

City Strolls

Toronto is one of the best walking cities in the world. I know I'm boasting, but look at the evidence: the patchwork of dynamic ethnic neighborhoods, the impressive architecture, and the many parks. Because the city is such a sprawling place, however, you'll need to pick your route carefully.

The walking tours in this chapter aren't designed to give you an overview. They offer a look at the most colorful, exciting neighborhoods in the city, as well as areas that are packed with sights on almost every corner.

Walking Tour 1: Harbourfront

Start: Union Station.
Finish: Harbourfront Antique Market.
Time: At least 2 hours, and possibly a lot more, depending on how entranced you are with the antiques market.
Best Times: Saturday and Sunday, when the Harbourfront Antique Market is bustling.
Worst Time: Monday, when the antiques market is closed.

As you start your tour, pause to look at the beaux-arts interior of **Union Station,** which opened in 1927. The hall has a cathedral-like ceiling, and 22 pillars that weigh 70 tons each. From here, either take the LRT to York Quay or walk south along York Street (away from the Royal York hotel to Queen's Quay West. The Gardiner Expressway looms overhead, making this a noisy, dark spot. When you reach the end of the street, you're at Queen's Quay West. Look across to:

1. **Queen's Quay Terminal,** a large complex that houses more than 100 shops and restaurants. On the third floor is a theater specially designed for dance performances. Built in 1927 when lake and railroad trade flourished, this eight-story concrete warehouse has been attractively renovated. The light, airy two-story marketplace has garden courts, skylights, and waterfalls. Condominium apartments occupy the floors above.

Although you'll find few bargains here, there are some charming stores on the street level. They include **Rainmakers,** which sells zillions of whimsical umbrellas and parasol hats, plus terrific insulated rainwear; **Oh Yes Toronto** (souvenirs and Toronto-centric clothing); **Crabtree & Evelyn** (soaps and other toiletries that appeal to the senses); and **Suitables** (reasonably priced silk fashions).

On the upper level, options include the classic Canadian **Tilley Endurables,** founded by Torontonian Alex Tilley (who invented the world's most adaptable hat). **First Hand Canadian Crafts** represents more than 200 contemporary folk artists who make both decorative and functional pieces, and **Table of Contents** sells all kinds of kitchen gear, napkins, tablecloths, and utensils.

☕ **TAKE A BREAK**   If you want to sit out and watch the lakefront traffic— boat and human—go for a light meal or a drink at **Spinnakers** (☎ 416/ 203-0559), or the **Boathouse Cafe** (☎ 416-203-6300), on the ground floor of Queen's Quay. More formal dining can be found at the **Pearl Harbourfront Chinese Cuisine** (☎ 416/203-1233). The Queen's Quay complex also has a variety of cafes, and there are food vendors just outside.

From Queen's Quay Terminal, walk along the water to:

2. **The Power Plant Contemporary Art Gallery.** This was indeed a power plant when it was built in 1927. Identifiable by its towering smokestack, the space has been converted to display modern art. The same building houses the Du Maurier Theatre Centre, which presents works in French.

Behind this building, adjacent to Queen's Quay West, is the Tent in the Park, where events take place during the summer season. Walk next door to the:

3. **York Quay Centre,** a complex converted from a 1940 trucking warehouse that contains a number of interesting restaurants and galleries. Spend some time in the Craft Studio watching the glassblowers, potters, jewelry makers, and other artisans at work, and browse in the store that sells their work.

On the waterfront side in front of York Quay, there's a pond where kids operate model boats in summer; in winter it turns into an ice-skating rink.

From York Quay, cross the Amsterdam Bridge above Marina 4, checking out the wealth that's bobbing down below. You'll arrive on:

4. **John Quay.** The first building you'll come to contains four restaurants, beyond which are the towers of the:

5. **Radisson Plaza Hotel Admiral** and **Admiralty Point Condominiums,** and, across Queen's Quay West, the HarbourPoint Condominiums. The ground level of the Admiralty Point Condos houses a few interesting stores. The **Nautical Mind** sells marine books, photographs, navigational charts, and boating videos; and the Dock Shoppe is filled with all kinds of sailing gear and fashions.

☕ **TAKE A BREAK**   Pop into the **Radisson Plaza Hotel Admiral** (☎ 416/ 203-3333), 249 Queen's Quay W., which has a couple of dining options (the **Commodore's Dining Room** and the **Gallery Café,** which serves light fare), plus a pleasant terrace if it's a sunny day.

Continue west along Queen's Quay West past:

6. **Maple Leaf Quay.** (You can stop at the Nautical Centre to sign up for sailing classes first; see chapter 6.) Continue west and you'll see the Maple Leaf Quay Apartments on your right and the Harbour Terrace Condominiums farther along on your left, on the waterfront. Next door to the westernmost tower of the Maple Leaf Quay Apartments is the:

Walking Tour—Harbourfront

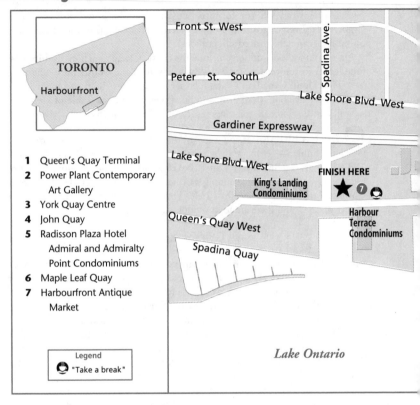

TORONTO

Harbourfront

1 Queen's Quay Terminal
2 Power Plant Contemporary
   Art Gallery
3 York Quay Centre
4 John Quay
5 Radisson Plaza Hotel
   Admiral and Admiralty
   Point Condominiums
6 Maple Leaf Quay
7 Harbourfront Antique
   Market

Legend
😊 "Take a break"

Front St. West

Peter St. South

Spadina Ave.

Lake Shore Blvd. West

Gardiner Expressway

Lake Shore Blvd. West

FINISH HERE
★ ❼ 😊

King's Landing
Condominiums

Harbour
Terrace
Condominiums

Queen's Quay West

Spadina Quay

Lake Ontario

7. Harbourfront Antique Market, a terrific destination where more than 100 dealers sell fine furniture, jewelry, books, clocks, and art deco items (in summer, there are often 150 or more dealers, as the market expands out-of-doors). On Sunday, there's also an outdoor market featuring less established dealers. The market is open Tuesday through Sunday 10am to 6pm. This is a wonderful place to test your bargaining skills, particularly when the market starts to shut down late in the day.

😊 **WINDING DOWN** In the Harbourfront Antique Market, **Sophie's** has great fresh salads, sandwiches, quiches, and desserts.

To return to downtown, board the LRT and head back to Union Station.

Walking Tour 2: The Financial District

This is the Wall Street of Toronto, the financial engine that has made Ontario the nation's strongest and wealthiest economy. For more information about the major sights mentioned below, see chapter 6.

Start: The CN Tower, near the corner of John and Front streets.
Finish: A Queen Street West watering hole.
Time: 2 to 4 hours.

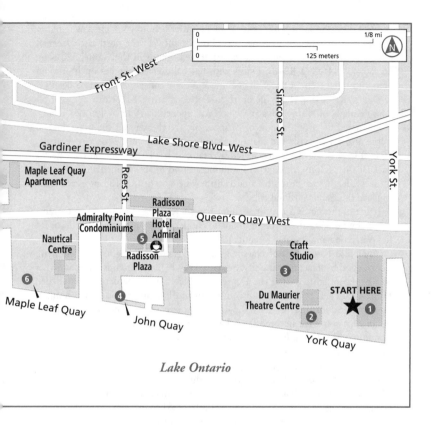

Best Time: Weekdays during business hours.

Worst Times: Weekends, when the Stock Market is closed and the Financial District is dead.

Start by going up the:

1. **CN Tower,** the tallest freestanding structure in the world. Although it has become a symbol of the city, the CN Tower drew a great deal of criticism when it was built in 1975. It has since been recognized as an important symbol of a city trying to forge a new identity. Robert Fulford writes about it in *Accidental City:* "In the 1970s [Toronto] was struggling to shake off the dowdy self-image that was part of its heritage as a colonial city . . . Torontonians were starting to consider, with shy pleasure, the novel idea that their city might be attractive, even enviable . . . At that happy moment, the tower reinforced local exuberance and asserted the city's claim to even more attention." However you view it, the most enjoyable thing is the view *from* it. On a clear day it feels like you can see forever . . . or is that Buffalo?

Once you're back down at the base, exit at the corner of John and Front streets. From here, look to the right along Front Street to see the glistening golden Royal Bank towers (part of the Royal Bank Centre). The CBC Centre stretches along the north side of Front Street for a whole long block. Inside, you can peek at the lobby radio studios and take a nostalgic radio-TV trip in the free museum.

Walk north on John Street (with the CN Tower behind you), cross Wellington Street, and continue up to King Street. Turn right. On the northeast corner of King Street, sports fans will want to stop in at **Legends of the Game,** 322 King St. W. (☎ **416/971-8848**). Doors with baseball-shaped handles open onto an emporium that features the Wall of Fame and every conceivable sports collectible. Continue walking along the north side of King Street 1 block to:

2. The Princess of Wales Theatre, which was opened in 1993 by Princess Diana. Constructed for a production of *Miss Saigon,* the theater was the brainchild of impresario Ed Mirvish and his son, David. Try to pop inside for a peek at the 10,000 square feet of murals created by Frank Stella. There's one on the exterior back of the building that's worth walking around to see. Immediately after the princess' death, the theater became a shrine where mourning Torontonians came to place thousands of floral tributes.

Exit the theater and continue along King Street past a cluster of restaurants owned by Ed Mirvish. (Drop in to one to check out the larger-than-life decor Ed has purchased at antiques closeouts.)

You'll also pass a wall of newspaper clippings about this gutsy Torontonian. Booster and benefactor of the city, he started out in bleak circumstances as owner of a bankrupt store during the Depression. He paid off the debt and launched **Honest Ed's** (see chapter 8), a discount store at Bloor and Bathurst that brought him fame and fortune. He saved the Royal Alex (see below) from demolition, and he and his son have become legendary theater impresarios in Toronto and in London, where Ed outbid Andrew Lloyd Webber in 1982 for the Old Vic. For this he was named a Commander of the Order of the British Empire.

Cross Duncan Street. Next you'll come to:

3. The Royal Alexandra. John M. Lyle built this beloved theater in 1906 and 1907 at a cost of C$750,000. In 1963, it was scheduled for demolition, but Ed Mirvish bought it for a mere C$200,000 (US$136,000) and refurbished it. Named after Queen Alexandra, wife of Edward VII, the magnificent beaux-arts structure is Edwardian down to the last detail. It abounds with gilt and velvet, and has an entrance foyer lined with green marble.

Across the street from these two theaters stands the new **Metro Hall,** 55 John St., designed by Brisbin Brook Beynon. Go in to see the interior art installations, especially the animal sculptures by Cynthia Short. Free tours (☎ **416/ 392-8000**) of the first three floors are available. Also on the south side of the street, at the corner of King and Simcoe streets, is:

4. Roy Thomson Hall, named after newspaper magnate Lord Thomson of Fleet (a Canadian press baron who wound up taking a seat in the British House of Lords). Built between 1972 and 1982 and designed by Arthur Erickson, the building's exterior looks very space age. Inside, the mirrored effects are dramatic. Tours (C$3/US$2.05)) of the fabulous concert hall are usually given at 12:30pm, but call ahead (☎ **416/593-4828**) to confirm the schedule. If you don't want to take a tour, at least go in for a look.

Continue walking east on King Street. You'll pass through the heart of the Financial District, surrounded by many towers owned and operated by banks and brokerage, trust, and insurance companies. On the northeast corner of King and Simcoe rises the first of the towers that make up the Sun Life Centre; on the southeast corner stands:

5. St. Andrew's Presbyterian Church (1874–75), a quietly inviting retreat from the city's pace and noise. It was designed by the city's premier architect of the

Walking Tour—Financial District

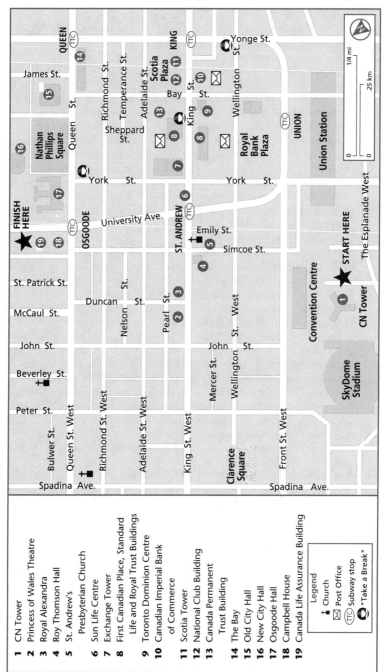

1 CN Tower
2 Princess of Wales Theatre
3 Royal Alexandra
4 Roy Thomson Hall
5 St. Andrew's
  Presbyterian Church
6 Sun Life Centre
7 Exchange Tower
8 First Canadian Place, Standard
  Life and Royal Trust Buildings
9 Toronto Dominion Centre
10 Canadian Imperial Bank
  of Commerce
11 Scotia Tower
12 National Club Building
13 Canada Permanent
  Trust Building
14 The Bay
15 Old City Hall
16 New City Hall
17 Osgoode Hall
18 Campbell House
19 Canada Life Assurance Building

Legend
+ Church
⊠ Post Office
(TTC) Subway stop
"Take a Break"

time, W. G. Storm, in an inspired picturesque Scottish Romanesque style. Sun Life paid C$4.3 million (US$2.9 million) for the church's air rights, doubtless contributing to its survival. Continue along King Street to University Avenue. Opposite, on the northeast corner, is the:

6. **Sun Life Centre's second tower,** marked by a sculpture by Sorel Etrog. Farther along the block you'll find another sculpture, *Parent I,* by British sculptor Barbara Hepworth. It's in a courtyard setting complete with splashing fountain at the northwest corner of York and King streets. On the northeast corner stands:

7. **2 First Canadian Place,** the north corner of which is the **Toronto Exchange Tower,** at the corner of Adelaide and York streets. The Sculptor's Society Gallery, which always has an interesting free show, is in 2 First Canadian Place. Then head up to the Stock Exchange's public gallery, in the Exchange Tower. From here, you can see the action on the floor and a presentation explaining how today's cyber-trading works. Also on the ground floor in the building, stop in to see the fabulous glass sculptures and other glass pieces in the **Sandra Ainsley** gallery (☎ 416/362-4480).

    Continue along King Street past:

8. **First Canadian Place,** on the north side, and the **Standard Life** and **Royal Trust buildings** (part of the Toronto Dominion Centre), on the south. At the end of this block, you'll reach Bay Street. The Standard Life building was designed by New York architect Edward Durell Stone with Bregman & Hamann and is faced with marble in contrast to the TD Centre, which is black. Again, there are views of the magnificent towers of the Royal Bank Centre from here.

    The intersection of Bay and King streets was once considered the precise geographical center of Toronto's financial power. During the mining booms in the 1920s and 1950s, Bay Street was lined with offices that were filled with commission salesmen peddling stocks to the equivalent of the little old lady from Dubuque. This is the hub that gave Torontonians their reputation as a voracious band of money-grubbing folks that Hugh McLennan portrayed in his marvelous novel about Quebec, *Two Solitudes.* Today it's called Mint Corner because a major bank occupies each corner.

    If it's near lunchtime and your stomach is rumbling, this isn't a bad place to:

    🫖 **TAKE A BREAK** Your best bet for a leisurely lunch in this neighborhood is a block south and a block east at **Jump Café and Bar,** 1 Wellington St. W. (☎ 416/363-3400; see chapter 5). For a quick snack, seek out one of the casual spots in the concourse of **First Canadian Place.**

    Our next stop, at King and Bay streets, is the:

9. **Toronto Dominion Centre,** built between 1963 and 1969 and designed by Mies van der Rohe in his sleek trademark style. The black steel and dark-bronze-tinted glass tower rises from a gray granite base. Go through the Royal Trust and Toronto Dominion Towers, stopping to browse in the **Toronto Dominion Gallery of Inuit Art,** 79 Wellington St. W. (☎ 416/982-8473), on the ground floor and mezzanine of the Toronto Dominion Tower. Close to 100 marvelous soapstone sculptures are on display. Exit the TD Centre on Wellington Street and walk right; you'll come to a small staircase that leads to the courtyard behind the Toronto Dominion Bank Tower. In this open space you'll find a patch of grass where half a dozen bronze cows are lazing. Artist Joe Fafard's Pasture serves as a reminder to the bankers and stockbrokers that Toronto's wealth was derived from other stock, too.

Walk through the Centre to the King Street exit. Exit onto King Street and turn right to continue east. Cross Bay Street. On the south side of King Street, you'll come to the entrance to Commerce Court. Architecture buffs will also want to go into the:

10. **Canadian Imperial Bank of Commerce** (1929–31), if only to see the massive banking hall—145 feet long, 85 feet wide, and 65 feet high—with its coffered ceiling, gilt moldings, and sculpted friezes. The main entrance is decorated with squirrels, roosters, bees, bears, and figures representing Industry, Commerce, and Mercury. For years, this 34-story building dominated the Toronto skyline. It was designed by New Yorkers York and Sawyer, with Darling and Pearson. Note the carved heads on the top of the building depicting courage, observation, foresight, and enterprise. In the early 1970s, I. M. Pei was asked to design a new complex while preserving the old building. He set the new mercury-laminated stainless-steel bank tower back from King Street, creating Commerce Court.

    Opposite, on the north side of King Street, note:

11. **Scotia Tower.** It's a red-granite building, designed by Webb Zerafa Menkes Housden between 1985 and 1988.

    Walk back to Bay Street and turn right. You're now going north. At no. 303, on the east side, is the:

12. **National Club Building.** In 1874 the Canada First Movement, which had started in Ottawa in 1868, became centered in Toronto. As its name suggests, the members were fervent nationalists. It established a weekly, *The Nation*, entered politics (as the Canadian National Association), and founded the National Club. The club moved here in 1907. Today, it's a prestigious private club.

    Across the street on the west side, at the corner of Bay and Adelaide streets, stands the:

13. **Canada Permanent Trust Building** (1928), 7 King St. E. Go in to view the beautifully worked art-deco brass and bronze, particularly the elevator doors, which are chased and engraved with foliage and flowers.

    Cross Adelaide Street. As you walk up Bay Street, the magnificent Old City Hall is clearly in view. First, on the east side of Bay Street between Richmond and Queen streets, look at—or stop in to:

14. **The Bay,** one of Canada's venerable retailers. The Bay, along with its arch-rival, Eaton's, has influenced the development of the downtown areas of most major Canadian cities.

    Across Queen Street looms:

15. **Old City Hall,** reflected dramatically in the Cadillac Fairview Office Tower at the corner of James and Queen streets. This solid, impressive building, designed by Edward James Lennox, was built out of Credit River Valley sandstone. The magnificent Romanesque Revival style shows the obvious influence of H. H. Richardson. Begun in 1885, it opened in 1899, and for years its clock tower was a skyline landmark. Today, the building houses the provincial criminal courts. Go in to see the impressive staircase, columns with decorative capitals, and mosaic floor. The stained-glass window (1898) by Robert McCausland depicts the union of Commerce and Industry watched over by Britannia. Note the carved heads on the exterior entrance pillars—supposedly portraits of the political figures and citizens of the period, including the architect.

    Exit along Queen Street and turn right. Pause at the intersection of Queen and Bay streets. Bay, Toronto's equivalent of Wall Street, curves at this intersection, offering a good view north and south. Cross Bay Street and you'll find yourself in Nathan Phillips Square, with New City Hall looming above.

16. New City Hall, the city's fourth, was built between 1958 and 1965 in modern sculptural style. It's the symbol of Toronto's postwar dynamism, although not everyone felt that way when it was built. According to Pierre Berton, Frank Lloyd Wright said of it, "You've got a headmarker for a grave and future generations will look at it and say: 'This marks the spot where Toronto fell.'" The truth is quite the opposite—this breathtaking building was the first architectural marker of an evolving metropolis. Finnish architect Viljo Revell won a design competition that drew entries by 510 architects from 42 countries, including I. M. Pei. The building has a great square in front with a fountain and pool; people flock here in summer to relax, and in winter to skate. The square is named after Nathan Phillips, Toronto's first Jewish mayor, who made it his mission to see the project through.

City Hall also has some art worth viewing. Look just inside the entrance for *Metropolis,* which local artist David Partridge fashioned from more than 100,000 common nails. You'll need to stand well back to enjoy the effect. Henry Moore's sculpture *The Archer* stands in front of the building—thanks to Mayor Phil Givens, who raised the money to buy it through public subscription after city authorities refused. The gesture encouraged Moore to bestow a major collection of his works on the Art Gallery of Toronto (see chapter 6). Two curved concrete towers, which house the bureaucracy, flank the Council Chamber. From the air, the whole complex supposedly looks like an eye peering up at the heavens.

☕ **TAKE A BREAK**   For some light refreshment, stop in at one of several dining spots in the **Sheraton Centre,** 123 Queen St. W., among them the pub **Good Queen Bess** (☎ **416/361-1000**).

From City Hall, walk west along Queen Street. On your right, behind an ornate wrought-iron fence that once kept out the cows, you'll see:

17. Osgoode Hall, since the 1830s headquarters of the Law Society of Upper Canada, a professional association. Named after the first chief justice of Upper Canada, the building was constructed in stages. It started with the East Wing (1831 to 1832), then the West Wing (1844 to 1845), and the center block (1856 to 1860). The last, designed by W. G. Storm, with a Palladian portico, is the most impressive. Inside is the **Great Library**—112 feet long, 40 feet wide, and 40 feet high—with stucco decoration and a domed ceiling. The Ontario Supreme Court is across the street on the south side of Queen Street.

Walk west 1 block to University Avenue. On the northwest corner you can visit:

18. Campbell House, the elegant Georgian residence of Sir William Campbell, a Scot who moved to York in 1811 and rose to become chief justice of Upper Canada. A handsome piece of Georgian architecture, it was moved to this location from a few miles farther east.

Stretching northward behind Campbell House, on the northwest side of University Avenue, is the:

Impressions

The real achievement of Toronto is to have remained itself.
—Jan Morris, *O Canada! Travels in an Unknown Country*

19. **Canada Life Assurance Building.** Atop the tower a neon sign provides weather reports—white flashes for snow, red flashes for rain, green beacon for clement weather, red beacon for cloudy weather. If the flashes move upward, the temperature is headed that way, and vice versa.

At University Avenue and Queen Street, you can end the tour by boarding the subway at Osgoode to your next destination, or you can continue walking west along Queen Street to explore its many shops and cafes.

Walking Tour 3: St. Lawrence & Downtown East

Start: Union Station.
Finish: King subway station.
Time: 2 to 3 hours.
Best Time: Saturday, when the St. Lawrence Market is in full swing.
Worst Time: Sunday, when it's closed.

At one time, this area was at the center of city life. Today it's a little off-center, and yet it has some historic and modern architectural treasures, and a wealth of history in and around the St. Lawrence Market. Begin at:

1. **Union Station.** Check out the interior of this classical revival beauty, which opened in 1927 as a temple to and for the railroad. Look up at the shimmering ceiling, faced with vitrified Guastavino tile. It soars 88 feet above the 260-foot-long hall.

Across the street, at York and Front streets, stands the:

2. **Royal York hotel,** a venerable railroad hotel and longtime gathering place for Torontonians. It's the home of the famous Imperial Room cabaret and nightclub, which used to be one of Eartha Kitt's favorite venues (it's still there, but open for dining and dancing only). The hotel was once the tallest building in Toronto and the largest hotel in the British Commonwealth. Check out the lobby, with its coffered ceiling and opulent furnishings, and the meeting rooms where so many of the city's banquets and other events have taken place.

As you leave the hotel, turn left and walk east on Front Street. At the corner of Bay and Front streets, look up at the absolutely stunning:

3. **Royal Bank Plaza,** two triangular gold-sheathed towers, one 41 floors, the other 26, joined by a 130-foot-high atrium. The mirrored glass is enhanced by 150 pounds of gold. It was designed by Webb Zerafa Menkes Housden and built between 1973 and 1977.

Cross Bay Street and continue east on Front Street. On the south side of the street is the impressive sweep of **One Front Street,** the main post office building (okay, not an exciting-sounding sight, but an attractive one). On the north side of the street is the city's latest financial palace and most impressive architectural triumph, Bell Canada Enterprises':

4. **BCE Place.** Go inside to view the soaring galleria. It was designed by Skidmore, Owings, and Merrill with Bregman & Hamann in 1993. The twin office towers are connected by a huge glass-covered galleria five stories high, spanning the block between Bay and Yonge streets. It connects the old Midland Bank building to the twin towers, and was designed by artist-architect Santiago Calatrava with Bregman & Hamann.

☕ **TAKE A BREAK** For an unusual dining experience, stop in at **BCE Place's Movenpick Marché** (☎ 416/366-8986), which turns diners into hunter-gatherers. Rather than waiting for table service, you forage for salads, pastas, and meat dishes at various counters. If you can't bear the thought of chasing down your grub, head across the courtyard to the dramatically designed **Acqua** (☎ 416/368-7171) for Italianate dishes. Downstairs, there's also a food court with a variety of fast-food and casual dining choices. If you prefer a deli sandwich, head for **Shopsy's,** 33 Yonge St. (☎ 416/365-3333; see chapter 5).

Back out on Front Street, turn left and continue to the northwest corner of Yonge and Front, stopping to admire the:

5. Bank of Montreal (1885–86), a suitably ornate building for the most powerful Canadian bank of the 19th century, banker to the colonial and federal governments. Inside, the banking hall rises to a beamed coffered ceiling with domed skylights of stained glass. It now houses the Stanley Cup and other hockey trophies, plus the **Hockey Hall of Fame** (see page 128), another example of the city's genius for architectural adaptation. The exterior, embellished with carvings, porthole windows, and a balustrade, is a sight.

From here, you can look ahead along Front Street and see the weird mural by Derek M. Besant that adorns the famous and highly photogenic:

6. Flatiron or Gooderham Building (1892). It was built as the headquarters of George Gooderham, who had expanded his distilling business into railroads, insurance, and philanthropy. At one time his liquor business was the biggest in the British Empire, and he was also president of the Bank of Toronto. The five-story building occupies a triangular site, and the western tip (and the windows) is beautifully curved and topped with a semicircular tower. The design is by David Roberts.

At the southwest corner of Yonge and Front streets, you can stop in at:

7. The Hummingbird Centre and, across Scott Street, the neighboring **St. Lawrence Centre.** The former is home to the National Ballet of Canada and, at the moment, to the Canadian Opera Company (a new opera house is currently under construction).

Continue east along Front Street to:

8. The Beardmore Building (1872), 35–39 Front St. E. This and the many other cast-iron buildings that line the street were the heart of the late-19th-century warehouse district, close to the lakefront and railheads. Now they're occupied by stores like **Frida Crafts,** which sells imports from Guatemala, India, and Bangladesh, as well as jewelry, bags, candles, and other knickknacks; and **Mountain Equipment Co-op,** stocked with durable outdoor adventure goods. At no. 41–43, note the **Perkins Building,** and at no. 45–49, look for the building with a totally cast-iron facade; the **Nicholas Hoare** bookstore, one of the coziest in the city, is at no. 45.

Continue browsing past Church Street. **Wonderful & Whites,** 83 Front St., features delicate pieces—Victorian linens, lace, pillows, china, and glass. They do cheat, though: Some of the pieces have beautiful, and colorful, patterns. Next door, **Ra** offers an array of Indian and other decorative accents—Indian bedspreads and pillows, along with apparel and jewelry.

Now cross Market Street to the:

9. St. Lawrence Market, in the old market building on the right. Enter this great market hall, which was constructed around the city's second city hall (1844–45).

Walking Tour—St. Lawrence & Downtown East

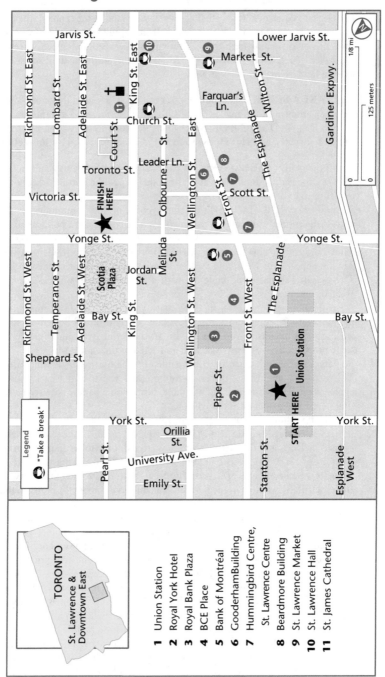

Jarvis St.

Lower Jarvis St.

Richmond St. East

Lombard St.

Adelaide St. East

King St. East

10

9

Market St.

Wilton St.

Gardiner Expwy.

Farquar's Ln.

Court St.

11

Church St.

Toronto St.

Leader Ln.

Colbourne St.

Wellington St. East

8

6

7

Front St.

Scott St.

The Esplanade

FINISH HERE

Victoria St.

7

Yonge St.

Yonge St.

Richmond St. West

Temperance St.

Adelaide St. West

Scotia Plaza

Jordan St.

Melinda St.

Wellington St. West

5

The Esplanade

King St.

Bay St.

Bay St.

Sheppard St.

Front St. West

3

Wellington St. West

4

Piper St.

2

1

Union Station

START HERE

York St.

York St.

Pearl St.

Orillia St.

University Ave.

Stanton St.

Esplanade West

Emily St.

1/8 mi

125 meters

TORONTO

St. Lawrence & Downtown East

1 Union Station
2 Royal York Hotel
3 Royal Bank Plaza
4 BCE Place
5 Bank of Montréal
6 Gooderham Building
7 Hummingbird Centre, St. Lawrence Centre
8 Beardmore Building
9 St. Lawrence Market
10 St. Lawrence Hall
11 St. James Cathedral

The elegant pedimented facade that you see as you stand in the center of the hall was originally the center block of the city hall. Today the market is filled with all kinds of vendors selling fresh eggs, Mennonite sausage, seafood, meats, cheeses, and baked goods. From Thursday to Saturday in the north building across the street, a farmers' market starts at 5am.

☕ **TAKE A BREAK**   The most fun place to stop is at one of the stands offering fresh produce in the market itself. Other choices include **Le Papillon,** 16 Church St. (☎ **416/363-0838;** see chapter 5), which features a raft of savory and dessert crepes, and **Hot House Cafe** at 35 Church St. (☎ **416/366-7800**).

Exit the market where you came in. Cross Wellington Street and cut through Market Lane Park and the shops at Market Square, past the north market building. Turn right onto King Street to:

10. St. **Lawrence Hall** (1850–51), the focal point of the community in the mid–19th century. This hall was the site of grand city occasions, political rallies, balls, and entertainment. Frederick Douglass delivered an antislavery lecture; Jenny Lind and Adelina Patti sang in 1851 and 1860, respectively; General Tom Thumb appeared in 1862; and George Brown campaigned for Confederation. The elegant Palladian-style building, with a domed cupola, was designed by William Thomas.

Cross King Street and enter the 19th-century garden. It has a cast-iron drinking fountain for people, horses, and dogs, and neatly trimmed flowerbeds filled with seasonal blooms. If you like, rest on a bench while you admire the handsome proportions of St. Lawrence Hall and listen to the chimes of:

11. St. **James Cathedral,** adjacent to the garden on the north side of King Street. This is one of my favorite places in Toronto, and you needn't be religious to appreciate it. The beautiful building and its surrounding park make a serene setting to rest and gather one's thoughts.

York's first church was built here from 1803 to 1807. Originally a frame building, it was enlarged in 1818 and 1819, and replaced in 1831. The second church burned in 1839, and the first cathedral was erected, only to be destroyed in the great fire of 1849. The present building was begun in 1850 and finished in 1874. It boasts the tallest steeple in Canada. Inside, at the northern end of the east aisle, there's a Tiffany window in memory of William Jarvis, one of Toronto's founding fathers.

St. James' first incumbent was the Rev. George O'Kill Stuart, who was succeeded by John Strachan (pronounced Strawn), later the first bishop of Toronto. Strachan wielded tremendous temporal as well as spiritual power. For 50 years, until his death in 1867, he was an indomitable spirit. He threatened the Americans with the vengeance of the British Navy after they occupied York (Toronto), defied the British prelates by keeping King's College open over their objections that the charter was too liberal, and dismissed Thomas Jefferson as "a mischief maker." He revered British institutions and abhorred anything Yankee.

From here, you can view one of the early retail store buildings, which were built when King Street was the main commercial street. **Nos. 129–35** were originally built as an Army and Navy Store, using cast iron, plate glass, and arched windows so that the shopper could see what was available in the store. Also note nos. 111 and 125. The **Toronto Sculpture Garden,** 115 King St. (☎ **416/ 485-9658**), is a quiet corner for contemplation.

☕ **WINDING DOWN**   From St. James, the venerable **Le Royal Meridien King Edward,** 37 King St. E. (☎ **416/863-9700**), is only a block away. You can stop for afternoon tea in the lounge, or light fare or lunch in the **Café Victoria.** Both **La Maquette,** 111 King St. E. (☎ **416/366-8191**), and **Biagio** (☎ **416/366-4040**), 157 King St. E., have appealing outdoor dining courtyards.

From St. James, go south on Church Street for 1 block and turn right into Colbourne Street. From Colbourne, turn left down Leader Lane to Wellington, where you can enjoy a fine view of the mural on the Flatiron Building and also of the rhythmic flow of mansard rooflines along the south side of Front Street.

Turn right and proceed to Yonge Street, then turn right and walk to King Street to catch the subway to your next destination.

Walking Tour 4: Chinatown & Kensington Market

This walk takes you through the oldest of Toronto's several Chinatowns. The original Chinatown was on York Street between King and Queen streets, but it has long since been replaced by skyscrapers. Although today there are at least four Chinatowns and most Chinese live in the suburbs, the intersection of Dundas Street and Spadina Avenue is still a major shopping and dining area for the Asian community. As a new wave of Asian immigrants has arrived from Southeast Asian countries—Thailand and Vietnam in particular—this old, original Chinatown has taken them in. Today, many businesses are Vietnamese or Thai.

Successive waves of immigration have also changed the face of the nearby Kensington Market. From the turn of the century until the 1950s, it was the heart of the Jewish community before the population dispersed to the suburbs. In the 1950s, Portuguese immigrants arrived to work in the food-processing and meatpacking industries and made it their home. In the '60s, a Caribbean presence was established. Today traces of all these communities remain in the vibrant life of the market.

Start: Osgoode subway station.
Finish: Toronto Public Reference Library and Queen's Park subway station.
Time: At least 2 hours. Depending on how long you want to linger at the Art Gallery of Ontario and at various stops, perhaps as long as 8 hours.
Best Times: Tuesday to Saturday during the day.
Worst Times: Sunday, when many of the stores in Kensington Market close, and Monday, when the Art Gallery is closed.

From the Osgoode subway station, exit on the northwest corner of Queen Street and University Avenue, and walk west on Queen Street. Turn right onto McCaul Street. If you're interested in crafts, you'll want to stop at 52 McCaul St., on the left side of the street, the:

1. **Prime Gallery.** It sells ceramics, jewelry, fabrics, and other art objects crafted by contemporary artisans.

On the right is:

2. **Village by the Grange,** an apartment and shopping complex that's laid out in a series of courtyards (one even contains a small ice-skating rink). Go into the complex at the southern end and stroll through, emerging from the food market. En route you'll come across some small fashion boutiques and **18 Karat**

(☎ **416/593-1648**), where the proprietors design and create jewelry behind the counter. Show them what you have in mind, and they will craft it for you beautifully.

☕ **TAKE A BREAK**   Also in Village by the Grange is one of the city's oldest and most popular Chinese restaurant, **Sun Lok** (☎ **416/593-8808**). The **Food Market** contains stalls that sell everything—12 varieties of freshly brewed coffee, schnitzels, satay, Japanese noodles, salads, falafel, hot dogs, Chinese food, kebabs, pizza, and fried chicken.

Exit at McCaul Street and turn right to continue walking north. You'll pass the Ontario College of Art on the other side of the street. At Dundas Street, you'll encounter a large Henry Moore sculpture, *Large Two Forms,* which describes precisely what it is.

Turn left onto Dundas Street. On the left is the entrance to the:

3. **Art Gallery of Ontario.** If you don't want to go in to see the collections, you can browse the gallery stores without paying admission. The wonderful restaurant, **Agora** (see chapter 5), is open for lunch.

Cross to the north side of Dundas Street, opposite the Art Gallery. A worthwhile stop is:

4. **Bau-Xi,** 340 Dundas St. W. (☎ **416/977-0600**), a gallery representing modern Canadian artists. From here, continue to Beverley and turn right. Walk to Baldwin Street, a short street containing so many ethnic restaurants that you can practically dine around the world, from China and Japan to France and Mexico. On the corner of Baldwin and Beverley streets is the:

5. **George Brown House,** 50 Baldwin St. This is the home of the founder of the reform newspaper, the *Globe* (1844), and a prominent politician. Brown's house, built in 1877, had a notable modern feature—a shower.

Backtrack to Dundas Street and turn right. You're now walking into the heart of Chinatown, with its abundance of grocery stores, bakeries, bookstalls, and emporiums selling foods, handcrafts, and other items from Asia.

What follows are some of my favorite browsing stops along the stretch of Dundas Street between Beverley Street and Spadina Avenue. On the south or left side as you go west is:

6. **Tai Sun Co.,** nos. 407–09, a supermarket displaying dozens of different mushrooms, all clearly labeled in English, as well as fresh Chinese vegetables, meats, fish, and canned goods. **Melewa Bakery,** no. 433, has a wide selection of pastries, like mung-bean and lotus-paste buns. Outside **Kiu Shun Trading,** no. 441, dried fish are on display; inside you'll find numerous varieties of ginseng and such miracle remedies as "Stop Smoking Tea" and delicacies such as swallows' nests.

On the north side of the street are:

7. **J & S Arts and Crafts,** no. 430. This is a good place to pick up souvenirs, including kimonos and happy coats, kung-fu suits, address books, cushion covers, and all-cotton Chinatown T-shirts. **Kim Moon,** no. 438, is an Asian bakery that features almond cookies, deep-fried taro pastries, and dim sum pork buns.

At the corner of Huron Street, on the north side of Dundas Street, is:

8. **Ten Ren Tea,** no. 454, which sells all kinds of tea—black, oolong, and so forth—stored in large canisters in the back of the store. Charming small ceramic teapots are priced from C$25 to $75 (US$17 to $51). You will probably be asked to sample some tea in a tiny cup. The large variety of gnarled ginseng root on display is

Walking Tour—Chinatown & Kensington Market

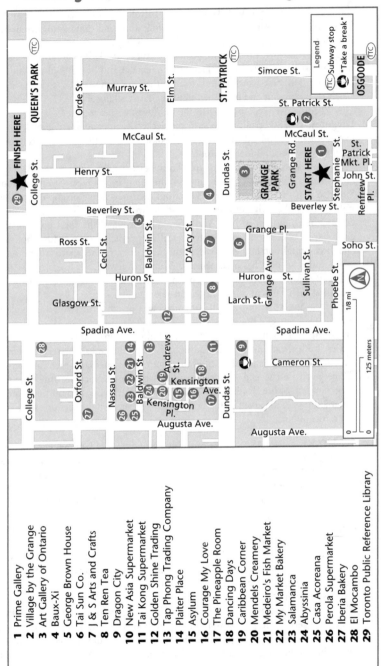

1 Prime Gallery
2 Village by the Grange
3 Art Gallery of Ontario
4 Baux-Xi
5 George Brown House
6 Tai Sun Co.
7 J & S Arts and Crafts
8 Ten Ren Tea
9 Dragon City
10 New Asia Supermarket
11 Tai Kong Supermarket
12 Golden Shine Trading
13 Tap Phong Trading Company
14 Plaiter Place
15 Asylum
16 Courage My Love
17 The Pineapple Room
18 Dancing Days
19 Caribbean Corner
20 Mendels Creamery
21 Medeiro's Fish Market
22 My Market Bakery
23 Salamanca
24 Abyssinia
25 Casa Acoreana
26 Perola Supermarket
27 Iberia Bakery
28 El Mocambo
29 Toronto Public Reference Library

also for sale. Next door, **W Y Trading Co., Inc.,** has a great selection of records, CDs, and tapes—everything from Chinese folk songs and cantatas to current hit albums from Hong Kong and Taiwan. This is one place a non-Chinese-speaking visitor can read what the recording contains. At no. 482A, **Po Chi Tong** is a fun store that sells exotic remedies, like deer-tail extract and liquid-gold ginseng or royal jelly. The best remedy of all time is the "slimming tea." Watch the staff weigh each item out and total the bill with a fast-clicking abacus.

At Spadina Avenue, cross over to the southwest corner to:

9. **Dragon City,** 280 Spadina Ave., a triple-decker Asian shopping complex complete with a food court. Here you'll find books, music, clothing, toys, and homeopathic remedies all under one roof.

Spadina Avenue is the widest street in the city because the wealthy Baldwin family had a 132-foot swath cut through the forest from Queen Street to Bloor Street so that they could view the lake from their new home on top of Spadina Hill. Later, in the early 20th century, Spadina Avenue became Toronto's garment center (the equivalent of New York's Seventh Ave.) and the focal point of the city's Jewish community. Although it's still the garment center, with wholesale and discount fashion houses, as well as the fur district (farther south around Adelaide), today Spadina has become more Asian than Jewish.

If you enjoy strolling through supermarkets filled with exotic Asian delights, including such fruits as durian in season, then go into the:

10. **New Asia Supermarket,** 293–97 Spadina Ave., or cross the street and explore the:

11. **Tai Kong Supermarket.** Look at all the different provisions—chili and fish sauces, fresh meat and fish (including live tilapia in tanks), preserved plums, chrysanthemum tea and other infusions, moon cakes, and large sacks of rice.

12. While you'll find several wholesalers on this block, one local favorite is at no. 349: **Golden Shine Trading** (☎ **416/979-7755**) boasts fashion accessories, ceramics, toys, and carved statuettes, but unlike many wholesalers this store will sell to the public.

☕ **TAKE A BREAK**   You're probably getting hungry by now. For fine and reasonably priced food, a Chinatown favorite is **Happy Seven,** 358 Spadina Ave. (☎ **416/971-9820;** see chapter 5). If you don't mind lining up, head for the ever-popular **Lee Garden,** 331 Spadina Ave. (☎ **416/593-9524;** see chapter 5). For speedy service, check out **Co Yen,** 334 Spadina Ave. (☎ **416/597-1573**), a Vietnamese takeout spot (there are no seats). Continuing north, cross St. Andrews Street.

13. **Tap Phong Trading Company,** 360 Spadina Ave., has terrific wicker baskets of all shapes and sizes, as well as woks and ceramic cookware; heavy, attractive mortars and pestles; and other household items.

Cross Baldwin Street and you'll come to:

14. **Plaiter Place,** 384 Spadina Ave., which has a huge selection of finely crafted wicker baskets, birdcages, woven blinds, bamboo steamers, hats, and other fun items. **Fortune Housewares,** no. 388, carries kitchen and household items—including all the good brand names—for at least 20% off prices elsewhere in the city.

Now double back to St. Andrews Street. Turn right onto St. Andrews and note the synagogue on the north side of the street.

Walk along St. Andrews to Kensington Avenue and turn right. You'll be in the heart of the **Kensington Market** area, which has always reflected the city's current ethnic scene. Once it was primarily a Jewish market; later it became more Portuguese; today, it is a blend of Portuguese, Jewish, Caribbean, and Asian.

You'll end up walking the length of Kensington Avenue, and I would suggest turning left first. This block has the greatest concentration of vintage clothiers in the city.

15. At 42 Kensington Ave., on the west side of the street, you'll seek Asylum (see chapter 8), which has good jeans as well as party frocks.

16. Courage My Love, no. 14 (see chapter 8), has the loveliest, wackiest dresses, all very reasonably priced.

17. The Pineapple Room, no. 2, stocks classic cocktail shakers and other doodads among the clothes.

18. Dancing Days, no. 17 (on the east side of the street), has party-ready glad rags that will make you look like an extra in *Grease!*.

Walk north on Kensington Avenue. There are several West Indian grocery stores on this street, including:

19. Caribbean Corner, 171 Baldwin St. (☎ **416/593-0008**), on the east side of the street. It sells such items as plantains, yuca, sugarcane, papaya, mangoes, and other tropical products.

On the west side is:

20. Mendels Creamery, at no. 72, sells smoked fish, herring, cheeses, and fine dill pickles. Another door down, **Global Cheese** offers an enormous selection at good prices.

Continue along Kensington Avenue to Baldwin Street, another prime food-shopping street. On the opposite side of Baldwin, you'll find:

21. Medeiro's Fish Market, Seven Seas, and Coral Sea. At these and other fish stores on the north side of the street, folks buy their supplies of salt cod.

Nearby, stick your nose in the air and sniff the comforting aromas wafting from:

22. My Market Bakery, 172 Baldwin St. (☎ **416/593-6772**), and the **Baldwin Street Bakery,** 173 Baldwin St. (☎ **416/971-5860**), which will doubtless lure you in to buy some bread. Focaccia, sourdough—you name it, they have it.

From here to the corner, small shops like:

23. Salamanca line the street. They sell an array of nuts, fruits, and grains. Pick up some dried papaya, mango, pineapple, or apricots as a snack.

On the south side of Baldwin, you'll pass:

24. Abyssinia, which specializes in African and West Indian products; and **Patty King,** which stocks Jamaican breads and other West Indian goods, including roti, bread pudding, and tamarind balls. Several **seafood stores** display what looks like an infinite variety of fresh fish and salted cod piled in boxes on the sidewalk; and the **Royal Food Centre** sells a variety of Jamaican specialties, including goat.

At the corner of Augusta Avenue and Baldwin Street is:

25. Casa Acoreana, (no. 235) an old-fashioned store that stocks a full range of fresh coffees, as well as great pecans and filberts. Just up the block at no. 214 is the **Alvand Food Mart** (☎ **416/597-2252**), which specializes in Middle Eastern foods and stocks imported goods from the region.

At the end of Baldwin, turn right onto Augusta Avenue into the heart of the old Portuguese neighborhood. In addition to the discount and used-clothing emporiums on the west side of the street, there are several Latino stores, such as:

26. Perola Supermarket, 247 Augusta Ave., which displays cassava and strings of peppers—ancho, arbol, pasilla—hung up to dry and sitting in bins, plus more exotic fruits and herbs. **Emporium Latino,** which sells cactus leaves, yuca, and chilies, among many other Latin American items, is part of Perola Super.

Cross Nassau Street to get to one of the Portuguese establishments:

27. Iberica Bakery, 279 Augusta Ave.—where you can enjoy coffee and pastries at a handful of tables—is on the east side of the street. It represents one of the few remaining traces of the Portuguese presence in the Kensington Market area, along with the Portuguese church over on Nassau Street and the Portuguese radio station around the corner on Oxford Street.

Turn right onto Oxford Avenue and walk to Spadina Avenue. Turn left and walk 1 block to reach:

28. El Mocambo, the rock-and-roll landmark where the Rolling Stones played on March 4 and 5, 1977. Now hop on the streetcar that runs east along College Street to the subway. (You can also continue on foot, but it's not an especially exciting area.) On the left (north) side of the street, you'll pass what used to be the:

29. Toronto Public Reference Library, an attractive classical revival building now occupied by the University of Toronto bookstore and Koffler Student Centre. On the south corner of College Street and University Avenue, you'll see the weird-looking mirrored-glass **Hydro Place.**

The streetcar will carry you to the Queen's Park subway station. The southbound train will take you back downtown.

Shopping

Shopping in Toronto can be a schizophrenic experience. The hautest international retailers like Armani, Chanel, Vuitton, and Tiffany compete for attention with discount emporiums like Honest Ed's. Megastores dominate the landscape, yet boutiques are blossoming. And while foreign chains stake their claim in shopping arcades and malls, they stand in close proximity to homegrown talent.

The result of this chaos is a cornucopia of shops that fit a wide range of budgets and tastes. The bad news: While window-shopping is a laudable pastime in Toronto, don't fool yourself that it will stop there. Just don't break the bank.

1 The Shopping Scene

While you may want to check out the impressive array of international retailers, it would be a mistake to overlook the homegrown talent. If your passion is fashion, do check out designers like Lida Baday, Ross Mayer, Misura by Joeffer Caoc, Linda Lundstrom, Crystal Siemens, and Frette by Michelle Secours.

Toronto also has a bustling arts and crafts community, with many art galleries, custom jewelers, and artisans. Some of the best buys are on native and Inuit art. Artwork can be imported into the United States duty-free.

Stores usually open at around 10am from Monday to Saturday, and closing hours change depending on the day. From Monday to Wednesday, most stores close at 6pm; on Thursday and Friday, hours run to 8pm or 9pm; on Saturdays, closings are quite early, usually around 6pm. Most stores are open on Sunday, though the hours may be restricted—11am or noon to 5pm is not unusual.

Almost everyone accepts MasterCard and Visa, and a growing number take American Express. U.S. cash is generally welcomed, and the exchange rate is a favorable one, especially downtown in the Eaton Centre area.

2 Great Shopping Areas

BLOOR STREET WEST This strip of real estate, bordered by Yonge Street to the east and Avenue Road to the west, is where most of the top international names in fashion set up shop in Toronto. If you're in the mood to see what Karl Lagerfeld is designing these days or have a whim to pick up some glittering bauble from Cartier or Tiffany, this is your hunting ground.

YORKVILLE   A far cry from its days as a hippie hangout and commune in the 1960s, this is now one of Toronto's best known—and most expensive—shopping neighborhoods. The streets are crisscrossed by little alleyways, giving Yorkville a romantic, old-fashioned appeal. The shops here tend to be small boutiques that specialize, say in beaded handbags or in fine handmade papers. Bistros and cafes abound, giving rise to Yorkville's other pastime: people-watching.

QUEEN STREET WEST   Grittier than its uptown siblings, Queen West between University and Spadina avenues is rich with cutting-edge design in both fashion and housewares. Locals will complain that this neighborhood isn't what it used to be before The Gap moved in, but it's still a great stomping ground for fashionistas in need of a fix.

THE EATON CENTRE   Okay, you're short on time, but you still want to fit in all your shopping. Where else can you go but the Eaton Centre? With more than 300 shops, including Tower Records, Browns, Danier, Nine West, La Vie en Rose, The Bombay Company, Eddie Bauer, Banana Republic, and Indigo, you'll be sure to find something. Just don't forget to step outside—local retailer Sam the Record Man is just up the street.

THE UNDERGROUND CITY   Subterranean Toronto is a hive of shopping activity. While you won't find too many shops down here that don't have an above-ground location, the Underground City is a popular place in winter, and with those whose schedules don't allow them out of the Financial District.

CHINATOWN   It's crowded and it's noisy, but don't let that put you off. Sure, there's the usual touristy junk, like cheapo plastic toys and jewelry, but the real China-town has a lot more to offer, including fine rosewood furniture, exquisite ceramics, and homeopathic herbs. Just don't try driving here: This is traffic purgatory, and is best navigated on foot.

3 Shopping A to Z

ANTIQUES

Toronto's antiques scene has exploded. Throw a stone in any direction and you're bound to hit an Edwardian console, or at least a classic Eames chair. For fine antiques, head north from Bloor Street along Avenue Road until you reach Davenport Avenue, or walk north on Yonge Street from the Rosedale subway station to St. Clair Avenue. Another top area is Mount Pleasant Road from St. Clair Avenue to Eglinton Avenue. For less pricey finds, head west on Queen Street to the Bathurst Street area. Merchandise at the Harbourfront Antique Market varies widely in quality and price.

At Home. 1156 Yonge St. ☎ **416/924-6590.** Subway: Summerhill.

An inviting, airy room filled with a mix of formal and rustic pieces. Many of the wrought-iron furnishings started out as garden furniture. There are also French decorative items, like the 19th-century candlestick lamps.

Belle Epoque. 1066 Yonge St. ☎ **416/925-0066.** Subway: Summerhill.

If you're feeling pretty and looking for furniture to match, this attic-like shop is worth a look. The furnishings are luxurious, and some pieces would not be out of place at Versailles, gilt and all. Some reproductions are mixed in with the real articles.

Bernardi's Antiques. 699 Mount Pleasant Rd. (south of Eglinton Ave). ☎ **416/483-6471.** www.bernardisantiques.com. Subway: Eglinton, then no. 34 bus to Mount Pleasant, and walk 1 block south.

The tiny showroom is jam-packed with furniture, silver flatware, paintings, bronzes, and carpets. Discontinued Royal Doulton figurines are a specialty.

Constantine. 112 Avenue Rd. ☎ **416/929-1177.** Subway: Bay or Museum.

A favorite of Toronto's decorating cognoscenti, this dimly lit, close-packed shop is in a Victorian building. It's stocked with imposing wood furniture and delicate baubles. Be sure to check out the selection of finely wrought light fixtures and gilt-trimmed glassware.

Decorum Decorative Finds. 1210 Yonge St. ☎ **416/966-6829.** Subway: Summerhill.

If you're going on an ocean voyage, can you resist a C$2,200 (US$1,500) vintage Louis Vuitton trunk? The wares here range from tables and chaise lounges to oil paintings and old books. All are top priced, but also top of the line.

Harbourfront Antique Market. 390 Queen's Quay W. ☎ **416/260-2626.** www.hfam. com. Subway: Union, then LRT to Rees St.

Renowned for its top-quality antiques, the market has its share of attic-worthy junk, too. With more than 100 dealers, what else would you expect? The variety is intriguing: furniture, glassware, art, silver, and jewelry dating back just a decade or as much as a century. Throughout the summer, itinerant dealers set up shop outside. Year-round, serious shoppers start early, but if you're looking for a bargain, start bidding just before closing time. The market is open 10am to 6pm Tuesday to Sunday.

Horsefeathers! 630 Mount Pleasant Rd. ☎ **416/486-4555.** Subway: Eglinton, then no. 34 bus to Mount Pleasant.

If your taste runs to English and French country house styles, this emporium's for you. Striking wooden pieces in walnut and mahogany share the spotlight with tapestries and Persian carpets.

✪ **L'Atelier.** 1224 Yonge St. ☎ **416/966-0200.** Subway: Summerhill.

This is about as glamorous as it gets. Napoleon III side tables share space with chrome bar stools and rococo Italian lamps. Many of the price tags hit four digits, but there are lovely accoutrements for as little as C$10 (US$6.80).

Mark McLaine Collection. Hazelton Lanes, 55 Avenue Rd. ☎ **416/927-7972.** Subway: Bay.

This shop features styles as diverse as art deco and chinoiserie (a blend of Asian and French design). Many of the furnishings, carvings, and jewelry are the real McCoy, though some fabulous fakes have worked their way into the mix, too.

Michel Taschereau Antiques. 176 Cumberland St. ☎ **416/923-3020.** Subway: Bay.

In business since 1955, this attic-like shop is filled with 18th-, 19th-, and early 20th-century pieces from England, France, and North America. There's also a collection of decorative glass objects, Asian porcelain, and prints.

Mostly Movables Inc. 785 Queen St. W. (west of Bathurst St.). ☎ **416/504-4455**. Subway: Osgoode, then any streetcar west to Euclid Ave.

Turn-of-the-century Canadiana and English Jazz Age furnishings fill this shop. The pieces are generally in fine form, and the prices are somewhat lower than those at many Yorkville and Rosedale competitors.

✪ **Putti.** 1104 Yonge St. ☎ **416/972-7652**. Subway: Summerhill.

Two generously portioned rooms are filled with European treasures old and new: dining sets, armoires, cushions, and china. This shop has been featured repeatedly in *Victoria* magazine.

Quasi-Modo. 789 Queen St. W. ☎ **416/366-8370**. Subway: Osgoode.

This shop defines *eclectic*. It runs the gamut of 20th-century design, favoring all things streamlined. Perennially on display are Noguchi paper lamps and Eames shelving units; there are also contemporary tables by Canadian designer Martha Sturdy.

Showcase Antique Mall. 610 Queen St. W. ☎ **416/703-6255**. Subway: Osgoode, then any streetcar west to Bathurst St.

Spanning four floors, this unusual mall has more than 300 dealers. There is no shortage of transferware, fine china, and jewelry (costume and real) among the collection of pop culture and rock memorabilia.

Whim Antiques. 561 Mount Pleasant Rd. ☎ **416/481-4474**. Subway: St. Clair, then Mount Pleasant bus to Belsize Ave.

The store is aptly named—whimsical it is. It's filled with beautiful baubles, silverware, and decorative *objets*, and walking through it feels rather like being let loose in great-grandma's attic.

Zig Zag. 1107 Queen St. E. ☎ **416/778-6495**. Subway: Queen, then any streetcar east to Pape Ave.

This shop carries a mélange of styles, but the specialty is early Modernist pieces. The names to watch out for are Eames, Saarinen, Arne Jacobsen, and Warren Platner. There are some bargains, with excellent pieces in the C$200 to $400 (US$136 to $272) range, with a few stellar finds that run as high as C$3,500 (US$2,380).

ART

Bau-Xi. 340 Dundas St. W. ☎ **416/977-0600**. Subway: St. Patrick.

After viewing the masterworks at the Art Gallery of Ontario, you can head across the street and buy your own. A West Coast native founded Bau-Xi, which features works by many artists from that region, with a few from Ontario in the mix.

Bay of Spirits Gallery. 156 Front St. W. ☎ **416/971-5190**. Subway: Union.

Here you'll find works by native Indians from across Canada. Most of the collection focuses on the art of the Pacific Northwest, including totem poles, masks, prints, and jewelry.

Eskimo Art Gallery. 12 Queens' Quay W. (opposite Westin Harbour Castle). ☎ **416/366-3000**. Subway: Union, then LRT to Queen's Quay.

This award-winning gallery has the largest collection of Inuit sculpture in Toronto. At any given time, it shows more than 500 pieces, with prices ranging from C$16 to $14,500 (US$10.90 to $9,860).

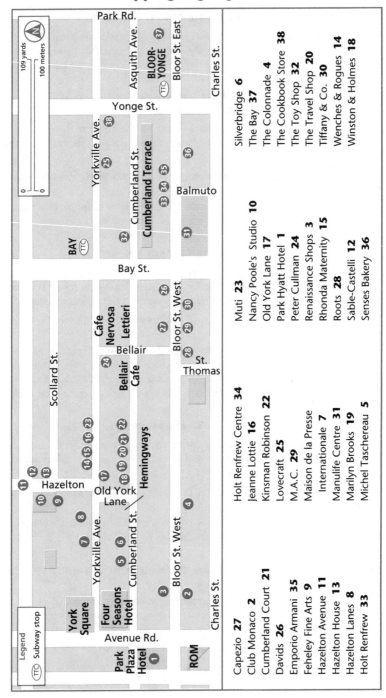

Capezio **27**
Club Monaco **2**
Cumberland Court **21**
Davids **26**
Emporio Armani **35**
Feheley Fine Arts **9**
Hazelton Avenue **11**
Hazelton House **13**
Hazelton Lanes **8**
Holt Renfrew **33**

Holt Renfrew Centre **34**
Jeanne Lottie **16**
Kinsman Robinson **22**
Lovecraft **25**
M.A.C. **29**
Maison de la Presse
  Internationale **7**
Manulife Centre **31**
Marilyn Brooks **19**
Michel Taschereau **5**

Muti **23**
Nancy Poole's Studio **10**
Old York Lane **17**
Park Hyatt Hotel **1**
Peter Cullman **24**
Renaissance Shops **3**
Rhonda Maternity **15**
Roots **28**
Sable-Castelli **12**
Senses Bakery **36**

Silverbridge **6**
The Bay **37**
The Colonnade **4**
The Cookbook Store **38**
The Toy Shop **32**
The Travel Shop **20**
Tiffany & Co. **30**
Wenches & Rogues **14**
Winston & Holmes **18**

Feheley Fine Arts. 14 Hazelton Ave. ☎ **416/323-1373.** Subway: Bay.

The Feheleys personally select every piece in their gallery, making this one of the most individualized collections of contemporary Inuit art anywhere. To commemorate the creation of the new Inuit-governed territory of Nunavut in 1999, the gallery has special exhibitions to highlight the diversity of Inuit art.

Gallery Moos. 622 Richmond St. W. ☎ **416/504-5445.** Subway: Osgoode, then any streetcar west to Bathurst St., and walk 1 block south.

German native Walter Moos has been a fixture on the Toronto art scene for 30 years. His gallery features top Canadian artists as well as an assortment of international figures.

✪ **Isaacs/Innuit Gallery.** 9 Prince Arthur Ave. ☎ **416/921-9985.** www.novator.com/ isaacs-innuit. Subway: Bay or St. George.

This is one of the finest galleries in the city. Top-quality Inuit sculpture, prints, drawings, and wall hangings are displayed with panache; the exhibitions change every six weeks. There is also an extensive collection of Native Canadian antiquities.

Jane Corkin Gallery. 179 John St. ☎ **416/979-1980.** Subway: Osgoode.

Most of the works here are historical and contemporary photographs from artists around the world. They include works by Cylla von Tiedemann, Irving Penn, and Herb Ritts. There is also a small collection of modernist painting and sculpture.

Kinsman Robinson. 108 Cumberland St. ☎ **800/895-4278** or 416/895-4278. Subway: Bay.

The two stories of this Yorkville gallery display 20th-century figurative paintings, sculpture, and drawings. Artists represented include Stanley Cosgrove, Robert Katz, Esther Wertheimer, and Donald Liardi. Native Canadians Robert Davidson and Norval Morrisseau also exhibit their work here. There are a few paperworks by Zuniga, Braque, and Chagall, among others.

Nancy Poole's Studio. 16 Hazelton Ave. ☎ **416/964-9050.** Subway: Bay.

This intimate gallery of painting and sculpture has been in business for three decades. Most of the art is contemporary, much of it Canadian in origin. The gallery launches solo exhibitions every three weeks.

Olga Korper Gallery. 17 Morrow Ave. (off Dundas St. W.). ☎ **416/538-8220.** Subway: Dundas West.

Established in 1973, this gallery houses contemporary Canadian and international works. Artists represented include Averbuch, John Brown, Sankawa, and the estate of Louis Comtois.

Ontario College of Art & Design Gallery. 291 Dundas St. W. ☎ **416/977-6000.** Subway: St. Patrick.

If you're interested in the work of an emerging generation of artists, check out the ongoing exhibitions at the OCAD. Students display sculpture, photography, and painting, as well as multimedia installations.

Sable-Castelli. 33 Hazelton Ave. ☎ **416/961-0011.** Subway: Bay.

This highly regarded gallery has been in business for a quarter century. It represents contemporary American and Canadian artists, including heavy hitters like Warhol and Oldenburg.

Shopping Highlights—Queen Street West

Bamboo **6**
Browns **12**
CityTV **2**
David Mason **7**
Du Verre Glass **4**
Lush **5**
Lynn Robinson **16**
Modrobes **8**
Mostly Moveables, Inc. **17**
Native Stone Art **1**
Osmosis Everyday
  Aromatherapy **10**
Preloved **13**
Price Roman **3**
Quasi Modo **18**
Record Peddler **14**
Showcase Antique Mall **15**
Stephen Bulger Gallery **19**
Stephen Temple Books **11**
The Silver Snail **9**

Ossington Ave.
Givins St.
Shaw St.
Crawford St.
Crawford St.
Massey St.
Trinity Dr.
Strachan Ave.
TRINITY BELLWOODS PARK
Stafford St.
Gorevale Ave.
Queen St.
Crocker Ave.
Bellwood Ave.
Dundas St. W.
Walnut Ave.
Niagara St.
Adelaide St.
Richmond St. W.
Robinson St.
Claremont St.
Manning St.
Euclid St.
Palmerston Ave.
Tecumseth St.
Wolseley St.
Markham St.
Mitchell St.
Bathhurst St.
ALEXANDRA PARK
Bathhurst St.
Toronto Western Hospital
Portland St.
Ryerson Ave.
Maud St.
Denison Ave.
King St.
Augusta Ave.
Brenner Blvd.
Camden St.
Vanauley St.
Cameron St.
Spadina Ave.
Peter St.
Huron St.
Sky Dome
Front St.
Phoebe St.
Dundas St. W.
D'Arcy St.
Beverly St.
John St.
McCaul St.
Nelson St.
Duncan St.
Queen St.
St. Patrick St.
Simcoe St.
University St.
Richmond St. W.
Chestnut St.
York St.
City Hall
Elizabeth St.
Barnaby Pl.
Brenner Blvd.
Union Station
Sheppard
Bay St.
Bay St.
0   1/4 mi
0   .25 km
N
Yonge St.
Legend
"Take a break"

✪ **Sandra Ainsley.** 2 First Canadian Place. ☎ **416/362-4480.** Subway: St. Andrew.

Specializing in glass sculpture, this renowned gallery represents more than 50 artists from across North America, including Dale Chihuly, Tom Scoon, and Susan Edgerley. The one-of-a-kind pieces have big price tags, but there are also some affordable items, such as paperweights, vases, and jewelry.

Stephen Bulger Gallery. 700 Queen St. W. (west of Bathurst St.). ☎ **416/504-0575.** Subway: Osgoode, then any streetcar west to Palmerston Ave.

This gallery displays contemporary Canadian and international photography, usually with a social commentary slant.

Susan Hobbs Gallery. 137 Tecumseth St. (at King St.) ☎ **416/504-3699.** Subway: St. Andrew, then any streetcar west to Tecumseth St.

This small gallery, in an unprepossessing warehouse far from the Yorkville crowd, is a major player in Canadian contemporary art. Hobbs represents 11 of Toronto's best artists, including Ian Carr-Harris, Shirley Wiitasalo, Robin Collyer, and Sandra Meigs.

Ydessa Hendeles Art Foundation. 778 King St. W. ☎ **416/413-9400.** Subway: St. Andrew, then any streetcar west to Bathurst St.

This is one of the most interesting contemporary art collections in the city. Hendeles features installations by international artists. Works on display include paintings, photography, and multimedia projects.

AUDIO-VISUAL & ELECTRONIC GOODS

Bay-Bloor Radio. Manulife Centre, 55 Bloor St. W. ☎ **416/967-1122.** Subway: Bay.

This 13,000-square-foot store carries all the latest and greatest audio equipment, from portable units to in-home theater systems.

Canadian Tire. 839 Yonge St. ☎ **416/925-9595.** Subway: Yonge/Bloor.

This is handyman heaven. The endless aisles overflow with gadgets for home, yard, office, car, and any place in between. This is where I head as Father's Day approaches.

Henry's. 119 Church St. ☎ **416/868-0872.** Subway: Queen.

This bi-level shop deals in analog and digital photography. The first floor has electronic equipment, darkroom supplies, and a photo processing lab. Upstairs, there's a wide selection of secondhand cameras and gear.

Spy Tech. 2028 Yonge St. ☎ **416/482-9938.** Subway: Davisville.

James Bond wannabes, welcome. Entering Spy Tech is like having a free pass to Q's lab. Looking for a gadget to modify your telephone voice or a spook-worthy camera? You'll find it all here, though the price tags do get a little steep—all the way up to C$100,000 (US$68,000) for a bulletproof car.

BOOKS

Another Man's Poison. 29 McCaul St. (just north of Queen St.). ☎ **416/593-6451.** Subway: Osgoode.

This shop boasts an international collection of books about graphic arts, interior design, and architecture. Anything you can't find on the shelves can be special ordered. There's also a substantial selection of out-of-print titles.

Atticus Books. 84 Harbord St. ☎ **416/922-6045.** Subway: Spadina, then walk south.

Bookworms can while away hours in this crowded shop filled with secondhand scholarly tomes. There are many volumes of philosophy, psychology, and psychoanalysis. Antiquarian books and illuminated manuscripts are at the back of the store.

Ballenford Books on Architecture. 600 Markham St. (south of Bloor St. W.) ☎ **416/ 588-0800.** Subway: Bathurst.

Interior designers, whether amateur or pro, will love this well-arranged store. There are books covering everything from antique furniture to architectural theory, from urban design to landscaping. The shop also displays sketches and drawings by local architects.

Bob Miller Book Room. 180 Bloor St. W., lower concourse. ☎ **416/922-3557.** Subway: St. George.

When I was a student at the University of Toronto, I would come into this academic bookstore looking for one text and end up browsing for ages. It stocks mainly literary fiction, humanities, and social sciences. Works in translation are carefully selected— these editions really *are* the best.

Book City. 501 Bloor St. W. ☎ **416/961-4496.** Subway: Bathurst.

All the books here are new, and many are discounted by 10% to 30%. There is also a good assortment of international magazines. Book City has branches at 1950 Queen St. E. (☎ **416/698-1444**) and 348 Danforth Ave. (☎ **416/469-9997**).

✪ **Chapters.** 110 Bloor St. W. ☎ **416/920-9299.** Subway: Bay.

While the scope of the Chapters store is monolithic, its user-friendly design nonetheless makes the place feel cozy. So cozy, in fact, that it's easy to while away hours loitering in the aisles. Eminently browse-worthy and well-stocked, Chapters boasts comfy chairs, a Starbucks café, and a host of free-of-charge special events. Celebrity authors Sophia Loren and Sarah, Duchess of York, had their Toronto engagements here. There are Chapters stores at 142 John St. (☎ **416/595-7349**) and 2400 Yonge St., just north of Eglinton (☎ **416/544-0625**). The stores are open late, usually 10 or 11pm on weeknights and midnight on weekends.

The Children's Book Store. 2532 Yonge St. (north of Eglinton Ave.). ☎ **416/480-0233.** Subway: Eglinton.

Stocked with every book, cassette, and video a kid could possibly want. Offerings are grouped by age, going up to early adolescence. On weekends there are author visits and other special events.

The Cookbook Store. 850 Yonge St. ☎ **416/920-2665.** Subway: Yonge/Bloor.

I call it food porn: lush, gooey close-ups of scallop ceviche and tiramisu. This store specializes in the kind of book that makes a gourmet's heart go pitter-patter. There are also tomes about wine, health, and restaurants.

David Mason. 342 Queen St. W. ☎ **416/598-1015.** Subway: Osgoode.

This charming used-book store is straight out of Dickens. There are large collections of books about art and travel, and a number of first editions of Canadian, American, and British works.

Glad Day Bookshop. 598A Yonge St., 2nd floor. ☎ **416/961-4161.** Subway: Wellesley.

This was the first gay-oriented bookstore in Canada, and it remains one of the best. The shelves hold a sizable collection of gay and lesbian fiction, biography, and history books, and the offerings have expanded to include magazines, videos, calendars, and cards.

✪ **Indigo Books Music & More.** 55 Bloor St. W. ☎ **416/925-3536.** Subway: Yonge/ Bloor or Bay.

While I'm partial to cubbyhole-like bookstores, I have to admit the Indigo is a serious draw. The Canadian-owned chain boasts an excellent selection of books, magazines, and videotapes. There are tables and chairs to encourage browsing, a café, and helpful staff. Best of all, there are special events almost daily. The store schedules author visits from the likes of Vikram Seth, live performances by luminaries like Diana Krall, and seminars about interior decorating, staying healthy, and even investing. There are also events for kids. The store is a favorite with night owls, as it's open until 11pm or midnight every day. There are locations at the Eaton Centre (☎ 416/591-3622) and at 2300 Yonge St., at Eglinton Avenue (☎ 416/544-0049).

✪ **Nicholas Hoare.** 45 Front St. E. ☎ 416/777-2665. Subway: Union.

This shop has the cozy feel of an English library, with hardwood floors, plush couches, and a fireplace. There's an extensive selection of Canadian and international fiction, as well as heavyweight art tomes and children's books.

Open Air Books & Maps. 25 Toronto St. ☎ 416/363-0719. Subway: King.

This shop caters to nature lovers and ecology buffs. It carries a vast assortment of travel guidebooks and maps.

Seekers Books. 509 Bloor St. W. ☎ 416/925-1982. Subway: Bathurst.

New and old books about Eastern religion, mysticism, meditation, and the occult are mixed on the shelves. The focus is definitely New Age, but you'll find general-interest fiction and nonfiction, too.

The Silver Snail. 367 Queen St. W. ☎ 416/593-0889. Subway: Osgoode.

Remember those comic books you read as a kid? Well, they're all here, with adult-oriented comics like the *Sandman* series. There is a sizable section of imported editions, and posters and movie memorabilia, too.

Smithbooks. Toronto Dominion Centre. ☎ 416/362-5967. Subway: King.

This general-interest bookstore stocks lots of best-sellers. There are also departments for food, travel, biography, and children's books. There are several locations scattered throughout the city.

Steven Temple Books. 489 Queen St. W., 2nd floor. ☎ 416/703-9908. Subway: Osgoode, then any streetcar west.

If you're looking for a rare first edition of a 19th- or 20th-century literary work in English, be sure to make an appointment at this shop. It also carries secondhand books about a variety of subjects.

Toronto Women's Bookstore. 73 Harbord St. ☎ 416/922-8744. Subway: Spadina, then walk south.

This small but well-stocked shop carries books on feminist literary and social criticism, fiction by female writers, titles about lesbian issues, and books by women of color.

The World's Biggest Bookstore. 20 Edward St. ☎ 416/977-7009. Subway: Dundas.

The debate about whether the World's Biggest is *really* the world's biggest rages on. Either way, the 17 miles of bookshelves do contain a good selection. Browsing is welcome, but be warned that the bright, bright lights are headache-inducing after a while. There are also software, video, and magazine departments; upstairs, tarot cards are on display in glass cabinets.

CHINA, SILVER & GLASS

Du Verre Glass. 280 Queen St. W. ☎ 416/593-0182. Subway: Osgoode.

The store name is a bit of a misnomer. Gorgeous glass works are on display, but they share this airy, open space with ceramics, wood and wrought-iron furniture, lamps, and candlesticks.

Muti. 88 Yorkville Ave. ☎ **416/969-0253.** Subway: Bay.

Murano glass designs and cheery ceramics from Italy dominate this store. Look a little closer and you'll find a few French tapestries and tablecloths, too.

✪ **William Ashley.** Manulife Centre, 55 Bloor St. W. ☎ **416/964-2900.** Subway: Bay.

The last word in luxe, whether it be fine china, crystal, or silver. All of the top manufacturers are represented, including Waterford, Baccarat, Christofle, Wedgewood, and Lenox. Even if you're not in a buying mood, the detailed displays are fascinating.

CRAFTS

✪ **The Algonquians Sweet Grass Gallery.** 668 Queen St. W. ☎ **416/703-1336.** Subway: Osgoode, then any streetcar west.

Ojibway-owned and -operated, this shop specializes in exquisitely made Native Canadian arts and crafts. The collection includes porcupine-quill jewelry, soapstone sculpture, Iroquois masks, prints, antique spearheads, and moccasins.

Arctic Canada. 207 Queen's Quay W. ☎ **416/203-7889.** Subway: Union, then LRT to Queen's Quay.

Here you'll find a wide range of arts and crafts, from soapstone carvings to jewelry and clothing, all hailing from the Arctic Circle. There's another branch at **Pearson International Airport, Terminal 2** (☎ **905/678-6064**).

Art Zone. 592 Markham St. (south of Bloor St. W.). ☎ **416/534-1892.** Subway: Bathurst.

Sisters Jane and Kathryn Irwin own and operate this gallery-like space. Their main medium is stained glass, and their style is colorful and modern. They also carry a limited number of glass gift items, including bowls, trays, masks, and jewelry.

Arts on King. 169 King St. E. ☎ **416/777-9617.** Subway: King.

This 10,000-square-foot complex consists of boutiques selling original art, folk crafts, and furniture. Connected to it is the Wagner Rosenbaum Gallery, which exhibits work by new and established Toronto artists every month.

Five Potters Studio. 131A Pears Ave. ☎ **416/924-6992.** Subway: St. George.

Phone ahead for an appointment, and once you're in the studio, you're free to watch the five ceramic artists—all women—at work. The pieces on display vary from functional earthenware to sculptural items. Prices range from C$15 to $300 (US$10.20 to $204).

Frida. 39 Front St. E. ☎ **416/366-3169.** Subway: Union.

Arts and crafts from Africa, Southeast Asia, and Latin America share space in this bi-level shop. It offers an assortment of colorful woven mats, clothes, carved statuettes, jewelry, and candelabras.

Lynn Robinson. 709 Queen St. W. ☎ **416/703-2467.** Subway: Osgoode, then any streetcar west to Bathurst St.

Robinson herself creates many of the bronze and raku (Japanese earthenware) objects on display. In addition to the sculpture and glass, wood, and clay pieces, you'll see objects by five jewelers working with precious metals. Visitors are often treated to the sight of a potter working near the entrance.

Native Stone Art. 4 McCaul St. (at Queen St. W.). ☎ **416/593-0924.** Subway: Osgoode.

This shop houses the creations of native Indian artisans from across North America. There are Mohawk and Iroquois carvings, Cree moccasins, and Zuni and Hopi jewelry. The quality is very high.

The Best Bargains

Maybe you can't get something for nothing . . . but the truth is that you can score some pretty fab finds on the cheap in Toronto. It's a treasure hunt of sorts, and the spoils are anything but certain, but when you find that perfect piece that's marked down to next-to-nothing, well, that just makes it all worthwhile. It's a well-kept secret that many Toronto retailers, including luxurious Holt Renfrew, have their own outlet shops. Here's my own little black book of favorite foraging grounds. Happy hunting!

✪ **Honest Ed's World Famous Shopping Centre.** 581 Bloor St. W. ☎ **416/537-2111**; Subway: Bathurst.

Ed's is a Toronto institution, framed with flashing red and yellow lights both outdoors *and* indoors. "Don't just stand there, buy something!" blurts out one brazen sign. This idiosyncratic store has a deal for you on everything from housewares to carpets, from clothing to sundries. Crazy-making as shopping here can be, the bargains are unbeatable—but be warned, the queues are, too.

Tom's Place. 190 Baldwin St. ☎ **416/596-0297.** Subway: Spadina, then LRT to Baldwin St.

After more than 40 years in business, Tom's Place looks sharper than ever. While the shop devotes an entire floor to ladies wear, the best buys here are in the men's department: You'll find brand-name merchandise by the likes of Armani and Valentino. Suits that cost C$495–$1,800 (US$337–$1,224) elsewhere ring up for C$299–$850 (US$203–$578) here, and stock is carried in sizes from 36 short to 50 tall.

Holt Renfrew Last Call. 370 Steeles Ave. W. ☎ **905/886-7444.** Subway: Finch, then Steeles West bus.

It might not be the best organized store you've laid eyes on, but what it lacks in tidiness it makes up for in bargains. The racks are laden with brand labels such as Donna Karan, Prada, and Versace, marked down to one-fifth of what they would normally cost. There have been rumors of Kate Spade handbags on sale here, but I have yet to arrive in time. May you have better luck.

Marilyn's. 130 Spadina Ave. ☎ **416/504-6777.** Subway: Spadina, then LRT to Queen St. W.

Here's a rare thing: knockdown prices paired with attentive service. The specialty is Canadian fashions for women, from sportswear to glamorous gowns. There are also in-store seminars about fashion-forward topics like traveling with just one suitcase.

Paris Samples. 101 Yorkville Ave. ☎ **416/926-0656.** Subway: Bay.

This store snaps up designers' samples and marks them down 20% to 75%. The clothes range from wool pants to velvet dresses to micro-miniskirts. *One caveat:* The sizes are all under 14, and many clothes come only in the smallest sizes.

Winner's. 57 Spadina Ave. ☎ **416/585-2052.** Subway: Spadina, then LRT to King St. W.

This chaotic store is worth the time it takes to sift through the haphazard racks—they do start out orderly in the morning, so try to go early. If you're patient, you may find designer clothes for men and women, and top-name togs for the kiddies. There's also an ever-changing selection of housewares, cookware, linens, toiletries, and toys.

✪ **Dixie Outlet Mall.** 1250 S. Service Rd., Mississauga. ☎ **905/278-7492.** Gardiner Expwy./Queen Elizabeth Way (QEW) west to Dixie Rd. exit. Turn left, follow Dixie Rd. south to S. Service Rd.

Ten minutes from Pearson International Airport is the answer to bargain-shoppers' prayers. It's hard to beat the Dixie Outlet Mall for number of bargains per square foot. There are more than 120 outlet shops here, so you're bound to find something. For clothing, check out Femme de Carriere, The Coat Club, The Kidz Store, and Jacob; for footwear, Bata Shoes and Pegabo; for housewares, The Bombay Company and Black & Decker; for underwear, La Vie en Rose and Warner's; and for candy, Laura Secord. There is also a Winner's department store on the premises.

Snow Lion Interiors. 575 Mount Pleasant Rd. ☎ **416/484-8859.** Subway: Davisville, then Mount Pleasant bus to Belsize Ave.

Specializing in handicrafts from Tibet, Snow Lion displays paintings, hand-knotted carpets, privacy screens, lamps, and silver jewelry. There is also a collection of Buddhist books and accessories.

DEPARTMENT STORES

Holt Renfrew. 50 Bloor St. W. ☎ **416/922-2333.** Subway: Yonge/Bloor.

Designers such as Donna Karan, Christian Lacroix, and Yves St. Laurent figure in Holt Renfrew's four levels of merchandise. The basement connects with an underground mall, and features a gourmet food department and a cafe.

The Hudson's Bay Company. 176 Yonge St. (at Queen St.). ☎ **416/861-9111.** Subway: Queen. Also at 2 Bloor St. E. (at Yonge St.). ☎ **416/972-3333.** Subway: Yonge/Bloor.

Started as a fur-trading business when the first French-speaking settlers came to Canada, the Bay boasts excellent selections of clothing and housewares. It has weekend sales every couple of weeks, though shoppers should be warned that winning the staff's attention requires patience. Besides the locations listed, there are others around the city.

FASHION

Also see the listings under "Shoes" and "Vintage Clothing," below.

CHILDREN'S

Kids Cats & Dogs. 508 Eglinton Ave. W. ☎ **416/484-1844.** Subway: Eglinton.

Not just for kids—the shop carries its signature T-shirts, pajamas, and sweats in sizes from infant to adult. Everything sports a cat or dog motif, including knapsacks and comforters.

Lovechild. 2523 Yonge St. ☎ **416/486-4746.** Subway: Eglinton

A favorite with tiny tots who are already developing fashion savvy, Lovechild offers a selection of groovy clothes in a rainbow of colors.

MEN'S & WOMEN'S

Club Monaco. 157 Bloor St. W. ☎ **416/591-8837.** Subway: Museum.

This is Club Monaco's flagship store in Toronto. It's an airy, high-ceilinged space filled with casual wear and sportswear, with a smattering of work-ready clothes. It also has its own accessories and makeup lines. There are 19 other outlets around the city, including 403 Queen St. W. (☎ **416/979-5633**).

Emporio Armani. 50 Bloor St. W. ☎ **416/703-5595.** Subway: Bay.

Clean, sleek lines are the sign of Armani—and this double-decker shop, divided into boutiques for women's apparel, men's clothes, and various accessories, showcases the designer's complete collections. This beautifully designed space is worth a look in itself.

George Bouridis. 193 Church St. ☎ **416/363-4868.** Subway: Dundas.

This is the place to go for top-notch custom-made clothing, including men's shirts, and women's blouses and dresses. Bouridis imports fabrics from England, France, and Germany, and has everything from high-grade cotton to the smoothest of silks at hand. A man's cotton shirt starts at C$130 (US$88.40) and takes 2 weeks (the store also accommodates rush requests in 1 week).

Irish Shop. 150 Bloor St. W. ☎ **416/922-9400.** Subway: Bay.

If you're yearning for the Emerald Isle, you'll welcome the sight of lace shawls, linens, fisherman's sweaters, and Celtic music, books, and decorations.

Modrobes. 329 Queen St. W. ☎ **416/340-1222.** Subway: Osgoode.

Renowned for its comfy, casual clothing, Canadian-owned Modrobes got its start when its founder, Steven Debus, was still in university. Debus designed "exam pants" —trousers so comfy you could spend a day writing exams in them without your bum going numb. Today the store's offerings include T-shirts, jackets, and hats.

Roots. Eaton Centre, 95A Bloor St. W. ☎ **416/323-3289.** Subway: Bay.

This is one Canadian retailer that Hollywood types love. The clothes are casual, from hooded sweats to fleece jackets, and there's a good selection of leather footwear. The slouchy Roots hat (available in red or black) is known far and wide. Don't overlook the tykes' department, which has the same stuff in tiny sizes. Other locations include the Eaton Centre (☎ **416/593-9640**).

✪ **Wenches & Rogues.** 110 Yorkville Ave. ☎ **416/920-8959.** Subway: Bay.

This upscale shop carries the latest and greatest in Canadian design for men and women. Featured labels include Misura by Joeffer Caoc, as well as up-and-coming talent from around the country.

X-Large. 170 Spadina Ave. ☎ **416/203-2123.** Subway: Spadina, then LRT to Queen St. W.

If you're baffled by current street-inspired trends—or longing to update your so-hip-it-hurts wardrobe—X-Large marks the spot. Glad rags from Haze, Mini, and Geek Boutique are in the mix, too.

MEN'S

Alan Cherry. Hazelton Lanes, 55 Avenue Rd. ☎ **416/923-9558.** Subway: Bay.

In addition to Cherry's own line of European-made clothes, this shop carries top-notch designer menswear. The clearance center at the back boasts some serious markdowns.

✪ **Harry Rosen.** 82 Bloor St. W. ☎ **416/972-0556.** Subway: Bay.

Designed like a mini department store, Harry Rosen carries the crème de la crème of menswear designers, including Hugo Boss, Brioni, and Versace. There's also a good selection of work-worthy footwear, and a famous "Great Wall of Shirts."

Moores. 100 Yonge St. ☎ **416/363-5442.** Subway: King.

There's something for everyone at this spacious shop. Most of the suits, sport coats, and dress pants are Canadian-made, and international designers like Oscar de la Renta are represented, too. Sizes run from extra short to extra tall and oversize. The prices tend to be reasonable, and bargains abound.

Rotman Hat Shop and Haberdasher. 345 Spadina Ave. ☎ **416/977-2806.** Subway: Spadina, then LRT to Baldwin St.

In business for more than 45 years, this shop is a reminder of Spadina's original Jewish community. Rotman's boasts a selection of top-quality headgear, including fedoras, tam-o'-shanters, and cool Kangol caps.

Thomas K.T. Chui. 754 Broadview Ave. ☎ **416/465-8538.** Subway: Broadview.

Established three decades ago, Chui's shop looks unremarkable from the street. Inside, however, you'll immediately see why he has such a following among the famous. The quality can't be beat, which is why a custom-made suit costs C$1,000 (US$680) and up, up, up.

WOMEN'S

Andrew's. Hazelton Lanes, 55 Avenue Rd. ☎ **416/969-9991.** Subway: Bay.

Smaller than nearby Holt Renfrew, this department store nonetheless stocks a competing collection of European sportswear, formal dresses, lingerie, and cosmetics.

Chanel. 131 Bloor St. W. ☎ **416/925-2577.** Subway: Bay.

This airy atelier is filled with Karl Lagerfeld's creations for the house that Coco built. There is also a selection of accessories, including handbags, belts, shoes, jewelry, and perfume.

✪ **Fresh Baked Goods.** 274 Augusta Ave. ☎ **416/966-0123.** Subway: Spadina, then LRT to Baldwin St., and walk 2 blocks west.

No, this isn't a bakery. Owner Laura Jean "the knitting queen" features a line of flirty knitwear made of cotton, mohair, wool, or lace. This is a favorite haunt of the celebrity set—stars like Neve Campbell drop by when they're in town.

F/X. 152 Spadina Ave. ☎ **416/703-5595.** Subway: Spadina, then LRT to Queen St. W.

The significance of the name is clear from the start: This is dressing for dramatic effect. Funkier pieces from the prêt-à-porter collections of Vivienne Westwood, Anna Sui, and Betsey Johnson are at the back of the store. There are also cutting-edge shoes and boots, a makeup collection, and candy.

Jeanne Lottie. 106 Yorkville Ave. ☎ **416/975-5115.** Subway: Bay.

Can you make a fashion statement with a handbag? Canadian designer Jane Ip thinks so. Her boutique is filled with purses for all occasions, from zebra-patterned boxy bags for day and glittering sequin-encrusted numbers for a night out. Prices are low, with most offerings in the C$50-$80 (US$34–$54) range.

Linda Lundstrom. 136 Cumberland St. ☎ **416/927-9009.** Subway: Bay.

Lundstrom has been designing women's clothing since the early 1970s. Her distinctive brand of sportswear incorporates native Canadian art and themes. The famous La Parka coat is still a best-seller.

Marilyn Brooks. 132 Cumberland St. ☎ **416/961-5050.** Subway: Bay.

Still going strong after almost 4 decades of designing, Brooks displays her own easy-fitting creations alongside the clothes of budding Canadian couturiers.

Maxi Boutique. 575 Danforth Ave. ☎ **416/461-6686.** Subway: Pape.

Homegrown talent takes center stage here, with designs from Lida Baday, Ross Mayer, and Misura by Joeffer Caoc. There's a full complement of suits, separates, and eveningwear.

Price Roman. 267 Queen St. W. ☎ **416/979-7363.** Subway: Osgoode.

The husband-and-wife team of Derek Price and Tess Roman produces sleek, tailored clothes with a sultry edge.

Rhonda Maternity. 110 Cumberland St. ☎ **416/921-3116.** Subway: Bay.

For the last of the red-hot mamas, there's this glamorous boutique. The stylish suits, sweater sets, and sportswear are this store's exclusive designs.

Suitables. 207 Queen's Quay W. ☎ **416/203-0655.** Subway: Union, then LRT to Queen's Quay.

Silk, glorious silk, is the mainstay of this popular shop. In addition to blouses in a variety of colors, there are hand-painted vests, sweaters, jerseys, and jackets, many of them Canadian-made. Most prices are in the C$50–$100 (US$34–$68) range. The store also stocks some contemporary costume jewelry, including unusual Austrian collar crystals.

FOOD

The Big Carrot. 348 Danforth Ave. ☎ **416/466-2129.** Subway: Chester.

Who says health food can't be fun? This large-scale emporium stocks everything from organic produce to vitamins to all-natural beauty potions. Stop in at the café for a power shake.

The Bonnie Stern School. 6 Erskine Ave. ☎ **416/484-4810.** Subway: Eglinton.

Crammed to the rafters with cooking accoutrements (such as stovetop grills) and exotic books, this store also features the raw ingredients you need to produce fine cuisine. It carries top-notch olive oil, balsamic vinegar, Asian sauces, and candied flower petals. If you take a course or seminar, you get a 10% discount on everything you buy.

Global Cheese Shoppe. 76 Kensington Ave. ☎ **416/593-9251.** Subway: Spadina, then LRT to Baldwin Ave.

Cheese, glorious cheese. More than 150 varieties are available, from mild boccocini to the greenest of Gorgonzola, and the staff is generous with samples.

House of Tea. 1017 Yonge St. ☎ **416/922-1226.** Subway: Rosedale.

Visitors to this shop can drink in the heady scent of more than 150 loose teas. And the selection of cups, mugs, and tea caddies runs from chic to comical.

Senses. 15 Bloor St. W. ☎ **416/961-0055.** Subway: Yonge/Bloor.

The food here is delicate, exquisite, and priced accordingly. There are counters of terrines and pâtés, caviar, pastries and chocolates, as well as grocery shelves filled with bottled Hong Kong sauces and boxed Dean & Deluca spices.

Simone Marie Belgian Chocolate. 126A Cumberland St. ☎ **416/968-7777.** Subway: Bay.

All of the rich truffles, colorful almond dragées, and fruit jellies in this shop are flown in from Belgium. If you're going to splurge, you may as well do it in style.

Sugar Mountain Confectionery Co. 320 Richmond St. W. ☎ **416/204-9544.** Subway: Osgoode.

Remember Pez, candy necklaces, and lollipop rings? Sugar Mountain carries the toothaching sweets of youth, several of which have been elevated to cult status. Teens are drawn to this store, but the biggest customers are nostalgic boomers.

FURS

In addition to the shops listed here, the Hudson's Bay Company has a well-stocked fur department. Look for summer and January Boxing Day sales.

AlaMode. 686 Bathurst St. ☎ **416/539-9999.** Subway: Bathurst.

This 13,000-square-foot space consists of smaller boutiques, with coats and jackets in mink, beaver, raccoon, fox, and sable, among others. All of the prices are wholesale.

Magder Furs. 202 Spadina Ave. ☎ **416/504-6077.** Subway: Spadina, then LRT to Dundas St. W.

This shop carries excellent new and previously worn furs in sizes from 2 to 50. Paul Magder is a legend in Toronto for his year-in-year-out battles with the government to allow Sunday shopping; he finally prevailed a decade ago.

GIFTS & MORE

Down East Gifts and Gallery. 508 Bathurst St. ☎ **416/925-1642.** Subway: Bathurst.

If your travels won't take you any farther east than Toronto, drop in on this shop to check out the folk art of the Atlantic provinces. The carvings, prints, and knickknacks are whimsical and charming.

✪ **French Country.** 6 Roxborough St. W. ☎ **416/944-2204.** Subway: Rosedale.

Owner Viola Jull spent several years living in France, and she re-creates a Parisian atmosphere in her shop. Many items are unique, including painted lampshades, antique silver, and framed prints. There are also a few gourmet food products and hand-milled soaps.

Ice. 163 Cumberland St. ☎ **416/964-6751.** Subway: Bay.

This small store is a big lure for visiting celebs. Are they drawn in by the Hard Candy and Urban Decay cosmetic lines? Maybe it's the Beanie Babies or the fab costume jewelry.

Japanese Paper Place. 887 Queen St. W. ☎ **416/703-0089.** Subway: Osgoode, then any streetcar west to Ossington Ave.

The Japanese have elevated gift-wrapping to an art form, and this shop has all the boxes, papers, and handmade cards you need to follow suit. Better yet, it also stocks instruction books.

Legends of the Game. 322A King St. W. ☎ **416/971-8848.** Subway: St. Andrew.

This collectibles store, just 2 blocks north of SkyDome, houses memorabilia of Babe Ruth, Wayne Gretzky, Muhammad Ali, and Michael Jordan, among others. There are trading cards, team jerseys, and other souvenirs.

Oh Yes, Toronto. Eaton Centre. ☎ **416/593-6749.** Subway: Dundas or Queen.

Looking for souvenirs for the folks back home? Oh Yes, Toronto stocks no end of Hogtown knickknacks, as well as quality T-shirts and sweatshirts. There are also branches at Queen's Quay West (☎ **416/203-0607**), and at Terminal 2 (☎ **905/612-0175**) and Terminal 3 (☎ **905/672-8594**) at **Pearson International Airport.**

Pencraft. 159 Yonge St. ☎ **416/364-8977.** Subway: Dundas or Queen.

If you take your writing implements seriously—and cringe at the thought of a disposable ballpoint—check out this small store. It carries top-of-the-line pens from Mont Blanc and Waterman, as well as secondhand fountain pens.

HEALTH & BEAUTY

Lush. 312 Queen St. W. ☎ **416/599-5874.** Subway: Osgoode.

This clever U.K. emporium looks like a gourmet grocery store. The heady scent of mingled perfumes is the giveaway. Lush stocks a selection of fizzy bath bombs, skin lotions and potions, and aromatherapy-oriented items. All products are sold by weight.

✪ **M.A.C.** 89 Bloor St. W. ☎ **416/929-7555.** Subway: Bay.

This makeup line used to be a trade secret among models and actors, though the word has been out for a while (the company was originally founded in Toronto, but is now owned by Estée Lauder). M.A.C's flagship store is perpetually packed, especially on weekends, but if you call ahead you can schedule an appointment for a complimentary makeup lesson—with no pressure to buy (really!). In addition to cosmetics, there are skin- and hair-care supplies.

Noah's. 322 Bloor St. W. ☎ **416/968-7930.** Subway: Spadina.

This is mecca for health nuts. Noah's boasts aisle after aisle of vitamins and dietary supplements, organic foods and "natural" candies, skin care and bath products, and books and periodicals. The staff is well-informed and helpful.

Osmosis Everyday Aromatherapy. 502 Queen St. W. ☎ **800/IRISES-5** or 416/504-ROSE. Subway: Osgoode.

I'm not sure that I believe everything I've heard about the powers of aromatherapy, but walking into this Canadian-owned store almost converted me. Everything smells delicious, from the bath scents to the jet-lag therapies to the sleeping potions. There are also some special products for kids.

Thompson's Homeopathic Supplies. 844 Yonge St. ☎ **416/922-2300.** Subway: Yonge/Bloor.

This is just like an old-fashioned apothecary, with endless rows of potions behind a wooden counter. It has a homeopathic remedy for everything from the common cold to dermatitis or conjunctivitis. The staff is friendly and knowledgeable.

HOUSEWARES & FURNISHINGS

The Art Shoppe. 2131 Yonge St. ☎ **416/487-3211.** Subway: Eglinton.

This is one of the prettiest stores in the city, with top-notch furniture arranged into suites of rooms. A wide range of styles is on display, from gilty baroque to streamlined art deco. The price tags are high, but the store is well worth browsing.

✪ **Elte Carpet & Home.** 80 Ronald Ave. (just west of Dufferin St.). ☎ **416/785-7885.** Subway: Eglinton W., then any westbound bus to Ronald Ave.

With 130,000 square feet of showroom space, Elte has room for a lot more than rugs. This megastore is divided into boutiques where big names like Ralph Lauren and Calvin Klein flog their home-design lines. History-spanning reproductions abound, and there are a few antiques finds, too.

Kitchen Stuff Plus. 703 Yonge St. ☎ **416/944-2718.** Subway: Yonge/Bloor.

This housewares shop sells brand-name goods from the likes of Umbra at discount prices. It offers a good selection of picture frames, wine racks, area rugs, candles, painted ceramics, and kitchen accessories.

Sonoma Interiors. 146 Dupont St. ☎ **416/923-1994.** Subway: Museum, then any Avenue Rd. bus north.

With 15,000 square feet spread over two floors, Sonoma really does try to cover its bases. Divided into departments, it specializes in 19th-century Russian design, 1940s French-style furniture, and Anglo-Indian Raj–inspired pieces. There are also reproductions of pieces from the Victoria and Albert Museum in London, and a Frank Lloyd Wright collection.

Souleiado En Provence. 20 Hazelton Ave. ☎ **416/975-9400.** Subway: Bay.

Anyone who has been carried away by reading about the south of France—think of Peter Mayle's *A Year in Provence*—will feel right at home here. It stocks brightly colored dinnerware, tasseled lamps, printed bed linens, and wrought-iron furniture.

Tap Phong Trading Co. 360 Spadina Ave. ☎ **416/977-6364.** Subway: Spadina, then LRT to Baldwin St.

If you have only a few minutes in Chinatown, spend them here. There are beautiful hand-painted ceramics, earthenware, decorative items, kitchen utensils, and small appliances. Best of all, just about everything is inexpensive and of reliable quality.

UpCountry. 214 King St. E. ☎ **416/777-1700.** Subway: King.

The style tends mainly toward Arts & Crafts and Mission; most pieces are new, but a few are restored antiques. The sizable selection of decorative touches includes antique globes and pretty bath products.

JEWELRY

Birks. Manulife Centre, 55 Bloor St. W. ☎ **416/922-2266.** Subway: Bay.

This Canadian institution, founded in 1879, is synonymous with top quality. Among the silver, crystal, and china is an extensive selection of top-quality jewelry, including exquisite pearls and knockout diamond engagement rings. There's even a children's section, filled with keepsake gifts like Royal Doulton Bunnykins china and whimsical picture frames by Nova Scotia's Seagull Pewter. There are Birks branches at the Eaton Centre (☎ **416/979-9311**) and at First Canadian Place (☎ **416/363-5663**).

Experimetal. 588 Markham St. (south of Bloor St. W.). ☎ **416/538-3313.** Subway: Bathurst.

Some of proprietor Anne Sportun's sterling silver, gold, and platinum creations have won design awards. She will also fashion custom engagement and wedding bands. Also on display are pieces by other North American jewelers.

Peter Cullman. Cumberland Court, 99 Yorkville Ave. ☎ **416/964-2196.** Subway: Bay.

Cullman has traveled to and apprenticed in different parts of the world, including Germany, southern Africa, and Mexico. You can watch him create his unique mini-masterpieces in his shop.

Royal de Versailles Jewellers. 101 Bloor St. W. ☎ **416/967-7201.** Subway: Bay.

This European-style shop carries an eye-catching assortment of pearls, gold, and platinum. The designs range from classic to funkier, playful styles.

Silverbridge. 162 Cumberland St. ☎ **416/923-2591.** Subway: Bay.

Most of the necklaces, bracelets, rings, and earrings here are fashioned of silver, and the sensibility is modern. Most of the designs are the work of Costin Lazar, and they are produced in Toronto; Lazar will also take on custom work. There are also a few pieces in 18-karat gold and platinum, as well as watches by Georg Jensen and Ole Mathiesen.

Tiffany & Co. 85 Bloor St. W. ☎ **416/921-3900.** Subway: Bay.

Diamonds are still a girl's best friend at this art deco–style shop. Precious gems and designs by Elsa Peretti and Paloma Picasso are on the first level; the second floor has silver jewelry, stationery, and housewares.

LEATHER GOODS

Danier. Eaton Centre. ☎ **416/598-1159.** Subway: Queen.

This Canadian chain carries suede and leather coats, suits, pants, and skirts at reasonable prices. Not-uncommon sales knock the prices down 20% to 50%.

Taschen! Hazelton Lanes, 55 Avenue Rd. ☎ **416/927-8802.** Subway: Bay.

Exclusive designer handbags, luggage, wallets, and other accessories are mainstays here. Many are European imports, and quality is high.

LINGERIE

La Vie en Rose. Eaton Centre. ☎ **416/595-0898.** Subway: Queen.

There's quite the eclectic collection of undies here, from sensible cotton briefs to maribou-trimmed teddies, and from retro PJs to up-to-the-minute cleavage enhancers. The items at the front of the store are inexpensive, but the farther back you go, the pricier it gets.

La Senza. Holt Renfrew Centre, 50 Bloor St. W. ☎ **416/972-1079.** Subway: Yonge/Bloor.

This Montreal-based chain carries inexpensive but eye-catching bra-and-panty sets and naughty-looking nighties. There are also plush unisex robes and patterned boxers. An assortment of slippers, candles, bath mousse, and picture frames rounds out the offerings.

MAGAZINES & INTERNATIONAL NEWSPAPERS

Great Canadian News Company. BCE Place, 30 Yonge St. (at Front St.). ☎ **416/363-2242.** Subway: Union.

This shop has a great selection, with more than 2,000 magazines filling its shelves, but it's no place for a lengthy browse.

Maison de la Presse Internationale. 124 Yorkville Ave. ☎ **416/928-2328.** Subway: Bay.

While this store fills up fast on weekends, drawing expats and locals alike, it's still a great place to while away an hour. The many international magazines and newspapers are as current as you'll find.

MALLS & SHOPPING CENTERS

Atrium on Bay. Bay and Dundas sts. ☎ **416/980-2801.** Subway: Dundas.

This two-level complex has more than 60 shops selling clothing, jewelry, furniture, and more.

College Park Shoppes. 444 Yonge St. ☎ **416/597-1221.** Subway: College.

With more than 100 stores on its two levels, College Park is like a mini Eaton Centre, minus the teenagers.

✪ **Eaton Centre.** 220 Yonge St. ☎ **416/598-2322.** Subway: Dundas or Queen.

It's odd that one of urban Toronto's main attractions is a mall—but, oh, what a mall. More than 300 shops and restaurants spread over four levels in the Eaton Centre, which takes up 2 entire city blocks.

First Canadian Place. King and Bay sts. ☎ **416/862-8138.** Subway: King.

Another piece of the labyrinth that makes up the underground city, this complex houses 120 shops and restaurants. It also stages free noontime events each week, with performances as diverse as Opera Atelier's Handel recital and the dancing monks of the Tibetan Drikung Monastery. There are also ongoing art exhibitions.

Hazelton Lanes. 55 Avenue Rd. ☎ **416/968-8602.** Subway: Bay.

A byword for elegance and extravagance, Hazelton is a two-level complex with about 90 shops. The wares are uniformly exquisite, right down to the Swiss chocolates at Teuscher's. The charming courtyard at the center transforms into a skating rink in winter.

Holt Renfrew Centre. 50 Bloor St. W. ☎ **416/923-2255.** Subway: Yonge/Bloor.

Anchored by the chic Holt Renfrew department store, this small underground concourse is more down to earth. It connects with the Manulife Centre and the Hudson's Bay Centre.

✪ **Manulife Centre.** 55 Bloor St. W. ☎ **416/923-9525.** Subway: Bay.

More than 50 posh shops—including William Ashley, Indigo Books Music & More, and a top-notch LCBO outlet—occupy this complex. The Manulife connects to the Holt Renfrew Centre underground.

Queen's Quay Terminal. 207 Queen's Quay W. No phone. Subway: Union, then LRT to Queen's Quay.

This is waterfront shopping at its best, with more than 100 shops and cafes. Queen's Quay caters to tourists—while you'll find some unique items, the prices tend to be moderate to high.

Royal Bank Plaza. Bay and Front sts. ☎ **416/974-5570.** Subway: Union.

Part of Toronto's underground city, the Royal Bank Plaza connects to Union Station and to the Royal York Hotel. Its 60-plus outlets include a variety of shops, two full-service restaurants, and a food court. The building above it is worth a look, too.

Scarborough Town Centre. Hwy. 401 and McCowan Ave. ☎ **416/296-0296.** Subway: Scarborough Town Centre.

This is a megamall to rival the Eaton Centre; if you're staying on the city's eastern fringe, you can't miss it. It has more than 200 shops, including branches similar to those at the Eaton Centre.

Village by the Grange. 122 St. Patrick St. ☎ **416/598-1414.** Subway: St. Patrick.

Cheek-by-jowl to the Art Gallery of Ontario, the Grange contains more than 40 shops. Its International Food Market has decent Middle Eastern and Asian selections.

MARKETS

✪ **Kensington Market.** Along Baldwin, Kensington and Augusta aves. No phone. Subway: Spadina, then LRT to Baldwin St. or Dundas St. W.

This neighborhood has changed dramatically in the past 40 years. Originally a Jewish community, it now borders on Chinatown. There are several Asian herbalists and grocers, as well as West Indian and Middle Eastern shops. Kensington Avenue has the greatest concentration of vintage clothing stores in the city. For a full description, see "Walking Tour 4: Chinatown & Kensington Market" in chapter 7.

St. Lawrence Market. 92 Front St. E. ☎ **416/392-7219.** Subway: Union.

This market is a local favorite for fresh produce, and it even draws people who live a good distance away. Hours are Tuesday to Thursday 9am to 7pm, Friday 8am to 8pm, Saturday 5am (when the farmers arrive) to 5pm. See chapter 6 for a complete description.

MUSIC

HMV. 333 Yonge St. ☎ **416/596-0333.** Subway: Dundas.

This is the flagship Toronto store of the British chain. (You'll find smaller outlets throughout the city.) The selection of pop, rock, jazz, and classical music is large. Best of all, you can listen to a CD before you buy it.

The Music Store. In Roy Thomson Hall, 60 Simcoe St. ☎ **416/593-4822.** Subway: St. Andrew.

On the Toronto Symphony Orchestra's home turf, this attractive shop includes several TSO CDs and cassettes in its collection of classical and choral music.

Record Peddler. 619 Queen St. W. ☎ **416/504-3828.** Subway: Osgoode, then any streetcar west to Bathurst St.

This specialty store is packed with British and other European imports. The selection is mostly techno-infused rock and experimental jazz.

✪ **Sam the Record Man.** 347 Yonge St. ☎ **416/977-4650.** www.samscd.com Subway: Dundas.

Its megastore competition may look more chic, but Sam's three-story emporium has the most extensive music collection in the city. The store is beloved by Canadian artists like Joni Mitchell, Rush, Liona Boyd, and the Guess Who because it has always promoted homegrown talent. There is also a well-stocked video department.

SEX TOYS

Lovecraft. 27 Yorkville Ave. ☎ **416/923-7331.** Subway: Bay.

Believe it or not, Lovecraft is downright wholesome. Sure, there are the requisite badgirl (and -boy) lingerie and toys, but much of the shop stocks joke gifts, T-shirts with suggestive slogans, and an impressive collection of erotic literature (no porn mags). The staff is friendly and the atmosphere playful.

SHOES

Browns. Hazelton Lanes, 55 Avenue Rd. ☎ **416/968-1806.** Subway: Bay.

To treat your feet to fabulous footwear by Manolo Blahnik, Prada, or Ferragamo, beat a path to this shop for men and women. There's also a selection of dressy handbags from Canadian label Jeanne Lottie, among others. Browns has several branches around the city, including one at the Eaton Centre (☎ **416/979-9270**).

Capezio. 70 Bloor St. W. ☎ **416/920-1006.** Subway: Bay.

Whether you're looking for the perfect pair of ballet slippers or an up-to-the-minute design from Steve Madden or Guess, you'll find it here. All the shoes and other leather goods are for women.

David's. 66 Bloor St. W. ☎ **416/920-1000.** Subway: Bay.

For serious shoppers only. This high-end store stocks elegant footwear for men and women—from Bruno Magli, Bally, and Sonia Rykiel, as well as the store's own collection—but prices are accordingly steep.

Mephisto. 1177 Yonge St. ☎ **416/968-7026.** Subway: Summerhill.

These shoes are made for walking—particularly because they're made from all natural materials. Devotees of this 30-year-old shop swear that it's impossible to wear out Mephisto footwear.

Petit Pied. 890 Yonge St. ☎ **416/963-5925.** Subway: Rosedale.

For especially tiny tootsies, check out this elegant shop. Petit Pied carries children's shoes for newborns to adolescents. Many of the brands are European, including Minibel and Elefanten, but there are also sporty designs from Nike and Reebok.

✪ **The Shoe Company.** 711 Yonge St. ☎ **416/923-8388.** Subway: Yonge/Bloor.

This is every foot fetishist's dream: great shoes for men and women from Unisa, Nine West, and others, marked down to unbeatable prices. There are lots of funky styles that won't be stylish for long, but it won't hurt your pocketbook to splurge. There are outlets around the city, including First Canadian Place.

TOBACCO

Thomas Hinds. 8 Cumberland St. ☎ **416/927-7703.** Subway: Yonge/Bloor.

This is Havana heaven for the stogie set. Thomas Hinds carries a wide range of Cuban cigars and cigarillos, as well as pipes and the other smoking accouterments. Upstairs there's a lounge and humidor.

TOYS

George's Trains. 510 Mount Pleasant Ave. ☎ **416/489-9783.** Subway: St. Clair, then Mount Pleasant bus to Belsize Ave.

Everything the young (or young at heart) could want to spruce up a model train set is here, including tracks, stations, and scenic backdrops. There are wooden trains as well as train kits.

Just Bears. 29 Bellair St. ☎ **416/928-5963.** Subway: Bay.

The name tells you all you need to know about this upscale shop. Anything that isn't a teddy has a bear motif.

Kidding Awound. 91 Cumberland St. ☎ **416/926-8996.** Subway: Bay.

Yo-yos and wind-up gadgets are the specialty here. There are also some antique toys (which you won't let the kids near) and gag gifts.

The Little Dollhouse Company. 617 Mt. Pleasant Rd. ☎ **416/489-7180.** Subway: Eglinton, then no. 34 bus east to Mount Pleasant, and walk 2 blocks south.

This toy store isn't really for kids. It's beloved by adults in search of miniature tea services and wicker furniture. It also sells nine different dollhouse kits, from a stately Victorian mansion to a ranch bungalow.

✪ **Science City.** 50 Bloor St. W. ☎ **416/968-2627.** Subway: Yonge/Bloor.

Kids and adults alike will love this tiny store filled with games, puzzles, models, kits, and books—all related to science. Whether your interest is astronomy, biology, chemistry, archaeology, or physics, you'll find something here.

Top Banana. 639 Mount Pleasant Rd. ☎ **416/440-0111.** Subway: Eglinton, then no. 34 bus east to Mount Pleasant, and walk 2 blocks south.

Fun for kids—and their parents. The toys range from Thomas the Tank Engine to Stomp Rockets. There are also games and books galore.

The Toy Shop. 62 Cumberland St. ☎ **416/961-4870.** Subway: Bay.

This double-decker shop carries toys, many of them educational, from around the world. There is also a good selection of books, games, and videos.

TRAVEL GOODS

The Travel Stop. 130 Cumberland St. ☎ **416/961-6088.** Subway: Bay.

If an item is made in travel size, The Travel Stop stocks it. Offerings include steamers and hair dryers, travel guides, and luggage. There is a discount travel agency at the back of the store.

VINTAGE CLOTHING

Asylum. 42 Kensington Ave. ☎ **416/595-7199.** Subway: Spadina, then LRT to Baldwin St.

Secondhand jeans and vintage dresses line the racks in this Kensington Market stalwart. Bargains turn up in odd places, like the Anne Klein scarf at the bottom of a $C1 (US68¢) bin. There's also an assortment of toys and candy.

Courage My Love. 14 Kensington Ave. ☎ **416/979-1992.** Subway: Spadina, then LRT to Dundas St. W.

With its mix of vintage clothing and new silver jewelry, Courage is a Kensington Market favorite. Dresses run from '50s velvet numbers to '70s polyester, and almost everything is priced under C$20 (US$13.60). There's also a good selection of tweedy jackets and starchy white shirts. The owners' cat makes an occasional furtive appearance.

✪ **Divine Decadence.** Manulife Centre, 55 Bloor St. W. ☎ **416/324-9759.** Subway: Bay.

Owner Carmelita Krum has a unique line on vintage clothes: She imports them from her native Peru. Chic Peruvians had previously brought these glad rags in from Europe, so it's not unusual to find great French couture. The price tags are uniformly high, but so is the quality.

Ex-Toggery. 115 Merton St. ☎ **416/488-5393.** Subway: Davisville.

This is a consignment shop with outlets around the city. Items don't last long, particularly because the price drops every week. Scour the racks for designer names like Versace and Donna Karan. There are also a variety of vintage items on display, from clothing to accessories.

WINE

In Ontario, Liquor Control Board of Ontario (LCBO) outlets and small boutiques at upscale grocery stores sell wine; no alcohol is sold at convenience stores. There are LCBO outlets all over the city, and prices are the same at all of them. The loveliest shop is at the **Manulife Centre,** 55 Bloor St. W. (☎ **416/925-5266**). Other locations are at 20 Bloor St. E. ☎ **416/368-0521**); the **Eaton Centre** (☎ **416/979-9978**); and **Union Station** (☎ **416/925-9644**).

 Vintages stores have a different name, but they're still LCBO outlets. Check out the one at **Hazelton Lanes** (☎ **416/924-9463**) and at **Queen's Quay** (☎ **416/864-6777**).

Toronto After Dark

9

Toronto may not have a reputation for being a city that never sleeps, but it does have a vital and varied nightlife scene. It's a mecca for top-notch theater—you can sometimes see Broadway shows *before* they reach Broadway. The Toronto Symphony Orchestra is world renowned, and the city's many dance and music venues host the crème de la crème of international performers. Some of the best entertainment can be found in Toronto's comedy clubs, which have served as training grounds for stars such as Jim Carrey, Mike Myers, Dan Aykroyd, and John Candy.

The nightclub scene moves at a frenetic pace. Salsa music is all the rage right now, as swing was a couple of year ago. Cigar and martini bars are still popular, though lower-key pool bars are in vogue, too.

MAKING PLANS For listings of local performances and events, check out *Where Toronto* and *Toronto Life,* as well as *The Globe & Mail,* the *Toronto Star,* and the *Toronto Sun.* For an up-to-the-minute list of hot-ticket events, check out the free weeklies *Now* and *Eye,* available around town in newspaper boxes, and at bars, cafes, and bookstores. If you have Internet access, surf over to *Toronto Life's* site (www.torontolife. com), or the *Toronto Star's* site (www.toronto.com) for lengthy lists of performances. (You should also look for MyToronto's Web site, www.myto.net, which at press time was set to launch any day.) Events of particular interest to the gay and lesbian community are listed in *Xtra!,* another free weekly available in newspaper boxes and many bookstores.

GETTING TICKETS For almost any theater, music, or dance event, you can buy tickets from **Ticketmaster** (☎ 416/870-8000; www.ticketmaster.ca). There's a service charge on every ticket (not every order) sold over the phone. To avoid the charge, head to a ticket center. They're scattered throughout the city; call the information line for the lengthy list of locations.

DISCOUNT TICKETS Ticketmaster (☎ 416/870-8000) also runs the **T.O. Tix** booth, which sells half-price day-of-performance tickets. Cash and credit cards are accepted; all sales are final. T.O. Tix is open Tuesday to Friday from noon to 7:30pm and on Saturday from noon to 6pm; the booth is closed Sunday and Monday. T.O. Tix is located at the Eaton Centre Dundas Mall on Level 2 (that actually one level below street level); the easiest access to the booth is from Dundas Street.

Downtown After Dark

ARTS & ENTERTAINMENT:
Buddies in Bad Times Theatre **38**
Canadian Stage Company/
  Berkeley Theatre **76**
Cinematheque Ontario **3**
Elgin & Winter Garden Theatre **57**
Factory Theatre **28**
Glenn Gould Studio **70**
Hummingbird Centre/
  St. Lawrence Centre **80**
Laugh Resort **72**
La Cage Dinner Theatre **55**
Maple Leaf Gardens **39**
Massey Hall **54**
Pantages Theatre **56**
Premiere Dance Theatre **82**
Princess of Wales Theatre **67**
Roy Thomson Hall **69**
Royal Alexandra Theatre **68**
Second City **36**
SkyDome **37**
St. James's Cathedral **74**
St. Patrick's Church **52**
Theatre Centre West **6**
Theatre Passe Muraille **5**
Young People's Theatre **77**

MUSIC, BARS & CLUBS:
Al Frisco's **23**
Alice Fazooli's **26**
Amsterdam **29**
BamBoo **13**
Bar 501 **46**
The Barn/The Stables **40**
Bauhaus **34**
Ben Wick's **50**
The Bishop Belcher **14**
Bovine Sex Club **7**
Byzantium **41**
Cameron Public House **10**
C'est What? **78**
Chartroom **81**
The Chelsea Bun **51**
Churchill's Cigar &
  Wine Bar **66**
Club Lucky Cafe & Bar **24**
The Coloured Stone **61**
Consort Bar **73**
Crews/Tango **47**
Crocodile Rock **65**
Delux **22**
The Devil's Martini **63**
The Duke of
  Westminster **71**
Easy & the Fifth **59**
El Mocambo **2**

Fez Batik **20**
Fluid Lounge **60**
G-Spot **18**
Garage Paradise **62**
The Good Queen
  Bess **58**
Hard Rock Cafe **37**
The Hooch **8**
Horseshoe Tavern **11**
Industry **30**
The Joker **19**
Left Bank **9**
Life **16**

Limelight **64**
Mambo Lounge **27**
Milano **32**
Montana **15**
Montréal Bistro
  Jazz Club **75**
Plastique **21**
Phoenix Concert
  Theatre **49**
The Rivoli **12**
Sailor **43**
Slack Alice **48**
Sneaky Dee's **1**

Tallulah's Cabaret **44**
Top O' the Senator **53**
Up & Down **25**
Vines **79**
Vineyards Wine Bar
  & Bistro **33**
Wayne Gretzky's/
  Oasis **35**
Wheat Sheaf
  Tavern **31**
Whisky Saigon **17**
Wilde Oscar's **42**
Woody's **45**

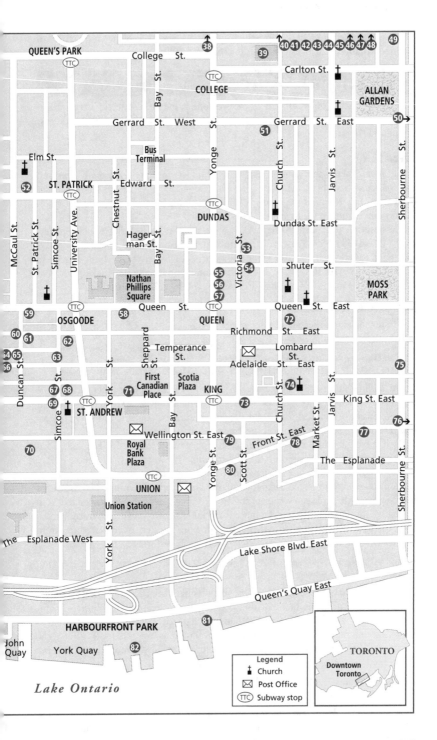

Discount tickets for a limited number of shows are also available from the **Toronto Theatre Alliance,** 720 Bathurst St. (☎ **416/536-6468**).

1 The Performing Arts

Toronto's arts scene offers something for everyone year-round. The city's arts institutions are widely renowned, and many top-notch international performers pass through town.

THEATER

While it may seem that Toronto favors big-budget musicals—*The Lion King* and *Mamma Mia!* have both made a big splash here—there are many excellent smaller companies, too. Many of the smaller troupes have no permanent performance space, so they move from venue to venue.

The best time to capture the flavor of Toronto's theater life is during the **Fringe Festival** (☎ **416/534-5919;** e-mail: fringeto@interlog.com), usually held for 10 days starting in early July. If you visit Toronto in July or August, try to catch the **Dream in High Park** (☎ **416/368-3110**). It mounts stunning productions of Shakespearean or Canadian plays from the Canadian Stage Company in an outdoor setting.

LANDMARK THEATERS

The following major theaters all offer guided tours, usually for C$5 (US$3.40) or less; call ahead for schedules.

✪ **The Elgin and Winter Garden Theatres.** 189 Yonge St. ☎ **416/872-5555** for tickets, 416/314-2871 for tour info. Tickets C$15–$90 (US$10.20–$61.20). Subway: Queen.

These landmark theaters first opened their doors in 1913, and today they vie with the Royal Alex and the Princess of Wales Theatre for major shows and attention. Recent productions have included *Stomp* and *Aladdin.* Both book concerts and opera performances, and are favorite venues of the Toronto International Film Festival.

Both the Elgin and the Winter Garden have been restored to their original gilded glory at a cost of C$29 million (US$19.8 million). They are the only double-decker theaters in Toronto. The downstairs Elgin is larger, seating 1,500 and featuring a lavish domed ceiling and gilded decoration on the boxes and proscenium. Hand-painted frescoes adorn the striking interior of the 1,000-seat Winter Garden. Suspended from its ceiling and lit with lanterns are more than 5,000 branches of beech leaves, which have been preserved, painted, and fireproofed. Both theaters offer everything from Broadway musicals and dramas to concerts and opera performances.

Pantages Theatre. 244 Victoria St. ☎ **416/872-2222.** Tickets normally C$60–$110 (US$40.80– $74.80). Subway: Dundas.

The Pantages is one of the theaters whose fortunes have been adversely affected by the collapse of Livent; at the moment the space is virtually empty. The glorious, glamorous building, which opened in 1920, had been restored to the tune of C$18 million (US$12.2 million) by Livent. Originally a silent film house and vaudeville theater, the 2,250-seat Pantages has made a mint presenting the splashy Andrew Lloyd Webber show *The Phantom of the Opera* for too many years to count.

Princess of Wales Theatre. 300 King St. W. ☎ **416/872-1212.** www.onstagenow.com. Tickets C$25–$125 (US$17–$85). Subway: St. Andrew.

This spectacular 2,000-seat state-of-the-art theater was built for the production of *Miss Saigon* and has a stage that was large enough to accommodate the landing of the helicopter in that production. Currently it is home of *The Lion King.* The exterior and

Farther Afield

Don't forget that two major theater festivals—the **Shaw Festival** in Niagara-on-the-Lake and the **Stratford Festival** in Stratford—are only an hour or two away. See chapter 10 for details.

interior walls were spectacularly decorated by Frank Stella, who painted 10,000 square feet of colorful murals. All levels of the theater are accessible to people in wheelchairs.

✪ **Royal Alexandra Theatre.** 260 King St. W. ☎ **800/593-4225** to order tickets, or 416/872-1212. www.onstagenow.com. Tickets C$25–$125 (US$17–$85). Subway: St. Andrew.

When shows from Broadway migrate north, they usually head for the Royal Alex. Tickets are often snapped up by subscription buyers, so your best bet is to call or write ahead (260 King St. W., Toronto, ON M5V 1H9). Recent favorites have included *Masterclass, Fame,* and *Mamma Mia!,* the ABBA-inspired musical.

The 1,495-seat Royal Alex is a magnificent spectacle. Constructed in 1907, it owes its current lease on life to discount-store czar and impresario Ed Mirvish, who refurbished it (as well as the surrounding area) in the 1960s. Inside it's a riot of plush reds, gold brocade, and baroque ornamentation. You're wise to avoid the second balcony and the seats "under the circle," which don't have the greatest sightlines.

St. Lawrence Centre for the Arts. 27 Front St. E. ☎ **416/366-7723.** Tickets C$32–$57 (US$21.75–$38.75). Mon night pay what you can. Senior and student discounts may be available 30 min. before performance. Subway: Union.

For three decades the St. Lawrence Centre has presented top-notch theater, music, and dance performances. The Bluma Appel Theatre is home to the Canadian Stage Company, and the smaller Jane Mallet Theatre features the Toronto Operetta Theatre Company, among others. This is a popular spot for lectures, too.

Toronto Centre. 5040 Yonge St. ☎ **416/872-2222.** Tickets C$15-$75 (US$10.20–$51). Subway: North York Centre.

This gigantic complex is home to the North York Symphony and the Amadeus Choir. It contains several performance venues. The 1,850-seat Apotex Theatre has featured award-winning musicals such as *Sunset Boulevard* and *Ragtime;* the 1,025-seat George Weston Recital Hall books music events. There are a 250-seat studio theater and an art gallery. Since the collapse of theater giant Livent, the Toronto Centre (formerly called the Ford Centre for the Performing Arts) has been sadly underused.

THEATER COMPANIES & SMALLER THEATERS

Buddies in Bad Times. 12 Alexander St. ☎ **416/975-8555.** www.buddies.web.net. Tickets C$12–$25 (US$8.15–$17). Subway: Wellesley.

This gay, or queer (as the company prefers to be called), theater company produces radical new Canadian works that celebrate difference and blur as well as reinvent the boundaries between gay and straight, gay and lesbian, male and female. American Sky Gilbert has built its cutting-edge reputation.

✪ **Canadian Stage Company.** Performing at the Berkeley Theatre, 26 Berkeley St., and St. Lawrence Centre, 27 Front St. E. ☎ **416/368-3110.** Tickets C$32–$57 (US$21.75–$38.75). Mon night pay what you can. Senior and student discounts may be available 30 min. before performance. Subway: Union for St. Lawrence Centre. King, then any streetcar east to Berkeley St. for Berkeley Theatre.

The Canadian Stage Company performs an eclectic variety of Canadian and international plays. Recent productions included the premiere of Pulitzer-winner Carol

Shield's *Thirteen Hands,* Tony Kushner's *Angels in America,* and Tom Stoppard's *Arcadia.* The St. Lawrence Centre seats 500 to 600; the Berkeley Theatre is a more avant-garde, intimate space.

The Canadian Stage Company also presents open-air summer theater—traditionally Shakespeare—in High Park. It's known as the **Dream in High Park.** The company plans to focus more on Canadian-written works in the near future.

Factory Theatre. 125 Bathurst St. ☎ **416/504-9971.** Tickets C$10–$28 (US$6.80–$19.05). Subway: St. Andrew, then streetcar west.

Since it opened in 1970, the Factory Theatre has focused its efforts on presenting Canadian plays, from political dramas to over-the-top comedies. Performances showcase up-and-coming scribes as well as established playwrights. George F. Walker started his career at the factory, and the clown duo Mump and Smoot appears occasionally.

Native Earth Performing Arts Theatre. 720 Bathurst St. ☎ **416/531-1402.** Tickets C$10–$20 (US$6.80–$13.60). Subway: Bathurst.

This small company is dedicated to performing works that express and dramatize the native Canadian experience. Recent shows have included the play *Red River* by Jim Millan and Daniel David Moses, and the dance performance *Chinook Winds* by Alejandro Ronceria.

Tarragon Theatre. 30 Bridgman Ave. (near Dupont and Bathurst sts.). ☎ **416/531-1827,** or 416/536-5018 for administration. Tickets C$15–$25 (US$10.20–$17). Sun pay what you can. Subway: Bathurst.

The Tarragon Theatre opened in 1971. It produces original works by such famous Canadian literary figures as Michel Tremblay, Michael Ondaatje, and Judith Thompson, and an occasional classic or off-Broadway play. It's a small, intimate theater.

Theatre Centre. 1032 Queen St. W. ☎ **416/538-0988.** Tickets C$12–$16 (US$8.15–$10.90), or pay what you can. Subway: Osgoode, then streetcar west.

The Theatre Centre operates this venue and a performance development program. This is the place to see grassroots performances.

Theatre Passe Muraille. 16 Ryerson Ave. ☎ **416/504-7529.** Tickets C$14–$28 (US$9.50–$19.05) Subway: Osgoode, then streetcar west to Bathurst.

This theater started in the late 1960s, when a pool of actors began experimenting and improvising original Canadian material. It continues to produce innovative, provocative theater by such contemporary Canadian playwrights as John Mighton, Daniel David Moses, and Wajdi Mouawad. There are two stages—the Mainspace seats 220, the more intimate Backspace 70. The recent performance of *The Drawer Boy* by Michael Healey won widespread critical acclaim.

Toronto Truck Theatre. 94 Belmont St. ☎ **416/922-0084.** Tickets C$23 (US$15.65). Subway: Rosedale.

The Toronto Truck Theatre is the home of Agatha Christie's *The Mousetrap,* now in its 25th year. It's Canada's longest-running show—and it shows no signs of losing steam.

✪ **Young Peoples Theatre.** 165 Front St. E. ☎ **416/862-2222.** www.toronto.com/ypt. Tickets C$14–$25 (US$9.50–$17). Subway: Union.

Toronto's such a theater town that even tiny tots (and the rest of the family) get their own performance center. The always-enjoyable Young Peoples Theatre mounts whimsical productions such as *Jacob Two-Two's First Spy Case* (a musical by Mordecai Richler), and children's classics such as Mark Twain's *The Prince and the Pauper*. Some performances highlight Native culture, African storytelling, and dance.

DINNER THEATER

✪ Famous People Players Dinner Theatre. 110 Sudbury St. ☎ **416/532-1137.** www.fpp.org. Dinner and show C$39 (US$26.50) adults, C$36 (US$24.50) seniors and youths, C$28 (US$19) children under 13. Subway: Osgoode, then streetcar west.

This group mounts unique, visually fantastic "black light" shows. Famous People Players is renowned not just for the quality of its shows, but for bringing out the creative potential in disabled performers. The price of the show includes a four-course dinner and backstage tour.

La Cage Dinner Theatre. 278 Yonge St. ☎ **416/364-5200.** Dinner and show C$39–$44 (US$26.50–$29.90); show only C$24–$28 (US$16.30–$19). Subway: Dundas.

For the best in campy impersonations, head to La Cage. Buddy Holly, Roy Orbison, and Elvis may never have performed together, but their mimics get along famously here.

Medieval Times Dinner & Tournament. Exhibition Place. ☎ **416/260-1170.** www.MedievalTimes.com. Tickets C$45 (US$31) adults, C$35 (US$23.80) children under 13. Subway: Bathurst, then Bathurst streetcar south to Exhibition Place (last stop).

Milord and Milady welcome you to their castle, where you'll be brought a cutlery-free meal by "serving wenches," view knights on horseback, and witness medieval games in the company of 1,000 of your closest friends. Adults may have trouble getting into the spirit of things, but it's always a hit with kids.

Mysteriously Yours. Royal York Hotel, 100 Front St. W. ☎ **416/486-7469.** www.MysteriouslyYours.com. Dinner and show C$65 (US$44.20); show only C$35 (US$23.80). Subway: Union.

The action at this interactive whodunit gets under way around dessert time. Actors are scattered at tables around the room, and guests try to solve the crime with the aid of a detective who leads the investigation.

MAJOR CONCERT HALLS & AUDITORIUMS

In addition to the Elgin and Winter Garden Theatres, the Ford Centre for the Performing Arts, and the St. Lawrence Centre, these are the city's top performance venues.

Hummingbird Centre for the Performing Arts. 1 Front St. E. ☎ **416/872-2262.** Tickets C$40–$125 (US$27.20–$85). Subway: Union.

If you visited Toronto before 1997, you might remember this as the O'Keefe Centre. It became famous in 1974 when Mikhail Baryshnikov defected after performing here. Since then Hummingbird Communications has invested in renovations and refurbishing. This 3,223-seat center is still the home of the National Ballet of Canada. It also books headlining acts like Canadian chanteuse Celine Dion, and international performing-arts companies such as *Riverdance*. The Canadian Opera Company also performs here, though it has been trying to find another home.

Glenn Gould Studio. 250 Front St. W. ☎ **416/205-5555.** Tickets C$20–$75 (US$13.60–$51). Subway: Union.

This 340-seat radio concert hall offers chamber, jazz, and spoken-word performances. It was named to celebrate the great, eccentric Toronto pianist whose life was cut short by a stroke in 1982.

Massey Hall. 178 Victoria St. ☎ **416/593-4822.** www.masseyhall.com. Tickets C$25–$100 (US$17–$68). Subway: King.

This landmark building is one of Canada's premier music venues. The 2,800 seats aren't the most comfortable, but the flawless acoustics will make you stop squirming. The music performances run from classical to pop to rock to jazz. This is also a popular stop for lectures.

Premiere Dance Theatre. Queen's Quay Terminal, 207 Queen's Quay W. ☎ **416/973-4000.** Tickets C$30–$95 (US$20.40–$64.60). Subway: Union, then LRT to Queen's Quay.

This hall, specifically designed for dance performances, is where you can catch Toronto's leading contemporary dance companies. Toronto Dance Theatre, Dancemakers, and the Danny Grossman Dance Company all perform here.

✪ **Roy Thomson Hall.** 60 Simcoe St. ☎ **416/593-4822.** www.roythomsonhall.com. Tickets C$25–$100 (US$17–$68). Subway: St. Andrew.

This stunning concert hall is home to the Toronto Symphony Orchestra, which performs here from September to June, and to the Mendelssohn Choir. Since it opened in 1982 it has also played host to an array of international musical artists. The hall was designed to give the audience a feeling of unusual intimacy with the performers—none of the 2,812 seats is more than 107 feet from the stage. The exterior of the building is gorgeous—dove-colored, petal-shaped, and enveloped in a huge glass canopy that's reflective by day and transparent by night. Roy Thomson was a Canadian newspaper baron who was named to the British House of Lords and became Lord Thomson of Fleet.

CLASSICAL MUSIC & OPERA

In addition to the major musical venues mentioned above, visitors can check to see what's playing at churches around town. Possibilities include **Trinity-St. Paul's,** 427 Bloor St. W. (☎ **416/964-6337**), the home of the Toronto Consort, performers of early music; **St. Patrick's,** Dundas and McCaul streets (☎ **416/483-0559**); and **St. James' Cathedral,** King Street East and Jarvis Street, where the Orpheus Choir sings. The **University of Toronto** (☎ **416/978-3744** for the box office) offers a full range of instrumental and choral concerts and recitals in Walter Hall and the Macmillan Theatre. It's also worth checking out who's performing at the **Royal Conservatory of Music,** 273 Bloor St. W. (☎ **416/408-2825**).

If you're a fan of new music, look out for the **Sonic Boom concert series** (☎ **416/944-3100**), which produces concerts of new opera and other contemporary music.

Canadian Opera Company. 227 Front St. E. ☎ **416/872-2262.** Tickets C$30–$125 (US$20.40–$85). Subway: Union.

The Canadian Opera Company, which dates to 1950, is Canada's largest opera company and the sixth largest in North America. It stages six operas at the Hummingbird Centre from September to April.

✪ **Tafelmusik Baroque Orchestra.** 427 Bloor St. W. ☎ **416/964-6337.** Tickets C$20–$45 (US$13.60–$30.60). Subway: Yonge/Bloor for Trinity/St. Paul's; King for Massey Hall.

This internationally acclaimed group plays baroque compositions by the likes of Handel, Bach, and Mozart on authentic period instruments. Visiting musicians frequently join the 19 permanent performers. It gives a series of concerts at **Trinity/St. Paul's United Church,** 47 Bloor St. W., and stages other performances in Massey Hall (see above).

Toronto Mendelssohn Choir. 60 Simcoe St. ☎ **416/598-0422.** Tickets C$22–$49 (US$14.95–$33.30). Subway: St. Andrew.

This world-renowned group first performed in Massey Hall in 1895. Its repertoire ranges from Verdi's *Requiem,* Bach's *St. Matthew Passion,* and Handel's *Messiah* to the soundtrack of *Schindler's List.*

Toronto Symphony Orchestra. 60 Simcoe St. ☎ **416/593-4828.** Tickets C$15–$75 (US$10.20–$51). Subway: St. Andrew.

The symphony, under the direction of innovative music director Jukka-Pekka Saraste, performs at Roy Thomson Hall from September to June. Its repertoire ranges from classics to jazzy Broadway tunes and new Canadian works. In June and July, free concerts take place at outdoor venues throughout the city.

POP & ROCK MUSIC VENUES

Everyone comes to Toronto—even Madonna, who ran into some trouble with the obscenity police a while back. Tickets are available through **Ticketmaster** (☎ **416/870-8000**). In addition to the previously mentioned Hummingbird Centre, these are the major pop and rock music venues.

Kingswood Music Theatre. Paramount Canada's Wonderland, 9580 Jane St., Vaughn. ☎ **905/832-8131.** Subway: Yorkdale or York Mills, then GO Express Bus to Wonderland. By car: Take Yonge St. north to Hwy. 401 and go west to Hwy. 400. Go north on Hwy. 400 to Rutherford Rd. exit and follow signs. By car from the north, exit at Major Mackenzie.

From May through September, Kingswood's open-air theater plays host to diverse, top-notch talent. Don Henley, the Beach Boys, the Scorpions, Barry Manilow, and Public Enemy have all played here. The bandshell is covered, but the lawn seats aren't—so beware in bad weather.

Maple Leaf Gardens. 60 Carlton St. ☎ **416/977-1641.** Subway: College.

The good old Gardens just haven't been the same since the Leafs left. Nonetheless, this is a popular site for rock concerts. Don't expect cushy seats, but the sight lines are generally good. The exceptions are gray seats and green seats that bracket the stage (sections 94–97 and 76–77); avoid these if you actually care about seeing the show.

Molson Amphitheatre. Ontario Place, 955 Lakeshore Blvd. W. ☎ **416/314-9900.** Subway: Bathurst, then Bathurst streetcar south to Exhibition Place (last stop).

This is a favorite summer spot because you can listen to music by the side of Lake Ontario. Most of the seating is on the lawn, and it's usually inexpensive.

SkyDome. 1 Blue Jays Way. ☎ **416/341-3663.** Subway: Union.

The biggest venue in the city, SkyDome is where the biggest acts usually play. Ticket prices frequently rise into the stratosphere. This venue is about as intimate as a parking lot. If you're seated in the 400 (Upper SkyBox) or 500 (SkyDeck) levels, you'll be watching the show on the JumboTron, unless you bring your binoculars. And remember to steer clear of the seats next to the JumboTron, or you won't see anything at all.

DANCE

Dancemakers. Performing at Premiere Dance Theater, Queen's Quay Terminal, 207 Queen's Quay W. ☎ **416/973-4000.** Office: 927 Dupont St. ☎ **416/535-8880.** Tickets C$20–$35 (US$13.60–$23.80).

Artistic director Serge Bennathan's company has gained international recognition for its provocative mix of stylized physical movement and theater. The most recent and most exciting work in its repertoire is the Sable/Sand trilogy performed to music by

---

Good to Know: Nightlife
_____

The drinking age in Ontario is 19, and most establishments enforce the law. Expect long queues on Friday and Saturday after 10pm at clubs in the downtown core. Bars and pubs that serve drinks only are open Monday to Saturday 11am to 2am. Establishments that also serve food are open Sunday, too. If you're out at closing time, you'll find the subway shut down, but special late-night buses run along Yonge and Bloor streets. Major routes on streets such as College, Queen, and King operate all night. To find out what's on, see "Making Plans," earlier in this chapter.

Toronto composer Ahmed Hassan. (*Dance* magazine described it as evoking images "at once earthy, smoldering, vulnerable, and proud.")

Danny Grossman Dance Company. Performing at Premiere Dance Theater, Queen's Quay Terminal, 207 Queen's Quay W. ☎ **416/973-4000.** Office: 511 Bloor St. W. ☎ 416/408-4543 or 416/531-5268. Tickets C$22–$38 (US$14.95–$25.85).

The choreography of this local dance favorite is noted for its athleticism, theatricality, humor, and passionate social vision. The company performs both new works and revivals of modern-dance classics. Refreshing, fun, and exuberant.

✪ **National Ballet of Canada.** Performing at Hummingbird Centre for the Performing Arts, 1 Front St. E. ☎ **416/872-2262,** and Ontario Place, 955 Lakeshore Blvd. W. Office: 157 King St. E. ☎ 416/366-4846. Tickets C$15–$85 (US$10.20–$57.80).

Perhaps the most beloved and famous of Toronto's cultural icons is the National Ballet of Canada. English ballerina Celia Franca launched the company in Toronto in 1951, and served initially as director, principal dancer, choreographer, and teacher. Over the years, the company has achieved great renown. Among the highlights of its history are its 1973 New York debut (which featured Nureyev's full-length *Sleeping Beauty*), Baryshnikov's appearance with the company soon after his defection in 1974, and the emergence of such stars as Karen Kain.

The company performs at the Hummingbird Centre in the fall, winter, and spring; tours internationally; and makes summer appearances before enormous crowds at the open theater at Ontario Place. Its repertoire includes the classics and works by Glen Tetley (*Alice*), Sir Frederick Ashton, and Jerome Robbins. James Kudelka, who has created *The Miraculous Mandarin, The Actress,* and *Spring Awakening,* was appointed artist-in-residence in 1991.

Toronto Dance Theatre. Performing at Premiere Dance Theatre, Queen's Quay Terminal, 207 Queen's Quay W. ☎ **416/973-4000.** Office: 80 Winchester St. Tickets C$22–$37 (US$15–$25.15).

The leading contemporary dance company in Toronto burst onto the scene in 1972, bringing an inventive spirit and original Canadian dance to the stage. Director Christopher House joined in 1979 and has contributed more than 35 new works to the repertoire. Exhilarating, powerful, and energetic—don't miss *Handel Variations, Four Towers, Sacra Conversazione,* or *Pingo Slink.* The company performs two seasonal programs per year.

2 The Club & Music Scene

COMEDY CLUBS

Toronto must be one heck of a funny place. That would explain why a disproportionate number of comedians, including Jim Carrey and Mike Myers, hail from here. This is one true Toronto experience you shouldn't miss.

The Laugh Resort. 26 Lombard St. ☎ **416/364-5233.** Dinner and show C$23–$33 (US$15.65–$22.45); show only C$7–$15 ($4.75–$10.20). Subway: Queen.

If you get your kicks from incisive humor with occasional dashes of social commentary, this is your place. Gilbert Gottfried, Paula Poundstone, Ray Romano, and George Wallace have all performed here. Most of the acts are stand-up solos, though there are sometimes inspired improvs, too.

The Rivoli. 332 Queen St. W. ☎ **416/597-0794.** Cover C$10 (US$6.80) or less. Subway: Osgoode.

While the Riv is well known for its music performances and poetry readings, the Monday night ALT.COMedy Lounge is its biggest draw. It features local and visiting stand-ups, and is best known as the place where the Kids in the Hall got their start. Shows take place in the intimate 125-seat back room. See chapter 5 for a restaurant review.

✪ **Second City.** 56 Blue Jays Way. ☎ **416/343-0011.** Dinner and show from C$33 (US$22.45); show only C$15 (US$10.20). Reservations required. Subway: St. Andrew.

This was where Mike Myers, otherwise known as Austin Powers, received his formal—and improvisational—comic training. Over the years, the legendary Second City has nurtured the likes of John Candy, Dan Aykroyd, Bill Murray, Martin Short, Andrea Martin, and Eugene Levy. It continues to turn out talented young actors. The scenes are always funny and topical, though the outrageous post-show improvs usually get the biggest belly laughs. Next door is the **Tim Simms Playhouse** (☎ **416/343-0022**), an intimate space that features fledgling local stand-up talent.

Yuk Yuk's Superclub. 2335 Yonge St. ☎ **416/967-6425.** Dinner and show from C$25 (US$17); pizza and show from C$15 (US$10.20); show only C$5–C$8 (US$3.40–$5.45) Sun–Thurs, C$15 (US$10.20) Fri–Sat. Subway: Eglinton.

Yuk Yuk's is Canada's original home of stand-up comedy. Comic Mark Breslin founded the place in 1976, inspired by New York's Catch a Rising Star and Los Angeles's Comedy Store. Some famous alumni include Jim Carrey, Harland Williams, Howie Mandel, and Norm MacDonald. Other headliners have included Jerry Seinfeld, Robin Williams, and Sandra Bernhard. Monday is new talent night, and Tuesday is all improv. There's another Yuk Yuk's in **Mississauga,** not far from Pearson International Airport (☎ **905/434-4985**).

COUNTRY, FOLK, ROCK & REGGAE

The BamBoo. 312 Queen St. W. ☎ **416/593-5771** (staffed 10am–5pm). Cover C$5–$10 (US$3.40–$6.80). Subway: Osgoode.

Colorful confusion reigns here. The granddaddy of Toronto's reggae scene, the 'Boo also books calypso, salsa, jazz, soul, and R&B. Tables set for dinner surround the teensy dance floor, and the menu is as diverse as the music. Pad Thai, barbecued burgers, and jerk chicken are top choices. Forget quiet conversation, even if you score a seat on the rooftop patio—you're here for the music.

C'est What? 67 Front St. E. ☎ **416/867-9499.** Cover C$2–$10 (US$1.35–$6.80). Subway: Union.

About as cozy as the basement of a historic warehouse can be, this casual spot attracts young and old alike. It offers 28 draught beers and a broad selection of single malts. Half pub and half performance space, C'est What? has played host to up-and-comers like Barenaked Ladies and Jewel. If the nightly acoustic music doesn't suit, you can always start on the abundant board games.

El Mocambo. 464 Spadina Ave. ☎ **416/968-2001.** Cover C$4–$12 (US$2.70–$8.15). Subway: Spadina, then LRT to College St.

This rock-and-roll institution has played peekaboo in recent years—it regularly closes and reopens. But the El Mo can never really die. It's where the Rolling Stones rocked in the '70s and Elvis Costello jammed in the '80s. Today it books artists such as alternative diva Liz Phair. Its rough-and-tumble atmosphere won't suit all comers; the genteel should steer clear of the washrooms.

Free Times Café. 320 College St. (between Major and Robert sts.). ☎ **416/967-1078.** Cover C$4–$8 (US$2.70–$5.45). Subway: Queen's Park, then any streetcar west to Robert St.

The back room is one of the city's regular folk and acoustic music venues. Performances start at around 9pm nightly. Monday night is open house. The restaurant up front (see chapter 5) offers a health-oriented menu.

The Horseshoe Tavern. 368 Queen St. W. ☎ **416/598-4753.** No cover; cover from C$10 (US$6.80) for special concerts. Subway: Osgoode.

This old, traditional venue has showcased the sounds of the decades: blues in the '60s, punk in the '70s, New Wave in the '80s, and everything from ska to rockabilly to Celtic to alternative rock in the '90s. It's the place that launched Blue Rodeo, the Tragically Hip, the Band, and Prairie Oyster, and staged the Toronto debuts of the Police and Hootie & the Blowfish. It attracts a cross section of 20- to 40-year-olds.

Lee's Palace. 529 Bloor St. W. ☎ **416/532-1598.** Cover C$10 (US$6.80) or less. Subway: Bathurst.

Versailles this ain't. Still, that hasn't deterred the crème de la crème of the alternative music scene. Nirvana, Red Hot Chili Peppers, the Tragically Hip, and Alanis have performed here. Despite the graffiti grunge, Lee's does boast the best sight lines in town. The audience is young and rarely tires of slam-dancing in the mosh pit in front of the stage.

✪ The Rivoli. 332 Queen St. W. ☎ **416/597-0794.** Cover C$10 (US$6.80) or less. Subway: Osgoode.

Currently this is the club for an eclectic mix of performances, including grunge, blues, rock, jazz, comedy, and poetry reading. Holly Cole launched her career here, Tori Amos made her Toronto debut in the back room, and the Kids in the Hall still consider it home (see "Comedy Clubs," above). Shows begin at 8pm and continue until 2am. People dance if they're inspired. Upstairs, there's a billiards room and espresso bar.

JAZZ, RHYTHM & BLUES

Toronto knows how to jazz things up—especially on Saturday, when many a hotel lounge or restaurant lays on an afternoon of rip-roaring rhythm. The best time to hear jazz is in late June during the 11-day **Du Maurier Downtown Jazz Festival** (☎ **416/363-8717** for information, or 416/973-3000 for tickets). Legendary international

---

Impressions

Toronto is known as Toronto the Good, because of its alleged piety. My guess is that there's more polygamy in Toronto than Baghdad, only it's not called that in Toronto.
                                                        —Austin F. Cross, *Cross Roads* (1936)

artists perform traditional and fusion jazz, blues, and gospel at 50 venues around town. In addition to the clubs listed below, the **BamBoo** (see "Country, Folk, Rock & Reggae," above) also offers some of the hottest jazz in town.

Ben Wick's. 424 Parliament St. (at Gerrard St.). ☎ **416/961-9425.** No cover. Subway: College, then any streetcar east to Parliament St.

This comfortable English-style pub is named after local cartoonist Ben Wick. Jazz, usually on Saturday only, begins at 8:30pm.

The Black Swan. 154 Danforth Ave. ☎ **416/469-0537.** Cover C$10 (US$6.80) or less. Subway: Broadview.

This friendly, laid-back locale for both local and visiting blues performers is casual and reasonably priced. There's pool, too.

✪ **Montreal Bistro and Jazz Club.** 65 Sherbourne St. ☎ **416/363-0179.** Cover C$8 (US$5.45) or less. Subway: King, then any streetcar east to Sherbourne St.

Here's a great two-for-one deal. Top performers like Oscar Peterson, Ray McShann, and George Shearling perform in a small room lit by rose-tinted lamps; the neighboring room (see chapter 5) is a Quebecois eatery that features tourtiere and smoked-meat sandwiches.

✪ **Reservoir Lounge.** 44 Wellington St. E. ☎ **416/955-0887.** Cover C$10–$15 (US$6.80–$10.20). Subway: St. Andrew.

This perennial favorite is a modern-day speakeasy. The cramped space—it only seats 100—is below street level, and feels intimate rather than claustrophobic. Live jazz, whether Dixieland, New Orleans, or swing, belts out six nights a week. The epicenter for the short-lived swing dance craze in Toronto, this is still the place to watch glam hepcats groove.

Southern Po Boys. 159 Augusta St. ☎ **416/993-6768.** Cover C$2–$5 (US$1.35–$3.40). Subway: Spadina, then LRT south to Dundas.

This new restaurant and club bills itself as the "Mardi Gras of the North." The menu is strictly rich Southern fare, and the sounds are bluesy and soulful.

Top O' the Senator. 249 Victoria St. ☎ **416/364-7517.** Cover C$10–$20 (US$6.80–$13.40). Subway: Dundas.

One of the classiest jazz joints in town, this long, narrow club schedules top performers, such as vocalist Molly Johnson and sax goddess Jane Bunnett. Leathery couches and banquettes add to the lounge-lizard ambiance. For those who still care, the third-floor humidor has a premium collection of Cuban smokes.

DANCE CLUBS

Dance clubs come and go at an alarming pace—the hottest spot can close or turn into a decidedly unhip place almost overnight—so keep in mind that some of the spots listed below may have disappeared or changed entirely by the time you visit. Some things stay constant, though. One is that, with few exceptions, everyone lines up to get into a club—so don't get the idea that charming the bouncer will get you in faster. Most clubs don't have much of a dress code, though "no jeans" rules are not uncommon. I have indicated what the current scene looks like, but it will almost certainly change, so be sure to call ahead. The club listings in the free weekly *Now* are consistently the best.

Bauhaus. 31 Mercer St. ☎ **416/977-9813.** Cover C$10-$15 (US$6.80–$10.20). Subway: St. Andrew.

The unfinished metal-and-rivet décor gives this space an industrial feel. A young PVC-clad crowd dances to R&B and soul on the first floor, and to house and hip-hop on the second.

Berlin. 2335 Yonge St. ☎ **416/489-7777.** Cover C$10 (US$6.80). Subway: Eglinton.

As sophisticated and soigné as it tries to be—it has a smashing dining room and Tuesday-night salsa lessons—Berlin is best known as an upscale meat market. A perennial favorite in the Young-and-Eligible—oops, Yonge-and-Eglinton neighborhood, the crowd is a little older (late 20s to mid 40s) than at most of the downtown clubs. Most nights the house DJ takes charge, though live Latin bands play a mean mambo here, too.

Chick 'n' Deli. 744 Mount Pleasant Rd. ☎ **416/489-3363.** No cover. Subway: Eglinton, then no. 34 bus east to Mount Pleasant.

There's no queue outside and no bouncers in sight. Chick 'n' Deli is a low-key place, a pub-style eatery that also attracts a crowd that wants to dance. Tiffany-style lamps set the background for Top 40 or R&B tunes every night. Chicken wings and barbecue are the specialties, along with nachos, salads, and a selection of sandwiches. Jeff Healy has been known to drop by.

Crocodile Rock. 240 Adelaide St. W. ☎ **416/599-9751.** No cover. Subway: St. Andrew.

Casual and laid-back, without any trace of attitude, this place spins '70s and '80s dance sounds for the 25- to 40-year-old crowd, which includes a sprinkling of suits from Bay Street. Eclectic sounds and scene, and pool tables, too.

Cutty's Hideaway. 538 Danforth Ave. ☎ **416/463-5380.** Cover C$10–$15 (US$6.80–$10.20). Subway: Chester or Pape.

This has been a Caribbean hot spot on the Danforth for a decade. Calypso and reggae bands entertain on weekends, easily luring the many island regulars out onto the dance floor. It's popular with young and old alike.

Deluge at Atlantis. Ontario Place, 955 Lakeshore Blvd. W. ☎ **416/260-8000.** Cover C$10 (US$6.80). Subway: Bathurst, then Bathurst streetcar south to Exhibition Place (last stop).

House dancers get the crowd going at this waterfront venue where casually put-together yuppies come to party and check each other out. The dance floor revolves; in summer there's also rooftop lounging. Open Thursday to Saturday year-round.

Delux. 322 Adelaide St. W. ☎ **416/596-2212.** No cover. Subway: St. Andrew.

The white-on-white decor is the first clue that this hot spot takes itself a tad seriously. On the first floor a mirror is stenciled with the words "Lack of charisma can be fatal." The dance floor is upstairs, and the sounds are progressive house and disco.

The Docks. 11 Polson St. (off Cherry St.). ☎ **416/461-DOCKS.** Subway: Union, then taxi (about C$7/US$4.75) to Lakeshore Blvd. E. and Cherry St.

This vast waterfront party is a complex that books live entertainers like James Brown, Blue Rodeo, and the Pointer Sisters. The dance club boasts more than a dozen bars, the latest in lighting, and other party effects. Thursday night is foam fun (that is, beer). There's a restaurant and a full raft of sports facilities, too. Open Tuesday to Sunday.

Easy & the Fifth. 225 Richmond St. W. ☎ **416/979-3000.** Cover C$8–$10 (US$5.45–$6.80). Subway: Osgoode.

This is the place to come if you're looking for a more sophisticated crowd. The music is less frenzied, and you might even manage a conversation. The dance area is a loft-like space. In the back, there's a cigar bar furnished with Oriental rugs and comfortable armchairs, plus two pool tables.

Fluid Lounge. 217 Richmond St. W. ☎ **416/593-6116.** Cover C$10 (US$6.80). Subway: Osgoode.

Having been around for ages (in dance-club time), the Fluid Lounge is still hot. Only the dressed-to-kill gain entry to this haven for the beautiful and hip, with moody lighting and a decor that features leopard *and* tiger prints (grrr). Sports and music celebrities sometimes drop by to groove to the neo-funk, industrial, and mainstream dance sounds. No running shoes or sportswear.

G-Spot. 296 Richmond St. W. ☎ **416/351-7768.** Cover C$10 (US$6.80). Subway: Osgoode.

Triple the fun: On weekends this three-story club is packed to the rafters with people dancing to R&B, hip-hop, and house sounds. A club kid favorite, G-Spot also draws thirty-somethings to the humidor in the top-floor lounge.

Garage Paradise. 175 Richmond St. W. ☎ **416/351-8101.** No cover. Subway: Osgoode.

If the thought of getting all gussied up to spend the night *waiting* to get into a trendy club leaves you cold, drop by Garage Paradise. The low-key jeans-clad crowd here just wants to have fun, and they fill the dance floor for contemporary and classic rock. In case you're wondering, this club was a garage in another lifetime; now license plates decorate its walls.

The Hangar. 100 St. George St. ☎ **416/978-4701.** Cover usually C$2–$4 (US$1.35–$2.70). Subway: St. George.

The University of Toronto Students' Administrative Council operates this venue. Live bands, pool tables, pub grub, and plenty of cheap beer.

Indian Motorcycle Café and Lounge. 355 King St. W. ☎ **416/593-6996.** No cover. Subway: St. Andrew.

It's got a bar, pool tables, and a dance floor—who could ask for anything more? When the twenty- and thirty-something crowd gets tired of dancing to R&B and rock, they take refuge on one of the several comfy couches in the bar.

Industry. 901 King St. W. ☎ **416/260-2660.** Cover C$12 (US$8.15). Subway: St. Andrew, then any streetcar west to Strachan Ave.

A shrine to the strobe light. Saturday is the night to go—the place fills with everyone from ravers and queens to the seemingly "normal," all jumping to the sounds of house. On Friday night, for R&B and hip-hop, there's a dress code (no jeans, running shoes, or hats).

The Joker. 318 Richmond St. W. ☎ **416/598-1313.** Cover C$5–$10 (US$3.40–$6.80). Subway: Osgoode.

This multilevel complex used to have a frenzied feel. Now its numerous pool tables, Net-nerd terminals, and crash-worthy couches boost the languid look. University kids get shaking to rock and house music on the second- and third-floor dance floors.

Life. 240 Richmond St. W. ☎ **416/977-4116.** Cover C$5–$10 (US$3.40–$6.80). Subway: Osgoode.

Good luck getting in—this club is perpetually packed. If you're patient for an hour or two, you may be admitted to the gorgeous space and groove to house and progressive rock.

Limelight. 250 Adelaide St. W. ☎ **416/593-6126.** Cover C$5–$10 (US$3.40–$6.80). Subway: St. Andrew.

The Limelight's first floor is for dancing, the second for pool, and the third for lounging in the "Greek Room." Wednesday is progressive; alternative and retro sounds play on weekends. The crowd is predominantly 18- to 25-year-olds, mostly from the suburbs. No jeans.

Misty's. At the Hilton Toronto Airport, 5875 Airport Rd., Mississauga. ☎ **416/677-9900.** Cover C$5 (US$3.40) or less.

A successful club for more than 20 years, Misty's is still popular thanks to its music, theme nights, pool tables, big-screen TVs, and cool martini bar. Open Wednesday through Sunday.

Moments. 111 Yorkville Ave. ☎ **416/924-9955.** Cover $5–$10 (US$3.40–$6.80). Subway: Bay.

If you need any evidence that all things Latin are still hot, hot, hot, drop by this subterranean club. The Venezuelan-born DJ spins a mix of Latino rock and pop for a twentysomething crowd. Thursday—Brazilian Night—is the most popular of the week.

Money. 199 Richmond St. W. ☎ **416/591-9000.** Cover $10 (US$6.80). Subway: Osgoode.

Self-consciously cool, with its pearly white decor and glass dance floor. The sounds are chart-topping dance and R&B hits.

Phoenix Concert Theatre. 410 Sherbourne St. ☎ **416/323-1251.** Cover C$4–$15 (US$2.70–$10.20). Subway: College, then any streetcar east to Sherbourne St.

One of the oldest dance halls in Toronto, the Phoenix attracts an all-ages, all-races crowd that includes straights and gays. As a rock venue, it showcases such artists as Screaming Headless Torsos, Patti Smith, and the Smashing Pumpkins. On the weekends, it gets the crowds dancing with a mixture of retro, Latin, alternative, and funk. Thursday is gay night.

Plastique. 128 Peter St. ☎ **416/506-9481.** Cover C$10–$15 (US$6.80–$10.20). Subway: Osgoode.

Fickle though the Beautiful People may be, they haven't tired yet of this double-decker gilt wonder. Everyone at this upscale meat market is dressed to the nines. Celebrity sightings are common—Antonio Banderas apparently has graced the dance floor.

Sneaky Dees. 431 College St. ☎ **416/603-3090.** No cover. Subway: Queen's Park, then any streetcar west to Bathurst St.

Pool tables and Mexican food complement alternative rock spun by a DJ in the club upstairs until 1:30am. Downstairs, the bar is open until 3am on weekdays, 5am on weekends.

Whiskey Saigon. 250 Richmond St. W. ☎ **416/593-4646.** Cover C$2–$10 (US$1.35–$6.80). Subway: Osgoode.

Crowds frolic to their heart's content in Euro-disco style to a variety of sounds on multiple floors—alternative, house, and retro. Open Thursday (cheap night) to Sunday.

3 The Bar Scene

The current night scene encompasses a flock of attractive bistros with billiard tables. You can enjoy cocktails, a reasonably priced meal, and a game of billiards in comfortable, aesthetically pleasing surroundings. The cigar bar is still in vogue, and most clubs have a humidor for the stogie set. Unlike dance clubs, the bars and lounges in Toronto are a pretty stable bunch.

BARS & LOUNGES

Al Frisco's. 133 John St. ☎ **416/595-8201.** Subway: Osgoode.

This is one of the few Toronto bars with its own microbrewery. Upstairs, people crowd around the pool tables or jam the dance floor, moving to retro sounds. Downstairs, cozy fireplaces enhance the gathering-spot atmosphere. The food is Mediterranean—pizza, pasta, salads, and antipasti. The extra-large outdoor patio is jammed in summer with a mix of tourists, suits, and casual professionals in their late 20s and beyond.

Alice Fazooli's. 294 Adelaide St. W. ☎ **416/979-1910.** Subway: Osgoode.

Baseball art and memorabilia, including a full-scale model of an outfielder making a catch against the wall, fill this large bar and dining room. It's usually packed with an older business crowd. The back room serves crabs cooked in many different styles, pizza, pasta, and raw-bar specialties. The garden patio with a fountain is great in the summer. There are more than 50 wines by the glass.

Bar Italia & Billiards. 582 College St. ☎ **416/535-3621.** Subway: Queen's Park, then streetcar west.

Downstairs, a young, trendy, good-looking crowd quaffs drinks or coffee and snacks on Italian sandwiches. Upstairs, guys gather around six pool tables. If you're seeking quiet, go early in the evening before the scene changes to a veritable fiesta.

Bovine Sex Club. 542 Queen St. W. ☎ **416/504-4239.** Subway: Osgoode, then any streetcar west to Bathurst St.

This alternative rock venue is not for the faint of heart. Intimidating metal sculptures and other shock-value art contribute to the funky atmosphere. Strictly for the nose-ring and body-pierced set. You'll recognize it by the tangle of bizarre metal outside.

✪ **Centro.** 2472 Yonge St. ☎ **416/483-2211.** Subway: Eglinton.

Downstairs at the restaurant, this comfortable bar is a see-and-be-seen spot for a dressed-up crowd in their 30s and up. Closed Sunday.

Club Lucky Cafe & Bar. 117 John St. ☎ **416/977-8890.** Subway: Osgoode.

This sophisticated cigar and piano bar, open only on weekends, draws a crowd in their 30s and 40s, and some 20-somethings.

✪ **Corso Italia.** 584 College St. ☎ **416/532-3635.** Subway: Queen's Park, then any streetcar west to Clinton.

This place positively glows. Up front you can sink into the couches and enjoy good, thick coffee. The orange and yellow walls brighten the day. Four pool tables await in the back. The mural depicting a bunch of guys clinging precariously to a girder is too cool for words.

The Devil's Martini. 136 Simcoe St. ☎ **416/591-7541.** Subway: St. Andrew.

Despite the ominous name, this is a great spot to slurp up a generous martini. The scene aims for hip, but is fairly relaxed.

✪ **Fez Batik.** 129 Peter St. ☎ **416/977-7544.** Cover C$10 (US$6.80) or less. Subway: Osgoode.

Fashion-conscious singles in their 30s gather in this Moroccan-inspired space. They fill the sidewalk patio, jam into the downstairs bar area, or hang out upstairs, where there's a small area for dancing to recorded funk and rock. For fun, you can have your tarot cards read. Thursday through Sunday nights, a DJ plays house music.

Hard Rock Cafe. 1 Blue Jays Way (enter through SkyDome Gate 1). ☎ **416/341-2388.** No cover. Subway: Union, then walk west (toward CN Tower).

This is the only Hard Rock Cafe in a sports stadium. It boasts a close-up view of the field and of other events held in the stadium. It offers a typical Hard Rock menu and the familiar rock and roll memorabilia decor.

Hemingway's. 142 Cumberland St. ☎ **416/968-2828.** Subway: Bay.

This Yorkville watering hole has a large, heated rooftop patio. It features piano or other entertainment Thursday to Saturday in winter. A pint of beer is C$5 (US$3.40).

The Hooch. 817 Queen St. W. ☎ **416/703-5069.** Subway: Osgoode, then streetcar west.

This relaxed spot is a great place to watch hepcats doing the swing thing. If you arrive before 7pm, you might even be able to take a dance lesson. The Hooch is upstairs at the **Gypsy Co-op** (see "Coffeehouses," later in this chapter).

Left Bank. 567 Queen St. W. ☎ **416/504-1626.** Subway: Osgoode, then any streetcar west to Bathurst.

An over-25 crowd gathers in the lower-level bar at this restaurant. It's especially inviting in winter, when the fire warms folks playing billiards or lolling on the comfortable banquettes.

Madison. 14 Madison Ave. ☎ **416/927-1722.** Subway: Spadina.

Madison has to be one of the city's most popular gathering places, with people (many of them students) jamming every floor and terrace. The newest development is the billiard room, with 10 tables. Everyone in the friendly crowd seems to know everyone else.

Mambo Lounge. 106 John St. ☎ **416/593-4407.** Subway: St. Andrew.

Upstairs at Xango, this is a sophisticated Cuban-style piano bar and smoking lounge that attracts an older (30s to 50s) crowd. It has live entertainment and dancing to a DJ. Leather couches and wrought-iron-and-glass coffee tables set the tone.

Milano. 325 King St. W. ☎ **416/599-9909.** Subway: St. Andrew.

Up front there's a bar, and beyond it stand several billiard tables. The dining area is off to the side. In summer, French doors open to the street, making for a pleasant Parisian atmosphere. The bistro-style food includes pizza, pasta, sandwiches, and such items as salmon with oven-roasted beet sauce.

Montana. 145 John St. ☎ **416/595-5949.** Subway: St. Andrew.

This kicky Western saloon has a log-cabin-style nook with a fireplace and a bison trophy upstairs. Live bands play mostly nostalgic music from the '70s and early '80s. There's a cigar lounge, the Big Smoke, and billiards, too. The relaxed, casual crowd also hangs out on the sidewalk patio.

Panorama. In the Manulife Centre, 55 Bloor St. W. ☎ **416/967-0000.** Subway: Bloor/Yonge.

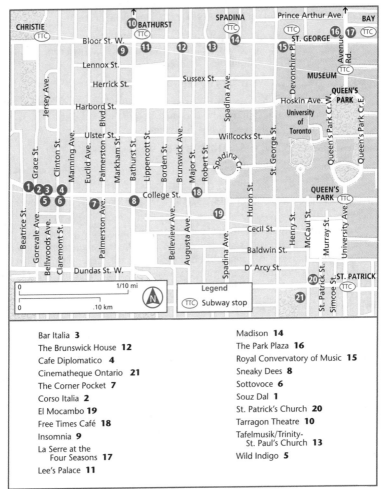

Legend

TTC Subway stop

Bar Italia **3**
The Brunswick House **12**
Cafe Diplomatico **4**
Cinematheque Ontario **21**
The Corner Pocket **7**
Corso Italia **2**
El Mocambo **19**
Free Times Café **18**
Insomnia **9**
La Serre at the
   Four Seasons **17**
Lee's Palace **11**

Madison **14**
The Park Plaza **16**
Royal Convervatory of Music **15**
Sneaky Dees **8**
Sottovoce **6**
Souz Dal **1**
St. Patrick's Church **20**
Tarragon Theatre **10**
Tafelmusik/Trinity-
   St. Paul's Church **13**
Wild Indigo **5**

From this 51st-floor perch above Bloor and Bay, visitors can see north and south for 150 miles (at least on a clear day). Go for the lit skyline and the Latin ambiance (check out the Rio carnival mural) and music. The seating is comfortable, and more than a dozen types of cigars are available. Arrive early if you want a window seat.

The Pilot. 22 Cumberland St. ☎ **416/923-5716.** Subway: Yonge/Bloor.

This watering hole dates to the early years of the Second World War. It's an unpretentious place with pool tables and a wonderful rooftop patio.

✪ **The Real Jerk.** 709 Queen St. E. ☎ **416/463-6055.** Reservations not accepted. Mon–Fri 11:30am–midnight, Sat 2pm–1am, Sun 3pm–11pm. Subway: Queen, then streetcar east.

The original Real Jerk became so popular that it moved to this larger space. The hip crowd digs the hot background music, the lively ambiance, and the moderately priced, super-spiced Caribbean food—jerk chicken, curries, shrimp Creole, rotis, and patties.

Sassafraz. 100 Cumberland St. ☎ **416/964-2222.** Subway: Bay.

In Yorkville, this classy gathering spot operates as a bar and bistro during the day and early evening. Later on, it's a club called the Catwalk, which has two bars, a double-sided gas fireplace, and a dance floor.

Shark City. 117 Eglinton Ave. E. ☎ **416/488-7899.** Subway: Eglinton.

Forget *Jaws*—the sharks here sport well-cut suits and smoke Havanas. When not busy striking a pose, the young, hip crowd shoots some pool at the basement tables. There's also a restaurant with basic pizza and pasta offerings, and a small patio.

Smokeless Joe's. 125 John St. ☎ **416/591-2221.** Subway: St. Andrew.

This is Toronto's only smoke-free bar. It stocks more than 175 brews from around the globe, and has a patio where the desperate can get a nicotine fix.

✪ **Souz Dal.** 636 College St. ☎ **416/537-1883.** Subway: Queen's Park, then any street-car west to Clinton St.

Located in Little Italy, Souz Dal stands out. It's dark and intimate, painted deep purple and mustard, and decorated in exotic Moroccan fashion. Kilims adorn the walls; the bar is fashioned out of copper. Candles light the small, trellised patio. There's a great selection of martinis and margaritas, as well as tropical drinks, like the Havana (rum, guava juice, and lime). Thursday is acid-jazz night.

Swingers. 57 Duncan St. ☎ **416/597-0202.** Subway: St. Andrew.

Despite the Hollywood-inspired name, this is a low-key joint with a pool table and a pretty aquarium. The patrons, in their 20s and 30s, are frequently suited up.

Up & Down. 270 Adelaide St. W. ☎ **416/977-4038.** Subway: St. Andrew.

Velvet, leather, and other plush textures create the sultry atmosphere. Relax, play some chess, or just listen to the eclectic music.

Wayne Gretzky's. 99 Blue Jays Way. ☎ **416/979-7825.** Subway: Union.

Hockey fans will want to visit this shrine to the Great One, who hails from the nearby town of Brantford. It's filled with memorabilia—photos, uniforms, and equipment are displayed in several cases. They trace Gretzky's rise from the junior leagues in Sault Ste. Marie, through his professional debut with the Indianapolis Racers, to his career in the NHL. Forget the food, unless you simply have to say that you dined at *his* place. Better to have a drink at the long bar or head upstairs to the rooftop Oasis. There, you can sit at the cabana-style bar, which affords a fine view of the CN Tower.

Wild Indigo. 607 College St. ☎ **416/536-8797.** Subway: Queen's Park, then any street-car west to Clinton St.

This intimate Little Italy bar has a small, atmospheric patio in the back. It attracts a youngish, intellectual crowd and features a DJ on weekends.

PUBS & TAVERNS

Allen's. 143 Danforth Ave. ☎ **416/463-3086.** Subway: Broadview.

Allen's sports a great bar that offers more than 80 beer selections and 80-plus single-malts. Guinness is the drink of choice on Tuesday and Saturday nights, when folks reel and jig to the Celtic-Irish entertainment. Readers have written in to recommend the steaks here.

The Amsterdam. 600 King St. W. (at Portland St.). ☎ **416/504-6882.** Subway: St. Andrew, then streetcar west.

Cueing Up

It's not hard to find a bar or a restaurant with a token pool table—it's a must-have accessory in some quarters—but real shark shops aren't so easy to come by. If you've got a serious pool habit, try one of the following clubs.

Academy of Spherical Arts. 38 Hanna St. ☎ **416/532-2782.** Subway: St. Andrew, then streetcar west along King St. to Atlantic Ave. and walk one block south.

Okay, maybe this isn't your typical pool hall, but it's got a great pedigree: The 5,000-square-foot space used to house billiard manufacturer Brunswick. Now it looks more like a turn-of-the-century gentlemen's club (there are even a few antique pool tables). This is a popular celebrity-sighting spot, and the likes of Kevin Bacon, Minnie Driver, Dennis Hopper, and Lennox Lewis have been known to drop by. (Because the Academy hosts private parties, always call before you drop by to make sure it's open that day.)

Charlotte Room. 19 Charlotte St. ☎ **416/598-2882.** Subway: St. Andrew.

Billiards Digest has called the Charlotte Room one of the ten best billiard rooms in North America. It's got the feel of an old-fashioned old-boys' club. In addition to the ten tables, there's a pub-grub menu and, on occasion, live jazz music.

The Coloured Stone. 205 Richmond St. W. ☎ **416/351-8499.** Subway: St. Andrew.

This pool hall offers curious mix of billiards and art. (No, that's not a misprint.) The Stone boasts an Art Nook where Ojibway artist Duke Redbird presents his sculptures and paintings. The billiard rooms are works of art themselves, with patterned rugs and brightly colored walls. The atmosphere throughout is relaxed and friendly.

The Corner Pocket. 533 College St. ☎ **416/928-3540.** Subway: Queen's Park.

Smack dab in the middle of Little Italy—the neighborhood where's every restaurant believes it's got the have its own pool table—there's the Corner Pocket. Unpretentious and low-key, the hall has seventeen billiard tables (and one foosball table, in case you're interested). The big-screen television is always tuned to the sports channel.

This brew pub is a beer-drinker's heaven, serving more than 200 labels as well as 30 types on draft. By 8pm the tables in the back are filled, and the long bar is jammed. In summer the patio is fun, too.

The Bishop and the Belcher. 361 Queen St. W. ☎ **416/591-2352.** Subway: Osgoode.

This British-style pub offers 14 drafts on tap and a decent selection of single malts. The classic pub fare includes bangers and mash, shepherd's pie, and a ploughman's lunch.

The Brunswick House. 481 Bloor St. W. ☎ **416/964-2242.** Subway: Spadina or Bathurst.

This cavernous room is a favorite with University of Toronto students. The Brunny House, as it's affectionately known, has been described as a cross between a German beer hall and an English north-country workingmen's club. Waiters carry trays of frothy suds between the Formica tables. Impromptu dancing to background music and pool and shuffleboard playing drown out the sound of at least 2 of the large-screen

Returning to Toronto was like finding a Jaguar parked in front of the vicarage and the padre inside with a pitcher of vodka martinis reading Lolita.
                                                                    —*Maclean's* magazine, January 1959

TVs, if not the other 18. This is an inexpensive place to down some beer. Upstairs, there's live-broadcast thoroughbred and harness racing from international tracks, including Hong Kong.

Cameron Public House. 408 Queen St. W. ☎ **416/703-0811.** Subway: Osgoode.

Old and new hippies hang in the front room, with its rococo bar. Local bands try out in the back room. On Sunday, the Cameron serves an amazingly good brunch.

The Duke of Westminster. First Canadian Place, 100 King St. W. ☎ **416/368-1555.** Closed weekends. Subway: King.

Designed in England and shipped and assembled here, this pub offers 16 beers and ales on tap. Imported premium beers usually cost about C$4 (US$2.70) per half-pint, C$6 (US$4.10) per pint. The Duke of Westminster offers a classy English atmosphere that seems to attract very English types for a good, frothy pint and a game of darts or pool.

The Rebel House. 1068 Yonge St. ☎ **416/927-0704.** Subway: Rosedale.

The youngish crowd here dresses in designer sportswear. They're drawn to this neighborhood pub by the impressive selection of microbrews and the reasonably priced grub.

The Unicorn. 175 Eglinton Ave. E. ☎ **416/482-0115.** Subway: Eglinton.

This Celtic pub is named for the Irish Rovers' song. Along with the usual pub staples, there's Irish stew and a great list of imported dark ales. It's a fun, relaxed place to unwind.

Wheat Sheaf Tavern. 667 King St. W. ☎ **416/504-9912.** Subway: St. Andrew, then any streetcar west to Bathurst St.

Designated a historic landmark, this is the city's oldest tavern—it's been in operation since 1849. For fans, eight screens show great moments in sports. The jukebox features 1,200 choices, and there are two pool tables and an outdoor patio.

WINE BARS

Centro. 2472 Yonge St. ☎ **416/483-2211.** Subway: Eglinton.

Upstairs is the gorgeous dining room (see review in chapter 5), downstairs is the upscale wine bar. A well-dressed crowded drop by for the convivial atmosphere, the gourmet pizzas and pastas, and the extensive selection of wines: there are more than 600 varieties from around the globe.

Sottovoce. 595 College St. ☎ **416/536-4564.** Subway: Queen's Park, then any streetcar west to Clinton St.

The name (a musical direction that translates as "very softly") must be an in-joke, because the decibel level here is outrageous. This wine bar is still a great find, not the least because it serves truly inspired focaccia sandwiches and salads.

Vines. 38 Wellington St. E. ☎ **416/955-9833.** Subway: King.

Vines provides a pleasant atmosphere in which to sample a glass of champagne or any one of 30 wines, priced from C$6 to $10 (US$4.10 to $6.80) for a 4-ounce glass.

Salads, cheeses, and light meals, served with fresh French sticks (mini baguettes), are available.

HOTEL BARS

Accents. At the Sutton Place Hotel, 955 Bay St. ☎ **416/924-9221.** Subway: Museum or Wellesley.

This wine bar offers a great selection by the glass. A pianist entertains throughout the evening.

The Chartroom. At the Westin Harbour Castle, 1 Harbour Sq. ☎ **416/869-1600.** Subway: Union, then LRT to Queen's Quay.

This casual meeting spot enjoys a lovely view of the lake and of the island ferry.

The Chelsea Bun. At the Delta Chelsea Inn, 33 Gerrard St. W. ☎ **416/595-1975.** Subway: College or Dundas.

As if the fine selection of single-malt whiskeys weren't enough of a draw, the Bun also features live musical entertainment. This is a great spot for jazz on Saturday from 3pm until around 7; 6 nights a week, a pianist and a band play Top 40 tunes from 9pm to 1am.

Club 22. At the Windsor Arms, 18 St. Thomas St. ☎ **416/971-9666.** Subway: Bay.

The newly rebuilt Windsor Arms caters to rarefied tastes with one of the most expensive bars in the city. At Club 22 you can order from a menu of caviar and champagne; a 4-ounce glass of Cristal goes for C$35 (US$23.80).

The Consort Bar. At Le Royal Meridien King Edward, 37 King St. E. ☎ **416/863-9700.** Subway: King.

This is a wonderfully clubby, old-fashioned bar. Not only does it boast comfortable wing chairs, but its 8-foot-high windows afford excellent people watching.

Good Queen Bess. At the Sheraton Centre, 123 Queen St. W. ☎ **416/361-1000.** Subway: Osgoode.

A true English pub, the Good Queen Bess was shipped over in sections from England. The list of dark ales is impressive.

La Serre. At the Four Seasons Hotel Toronto, 21 Avenue Rd. ☎ **416/964-0411.** Subway: Bay.

This charming piano bar offers a full range of single malts and martinis, and welcomes cigar aficionados. Located on street level, it's a great place to people-watch along Yorkville Avenue. *Newsweek* named it one of the world's best bars.

✪ **The Library Bar.** At the Royal York, 100 Front St. W. ☎ **416/863-6333.** Subway: Union.

This small, wood-paneled bar is simply the best place in the city to order a top-quality martini, which is served in a "fishbowl" glass. Slurp.

Matisse. At the Radisson Plaza Hotel, 90 Bloor St. E. ☎ **416/961-8000.** Subway: Yonge/Bloor.

This casual bar has a good selection of wines by the glass. It's attached to the dining room, which is also called Matisse.

✪ **The Roof. At the Park Hyatt Toronto.** 4 Avenue Rd. ☎ **416/924-5471.** Subway: Museum or Bay.

Author Mordecai Richler called this the only civilized spot in Toronto. It's an old literary haunt, with comfortable couches in front of a fireplace and excellent drinks. The walls sport caricatures of members of Canada's literary establishment, including luminaries such as Margaret Atwood. The James Bond martini—vodka with a drop of lillet—is well worth a try. The view from the outdoor terrace is one of the best in the city.

4 The Gay & Lesbian Scene

Toronto's large, active gay and lesbian community has created a varied nightlife scene.

Boots Complex. Selby Hotel, 592 Sherbourne St. ☎ **416/921-0665.** Subway: Wellesley.

This 12,000-square-foot club is popular with a young crowd that wants to dance. There's also a large patio area.

Bar 501. 501 Church St. ☎ **416/944-3272.** Subway: Wellesley.

This bar is famous for its Sunday evening drag shows, which often attract crowds that watch from the sidewalk through the large front window. There's also Saturday afternoon bingo with the infamous Sister Bedelia.

The Barn/The Stables. 418 Church St. ☎ **416/977-4702.** Subway: Wellesley.

This is one of the city's oldest gay bars. The second-floor dance floor is always jammed. There are afternoon underwear parties on Sundays, and sex videos, too. The favored look is denim with occasional ranch-style allusions (you'll see a few spurs). There's also an on-site leather shop selling fetish gear and clothing.

Byzantium. 499 Church St. ☎ **416/922-3859.** Subway: Wellesley.

An attractive bar-restaurant, Byzantium attracts an affable crowd for cocktails followed by dinner in the adjacent dining room. This is a comfortable, relaxed space, and the cooking draws straight patrons, too.

Crews/Tango. 508 Church St. ☎ **416/972-1662.** Subway: Wellesley.

Located in a renovated Victorian house, this two-in-one club boasts a large outdoor patio. Crews is a gay bar known for its drag shows, which start at 11pm on nights from Wednesday through Sunday. The adjoining Tango bar draws a lesbian crowd; it hosts Wednesday night karaoke; on Saturday, the crowd heads for the dance floor.

The Phoenix. 410 Sherbourne St. ☎ **416/323-1251.** Subway: College, then any streetcar east to Sherbourne St.

The Phoenix attracts an all-ages, all-races crowd that includes gays and straights on most nights. Thursday is specifically gay night.

Pope Joan. 547 Parliament St. (at Winchester St.). ☎ **416/925-6662.** Subway: Wellesley, then any streetcar east to Parliament St. and walk 2 blocks south.

This is the city's most popular lesbian bar. Downstairs, there are a pool table and a game room furnished with old, cozy couches, and there are a restaurant and dance area upstairs. On Saturday there's a hearty buffet brunch for C$6 (US$4.10). In summer, the fenced-in patio is the place to cool off. There are occasional performances by a group called the Drag Kings.

Sailor. 465 Church St. ☎ **416/972-0887.** Subway: Wellesley.

This bar-restaurant is attached to Woody's (see below), but has a livelier atmosphere. Every Thursday there's a Best Chest competition, and on Sunday the draw is the drag show. In the evening, a DJ spins an assortment of retro and alternative tunes.

Cyberfun: Internet Cafes

As in most other North American cities, the Web is a social magnet in Toronto. The **Cyberland Cafe,** Yonge St. (☎ **416/955-9628**), is one of the biggest Net cafes. In addition to the 20 networked computers, there's a billiards room and an attached restaurant and bar. Purchase C$9 (US$6.15) worth of food, and you'll get a free hour of Net-surfing. (Subway: Queen.)

Insomnia, 563 Bloor St. W. (☎ **416/588-3907**), is more social than your average Net cafe—maybe it's the sign over the door that reads, "The Internet is a strange place. Don't surf alone." There are several curtained computer terminals, as well as comfortable couches and a big-screen TV. The pizza and panini are usually pretty good. (Subway: Bathurst.)

Along Church Street, the heart of Toronto's gay and lesbian community, there's **Ciber Village** (449 Church St. at Alexander St., ☎ **416/928-6060**). Open only from 10am to 10pm, it offers Web-surfing more a mere C$6 (US$4.10) an hour, or 10 cents (US7 cents) per minute, with no minimum times. (Subway: College.)

Slack Alice. 562 Church St. ☎ **416/969-8742.** Subway: Wellesley.

This incredibly popular bar draws a gay and lesbian crowd. The menu features homestyle comfort food; on weekend evenings, a DJ gets the crowd on its feet.

Tallulah's Cabaret. 12 Alexander St. ☎ **416/975-8555.** Subway: Wellesley.

This is the place to let it all hang out. Alternative music, flamboyant dancing, and reasonably priced drinks make certain everyone has a good time. Friday is ostensibly women's night, but don't count on it.

Wilde Oscar's. 518 Church St. ☎ **416/921-8142.** Subway: Wellesley.

Decked out like an Edwardian salon, this popular spot is known for its gourmet pizzas and pastas.

Woody's. 467 Church St. (south of Wellesley St.). ☎ **416/972-0887.** Subway: Wellesley.

A friendly, very popular local bar, Woody's is frequented mainly by men, but welcomes women. It's a popular meeting spot, especially for brunch on the weekend.

5 Cinemas & Movie Houses

There is no shortage of movie theaters—in fact, monster megaplexes are the rage at the moment. The largest theaters are at the Eaton Centre, St. Lawrence Market Square, and Yonge and Eglinton. Cinemas with a mere pair of screens can be found at the Sheraton Centre, Bloor and Yonge, and Yonge and St. Clair. Check *Now, Eye,* or one of the newspapers for listings.

Carlton Cinemas. 20 Carlton St. ☎ **416/964-2463.** Tickets C$8.50 adults (US$5.80), C$6 (US$4.10) seniors and children. Tues discounts. Subway: College.

Home to the subtitled set, the Carlton plays films—many of them superb—that frequently don't see the light of day anywhere else. Many of the offerings originate in France, Italy, Russia, or China; there's also a smattering of independent North American films. Buy tickets early on weekends.

Sweet Treats: Toronto's Dessert Cafes

Nightlife doesn't have to mean high culture, barhopping, or anything in between. It doesn't even mean you have to stop eating. Here are some of the city's most agreeable places to satisfy a sweet tooth and do some people watching.

Demetre Caffe. 400 Danforth Ave. ☎ **416/778-6654.** Subway: Broadview.

In the heart of Greektown on the Danforth, Demetre is known for its Old World ambiance as well as its sweets: Belgian waffles, oversized sundaes, cakes, tortes, and baklava. It's popular at all hours of the evening with a casual crowd, and on weekends it draws families. Closing time is midnight Sunday through Thursday, 3am Friday and Saturday.

Desserts by Phipps. 420 Eglinton Ave. W. ☎ **416/481-9111.** Subway: Eglinton.

The cafe serves salads and sandwiches, but what really draws the crowds are the decadent desserts. Cappuccino chiffon cake is a direct hit, as are the moist but not gooey apple confections.

✪ **Dufflet Pastries.** 787 Queen St. W. ☎ **416/504-2870.** Subway: Osgoode, then any streetcar west to Euclid Ave.

On menus around town, you'll sometimes see mention of "desserts by Dufflet." *Divine* is the word that best applies to these confections. Owner Dufflet Rosenberg bakes some of the most delectable tortes, tarts, and pastries in the city. The

Cinematheque Ontario. Screenings at Art Gallery of Ontario, 317 Dundas St. W. (between McCaul and Beverley sts.). Office: 2 Carlton St. ☎ **416/967-7371** or 416/923-3456 (box office). Tickets C$8 (US$5.45) adults, C$4.25 (US$2.90) seniors and students.

This organization shows the best in contemporary cinema. The programs include directors' retrospectives, plus new films from France, Germany, Japan, Bulgaria, and other countries that you won't find in the first-run theaters around town.

6 Coffeehouses

While Starbucks has certainly staked out territory in Toronto, the Canadian chain the **Second Cup** is holding its ground. It offers a full range of flavored coffees and espresso varieties, plus cakes, muffins, croissants, and gift items. Another chain, **Timothy's,** invites you to pour your own selection from about 10 varieties. My favorite coffeehouses are all independents, though.

✪ **Cafe Diplomatico.** 594 College St. ☎ **416/534-4637.** Subway: Queen's Park.

One of the oldest cafes in Toronto, this Little Italy gem has mosaic marble floors, wrought-iron chairs, and an extra-large sidewalk patio. Many longtime area residents get their caffeine fix here in the morning; the patio attracts a trendier crowd.

Daily Express Café. 280 Bloor St. W. ☎ **416/944-3225.** Subway: St. George.

Near the student ghetto in the Annex neighborhood, this lively cafe draws most of its crowd from nearby U of T.

Future Bakery. 483 Bloor St. W. ☎ **416/922-5875.** Subway: Spadina.

This rambling cafe attracts an artsy crowd with fine breads and a selection of coffees. Would-be writers scribble away by the hour in well-lit corners.

problem is deciding where to start. Chocolate raspberry truffle? Cappuccino dacquoise? Your call. There are a few selections for people with gluten or nut allergies, and the cafe also serves light fare.

✪ **Greg's Ice Cream.** 200 Bloor St. W. ☎ **416/961-4734.** Subway: Museum or St. George.

One taste of Greg's homemade ice cream will turn you into an addict. (I should know—I've been one for years.) Different flavors are available each day, and the staff is generous about handing out samples. It's hard to pick one favorite flavor, but the roasted marshmallow would definitely be up there.

Just Desserts. 137 John St. (at Richmond St.). ☎ **416/599-0655.** Subway: Osgoode.

This cafe stays open practically around the clock on weekends for those in need of a sugar fix. Around 40 desserts are available—as many as 12 different cheese-cakes, 10 or so pies, plus an array of gâteaux, tortes, and meringues. All cost around C$6 (US$4.10).

Sicilian Ice Cream Company. 712 College St. ☎ **416/531-7716.** Subway: Queen's Park, then streetcar west.

This old-fashioned ice cream parlor is Toronto's top purveyor of Italian *gelati*. The wonderful patio is open in the summer.

Gypsy Co-op. 817 Queen St. W. ☎ **416/703-5069.** Subway: Osgoode, then streetcar west.

Coffee is not the only king here. Many teas and herbal infusions (for everything from stress to colds and flu) are available, as are super-rich brownies. Upstairs is the Hooch, the epicenter of the swing craze in Toronto.

Lettieri. 94 Cumberland St. ☎ **416/515-8764.** Subway: Bay.

The house rule is that after 7 minutes, a pot of coffee is no longer fresh. This place takes the bean seriously. In addition to the wide range of coffees, there are focaccia sandwiches, tarts, cookies, and pastries.

Nine of Cups. 1522 Queen St. W. ☎ **416/532-2216.** Subway: Osgoode, then streetcar west.

Off the beaten track but close to High Park is this unusual coffeehouse. The theme veers to the mystical, with sun and moon logos, and an upstairs salon where you can have your tea leaves read. But the bottom line is, they make a great cup of joe.

10

Side Trips from Toronto

I have got bad news for anyone who's come up with a plan to shoe-horn Toronto's many attractions into a week-long stay: There are several don't-miss sights within a 2-hour drive of the city. The big three—Niagara-on-the-Lake, Niagara Falls, and Stratford—as well as the less well-known city of Hamilton are described in this chapter.

For information about the areas surrounding Toronto, contact **Tourism Ontario,** P.O. Box 104, Toronto ON M5B 2H1 (☎ **800/ONTARIO** or 416/314-0944), or visit the travel center in the Eaton Centre on Level 1 at Yonge and Dundas. It's open Monday to Friday 10am to 9pm, Saturday 9:30am to 6pm, Sunday noon to 5pm. You can view the Web site at www.travelinx.com.

1 Stratford

145km (90 miles) NW of Toronto

The Stratford Festival was born in 1953 when director Tyrone Guthrie lured Alec Guinness to perform. The festival has become one of the most famous in North America, and it has put this scenic town on the map. While visitors will notice the Avon River and other sights named in honor of the Bard, they may not realize that Stratford has another claim to fame. It's home to one of the best cooking schools in the country, making it a delight to dine at many of the spots in town.

ESSENTIALS

VISITOR INFORMATION   For first-rate visitor information, go to the **Information Centre** (☎ **519/273-3352**) by the river on York Street at Erie. From May to early November, it's open Sunday to Wednesday 9am to 5pm, Thursday to Saturday 9am to 8pm. At other times, contact **Tourism Stratford,** 88 Wellington St., P.O. Box 818, Stratford, ON N5A 6W1 (☎ **800/561-SWAN** or 519/271-5140; www.georgianbay.com/sites/1305-001.htm).

GETTING THERE   Driving from Toronto, take Highway 401 west to Interchange 278 at Kitchener. Follow Highway 8 west onto Highway 7/8 to Stratford.

Amtrak and **VIA Rail** (☎ **416/366-8411**) operate several trains daily along the Toronto–Kitchener–Stratford route. Call ☎ **800/361-1235** in Canada or **800/USA-RAIL** in the United States.

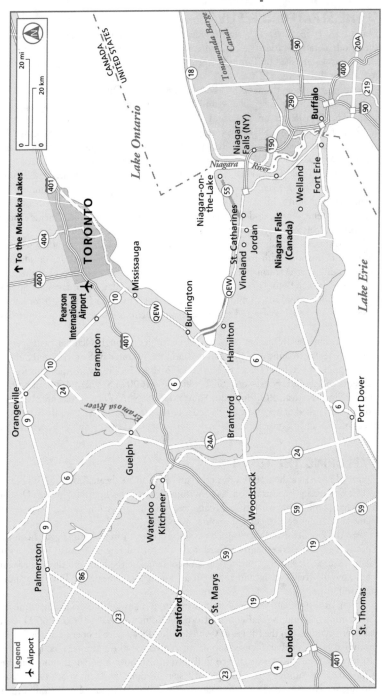

✪ THE STRATFORD FESTIVAL

On July 13, 1953, *Richard III,* starring Alec Guinness, was staged in a huge tent. From that modest start, Stratford's artistic directors have built on the radical, but faithfully classic, base established by Tyrone Guthrie to create a repertory theater with a glowing international reputation.

Stratford has three theaters. The **Festival Theatre,** 55 Queen St., in Queen's Park, has a dynamic thrust stage. The **Avon Theatre,** 99 Downie St., has a classic proscenium. The **Tom Patterson Theatre,** Lakeside Drive, is an intimate 500-seat theater.

World famous for its Shakespearean productions, the festival also offers classic and modern theatrical masterpieces. Recent productions have included *West Side Story, Oedipus Rex, Death of a Salesman, Dracula,* and *Glenn* (about the legendary, eccentric Canadian pianist Glenn Gould). Offerings from the Bard have included *The Taming of the Shrew, The Tempest,* and *Macbeth.* Among the company's famous alumni are Dame Maggie Smith, Sir Alec Guinness, Sir Peter Ustinov, Alan Bates, Christopher Plummer, Irene Worth, and Julie Harris. Present company members include Brian Bedford, Al Waxman, Cynthia Dole, Martha Henry, and Barbara Byrne.

In addition to attending plays, visitors may enjoy "Meet the Festival," a series of informal discussions with members of the acting company, production, or administrative staff. "Post Performance Discussions" follow Thursday evening performances. Backstage or warehouse tours are offered every Wednesday, Saturday, and Sunday morning from early June to mid-October. The tours cost C$5 (US$3.40) for adults, C$3 (US$2.05) for seniors and students; make tour reservations when you purchase tickets.

The season usually begins in May and continues through October, with performances Tuesday to Sunday nights and matinees on Wednesday, Saturday, and Sunday. Ticket prices range from C$39 to $64 (US$26.50 to $43.50), with special prices for students and seniors. For tickets, call ☎ **800/567-1600** or 519/273-1600; or write to the Stratford Festival, P.O. Box 520, Stratford, ON N5A 6V2. Tickets are also available in the United States and Canada at Ticketmaster outlets. The box office opens for mail and fax orders only in late January; telephone and in-person sales begin in late February.

EXPLORING THE TOWN

Stratford has a wealth of attractions that complement the theater offerings. It's a compact town, easily negotiable on foot. Within sight of the Festival Theatre, **Queen's Park** has picnic spots beneath tall shade trees and by the Avon River. There are also some superb dining and good shopping prospects.

Past the Orr Dam and the 90-year-old stone bridge, through a rustic gate, lies a very special park, the **Shakespearean Garden.** In the formal English garden, where a sundial measures the hours, you can relax and contemplate the herb and flower beds and the tranquil river lagoon, and muse on a bust of Shakespeare by Toronto sculptor Cleeve Horne.

If you turn right onto Romeo Street North from highways 7 and 8 as you come into Stratford, you'll find the **Gallery/Stratford,** 54 Romeo St. (☎ **519/271-5271**). It's in a historic building on the fringes of Confederation Park. Since it opened in 1967, it has mounted fine Canadian-focused shows, often oriented to the theater arts. If you're an art lover, do stop in—you're sure to find an unusual show in one of the four galleries. Open daily in summer 9am to 6pm; Tuesday to Sunday 10am to 5pm off-season. Admission is C$4 (US$2.70) for adults, C$3 (US$2.05) for seniors and students 12 and up.

Stratford

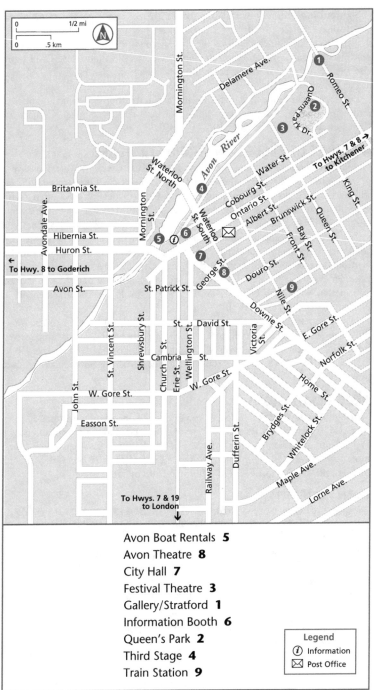

Avon Boat Rentals **5**

Avon Theatre **8**

City Hall **7**

Festival Theatre **3**

Gallery/Stratford **1**

Information Booth **6**

Queen's Park **2**

Third Stage **4**

Train Station **9**

Legend
- (i) Information
- ✉ Post Office

Stratford is a historic town, dating to 1832. Free 1-hour **guided tours of early Stratford** take place Monday to Saturday from July to Labour Day. They leave at 9:30am from the visitors' booth by the river. Many fine shops lie along Ontario and Downie streets and are tucked down along York Street. Antiques lovers will want to visit the nearby town of Shakespeare (7 miles out of town on Highway 7/8), which has several stores.

Paddleboat and canoe rentals are available at the **Boathouse,** behind and below the information booth. It's open daily from 9am until dark in summer. Contact **Avon Boat Rentals,** 40 York St. (☎ **519/271-7739**).

A COUPLE OF EXCURSIONS FROM STRATFORD

Only half an hour or so away, the twin cities of **Kitchener** and **Waterloo** have two drawing cards: the **Farmer's Market** and the famous 9-day **Oktoberfest.** The cities still have a German-majority population (of German descent, and often German speaking), and many citizens are Mennonites. On Saturdays starting at 6am, you can sample shoofly pie, apple butter, kochcase, and other Mennonite specialties at the market in the Market Square complex, at Duke and Frederick streets in Kitchener. For additional information, contact the **Kitchener–Waterloo Area Visitors and Convention Bureau,** 2848 King St. E., Kitchener, ON N2A 1A5 (☎ **519/748-0800**). It's open 9am to 5pm weekdays only in winter, daily in summer. For Oktoberfest information, write **K-W Oktoberfest,** P.O. Box 1053, 17 Benton St., Kitchener, ON N2G 4G1 (☎ **519/570-4267**).

Five miles north of Kitchener is the town of **St. Jacobs.** It has close to 100 shops in venues such as a converted mill, silo, and other factory buildings. For those interested in learning more about the Amish-Mennonite way of life, the **Meetingplace,** 33 King St. (☎ **519/664-3518**), shows a short film about it (daily in summer, weekends only in winter).

ACCOMMODATIONS

When you book your theater tickets, you can book your accommodations at no extra charge. The festival will reserve the type of accommodation and price category you prefer, from guest homes for as little as C$40 (US$27) to first-class hotels charging more than C$125 (US$85). Call or write the **Festival Theatre Box Office,** P.O. Box 520, Stratford, ON N5A 6V2 (☎ **800/567-1600** or 519/273-1600).

HOTELS & MOTELS

Bentley's. 107 Ontario St., Stratford, ON N5A 3H1. ☎ **519/271-1121.** 13 units. A/C TV TEL. Apr–Nov C$145 (US$99) double; Nov–June C$90 (US$61) double. Extra person C$20 (US$13.60). AE, DC, ER, MC, V.

The soundproof rooms here are luxurious duplex suites with efficiency kitchens. Period English furnishings and attractive drawings, paintings, and costume designs on the walls make for a pleasant ambiance. Five units have skylights. The adjoining British-style pub, also called Bentley's, is popular with festival actors (see "Dining," below).

Festival Inn. 1144 Ontario St. (P.O. Box 811), Stratford, ON N5A 6W1. ☎ **519/273-1150.** Fax 519/273-2111. www.festivalinnstratford.com. 182 units. A/C TV TEL. C$125–$200 (US$85–$136) double. Extra person C$10 (US$6.80). Winter discounts (about 30%) available. AE, DC, MC, V. Free parking.

The Festival Motor Inn is set back off highways 7 and 8, on 20 acres of landscaped grounds. The place has an Old English air, with stucco walls, Tudor-style beams, and high-backed red settees in the lobby. Tudor style prevails throughout the large, motel-style rooms. All have wall-to-wall carpeting, matching bedspreads, and floor-to-ceiling drapes, and reproductions of old masters on the walls. Some units have charming bay windows with sheer curtains, and all rooms in the main building, north wing, and annex have refrigerators. The inn has a dining room, a coffee shop, and an indoor pool with outdoor patio.

The Queen's Inn. 161 Ontario St., Stratford, ON N5A 3H3. ☎ **800/461-6450** or 519/271-1400. Fax 519/271-7373. 31 units. A/C TV TEL. May–Nov 15 C$105–$130 (US$71–$88) double, C$165–$190 (US$112–$129) suite; Nov 16–April C$65 (US$44) double, from C$85 (US$58) suite. AE, DC, MC, V.

Conveniently located in the town center, the Queen's Inn has recently been renovated and refurbished. The good-sized rooms are pleasantly decorated in pastels and pine. The Boar's Head Pub is on the premises.

23 Albert Place. 23 Albert St., Stratford, ON N5A 3K2. ☎ **519/273-5800.** Fax 519/273-5008. 34 units. A/C TV TEL. C$95–$105 (US$65–$71) double; C$115 (US$78) minisuite; from C$140 (US$95) suite. MC, V.

Around the corner from the Avon Theatre, the Albert Place has large rooms with high ceilings. Furnishings are simple and modern. Some units have separate sitting rooms. Complimentary coffee, tea, and doughnuts are available in the lobby for guests in the early morning.

A PICK OF THE BED & BREAKFASTS

For more information on the bed-and-breakfast scene, write to **Tourism Stratford,** P.O. Box 818, 88 Wellington St., Stratford, ON N5A 6W1 (☎ **519/271-5140**). It's open 9am to 5pm Monday to Friday.

Acrylic Dreams. 66 Bay St., Stratford, ON N5A 4K6. ☎ **519/271-7874.** www.bbcanada.com/3718.html. 4 units. A/C. C$90–$100 (US$61–$68) double; C$115–$135 (US$58–$92) suite. $25 extra for 3rd person in suite. Rates include breakfast. 2-night minimum on weekends. No credit cards.

As its name suggests, Acrylic Dreams has a fun, modern atmosphere, thanks to its artist owners. Most of the house is furnished with cottage-style antiques, but the living room is done in new wave style, with transparent acrylic furniture. Upstairs, there's a suite decorated in Provençal colors that has a separate sitting room with TV and refrigerator. On the ground floor, there are two doubles that share a refrigerator. The full breakfast varies from day to day, but might include peaches and peach yogurt, and homemade scones and preserves using ingredients from the garden (but no meat—the owners are vegetarians). There's a phone for guests' use. Yoga (C$10/US$6.80 per class) and reflexology are available.

Ambercroft. 129 Brunswick St., Stratford, ON N5A 3L9. ☎ **519/271-5644.** Fax 519/272-0156. www.bbcanada.com/2482.html. 4 units. A/C. C$95–$115 (US$65–$78.20) double. Rates include full breakfast. MC, V.

This inviting 1878 home in a quiet downtown area is convenient to the theaters and restaurants. The quirky, angular rooms are country cozy. There's a comfy front parlor, a small TV room, and front and rear porches. Guests have the use of a refrigerator. An extended continental breakfast is served—seasonal fruits, cereals, homemade baked goods, and more. No smoking, and no pets accepted.

Avonview Manor. 63 Avon St., Stratford, ON N5A 5N5. ☎ **519/273-4603.** www.avonviewmanor.on.ca. 4 units (2 with bathroom). C$85–$110 (US$57.80–$85) double; C$110–$160 (US$74.80–$109) suite. Rates include full breakfast. No credit cards, though personal checks are accepted.

In an Edwardian house on a quiet street, Avonview Manor has attractively and individually furnished rooms. Three have queen-size beds; the suite contains four singles, a sitting room, and a private bath. Breakfast is served in a bright dining room that overlooks the garden. A kitchen equipped with an ironing board is available on the first floor. The living room is very comfortable, particularly in winter, when guests can cozy up in front of the stone fireplace. Smoking is allowed only on the porch. There's also an in-ground pool and hot tub.

Brunswick House. 109 Brunswick St., Stratford, ON N5A 3L9. ☎ **519/271-4546.** 6 units (none with bathroom). From C$65 (US$44) double. Rates include full breakfast. No credit cards.

Here you'll stay in literate surroundings created by owners Geoff Hancock and Gay Allison—there are portraits of Canadian authors and poetry on the walls, and books everywhere. The six rooms share two baths. All six are nicely decorated and have ceiling fans. One is a family room with a double and two single beds. Each room has a personal decorative touch—a Mennonite quilt, posters by an artist friend, or a parasol atop a wardrobe. Smoking is restricted to the veranda. The building is within walking distance of the center of town and theaters.

✪ **Deacon House.** 101 Brunswick St., Stratford, ON N5A 3L9. ☎ **519/273-2052.** Fax 519/273-3784. www.bbcanada.com/1152.html. 6 units. A/C. C$105–$125 (US$71.40–$85) double. Extra person C$20 (US$13.60). Rates include breakfast. Off-season packages available. MC, V.

Deacon House, a shingle-style structure built in 1907, has been restored by Dianna Hrysko and Mary Allen. Rooms are decorated in country style, with iron-and-brass beds, quilts, pine hutches, oak rockers, and rope-style rugs. The living room, with a fireplace, TV, wingback chairs, and a sofa, is comfortable. The guest kitchen is a welcome convenience, as is the second-floor sitting and reading room. This is a great location, within walking distance of everything.

Woods Villa. 62 John St. N., Stratford, ON N5A 6K7. ☎ **519/271-4576.** Fax 519/271-7173. www.woodsvilla.orc.ca. 6 units. A/C TV TEL. C$120–$185 (US$81.60–$126) double. Rates include full breakfast. DISC, MC, V.

This handsome 1870 house is home to Ken Vinen, who collects and restores the Wurlitzers, Victrolas, and player pianos found throughout the house. In the large drawing room there are six—and they all work. Ken will happily demonstrate, drawing upon his vast library of early paper rolls and records. Five rooms have fireplaces, and the handsome suite boasts a canopy bed. Rooms are large and offer excellent value. Morning coffee is delivered to your room, followed by breakfast prepared to order and served in the dining room. There's an attractively landscaped outdoor pool and terrace.

A Nearby Place to Stay & Dine

✪ **Langdon Hall.** RR #3, Cambridge, ON N3H 4R8. ☎ **800/268-1898** or 519/740-2100. Fax 519/740-8161. 49 units. A/C TV TEL. C$259–$699 (US$176–$475) double. Rates include continental breakfast. AE, DC, ER, MC, V. From Hwy. 401, take Exit 275 south, turn right onto Blair Rd., follow signs.

This elegant house stands at the head of a curving, tree-lined drive. It was completed in 1902 by Eugene Langdon Wilks, a great-grandson of John Jacob Astor. It remained in the family until 1987, when its transformation into a small country-house hotel began. Today its 200 acres of lawns, gardens, and woodlands make for an ideal retreat. The main house, of red brick with classical pediment and Palladian-style windows, has a beautiful symmetry. Throughout, the emphasis is on comfort rather than grandiosity. Most rooms are around the cloister garden. Each is individually decorated; most have fireplaces. The furnishings consist of handsome antique reproductions, mahogany wardrobes, ginger-jar porcelain lamps, and armchairs upholstered with luxurious fabrics. Rooms boast such nice touches as live plants and terry bathrobes. Pets are accepted only in certain rooms, and there is a C$50 (US$34) extra charge for their stay.

Dining: The light, airy dining room serves fine regional cuisine. Main courses run C$22 to $30 (US$14.95–$20.40). Tea is served on the veranda, and there's a bar.

Amenities: The on-site spa offers a complete range of treatments; spa packages start at C$180 (US$122). Swimming pool, tennis court, croquet lawn, whirlpool, sauna, exercise room, billiard room, cross-country ski trails.

DINING
EXPENSIVE

✪ **The Church.** 70 Brunswick St. (at Waterloo St.). ☎ **519/273-3424.** www.churchrestaurant.com. Reservations strongly recommended. Fixed-price dinner (summer only) C$55–$69 (US$37.40–$46.95); main courses C$26–$40 (US$17.70–$27.20). AE, DC, MC, V. Tues–Sat 11:30am–1am, Sun 11:30am–11pm (hours vary and are generally shorter in the off-season). Call for Mon hours during special events. CONTINENTAL.

The Church is simply stunning. The organ pipes and the altar of the 1873 structure are intact, along with the vaulted roof, carved woodwork, and stained-glass windows. You can sit in the nave or the side aisles and dine to appropriate sounds—usually Bach. Fresh flowers and elegant table settings further enhance the experience.

In summer, there's a special four-course fixed-price dinner menu and an after-theater menu. Appetizers might include asparagus served hot with black morels in their juices, white wine, and cream; or sauté of duck foie gras with leeks and citron, mango, and ginger sauce. Among the selection of eight or so entrees you might find Canadian caribou with port and blackberry sauce, cabbage braised in cream with shallots and glazed chestnuts, or lobster salad with green beans, new potatoes, and truffles scented with caraway. Desserts are equally exciting—try charlotte of white chocolate mousse with summer fruit and dark chocolate sauce, or nougat glace with kiwi sauce.

To dine here during the festival, make reservations in March or April when you buy your tickets. The upstairs Belfry Bar is a popular pre- and post-theater gathering place.

✪ **The Old Prune.** 151 Albert St. ☎ **519/271-5052.** Reservations required. 3-course fixed-price dinner C$53 (US$36.05); main courses C$7–$12 (US$4.75–$8.15) at lunch, C$7–$14 (US$4.75–$9.50) at dinner. AE, MC, V. Wed–Sun 11:30am–1:30pm; Tues–Sat 5–9pm, Sun 5–7pm. After-theater menu Fri–Sat from 9pm. Call for winter hours. CONTINENTAL.

Two charming, whimsical women—Marion Isherwood and Eleanor Kane—run the Prune. In a lovely Edwardian home, it has three dining rooms and an enclosed garden patio. Former Montrealers, the proprietors demonstrate Quebec flair in both decor and menu. Marion's inspired paintings grace the walls.

Chef Bryan Steele selects the freshest local ingredients, many from the region's dedicated community of organic farmers, and prepares them simply to reveal their abundant flavor. Among the main courses, you might find Perth County pork loin grilled with tamari and honey glaze and served with shiitake mushrooms, pickled cucumbers, and sunflower sprouts; steamed bass in Napa cabbage with curry broth and lime leaves; or rack of Ontario lamb with smoky tomatillo–chipotle pepper sauce. Among the appetizers might be outstanding house-smoked salmon with lobster potato salad topped with Sevruga caviar, or refreshing tomato consommé with saffron and sea scallops. Desserts, such as rhubarb strawberry Napoleon with vanilla mousse, are always inspired. The Old Prune is also lovely for lunch or a late supper, when it offers such light specialties as sautéed quail with grilled polenta, Italian greens, mushrooms, roasted tomatoes, and balsamic *jus,* and smoked trout terrine.

✪ **Rundles.** 9 Cobourg St. ☎ **519/271-6442.** Reservations required. 3-course fixed-price dinner C$57.50 (US$39.10). AE, DC, ER, MC, V. Apr–Oct Wed and Sat–Sun 11:30am–1:30pm; Tues 5–7pm, Wed–Sat 5–8:30pm, Sun 5–7pm. Closed Mondays and throughout Nov–Mar. INTERNATIONAL.

Rundles provides a premier dining experience in a serene dining room overlooking the river. Proprietor Jim Morris eats, sleeps, thinks, and dreams food, and chef Neil Baxter delivers the exciting, exquisite cuisine to the table. The fixed-price dinner offers palate-pleasing flavor combinations. Among the five main dishes might be poached Atlantic salmon garnished with Jerusalem artichokes, wilted arugula, and yellow peppers in a light carrot sauce, or pink roast rib-eye of lamb with ratatouille and rosemary aioli. Appetizers might include shaved fennel, arugula, artichoke, and Parmesan salad or warm seared Quebec foie grass with caramelized endive, garlic-flavored fried potatoes, and tomato and basil oil. My dessert choice would be glazed lemon tart and orange sorbet, but hot mango tart with pineapple sorbet is also a dream.

MODERATE

Bentley's. 107 Ontario St. ☎ **519/271-1121.** Reservations not accepted. Main courses C$8–$13 (US$5.45–$8.85). AE, DC, ER, MC, V. Daily 11:30am–1am. CANADIAN/ENGLISH.

Bentley's is *the* local watering hole, and a favorite theater company gathering spot. The popular pastime is darts, but you can also watch TV. In summer you can sit on the garden terrace and enjoy the light fare—grilled shrimp, burgers, gourmet pizza, fish-and-chips, shepherd's pie, and pasta dishes. More substantial fare—including lamb curry, sirloin steak, and salmon baked in white wine with peppercorn-dill butter—is offered at dinner. The bar has 16 drafts on tap.

✪ **Keystone Alley Cafe.** 34 Brunswick St. ☎ **519/271-5645.** Reservations recommended. Main courses C$16–$25 (US$10.90–$17). AE, DC, MC, V. Mon–Sat 11am–3pm; Tues–Sat 5pm–9pm. CONTINENTAL.

Theater actors often stop here for lunch—perhaps a sandwich, like the maple-grilled chicken and avocado club, or a main dish like cornmeal-crusted Mediterranean tart. At dinner, entrees range from breast of Muscovy duck with stir-fried Asian vegetables and egg noodles in honey-ginger sauce, to escalopes of calf's liver accompanied by garlic potato puree and creamed Savoy cabbage with bacon. The short wine list is reasonably priced, and the food is better than the fare at some pricier competitors.

INEXPENSIVE

Let Them Eat Cake. 82 Wellington St. ☎ **519/273-4774.** www.letthemeatcake.on.ca. Reservations not accepted. Lunch items less than C$10 (US$6.80); desserts C$1–$4 (US70¢–$2.70). V. Apr–Oct Mon 7:30am–4pm, Tues–Sat 7:30am–12:30am, Sun 9am–6pm; Nov–Mar until 4pm daily. LIGHT FARE.

Let Them Eat Cake is great for breakfast (bagels and scones) and lunch (soups, salads, sandwiches, quiche, and chicken pot pie), but best of all for dessert. There are 15 to 20, including pecan pie, orange Bavarian cream, lemon bars, carrot cake, Black Forest cake, and chocolate cheesecake.

York Street Kitchen. 41 York St. ☎ **519/273-7041.** Reservations not accepted. Main courses C$8–$10 (US$5.45–$6.80). AE, V. Daily 8am–8pm from April to early Oct; daily 8am–5pm from mid-Oct to March; closed between Dec 24 and Jan 5. ECLECTIC.

This small, narrow restaurant is a fun, funky spot loved for its reasonably priced but high-quality food. You can come here for breakfast burritos and other morning fare, and for lunch sandwiches, which you build yourself by choosing from a list of fillings. In the evenings, expect to find comfort foods like meat loaf and mashed potatoes or barbecued chicken and ribs.

PICNICKING IN STRATFORD

Stratford is a picnicking place. Take a hamper down to the banks of the river or into the parks. Plenty of places cater to this business. **Rundles** (see above) will make you a super-sophisticated hamper. **Café Mediterranean,** 10 Downie St. in the Festival Square Building (no phone), has salads, quiches, crepes, and flaky meat pies and pastries. It's open Tuesday to Sunday, May to September 10am to 6pm, October to April noon to 4pm. Or go to **Picnics Gourmet Food Shop,** 40 Wellington St. (☎ **519/ 273-6000**). It offers all kinds of salads—pasta, grain, and vegetable—and pâtés; fish, chicken, and meat dishes; soups; and breads and pastries. Open May to September Tuesday to Friday 10am to 6pm, Saturday 10am to 4pm; October to April Tuesday to Friday 11am to 6pm (closed 2 weeks in January).

2 Niagara-on-the-Lake

130km (80 miles) SE of Toronto

Only 1½ hours from Toronto, Niagara-on-the-Lake is one of the best-preserved and prettiest 19th-century villages in North America. Handsome clapboard and brick period houses border the tree-lined streets. It's the setting for one of Canada's most famous events, the **Shaw Festival.** The town is the jewel of the **Ontario wine region.**

ESSENTIALS

VISITOR INFORMATION   The **Niagara-on-the-Lake Chamber of Commerce,** 153 King St. (P.O. Box 1043), Niagara-on-the-Lake, ON L0S 1J0 (☎ **905/ 468-4263;** www.niagara-on-the-lake.com/visit.html), provides information and can help you find accommodations at one of the 120 local bed-and-breakfasts. It's open Monday to Friday 9am to 5pm, Saturday and Sunday 10am to 5pm.

GETTING THERE   Niagara-on-the-Lake is best seen by **car.** From Toronto, take the Queen Elizabeth Way (signs read QEW) Niagara via Hamilton and St. Catharines, and exit at Highway 55. The trip takes about 1½ hours.

 Amtrak and **VIA** (☎ **416/366-8411**) operate **trains** between Toronto and New York, but they go only as far as St. Catharines and Niagara Falls. Call ☎ **800/ 361-1235** in Canada or **800/USA-RAIL** in the United States. From either place, you'll need to rent a car. Rental outlets in St. Catharines include **National Tilden,** 162 Church St. (☎ **905/682-8611**), and **Hertz,** 404 Ontario St. (☎ **905/682-8695**). In Niagara Falls, **National Tilden** is at 4523 Drummond Rd. (☎ **905/374-6700**).

THE SHAW FESTIVAL

The Shaw is devoted to the dramatic and comedic works of George Bernard Shaw and his contemporaries. From April through October, the festival offers a dozen plays in the historic Court House, the exquisite Festival Theatre, and the Royal George Theatre. Some recent performances have included *A Woman of No Importance* by Oscar Wilde, *The Matchmaker* by Thornton Wilder, *Brief Encounter* by Noel Coward, and Shaw's *The Doctor's Dilemma.*

 Free chamber concerts take place Sunday at 11am. Chats introduce performances on Friday evenings in July and August, and question-and-answer sessions follow Tuesday evening performances.

 The Shaw announces its festival program in mid-January. Tickets are difficult to obtain on short notice, so book in advance. Prices range from C$25 to $70 (US$17 to $47.60). For more information, contact the **Shaw Festival,** P.O. Box 774, Niagara-on-the-Lake, ON L0S 1J0 (☎ **800/511-7429** or 905/468-2172; www.shawfest.com).

EXPLORING THE TOWN

Niagara-on-the Lake is small, and most of its attractions are along one main street, making it easy to explore on foot.

Niagara Historical Society Museum. 43 Castlereagh St. (at Davy). ☎ **905/468-3912.** Admission C$3 (US$2.05) adults, C$2 (US$1.35) seniors, C$1 (US70¢) students, C50¢ (US35¢) children 5–12. Jan–Feb weekends 1–5pm; Mar–Apr and Nov–Dec daily 1–5pm; May–Oct daily 10am–5pm.

The Niagara Historical Society Museum houses more than 20,000 artifacts pertaining to local history. They include many possessions of United Empire Loyalists who first settled the area at the end of the American Revolution.

✪ **Fort George National Historic Park.** Niagara Pkwy. ☎ **905/468-6614.** Admission C$6 (US$4.10) adults, C$5 (US$3.20) seniors, C$4 (US$2.70) children 6–16, C$20 ($13.60) family, free for children under 6. Apr–June and Sept–Oct daily 10am–5pm; July–Aug Sun–Fri 10am–5pm, Sat 10am–8pm.

It's easy to imagine taking shelter behind Fort George's stockade fence and watching for the enemy from across the river—even though today there are only condominiums on the opposite riverbank.

The fort played a key role in the War of 1812, until the Americans invaded and destroyed it in May 1813. Although rebuilt by 1815, it was abandoned in 1828 and not reconstructed until the 1930s. You can view the guard room (with its hard plank beds), the officers' quarters, the enlisted men's quarters, and the sentry posts. The self-guided tour includes interpretive films and, occasionally, performances by the Fort George Fife and Drum Corps. Those who believe in ghosts, take note: The fort is one of Ontario's favorite "haunted" sites.

A NOSTALGIC SHOPPING STROLL

A stroll along the town's main artery, Queen Street, will take you by some entertaining, albeit touristy, shops. The **Niagara Apothecary Shop,** at no. 5 (☎ **905/468-3845**), dates to 1866. Its original black-walnut counters and the contents of the drawers are marked in gold-leaf script, and the original glass and ceramic apothecary ware is on display. **Loyalist Village,** no. 12 (☎ **905/468-7331**), stocks Canadian clothes and crafts, including Inuit art, native Canadian decoys, and sheepskins. **Maple Leaf Fudge,** no. 14 (☎ **905/468-2211**), offers more than 20 varieties that you can watch being made on marble slabs. At no. 16 is a charming toy store, the **Owl and the Pussycat** (☎ **905/468-3081**). At no. 35, **Greaves Jam** (☎ **905/468-7331**) is run by fourth-generation jam makers. The **Shaw Shop** (☎ **800/511-7429**), no. 79, next to the Royal George Theatre, has GBS memorabilia and more. There's also a Dansk outlet and several galleries selling contemporary Canadian and other ethnic crafts.

JET-BOATING THRILLS

Jet boat excursions leave from the dock across from 61 Melville St. at the King George III Inn. Don a rain suit, poncho, and life jacket, and climb aboard. The boat takes you out onto the Niagara River for a trip along the stone-walled canyon to the whirlpool downriver. The ride starts slow but gets into turbulent water. Trips, which operate from May to October, last an hour and cost C$49 (US$33.30) for adults, C$39 (US$26.50) for children 6 to 16. Reservations are required. Call the **Whirlpool Jet Boat Company** (☎ **905/468-4800**).

Niagara-on-the-Lake

Niagara River

Niagara Parkway

⑫

⑧

Melville St.

⑩

Ball St.

Delatre St.

Ricardo St.

Wellington St.

Byron St.

Picton St.

⑨

Davy St.

⑦

Platoff St.

⑪

Castlereagh St.

Nelles St.

King St.

④

⑥

⑬

⑤

Regent St.

Front St.

Prideaux St.

③

Queen St.

Johnson St.

Gage St.

Centre St.

Victoria St.

②

Gate St.

Anne St.

John St.

Mary St.

William St.

Simcoe St.

①

Mississauga St.

Butler St.

Dorchester St.

Lake Ontario

TORONTO

Niagara-on-the-Lake

ACCOMMODATIONS ■

Gate House Hotel **2**
Moffat Inn **9**
Oban Inn **1**
Old Bank House **4**
Pillar & Post Inn **13**
Prince of Wales Hotel **7**
Queen's Landing **8**

ATTRACTIONS ●

Court House/Court
  House Theatre **5**
Fort George National
  Historic Park **12**
Niagara Apothecary Shop **6**
Niagara Historical
  Society Museum **11**
Royal George Theatre **3**
Shaw Festival Theatre **10**

TOURING NIAGARA-ON-THE-LAKE WINERIES

Visiting a local winery is one of the loveliest (and tastiest) ways to pass an hour or two in this region. For maps of the area and information about all the region's vintners, contact the **Wine Council of Ontario,** 110 Hanover Dr., Suite B-205, St. Catharines, ON L2W 1A4 (☎ **888/5-WINERY** or 905/684-8070; www.wineroute.com). The wineries listed below are close to the town of Niagara-on-the-Lake. Tours are free. Prices for tastings vary with the winery and the wine you're sampling, and usually run C$3 to $10 (US$2.05 to $6.80).

Take Highway 55 (Niagara Stone Rd.) out of Niagara-on-the-Lake, and you'll come to **Hillebrand Estates Winery** (☎ **905/468-7123;** www.hillebrand.com), just outside Virgil. It's open year-round, plays host to a variety of special events (including a weekend concert series that features jazz and blues), and even offers bicycle tours. Hillebrand's Vineyard Café, with views of both the barrel-filled cellar and the Niagara Escarpment, is a delightful spot for lunch or dinner. Winery tours start on the hour daily from 10am to 6pm.

If you turn off Highway 55 and go down York Road, you'll reach **Château des Charmes,** west of St. Davids (☎ **905/262-5202**). The winery was built to resemble a French manor house, and its architecture is unique in the region. One-hour tours are given daily. Open 10am to 6pm year-round.

To reach the **Konzelmann Winery,** Lakeshore Road (☎ **905/935-2866**), take Mary Street out of Niagara-on-the-Lake. This vintner is famous for its award-winning ice wines. Tours are given from May to late September, Monday to Saturday.

ACCOMMODATIONS

In summer, hotel space is in high demand, but don't despair if you're having trouble nailing down a room. Contact the Chamber of Commerce, which provides an accommodations-reservations service. Your best bets are generally bed-and-breakfasts.

IN TOWN

Expensive

Gate House Hotel. 142 Queen St. (P.O. Box 1364), Niagara-on-the-Lake, ON L0S 1J0. ☎ **905/468-3263.** www.gatehouse-niagara.com. 10 units. A/C TV TEL. C$160–$180 (US$108–$124) double. AE, ER, MC, V.

Unlike many of the Canadiana-influenced lodgings in town, the Gate House Hotel is decorated in cool, clean-lined Milanese style. Guest rooms have a marbleized look, accented with ultramodern black lamps, block marble tables, leatherette couches, and bathrooms with sleek Italian fixtures. The effect is quite glamorous.

Dining: Ristorante Giardino, one of the best places to dine in town, is in the hotel; it's open daily 11:30am to 2:30pm and 5pm to 10pm.

✪ **Oban Inn.** 160 Front St. (at Gate St.), Niagara-on-the-Lake, ON L0S 1J0. ☎ **888/669-5566** or 905/468-2165. www.vintageinns.com. 25 units. A/C TV TEL. C$160 (US$108) standard double, C$220 (US$150) double with lake view. Winter packages available. AE, DC, MC, V.

With a prime location overlooking the lake, the Oban Inn is the place to stay. It's in a charming white Victorian house with a green dormer-style roof and windows, plus a large verandah. (The house is a re-creation of the original 1824 structure, which burned down in 1992.) The gorgeous gardens are the source of the bouquets throughout the house.

Each of the comfortable rooms is unique. They are furnished with antique reproductions—corn-husk four-poster beds with candlewick spreads, ginger-jar lamps, and club-style sofas. It's all very homey and old-fashioned. One recent change to take note of: the Oban Inn, which used to welcome pets, no longer allows them in the rooms.

Dining: Bar snacks and light lunches and dinners are available downstairs in the piano bar, which has leather Windsor-style chairs and a fireplace. Dinner main courses run C$20 to $25 (US$13.60 to $17).

Pillar & Post Inn. 48 John St. (at King St.), Niagara-on-the-Lake, ON L0S 1J0. ☎ **888/ 669-5566** or 905/468-2123. Fax 905/468-1472. www.vintageinns.com. 123 units. A/C MINIBAR TV TEL. C$235–$250 (US$160–$170) double; C$275–$335 (US$155–228) suite. Extra person C$20 (US$13.60). AE, DC, ER, MC, V.

The discreetly elegant Pillar & Post is a couple of blocks from the madding crowds on Queen Street. In recent years it has been transformed into one of the most sophisticated accommodations in town, complete with a spa that offers the latest in deluxe treatments. The light, airy lobby boasts a fireplace, lush plantings, and comfortable seating. The style is classic Canadiana: The spacious rooms all contain old-fashioned furniture, Windsor-style chairs, a pine cabinet (albeit with color TV tucked inside), and historical engravings. In the back, there's a secluded pool. Some rooms facing the pool on the ground level have bay windows and window boxes.

Dining: Warmed by fires on cool evenings, the two dining rooms occupy a former tomato and peach canning factory and basket manufacturing plant. Entrees run C$17 to $30 (US$11.55 to $20.40). The adjoining wine bar features a large selection of local and international wines.

Amenities: The spa offers a full range of body treatments and massage therapies (prices start at C$45/US$30.60), plus a Japanese-style warm mineral-spring pool, complete with cascading waterfall. Indoor pool, outdoor pool, sauna, whirlpool. Bike rentals available.

Prince of Wales Hotel. 6 Picton St., Niagara-on-the-Lake, ON L0S 1J0. ☎ **888/669-5566** or 905/468-3246. Fax 905/468-5521. www.vintageinns.com. 108 units. A/C TV TEL. From C$220 double. Extra person C$20 (US$13.60). Packages available. AE, MC, V.

The Prince of Wales has it all: a central location across from the lovely gardens of Simcoe Park; full recreational facilities; lounges, bars, and restaurants; and attractive rooms, all beautifully decorated with antiques or reproductions. It has a lively atmosphere yet retains the elegance and charm of a Victorian inn. Bathrooms have bidets, and most rooms have minibars. The hotel's original section was built in 1864; in 1999 the hotel was renovated and restored to its original glory, and it is now the most luxurious hotel in the district.

Dining: An impressive old oak bar dominates the quiet bar off the lobby. **Royals,** the elegant main dining room, offers a dozen classic entrees, priced from C$18 to $28 (US$12.25 to $19). Three Feathers, a luxuriant greenhouse cafe, is perfect for breakfast, lunch, or tea. The Queen's Royal lounge serves cocktails and light evening fare.

Amenities: Indoor pool, whirlpool, fitness center. Bike rental, aerobics classes, and massage therapy available. There's also an on-site spa.

Queen's Landing Inn. 155 Byron St., at Melville St., (P.O. Box 1180), Niagara-on-the-Lake, ON L0S 1J0. ☎ **888/669-5566** or 905/468-2195. www.vintageinns.com. 142 units. A/C MINIBAR TV TEL. C$145 double; C$275–$310 (US$187–$211) double with fireplace; from C$420 (US$286) double with fireplace and Jacuzzi. AE, DC, ER, MC, V.

Overlooking the river and within walking distance of the theaters, the Queen's Landing Inn is a modern, Georgian-style mansion. It has 71 rooms with fireplaces, and 32 with fireplaces and Jacuzzis. The spacious rooms are comfortably furnished with half-canopy or brass beds, wingback chairs, and large desks. This hotel attracts a business-oriented crowd, in part because of its excellent conference facilities, which include 20 meeting rooms.

Dining: The cozy Bacchu lounge has a fieldstone fireplace, copper-foil bar, and velvet-cushioned seating. The circular **Tiara** dining room, which serves three meals a day and Sunday brunch, looks out over the yacht-filled (in summer) harbor. Dinner main courses run C$24 to $36 (US$16.30 to $24.50).

Amenities: Indoor pool, room service (7am to 11pm), whirlpool, sauna, exercise room, lap pool, bicycle rentals.

White Oaks Conference Resort & Spa. Taylor Rd., Niagara-on-the-Lake, ON L0S 1J0. ☎ **800/263-5766** or 905/688-2550. Fax 905/688-2220. www.whiteoaksresort.com. 90 units. A/C TV TEL. July–Aug C$160–$190 double; C$185–$260 suite. Off-season discounts available. AE, DC, ER, MC, V. From QEW, exit at Glendale Ave.

Not far from Niagara-on-the-Lake, the White Oaks is a sports enthusiast's paradise. It's entirely possible to arrive here, be caught in a flurry of athletic activity all weekend, and not set foot outside the resort. The rooms are as good as the facilities, with oak furniture, vanity sinks, and niceties like a phone and hair dryer in the bathroom. Suites have brick fireplaces, marble-top desks, Jacuzzis (some heart-shaped), and bidets. Deluxe suites have sitting rooms.

In 2000, White Oaks added a full-service luxury spa, which has become one of its main attractions. The long list of treatments for men and women includes facials, massage, body wraps, and manicures. Some of the less orthodox therapies include reiki (a Japanese massage to "align your energy field"), and Danse de la Mains, a massage choreographed to music and performed by two therapists working in tandem.

Dining: A restaurant–wine bar, an outdoor terrace cafe, and a pleasant cafe and coffee shop.

Amenities: Four outdoor and eight indoor tennis courts, six squash courts, two racquetball courts, Nautilus room, jogging trails, sauna, tanning beds, bike rentals, massage therapist, day-care center with professional staff. Full-service spa facility.

Moderate

Moffat Inn. 60 Picton St. (at Queen St.), Niagara-on-the-Lake, ON L0S 1J0. ☎ **905/468-4116.** 22 units. A/C TV TEL. Apr 15–Oct and late Dec C$89–$159 double; Nov to mid-Dec and Jan–Apr C$69–$139 double. Packages available. AE, MC, V.

This is a fine choice in a convenient location. Most rooms are outfitted with brass-framed beds and furnishings in traditional-style wood, wicker, and bamboo. They have hair dryers, and a tea kettle and supplies. Seven rooms have fireplaces. Free coffee is available in the lobby, and there's a restaurant and bar. Smoking is allowed at the bar only.

✪ **The Old Bank House.** 10 Front St. (P.O. Box 1708), Niagara-on-the-Lake, ON L0S 1J0. ☎ **877-468-7136** or 905/468-7136. 9 units. A/C. C$125–$195 (US$85–$133) double; C$230 (US$156) 2-bedroom suite. Rates include breakfast. AE, MC, V.

Beautifully situated down by the river, this two-story Georgian was built in 1817 as the first branch of the Bank of Canada. Several tastefully decorated units have private entrances, like the charming Garden Room, which also has a private trellised deck. All but one have a refrigerator and coffee or tea supplies. The most expensive suite accommodates four in two bedrooms. The extraordinarily comfortable sitting room has a fireplace and eclectic antique pieces. The hotel will be under renovation in early 2001, but the work is expected to be completed before April, when theater season starts.

ALONG THE WINE ROAD

The Vintner's Inn. 3845 Main St., Jordan, ON L0R 1S0. ☎ **905/562-5336.** 9 units. A/C TEL. C$225–$315 (US$153–$214) double. AE, DC, ER, MC, V. From QEW, take Jordan Rd. exit; at first intersection, turn right onto 4th Ave., then right onto Main St.

In the village of Jordan, about 30km (18 miles) from Niagara-on-the-Lake, this modern accommodation consists entirely of handsome suites. Each has an elegantly furnished living room with a fireplace, and a whirlpool tub in the bathroom. Seven are duplexes—one of them, the deluxe loft, has two double beds on its second level—and three are single-level suites with high ceilings. The inn's restaurant, On the Twenty, is across the street (see "Dining: Along the Wine Road," below).

DINING
IN TOWN
In addition to the listings below, don't forget the dining rooms at the **Pillar & Post, Queen's Landing,** and the **Prince of Wales,** all listed above.

The stylish **Shaw Cafe and Wine Bar,** 92 Queen St. (☎ 905/468-4772), serves lunch and light meals, and has a patio. The **Epicurean,** 84 Queen St. (☎ 905/468-3408), offers hearty soups, quiches, sandwiches, and other fine dishes in a sunny Provence-inspired dining room. Service is cafeteria style. Half a block off Queen, the **Angel Inn,** 224 Regent St. (☎ 905/468-3411), is a delightfully authentic English pub. For an inexpensive down-home breakfast, go to the **Stagecoach Family Restaurant,** 45 Queen St. (☎ 905/468-3133). It also serves basic family fare, such as burgers, fries, and meat loaf. No credit cards are accepted. **Niagara Home Bakery,** 66 Queen St. (☎ 905/468-3431), is the place to stop for chocolate-date squares, cherry squares, croissants, cookies, and individual quiches.

The Buttery. 19 Queen St. ☎ **905/468-2564.** Reservations strongly recommended; reservations required for Henry VIII feast. Henry VIII feast C$49 (US$33.20); tavern main courses (available Tues–Sun 11am–5pm, all day Mon) C$8–$15 (US$5.45–$10.20); dinner main courses C$14–$22 (US$9.50–$14.95). MC, V. May–Sept daily 11am–midnight; Oct–Apr Sun–Thurs 11am–7:30pm. Afternoon tea year-round daily 2–5pm. CANADIAN/ENGLISH/CONTINENTAL.

The Buttery has been a dining landmark for years. It's known for its weekend Henry VIII feasts, when "serving wenches" bring food and wine while "jongleurs" and "musickers" entertain. You'll be served "four removes"—courses involving broth, chicken, roast lamb, roast pig, sherry trifle, syllabub, and cheese, all washed down with a goodly amount of wine, ale, and mead.

The tavern menu features spareribs, 8-ounce New York strip, shrimp in garlic sauce, and such English pub fare as lamb curry and steak, kidney, and mushroom pie. On the dinner menu, I highly recommend rack of lamb served with pan juices, or shrimp curry. Finish with mud pie or Grand Marnier chocolate cheesecake. You can take home fresh baked goods—pies, strudels, dumplings, cream puffs, or scones.

Fans Court. 135 Queen St. ☎ **905/468-4511.** Reservations recommended. Main courses C$10–$21 (US$6.80–$14.30). AE, DC, MC, V. Daily noon–10pm. CHINESE.

Some of the best food in town can be found in this comfortable spot, decorated with fans, cushioned bamboo chairs, and round tables spread with golden tablecloths. In summer, there's outdoor dining in the courtyard. The cuisine is primarily Cantonese and Szechwan. Singapore beef, moo shu pork, Szechwan scallops, and lemon chicken are just a few of the dishes available. Peking duck must be ordered 24 hours in advance.

Ristorante Giardino. In the Gate House Hotel, 142 Queen St. ☎ **905/468-3263.** www.gatehouse-niagara.com. Main courses C$24.50–$38 (US$16.70–$25.85). AE, ER, MC, V. May–Sept daily 11:30am–2:30pm and 5–10pm; Oct–Apr daily 5:30–9pm. ITALIAN.

On the ground floor of the Gate House Hotel is this sleek, ultramodern Italian restaurant with a gleaming marble-top bar and brass accents throughout. The food is

Northern Italian with fresh American accents. Main courses might include baked salmon seasoned with olive paste and tomato concasse, veal tenderloin marinated with garlic and rosemary, and braised pheasant in juniper-berry-and-vegetable sauce. There are several pasta dishes, plus such appealing appetizers as medallions of langostine garnished with orange and fennel salad. Desserts include a fine tiramisu, and panna cotta with seasonal berries.

IN NEARBY VIRGIL, ST. CATHARINES & WELLAND

✪ **Café Garibaldi.** 375 St. Paul St., St. Catharines. ☎ **905/988-9033.** Reservations recommended for dinner. Main courses C$13–$27 (US$8.85–$18.35). AE, DC, ER, MC, V. Tues-Sat 11:30am–2:30pm and 5pm–11pm. From QEW, exit at St. Paul St. and turn right. ITALIAN.

This relaxed spot is a favorite among locals. It serves Italian staples such as zuppa di pesce and veal scalloppine; homemade lasagna is the most-requested dish. The wine list features the local vintners' goods and some fine bottles from Italy.

Hennepin's. 1486 Niagara Stone Rd. (Hwy. 55), at Creek Rd., Virgil. ☎ **905/468-1555.** Tapas C$4–$8 (US$2.70–$5.45); main courses C$13–$25 (US$8.85–$17). AE, ER, MC, V. Sun–Wed 11:30am–9pm, Fri–Sat 11:30am–11pm. From QEW, exit at York Rd., turn left, follow to Niagara Stone Rd., turn right. CONTEMPORARY.

The region's first tapas bar, Hennepin's still stands out. The dining rooms display the works of local artists. The specialty of the house is Mediterranean- and Asian-inspired tapas—coconut shrimp, olive-stuffed meatballs, chicken satay, samosas—which are served all day. At dinner, there are always such temptations as escargots in Pernod, or pan-seared game pâté with blueberry kirsch sauce to start. Of the main courses, game and serious meats dominate—venison bordelaise, liver in chausseur sauce, steak, and pork tenderloin with portobello calvados sauce. The desserts are seriously rich—try the death by chocolate cake. The wine list is extensive; 28 selections are available by the glass.

Iseya. 22 James St. (between St. Paul and King sts.), St. Catharines. ☎ **905/688-1141.** Reservations recommended for dinner. Main courses C$12–$27 (US$8.15–$18.35). AE, MC, V. Mon–Fri 11:30am–2:30pm; Mon–Sat 5–11pm. From QEW, exit at St. Paul St., turn right, follow to St. James St., turn right. JAPANESE.

Chef Yasutoshi Hachoitori has had a virtual monopoly since he opened this eatery because Iseya is one of the region's few traditional Japanese restaurants. It serves fresh sushi and sashimi as well as teriyaki, tempura, and sukiyaki dishes.

Rinderlin's. 24 Burgar St., Welland. ☎ **905/735-4411.** Reservations recommended. Main courses C$21–$29 (US$14.30–$19.75). AE, DC, ER, MC, V. Mon-Fri 11:30am–1:30pm; daily 6–8pm. From QEW, take Hwy. 406 to Burgar St. exit, turn left. CONTINENTAL.

An intimate town-house restaurant, Rinderlin's has evolved from a traditional French restaurant to one with a continental flair. As a result, the dishes tend to be lighter; there are several vegetarian options. On the dinner menu, you might find sautéed shrimps and scallops in medium-hot curry sauce on a bed of basmati rice, roast pork tenderloin with honey-mustard-bacon sauce, herb polenta with grilled bell pepper, eggplant and zucchini, and local venison with wild mushrooms and game sauce. Desserts are seasonal—one favorite is the white chocolate torte flavored with brandy and served with raspberry sauce.

Wellington Court Restaurant. 11 Wellington St., St. Catharines. ☎ **905/682-5518.** Reservations recommended. Main courses C$11–$23 (US$7.50–16.75). ER, MC, V. Mon–Sat 11:30am–2:30pm; Tues–Sat 5:30–9:30pm. From QEW, exit at St. Paul St., turn right, follow to Wellington Ave., turn left. CONTINENTAL.

In an Edwardian town house with a flower trellis, the dining rooms here sport contemporary decor with modern lithographs and photographs. The menu features daily specials—fish and pasta of the day, for example—along with such items as a beef tenderloin in shallot-and-red-wine reduction, roasted breast of chicken served on gingered plum preserves, and grilled sea bass with cranberry vinaigrette.

ALONG THE WINE ROAD

✪ **Hillebrand's Vineyard Café.** Hwy. 55, near Niagara-on-the-Lake. ☎ **905/468-7123.** Fax 905/468-4789. www.hillebrand.com. Main courses C$23–$33 (US$15.65–$22.45). Open daily 11:30am–11pm (closes earlier in winter). CONTINENTAL.

This dining room is light and airy, and its floor-to-ceiling windows offer views over the vineyards to the distant Niagara Escarpment, or of wine cellars bulging with oak barrels. The food is excellent. The seasonal menu might feature such dishes as poached Arctic char with shellfish ragout, or prosciutto-wrapped pheasant breast atop linguine tossed with mushrooms, roasted eggplant, and shallot. The starters are equally luxurious. Try roasted three-peppercorn pear served warm with salad greens, pine nuts, and Parmesan slivers, or maybe spiced goat cheese and grilled portobello "sandwich" with walnuts and endive. My favorite among the irresistible desserts is chocolate tortellini with ice-wine ganache and stewed berries.

On the Twenty Restaurant & Wine Bar. At Cave Spring Cellars, 3836 Main St., Jordan. ☎ **905/562-7313.** Main courses C$22–$32 (US$14.95–$21.75). AE, DC, MC, V. Daily 11:30am–3pm and 5–10pm. CANADIAN.

This restaurant is a favorite among foodies. The gold-painted dining rooms cast a warm glow. The cuisine features ingredients from many producers, giving On the Twenty a small-town feel. For example, the quail is from Joe Speck, and the guinea fowl originates at Keyhole Ranch. Naturally, there's an extensive selection of Ontario wines, including some wonderful ice wines to accompany such desserts as lemon tart and fruit cobbler. On the Twenty is associated with the Vintner's Inn, across the street (see "Accommodations: Along the Wine Road," above).

✪ **Vineland Estates.** 3620 Moyer Rd., Vineland. ☎ **888/846-3523** or 905/562-7088. Fax 905/562-3071. www.vineland.com. Reservations recommended. Main courses C$19–$29 (US$12.95–$19.70). AE, DC, MC, V. Daily 11am–3pm and 5pm–9pm year-round. CONTINENTAL.

This inspired eatery serves some of the most innovative food along the wine trail. On warm days you can dine on a deck under a spreading tree, or you can stay in the airy dining room. The kitchen uses local ingredients wherever possible. Start with a goat cheese soufflé on local Cookstown greens, caramelized onion, and sweet pepper coulis. Follow with one of four pastas, including radiatore with sautéed sweetbreads and marinated artichokes in mustard jus. Those craving something meatier could go for venison with wild rice and mashed veggies in a juniper-thyme reduction. For dessert, there's a wonderful tasting plate of Canadian farm cheeses, including Abbey St. Benoit blue Ermite. Those with sweet tooths will probably prefer one of the decadent chocolate delights.

3 Niagara Falls

160km (100 miles) SE of Toronto

Niagara Falls was for decades the region's honeymoon capital. I say this in an attempt to explain its endless motels—each with at least one suite that has a heart-shaped pink bed. Today, it is better known for its casino, amusement parks, and wax museums. Nonetheless, nothing can steal the thunder of the falls. (Well, almost nothing—longtime locals fondly reminisce about Marilyn Monroe's coming here to film *Niagara* in

1953.) If the tacky commercial side starts to grate on your nerves, get out of town by driving along the Niagara Parkway. With its endless parks and gardens, it's an oasis for nature-lovers. (See "Along the Niagara Parkway," below.)

ESSENTIALS

VISITOR INFORMATION   Contact the **Niagara Falls Canada Visitor and Convention Bureau,** 5433 Victoria Ave., Niagara Falls, ON L2G 3L1 (☎ **905/ 356-6061**), or the **Niagara Parks Commission,** Box 150, 7400 Portage Rd. S., Niagara Falls, ON L2E 6T2 (☎ **905/356-2241**).

Summer information centers are open daily 9am to 6pm at Table Rock House, Maid of the Mist Plaza, Rapids View parking lot, and Niagara-on-the-Lake.

GETTING THERE   If you're driving from Toronto, take the Queen Elizabeth Way (signs read QEW) Niagara. The trip takes 1½ to 1¾ hours.

Amtrak and **VIA Rail** (☎ **416/366-8411**) operate trains between Toronto and New York, stopping in St. Catharines and Niagara Falls. Call ☎ **800/361-1235** in Canada or ☎ **800/USA-RAIL** in the United States.

GETTING AROUND   The best way to get around is aboard the **People Movers** (☎ **905/357-9340**), which cost C$4.50 (US$3.10) per person. Parking at Rapid View, several kilometers from the falls, is free. Preferred Parking (overlooking the falls) costs C$8 (US$5.45) with no in-out privileges. The People Mover, which serves both parking areas, is an attraction in itself. It travels in a loop, making nine stops from Rapid View to the Spanish Aero Car, from 8am to 10pm.

Shuttles to the falls also operate from downtown and Lundy's Lane; an all-day pass costs C$5 (US$3.40) for adults, C$2.50 (US$1.70) for children 6 to 12.

A MONEY-SAVING PASS   The **Explorer's Passport** includes admission to Journey Behind the Falls, Great Gorge Adventure, and the Niagara Spanish Aero Car, plus all-day transportation aboard the People Movers. It's available at information booths and costs C$21 (US$14.30) for adults, and C$11 (US$7.50) for children 6 to 12.

SEEING THE FALLS

You simply can't do anything else before you've seen the falls, the seventh natural wonder of the world. The most exciting way to do that is from the decks of the ✪ **Maid of the Mist,** 5920 River Rd. (☎ **905/358-5781**). The sturdy boat takes you right in—through the turbulent waters around the American Falls, past the Rock of Ages, and to the foot of the Horseshoe Falls, where 34.5 million Imperial gallons of water tumble over the 176-foot-high cataract each minute. You'll get wet, and your glasses will mist, but that won't detract from the thrill.

Boats leave from the dock on the parkway just down from the Rainbow Bridge. Trips operate daily from mid-May to mid-October. Fares are C$11 (US$7.50) for adults, C$7 (US$4.80) for children 6 to 12, free for children under 6.

Go down under the falls using the elevator at Table Rock House, which drops you 150 feet through solid rock to the **Journey Behind the Falls** (☎ **905/354-1551**). You'll appreciate the yellow biodegradable mackintosh that you're given. The tunnels and viewing portals are open all year. Admission is C$7 (US$4.80) for adults, C$3.50 (US$2.40) for children 6 to 12, free for children 5 and under.

To view the falls from a spectacular angle, take a 9-minute spin (C$175/US$119 for two) in a chopper over the whole Niagara area. Helicopters leave from the heliport, adjacent to the whirlpool at the junction of Victoria Avenue and Niagara Parkway, daily from 9am to dusk, weather permitting. Contact **Niagara Helicopters,** 3731 Victoria Ave. (☎ **905/357-5672**).

Niagara Falls

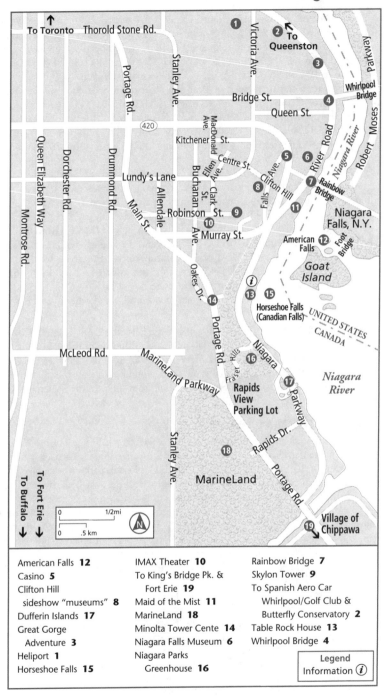

To Toronto ↑ Thorold Stone Rd.

Victoria Ave.

To Queenston ↖

Parkway

Whirlpool Bridge

Robert Moses

Bridge St.

Queen St.

Portage Rd.

Stanley Ave.

420

Kitchener St.

MacDonald Ave.

Centre St.

River Road

Niagara River

Lundy's Lane

Ellen Ave.

Clark St.

Buchanan Ave.

Falls Ave.

Clifton Hill

Rainbow Bridge

Niagara Falls, N.Y.

Queen Elizabeth Way

Dorchester Rd.

Drummond Rd.

Main St.

Allendale Ave.

Robinson St.

Murray St.

Oakes Dr.

American Falls

Foot Bridge

Goat Island

Montrose Rd.

Horseshoe Falls (Canadian Falls)

UNITED STATES
CANADA

McLeod Rd.

MarineLand Parkway

Portage Rd.

Fraser Hills

Niagara Parkway

Niagara River

Rapids View Parking Lot

Stanley Ave.

Rapids Dr.

Portage Rd.

MarineLand

0 ___ 1/2mi
0 ___ .5 km

N

To Fort Erie ↓
To Buffalo ↓

Village of Chippawa

American Falls **12**	IMAX Theater **10**	Rainbow Bridge **7**
Casino **5**	To King's Bridge Pk. & Fort Erie **19**	Skylon Tower **9**
Clifton Hill sideshow "museums" **8**	Maid of the Mist **11**	To Spanish Aero Car Whirlpool/Golf Club & Butterfly Conservatory **2**
Dufferin Islands **17**	MarineLand **18**	
Great Gorge Adventure **3**	Minolta Tower Cente **14**	Table Rock House **13**
Heliport **1**	Niagara Falls Museum **6**	Whirlpool Bridge **4**
Horseshoe Falls **15**	Niagara Parks Greenhouse **16**	Legend Information ⓘ

You can ride the external glass-fronted elevators 520 feet to the top of the **Skylon Tower Observation Deck,** 5200 Robinson St. (☎ 905/356-2651). The observation deck is open daily from 8am to midnight from June to Labour Day; hours vary in other seasons, so call ahead. Adults pay C$8 (US$5.45), seniors C$6.50 (US$4.40), children 6 to 12 C$4.50 (US$3.05), free for children 5 and under.

You can gain a similar perspective from the observation floors atop the 325-foot **Minolta Tower Centre,** 6732 Oakes Dr. (☎ 905/356-1501). On-site attractions include a Volcano Mine Ride, Galaxian Space Adventure, and Cybermind Virtual Reality. The free *Waltzing Waters*—a computerized music, light, and water show—runs nightly every 30 minutes from 9pm to midnight from May to October. The tower opens daily at 9am. It closes at 1am June to September, at 10pm March to April and October to December, at 9pm January to March. Admission is C$7 (US$4.80) for adults, C$5 (US$3.40) for students and seniors, free for children under 10. A day pass for the observation deck and unlimited entry to the games and rides costs C$20 (US$13.60). An unlimited play pass for the games and rides only is C$15 (US$10.20).

For a thrilling introduction to Niagara Falls, stop by the **IMAX Theater,** 6170 Buchanan Ave. (☎ 905/358-3611). You can view the raging, swirling waters in *Niagara: Miracles, Myths, and Magic,* shown on a six-story-high screen. Admission is C$8 (US$5.45) adults, C$7 (US$4.75) seniors and children 12 to 18, C$5.50 (US$3.75) children 5 to 11, free for children under 5.

The falls are also exciting in winter, when the ice bridge and other formations are quite remarkable.

THE FALLS BY NIGHT   Don't miss seeing the falls after dark. They're lit by 22 xenon gas spotlights (each producing 250 million candlepower of light), in shades of rose pink, red magenta, amber, blue, and green. Call ☎ 800/563-2557 (in the U.S.) or 905/356-6061 for schedules. The show starts around 5pm in winter, 8:30pm in spring and fall, and 9pm in summer. In addition, from July to early September, free fireworks start at 11pm every Friday.

✪ ALONG THE NIAGARA PARKWAY

Whatever you think of the tourist-oriented town, you can't help but love the Niagara Parkway, on the Canadian side of the falls. Unlike the American side, it is filled with natural wonders, including vast expanses of parkland. The 35-mile parkway, with bike path, makes a refreshing respite from the neon glow that envelops the town both day and night.

You can drive all the way from Niagara Falls to Niagara-on-the-Lake on the parkway, taking in attractions en route. The first diversion you'll come to is the **Great Gorge Adventure,** 4330 River Rd. (☎ 905/374-1221). The scenic boardwalk runs beside the raging white waters of the Great Gorge Rapids. Stroll along and wonder how it must have felt to challenge this mighty torrent, where the river rushes through the narrow channel at an average speed of 22 mph. Admission is C$5.25 (US$3.55) for adults, C$2.75 (US$1.85) for children 6 to 12, free for kids under 6.

Half a mile farther north, you'll arrive at the **Niagara Spanish Aero Car** (☎ 905/354-5711), a red-and-yellow cable-car contraption that whisks you on a 3,600-foot jaunt between two points in Canada. High above the whirlpool, you'll enjoy excellent views of the surrounding landscape. Admission is C$6 (US$4.10) for adults, C$3 (US$2.05) for children 6 to 12, free for kids 5 and under. Open daily May to the third Sunday in October. Hours are 9am to 6pm in May, 9am to 8pm in June, 9am to 9pm in July and August, 10am to 7:30pm in September, and 9am to 5pm in October.

At **Ride Niagara,** 5755 River Rd. (☎ 905/374-7433), you can experience what going over the falls must be like—without risking your life. Before going "over" the falls in the computerized motion simulator, you'll see a short video showing some of the weirder contraptions folks have devised for the journey. Then you take an elevator down to the simulator. Admission is C$12 (US$8.20) adults, C$7 (US$4.80) children 5 to 12. Children under the age of 5 aren't admitted. Open daily year-round; summer hours are 9:15am to 10:30pm.

After passing the **Whirlpool Golf Club,** stop at the **School of Horticulture** (☎ **905/356-8119**) for a free view of the vast gardens and a look at the Floral Clock, which contains 25,000 plants in its 40-foot-diameter face. The new **Butterfly Conservatory** is also in the gardens. In this lush tropical setting, more than 2,000 butterflies (50 international species) float and flutter among such nectar-producing flowers as lantanas and pentas. The large bright blue luminescent Morpho butterflies from Central and South America are particularly gorgeous. Interpretive programs and other presentations take place in the auditorium and two smaller theaters. The native butterfly garden outside attracts the more familiar swallowtails, fritillaries, and painted ladies. The school opens at 9am daily. It closes at 8pm in May and June; 9pm in July and August; 6pm in March, April, September, and October; and 5pm from November through February. It's closed December 25. Admission is C$6.50 (US$4.40) adults, C$3.50 (US$2.40) children 6 to 12, free for children under 6.

From here you can drive to **Queenston Heights Park,** site of a famous War of 1812 battle. You can take a walking tour of the battlefield. Picnic or play tennis (for C$6/US$4.10 per hour) in this shaded arbor before moving to the **Laura Secord Homestead,** Partition Street, Queenston (☎ **905/262-4851**). This heroic woman threaded enemy lines to alert British authorities to a surprise attack by American soldiers during the War of 1812. Her home contains a fine collection of Upper Canada furniture from the period, plus artifacts recovered from an archaeological dig. Stop at the candy shop and ice-cream parlor. Tours are given every half hour. Admission is C$1.50 (US$1). Open from late May to Labour Day, daily 10am to 6pm.

Also worth viewing just off the parkway in Queenston is the **Samuel Weir Collection and Library of Art,** R.R. #1, Niagara-on-the-Lake (☎ **905/262-4510**). The small personal collection is displayed as it was originally, when Samuel Weir occupied the house. Weir (1898–1981), a lawyer from London, Ontario, was an enthusiastic collector of Canadian, American, and European art as well as rare books. Open from Victoria Day to Canadian Thanksgiving (U.S. Columbus Day) Wednesday to Saturday 11am to 5pm, Sunday 1 to 5pm. Admission is free.

From here, the parkway continues into Niagara-on-the-Lake. It's lined with fruit farms, like **Kurtz Orchards** (☎ **905/468-2937**), and wineries. Two notable ones are the **Inniskillin Winery,** Line 3, Service Road 66 (☎ **905/468-3554** or 905/468-2187), and **Reif Winery** (☎ **905/468-7738**). Inniskillin is open daily 10am to 6pm from June to October, Monday to Saturday 10am to 5pm November to May. The self-guided free tour has 20 stops that explain the wine-making process. A free guided tour is also given at 2:30pm, daily in summer and Saturday only in winter. At Reif Winery, tours (C$2/US$1.35) are given daily from May through September at 1:30pm. The tasting room is open year-round.

The next stop between Niagara Falls and Niagara-on-the-Lake is the Georgian-style **McFarland House,** 15927 Niagara River Pkwy. (☎ **905/468-3322**). Built in 1800, it was home to John McFarland, "His Majesty's Boat Builder" to George III. It's open daily late May through June noon to 5pm, July to Labour Day 11am to 6pm. Admission is C$2 (US$1.35) adults, C$1 (US70¢) children. The last tour starts 30 minutes before closing.

A trip south from Niagara Falls along the parkway will take you by the Table Rock complex to the old-fashioned **Park Greenhouse,** a free attraction. It's open daily 9:30am to 7pm in July and August, 9:30am to 4:15pm September to June.

Farther along are the **Dufferin Islands.** The children can swim, rent a paddleboat, and explore the surrounding woodland areas while you play a round of golf on the illuminated 9-hole par-3 course. Open from the second Sunday in April to the last Sunday in October.

A little farther on, stop for a picnic in **King's Bridge Park** and stroll along the beaches. Continue to **Fort Erie,** 350 Lakeshore Rd., Fort Erie (☎ **905/871-0540**). It's a reconstruction of the fort that was seized by the Americans in July 1814, besieged later by the British, and finally blown up as the Americans retreated across the river to Buffalo. Guards in period costume stand sentry duty, fire the cannons, and demonstrate drill and musket practice. Open 10am to 6pm, daily from the first Saturday in May to mid-September, and weekends only to Canadian Thanksgiving (U.S. Columbus Day). Admission is C$6 (US$4.10) for adults, C$3.50 (US$2.40) for children 6 to 16, free for kids under 6.

Also in Fort Erie is the **Mildred M. Mahoney Dolls House Gallery,** 657 Niagara River Pkwy. (☎ **905/871-5833**). It displays more than 120 fully furnished dollhouses representing a variety of architectural styles, from Colonial to contemporary. Admission is C$3.50 (US$2.40) adults, C$2.50 (US$1.70) seniors, C$2 (US$1.35) children 6 to 17. Open daily May through December 10am to 4pm.

Another Fort Erie attraction, in the summer only, is the scenic, historic **Fort Erie horseracing track,** 320 Catherine St. (☎ **905/871-3200**). Take the Bertie Street exit from the QEW to get to the track.

MORE NIAGARA FALLS ATTRACTIONS

The biggest crowds aren't here for the falls; they head to **Casino Niagara,** 5705 Falls Ave. (☎ **905/374-3598**). The monolithic complex features 123 gambling tables that offer blackjack, roulette, baccarat, several different pokers, plus 3,000 slot and video poker machines. The casino contains five restaurants, including the Hard Rock Cafe, seven lounges, and several shops. It's open 24 hours a day, 365 days a year.

Founded in 1827, the **Niagara Falls Museum,** 5651 River Rd. (☎ **905/ 356-2151**), has exhibits ranging from Egyptian mummies to an odd mixture of Indian and Asian artifacts, shells, fossils, and minerals. There's also a Freaks of Nature display. Open in summer daily 8:30am to 11pm; in winter Tuesday to Sunday 10am to 5pm. Admission is C$9 (US$6.15) for adults, C$7.50 (US$5.10) for seniors, C$6.50 (US$4.45) for students 11 to 18, C$4 (US$2.70) for children 5 to 10, free for children 4 and under.

A popular family attraction is **White Water,** 7430 Lundy's Lane (☎ **905/ 357-3380**). You don your bathing suit and swoop around the corkscrew turns of the five slides into the heated pools at the bottom. If you prefer to frolic in the wave pool or wallow in the hot tub, you can do that, too. Tiny tykes can ride three small slides. Take a picnic (there's also a snack bar) and spend the greater part of the day. Admission is C$17 (US$11.60) for adults and youths (age 13 and up), C$12 (US$8.20) for children 12 and under. Open daily 9am to 6pm in July and August, 10am to 4pm in spring and fall. Closed mid-October to late April.

Another don't-miss spot for families is **Marineland,** 7657 Portage Rd. (☎ **905/ 356-9565**). At the aquarium-theater, King Waldorf, Marineland's mascot, presides over performances by killer whales, talented dolphins, and sea lions. Friendship Cove, a 4½-million-gallon breeding and observation tank, lets the little ones see killer whales up close. Another aquarium features displays of freshwater fish. At the small wildlife display, kids enjoy petting and feeding the deer and seeing bears and Canadian elk.

Marineland also has theme-park rides, including a roller coaster, Tivoli wheel, and Dragon Boat rides, and a fully equipped playground. The big thriller is Dragon

Mountain, a roller coaster that loops, double-loops, and spirals through 1,000 feet of tunnels. There are three restaurants, or you can picnic.

In summer, admission is C$25 (US$17) adults, C$22 (US$14.95) children 5 to 9 and seniors, free for children under 4. Off-season discounts are available. Open daily July and August 9am to 6pm; mid-April to mid-May and September to mid-October 10am to 4pm; mid-May to June 10am to 5pm. Closed November to April. Rides open in late May and close the first Monday in October. In town, drive south on Stanley Street and follow the signs; from the QEW, take the McCleod Rd. exit.

ACCOMMODATIONS

Every other sign in Niagara Falls advertises a motel. In summer, rates go up and down according to the traffic, and some proprietors will not even quote rates ahead of time. You can secure a reasonably priced room if you're lucky enough to arrive on a "down night," but with the casino in town that's becoming rare. Still, always request a lower rate and see what happens.

EXPENSIVE

Sheraton on the Falls. 5875 Falls Ave., Niagara Falls, ON L2E 6W7. ☎ **888/229-9961** or 905/374-4445. Fax 905/371-8349. www.niagarafallshotels.com. 670 units. A/C TV TEL. June to early Oct C$199–$629 (US$135–$428) double; mid-Oct–Apr C$119–$449 (US$80.95–$305) double; May C$159–$529 (US$108–$360) double. Extra person C$10 (US$6.80). Children under 18 stay free in parents' room. Packages available. AE, DC, DISC, ER, JCB, MC, V. Valet parking C$12 (US$8.20), self-parking C$6 (US$4.10).

A hotel to consider if you're looking for a room with a view—many of the rooms have balconies. In 1999, the hotel underwent extensive rebuilding and renovation, with the guestrooms being remodeled and redecorated in a tasteful manner. Each unit has in-room movies and individual climate control. The hotel is adjacent to Casino Niagara.

Dining: The 14th-floor penthouse dining room takes fair advantage of the view, with large glass windows. It serves a daily buffet for breakfast, lunch, and dinner, with nightly dancing to a live band (in season). The Steak and Burger serves reasonably priced fare.

Amenities: Outdoor rooftop pool.

Skyline Brock. 5685 Falls Ave., Niagara Falls, ON L2E 6W7. ☎ **800/263-7135** or 905/374-4444. 233 units. A/C TV TEL. Mid-June to Sept C$139–$239 (US$95–$163) double; Oct–Dec and Apr to mid-June C$99–$160 (US$67–$109) double; winter C$80–$115 (US$55–$78) double. Children under 18 stay free in parents' room. Extra person C$10 (US$6.80). Packages available. AE, DC, DISC, ER, MC, V. Parking C$7 (US$4.75).

For an unmarred view of the falls, try the Skyline Brock, which has entertained honeymooners and sightseers since 1929. It has a certain air of splendor, with a huge chandelier and marble walls in the lobby. About 150 of the rooms face the falls. City-view rooms are slightly smaller and less expensive.

Dining: The 10th-floor Rainbow Room, with a lovely view, serves a popular continental menu. The hotel also has a bar and a cafe.

MODERATE

The Americana. 8444 Lundy's Lane, Niagara Falls, ON L2H 1H4. ☎ **905/356-8444.** Fax 905/356-8576. 120 units. A/C TV TEL. Late June to Aug C$130–$180 double; Sept to mid-June C$80–$120 (US$55–$82) double. Extra person C$10 (US$6.80). AE, DISC, ER, MC, V. Free parking.

The Americana is one of the nicer moderately priced motels on this strip. It sits on 25 acres, with a pleasant picnic area, one tennis court, indoor and outdoor swimming pools, a whirlpool, sauna, and squash court. The large rooms are fully equipped and have vanity sinks. Some suites have whirlpool tubs and fireplaces. A dining room, lounge, and coffee shop are on the premises.

Holiday Inn by the Falls. 5339 Murray St. (at Buchanan), Niagara Falls, ON L2G 2J3. ☎ **905/356-1333.** 122 units. A/C TV TEL. Late June to Labour Day C$125–$195 (US$85–$133) double; spring and fall C$75–$155 (US$51–$105) double; winter C$64–$109 (US$44–$74) double. Extra person C$10 (US$6.80); rollaway bed C$10 (US$6.80); crib C$5 (US$3.40). AE, DC, DISC, ER, MC, V. Free parking.

The Holiday Inn by the Falls has a prime location right behind the Skylon Tower, only minutes from the falls. It's *not* part of the international hotel chain—the owner had the name first and refuses to sell it. Rooms are large and have ample closet space, an additional vanity sink, and modern furnishings. Most units have balconies. The restaurant, Mr. Coco's, is a steak house, pizzeria, and bar all in one. There's also a lounge, a gift shop, an indoor lap pool, an outdoor heated pool, and a patio.

Michael's Inn. 5599 River Rd., Niagara Falls, ON L2E 3H3. ☎ **800/263-9390** or 905/354-2727. Fax 905/374-7706. www.michaelsinn.com. 130 units. A/C TV TEL. June–Sept 15 C$98–$208 (US$67–$141) double; Sept 16–May C$59–$178 (US$40–$121) double. AE, CB, DC, ER, MC, V. Free parking.

At this four-story white building overlooking the Niagara River Gorge, the large rooms are nicely decorated and have modern conveniences. Many are whirlpool-theme rooms, like the Garden of Paradise or Scarlett O'Hara room. There's a solarium pool out back. The Ember's Open Hearth Dining Room boasts a glass-enclosed charcoal pit so that you can see all the cooking action. There's a lounge, too. A recent million-dollar renovation has resulted in the addition of a new indoor swimming pool, sauna, and fitness center.

INEXPENSIVE

Nelson Motel. 10655 Niagara River Pkwy., Niagara Falls, ON L2E 6S6. ☎ **905/295-4754.** 25 units. A/C TV. June 16–Sept 12 C$60–$100 (US$41–$68) double; mid-Mar to June 15 and Sept 13 to mid-Nov C$45–$55 (US$31–$44) double. Closed mid-Nov to mid-Mar. Rollaways and cribs extra. MC, V. Free parking.

For budget accommodations, try the Nelson Motel, run by John and Dawn Pavlakovich, who live in the large house adjacent to the motel. The lodgings have character, especially the family units—each has a double bedroom and an adjoining twin-bedded room for the kids. Regular units have modern furniture. None has a telephone, and singles have a shower only. All units face the fenced-in pool and neatly trimmed lawn. The Nelson Motel is a short drive from the falls, overlooking the Niagara River.

The Village Inn. 5685 Falls Ave., Niagara Falls, ON L2E 6W7. ☎ **800/263-7135** or 905/374-4444. 205 units. A/C TV TEL. Apr to mid-June C$70 (US$48) double; mid-June to Oct from C$90 (US$61) double; Nov–Mar C$60 (US$41) double. Packages available. AE, DC, DISC, MC, V. Parking C$4 (US$2.70).

Right by Casino Niagara, behind the Skyline and the Sheraton hotels, the Village Inn has unusually large rooms. Some suites measure 700 square feet and include a bedroom with two double beds and a living room. Because of its proximity to the casino, it's a popular choice with people who want to spend some time gambling.

A PLACE TO STAY IN NEARBY QUEENSTON

✪ **South Landing Inn.** Corner of Kent and Front sts. (P.O. Box 269), Queenston, ON L0S 1L0. ☎ **905/262-4634.** Fax 905/262-4639. 23 units. A/C TV. Mid-Apr to Oct C$95–$125 (US$64.60–$85) double; Nov to mid-Apr C$65–$75 (US$44.20–$51) double. AE, MC, V. Free parking. Follow Niagara Pkwy. to Queenston; turn right at Kent St.

The original section of Queenston's South Landing Inn was built in the 1800s. Today it has five attractive rooms with early Canadian furnishings, including four-poster beds. Other rooms are across the street in the modern annex. There's a distant view of the river from the inn's balcony. In the original inn, you'll also find a cozy dining room with red-gingham-covered tables, where breakfast is served for C$3.50 (US$2.40) per person.

DINING

Niagara Falls has never been a culinary hotbed, though you can fine standard fare at decent prices. If you want to dine well, reserve a table at one of the dining rooms in the wine-country towns of Jordan, Virgil, or Vineland (see above).

Alternatives in Niagara Falls include the **Pinnacle,** 6732 Oakes Dr. (☎ **905/ 356-1501**), which offers a Canadian and continental menu and a remarkable view from the top of the Minolta Tower. There's also a vista from atop the 520-foot tower at the **Skylon Tower Restaurants,** 5200 Robinson St. (☎ **905/356-2651,** ext. 259). Reasonably priced breakfast, lunch, and dinner buffets are served in the Summit Suite dining room, and pricier continental fare for lunch and dinner in the Revolving Restaurant.

EXPENSIVE

Casa d'Oro. 5875 Victoria Ave. ☎ **877/296-1178** or 905/356-5646. Reservations recommended. Main courses C$16–$40 (US$10.90–$27.20). AE, DC, DISC, ER, MC, V. Mon–Fri noon–3pm and 4–11pm, Sat 4pm–1am, Sun 4–10pm. ITALIAN.

Don't be intimidated by the wealth of kitsch. For Italian dining amid gilt busts of Caesar, Venetian-style lamps, statues of Roman gladiators, and murals of Roman and Venetian scenes, go to Casa d'Oro. Start with clams casino or *brodetto Antonio* (a giant crouton topped with poached eggs, floating on a savory broth garnished with parsley, and accompanied by grated cheese). Follow with specialties like saltimbocca alla romana or sole basilica (flavored with lime juice, paprika, and basil). Finish with a selection from the dessert wagon, or really spoil yourself with cherries jubilee or bananas flambé.

Happy Wanderer. 6405 Stanley Ave. ☎ **905/354-9825.** Reservations not accepted. Main courses C$10–$26 (US$6.80–$17.70). AE, MC, V. Daily 9am–11pm. GERMAN.

Warm hospitality reigns at the chalet-style Happy Wanderer, which offers a full selection of schnitzels, wursts, and other German specialties. Beer steins and game trophies adorn the walls. You might dine in the Black Forest Room, with a huge, intricately carved sideboard and cuckoo clock, or the Jage Stube, with solid wood benches and woven tablecloths. At lunch there are omelets, cold platters, sandwiches, and burgers. Dinner might start with goulash soup and proceed with bratwurst, knockwurst, rauchwurst (served with sauerkraut and potato salad), or a Wiener schnitzel, Holstein, or jaeger. All entrees include potatoes, salad, and rye bread. Desserts include, naturally, Black Forest cake and apple strudel.

MODERATE

Betty's Restaurant & Tavern. 8921 Sodom Rd. ☎ **905/295-4436.** Main courses C$8–$16 (US$5.45–$10.90). AE, MC, V. Mon–Sat 7am–10pm, Sun 9am–9pm. CANADIAN.

Betty's is a local favorite for hearty food at fair prices. It's a family dining room where the staff will attempt to stuff you to the gills with massive platters of fish-and-chips, roast beef, and seafood. All include soup or juice, vegetable, and potato. There are burgers and sandwiches, too. It's all but impossible to save room for the enormous portions of home-baked pies. Breakfast and lunch also offer good budget eating.

NIAGARA PARKWAY COMMISSION RESTAURANTS

The Niagara Parkway Commission has commandeered the most spectacular scenic spots, where it operates reasonably priced dining outlets. **Table Rock Restaurant** (☎ 905/354-3631) and **Victoria Park Restaurant** (☎ 905/356-2217) are both on the parkway right by the falls and are pleasant, if crowded. **Diner on the Green** (☎ 905/356-7221) is also on the parkway, at the Whirlpool Golf Course near Queenston. It's very plain. Queenston Heights offers the best dining experience.

Queenston Heights. 14276 Niagara Pkwy. ☎ **905/262-4274.** Reservations recommended. Main courses C$21–$30 (US$14.30–$20.40). AE, MC, V. Daily 11:30am–3pm; Sun–Fri 5–9pm, Sat 5–10pm. Closed Jan to mid-Mar. CANADIAN.

The star of the Niagara Parkway Commission's eateries stands dramatically atop Queenston Heights. Set in the park among firs, cypresses, silver birches, and maples, the open-air balcony affords a magnificent view of the lower Niagara River and the rich fruit-growing land through which it flows. Or you can sit under the cathedral ceiling in a room where the flue of the stone fireplace reaches to the roof. Dinner options might include fillet of Atlantic salmon with Riesling-chive hollandaise, prime rib, or grilled pork with apples and cider–Dijon mustard sauce. Afternoon tea is served from 3 to 5pm in the summer. If nothing else, go for a drink on the deck and the terrific view.

4 Hamilton

75km SW of Toronto

On a landlocked harbor spanned at its entrance by the Burlington Skyway's dramatic sweep, Hamilton has long been nicknamed "Steeltown" for its industrial roots. Since the early 1990s however, Hamilton has been making a name for itself with its ever-expanding list of attractions. It takes less than an hour to drive here from Toronto, and it's well worth a day trip for the whole family.

ESSENTIALS

VISITOR INFORMATION   The Greater Hamilton Tourist Information Centre, 127 King St. East., Hamilton, ON L8N 1B1 (☎ 800/263-8590 or 905/546-2666; www.city.hamilton.on.ca/visitor.htm) has a wealth of information about what to see and do, as well as where to dine and sleep. From early September till June 30, its hours are Monday through Saturday from 9am to 5pm; from July 1 through Labour Day, its hours are Monday through Saturday 10am-5pm and Sunday noon to 5pm.

There's also the Hamilton Chamber of Commerce, 555 Bay St. North, Hamilton, ON L8L 1H1 (☎ **905/522-1151;** www.hamilton-cofc.on.ca/links.asp), which has information about the city's attractions. It's open from Monday through Friday from 9am to 5pm.

GETTING THERE   Hamilton is easy to get to by car. From Toronto, take the Queen Elizabeth Way (signs read QEW) to Hamilton. The drive will take up to an hour.

GO (Government of Ontario) Transit is a commuter train that connects Toronto and Hamilton. Call ☎ **800/438-6646** or 416/869-3200 for information. Hamilton also has its own international airport, which has long been popular with cargo carriers and is now catching on with passenger carriers like US Airways and WestJet.

ATTRACTIONS ●
African Lion Safari **1**
Dundurn Castle **3**
Royal Botanical Gardens **2**

DINING ◆
Canadian Warplane
  Heritage Museum **6**
La Cantina **5**
Perry's Restaurant **4**

Hamilton Harbour

CITY OF BURLINGTON

TOWN OF DUNDAS

TOWN OF ANCASTER

Burlington St.
Barton St.
York Blvd.
Main St. W.
Main St. E.
Aberdeen Ave.
Fennell Ave. W.
Mohawk Rd. W.
Stone Church Rd. W.
Stone Church Rd. E.
Rymal Rd. W.
Rymal Rd. E.

Dundurn St.
Queen St.
Bay St.
James St.
John St.
Wellington St. N.
Wentworth St. N.
Sherman Ave. N.
Garth St.
West 5th St.
Upper James St.
Upper Wellington St.
Upper Wentworth St.
Upper Sherman Ave.

403
LINC
53

ATTRACTIONS

Hamilton's downtown core is best explored on foot, though you may want a car to visit attractions in the outlying areas.

Canadian Warplane Heritage Museum. Hamilton International Airport, 9280 Airport Rd. ☎ 877/347-3359 or 905/670-3347. www.warplane.com. Admission C$10 (US$6.80) adults, C$8 (US$5.45) seniors and youths 8–18; kids 7 and under are free; family admission for 2 adults and 2 youths is $30 (US$20.40). Open daily 9am–5pm.

This interactive museum charts the course of Canadian aviation from the beginning of World War II to the present. Visitors can climb into the cockpits of WWII trainer crafts or a CF-100 jet fighter. The most popular attractions are the flight simulators, which allow aspiring pilots to test their flight skills. There are also short documentary films, photographs, and other memorabilia. The aircraft on display include rarities like the Avro Lancaster bomber and the deHavilland Vampire fighter jet. The collection also includes a variety of military and transport craft.

Dundurn Castle. Dundurn Park, York Boulevard. ☎ **905/546-2872.** Admission C$8 (US$5.45) adults, C$6.50 (US$4.45) seniors, C$5.50 (US$3.75) students, and C$2.50 (US$1.70) children 6–14; children 5 and under are free. Open daily 10am–4pm from June 1 to Labour Day; the rest of the year, Tuesday to Sunday noon–4pm (closed Christmas and New Year's Day).

The castle affords a glimpse of the opulent life as it was lived in this part of southern Ontario in the mid-19th century. It was built between 1832 and 1835 by Sir Allan Napier MacNab, prime minister of the United Provinces of Canada in the mid-1850s and a founder of the Great Western Railway. MacNab was knighted by Queen Victoria for the part he played in the Rebellion of 1837. The 35-plus–room mansion has been restored and furnished in the style of 1855. The gray stucco exterior, with its classical Greek portico, is impressive enough, but inside, from the formal dining rooms to Lady MacNab's boudoir, the furnishings are rich. The museum contains a fascinating collection of Victoriana. In December, the castle is decorated splendidly for a Victorian Christmas.

✪ **Royal Botanical Gardens.** 680 Plains Rd. W., Burlington. ☎ **905/527-1158.** www.rbg.ca. Admission C$7 (US$4.80) adults, C$6 (US$4.10) for students 13–17 and for seniors, C$2 (US$1.40) for kids 5–12, free for children 4 and under. Open daily from 9:30am–dusk.

Situated just north of the city, the Royal Botanical Gardens spreads over 3,000 glorious acres. The Rock Garden features spring bulbs in May, summer flowers in June to September, and chrysanthemums in October. The Laking Garden blazes during June and July with irises, peonies, and lilies. The arboretum fills with the heady scent of lilac from the end of May to early June, and the exquisite color bursts of rhododendrons and azaleas thereafter. The Centennial Rose Garden is at its best late June to mid-September.

The gardens hosts many festivals during the year, including the Mediterranean Food & Wine Festival in February, the popular Ontario Garden Show in early April, the Tulip Festival in May, the Rose Society Show in June, and the Japanese Flower Society Show in September.

Should you work up an appetite while strolling the grounds, there are several on-site dining options, including the Gardens Café and the Rock Garden Tea House.

African Lion Safari. RR #1, Cambridge, Ontario Canada N1R 5S2. ☎ **800/461-WILD** or 519/623-2620. www.lionsafari.com. Admission C$18.95 (US$12.90) adults and youths, $15.95 (US$10.85) seniors, and $13.95 (US$9.50) children 3–12; children 2 and under are free. Open daily 10am–5:30pm from late June to Labour Day; from late April to mid-June and from early September to early October, daily from 9am–4pm; closed from mid-October through mid-April.

Just a half-hour drive northwest of Hamilton, you'll find a mirror image of a traditional zoo: At the African Lion Safari, visitors remain caged in their cars or in a tour bus while the animals roam wild and free. The 750-acre wildlife park contains rhino, cheetah, lion, tiger, giraffe, zebra, vultures, and many other species. In addition to the safari, the cost of admission covers other attractions like the cruise aboard the African Queen, during which a tour guide will take you around the lake and point out local inhabitants like spider monkeys, crested macaques, and ring-tailed lemurs. There's also a train that will take you through a forest populated by snapping turtles, among other wildlife.

Kids are particularly fascinated by the elephant bathing event, which occurs daily (the park has three baby Asian elephants: Samson, Albert, and George). There's also a Pets' Corner filled with frisky otters and pot-bellied pigs. There are several play areas for children as well, including a waterpark (bring bathing suits!).

ACCOMMODATIONS

Because Hamilton is so close to Toronto, it's easy to make a day trip here and back, rather than pulling up stakes and spending the night here. However, if you do want to stay in the area, several well-known chains have hotels here, including Sheraton (☎ **800/514-7101** or 905/529-5515) and Howard Johnson (☎ **800/263-8558** or 905/546-8111).

DINING

The suggested restaurants in St. Catharines and Welland, such as Café Garibaldi, Iseya, and Rinderlin's, are just a short drive away from Hamilton (see "Niagara-on-the-Lake," earlier in this chapter). However, Hamilton has a few restaurants worth checking out, too.

✪ **La Cantina.** 60 Walnut St. S.   ☎ **905/521-8989.** Reservations recommended. Main courses C$8–$25 (US$5.45–$17). AE, MC, V. Dining room Mon–Sat 11:30–2:30 and 6pm–10pm; Pizzeria Mon–Sat 11:30am–11pm. ITALIAN.

La Cantina is really two restaurants in one: there's a formal dining room, which serves up elegant plates like veal scaloppini in a dry Marsala sauce, and seared ostrich medallions cooked with Pinot Noir; equally elegant pasta plates include rotini with ham and peppers in a vodka sauce. Then there's the casual pizzeria, which serves up more than 20 varieties of pizza, ranging from the traditional Quattro Stagione (four seasons) with prosciutto, artichokes, olives, and mozzarella, to the unusual Gamberi, which is topped with shrimp, smoked, salmon, olives, eggplant, and pesto. This is a very popular spot, so try to make a reservation or arrive early, especially at lunch. If you're very lucky, you might just secure a seat in the restaurant's garden patio.

Perry's Restaurant. 1088 Main St. W.   ☎ **905/527-3779.** Main courses C$6–$13 (US$4.10–$8.85). MC, V. Open daily 11:30am–1am. BURGERS/INTERNATIONAL.

This casual family-style restaurant has a large menu that has something for everyone. It borrows from a range of cuisines, including Italian, French, Mexican, Greek, and American. Offerings include chicken souvlaki, rack of ribs, hearty sandwiches, and fish-and-chips. There are also lighter options such as salads, soups, and chicken fingers. There's a sunny patio at the front of the restaurant, too.

Appendix: Toronto in Depth

In less than 300 years, Toronto has grown from a trading post to a vibrant international capital. Read on to get a sense of how it happened.

History 101

FROM FUR TRADING POST TO MUDDY YORK As in most cities, geography, trade, and communications are the influences that have shaped Toronto and its history. Although the city today possesses a downtown core, it also sprawls across a large area—a gift of geography, for there are no physical barriers to stop it. When European settlement began, the flat broad plain rising from Lake Ontario to an inland ridge of hills (around today's St. Clair Ave.), and stretching between the Don River in the east and the Humber in the west, made the location ideal.

Native Canadians had long stopped here at the entrance to the Toronto Trail—a short route between the Lower and Upper lakes. French fur trader Etienne Brûleé was the first European to travel the trail in 1615. It wasn't until 1720 that the French established the first trading post, known as Fort Toronto, to intercept the furs that were being taken across Lake Ontario to New York State by English rivals. Fort Rouille, built on the site of today's CNE grounds, replaced the trading post in 1751. When the 1763 Treaty of Paris ended the Anglo-French War after the fall of Quebec, French rule in North America effectively ended, and the city's French antecedents were all but forgotten.

Only 20 miles across the lake from the United States, Toronto has always been affected by what happens south of the border. When the American Revolution established a powerful, potentially hostile new nation, Toronto's location became strategically more important, or so it seemed to John Graves Simcoe. He was lieutenant-governor of the newly formed province of Upper Canada, which had been established in 1791 to administer the frontiers—from Kingston and Quinte's Isle to Windsor and beyond—settled largely by Loyalists fleeing the Revolution. To Simcoe, Toronto was more defensible than Fort Niagara and a natural arsenal for Lake Ontario, which also afforded easy access to Lake Huron and the interior.

The governor had already purchased a vast tract of land from the Mississauga tribe for the paltry sum of £1,700 plus such baubles as blankets, guns, rum, and tobacco. In 1793, Lieutenant-Governor Simcoe, his wife, Elizabeth, and the Queen's Rangers arrived to build a settlement. Simcoe ordered a garrison built, renamed the settlement York, and laid it out in a 10-block rectangle around King, Front, George, Duke, and Berkeley streets. Beyond stretched a series of 100-acre lots from Queen to Bloor, which were granted to government officials to mollify their resentment about having to move to the mosquito-plagued, marshy outpost. Its muddiness was prodigious, and in fact a story is told of a fellow who saw a hat lying in the middle of a street, went to pick it up, and found the head of a live man submerged below it! In 3 short years a small hamlet had grown, and Simcoe had laid out Yonge Street—then a 33-mile oxcart trail. Four years later the first Parliament meeting confirmed York as the capital of Upper Canada.

FROM MUDDY YORK TO THE FAMILY COMPACT
The officials were a more demanding and finicky lot than the sturdy frontier farmers, and businesses sprang up to serve them. By 1812 the population had grown to 703 and included a brewer-baker, blacksmith, watchmaker, chair-maker, apothecary, hatter, and tailor.

During the War of 1812, despite initial victories at Queenston and Detroit, Canada was under siege. In April 1813, 14 ships carrying 1,700 American troops invaded York, blew up the uncompleted fort, burned the Parliament buildings, and carried off the mace (which was not returned until 1934). The British general burned a 30-gun warship, the *Sir Isaac Brock,* which was being built, and retreated, leaving young John Strachan to negotiate the capitulation. This event did much to reinforce the town's pro-British, anti-American attitude—an attitude that persists to some extent to this day. In retaliation for the burning of Fort York, some Canadians went down and torched the American president's residence. (The Americans later whitewashed it to hide the charred wood— hence, the White House.)

A conservative pro-British outlook permeated the official political oligarchy that dominated York, and that group was dubbed the Family Compact. Many of the names on street signs, subway stops, and maps derive from this august group of early government officers and their

Dateline

- **1615** Etienne Brûleé travels the Toronto Trail. "Toronto" is derived from a Huron term for "place of meeting."
- **1720** France establishes post at Toronto.
- **1751** French build Fort Rouille.
- **1759** Fort Rouille burned during British conquest.
- **1763** Treaty of Paris effectively ends French rule in Canada.
- **1787** Lord Dorchester, British governor of Quebec, purchases land from Scarborough to Etobicoke from the Mississauga tribe.
- **1793** Governor of Upper Canada, Col. John Simcoe, arrives and names settlement York. It becomes capital of Upper Canada.
- **1796** Yonge Street laid out, a 33-mile oxcart trail.
- **1812–1815** War of 1812 between United States and England, using Canada as a battleground. In 1813, Americans invade, blow up Fort York, and burn Parliament buildings. In 1814, U.S. troops are driven out of Canada; the British burn the White House.
- **1820s** Immigration of Nonconformists and Irish Catholics fosters reform politics.
- **1828** Erie Canal extended to Oswego on Lake Ontario.
- **1830s** Orange Order becomes prominent influence in politics.
- **1832–34** Cholera epidemics.
- **1834** City named Toronto; City Council replaces magistrates; William Lyon Mackenzie becomes first mayor.
- **1837** Former mayor Mackenzie leads rebellion sparked by bad economic times.

continues

- **1840s–50s** Mass Irish immigration.
- **1841** Act of Union establishes the United Province of Canada, with Kingston as ruling seat; Toronto loses status as a capital.
- **1843** The university, King's College, opens.
- **1844** City Hall built. George Brown founds the *Globe.*
- **1849** Great fire destroys much of city. Anglican King's College converts to secular University of Toronto.
- **1851** Population 30,000 (33% Irish); Anglican Trinity College founded; St. Lawrence Hall built.
- **1852** Toronto Stock Exchange opens; Grand Trunk Railroad charted, linking Quebec, Montreal, Toronto, Guelph, and Sarnia.
- **1853** St. James Cathedral completed.
- **1858** Storm creates the Toronto Islands.
- **1861** Horse-powered street railway runs along Yonge to Yorkville.
- **1867** Canadian Confederation; Toronto becomes capital of new province of Ontario.
- **1868** Canada First movement begins.
- **1869** Eaton's department store opens.
- **1871** Population 56,000.
- **1872** Simpson's department store opens.
- **1876** John Ross Robertson starts *Evening Telegram,* which wields influence for next 90 years.
- **1886** Provincial parliament buildings erected in Queen's Park.
- **1893** First Stanley Cup played.
- **1896** *Maclean's* newsmagazine started.
- **1901** Population 208,000.

continues

families. Among them were William Jarvis, a New England Loyalist who became provincial secretary; John Beverley Robinson, son of a Virginia Loyalist, who became attorney general at age 22 and later chief justice of Upper Canada; and Scottish-educated Dr. John Strachan, who rose from being a schoolmaster to an Anglican rector and the most powerful figure in York. Anglo-Irish Dr. William Warren Baldwin, doctor, lawyer, architect, judge, and parliamentarian, laid out Spadina Avenue as a thoroughfare leading to his house of that name in the country; and the Boultons were prominent lawyers, judges, and politicians—Judge D'Arcy Boulton built a mansion, the Grange, which later became the core of the art museum and still stands today.

These men, extremely conscious of rank, were conformist, conservative, pro-British, Tory, and Anglican. Their power was broken only later in the 19th century, as a larger and more diverse population gave reformers a chance to challenge their control. But even today their influence lingers in the corporate world, where a handful of companies and individuals control 80% of the companies on the Toronto Stock Exchange.

THE EARLY 19TH CENTURY—CANAL, RAILROAD & IMMIGRATION The changes that eventually diluted their control began in the early 19th century, especially during the 1820s, 1830s, and 1840s, when immigrants— Irish Protestants and Catholics, Scots, Presbyterians, Methodists, and other Nonconformists— poured in to settle the frontier farmlands. By 1832 York had become the largest urban community in the province, with a population of 1,600. Already well established commercially as a supply center, York gained another boost when the Erie Canal was extended to Oswego on Lake Ontario, giving it direct access to New York, and the Welland Canal was built across the Niagara Peninsula, allowing access to Lake Erie and points beyond. In 1834 the city was incorporated and York became Toronto, a city bounded by Parliament Street to the east, Bathurst to the west, the lakefront to the south, and 400 yards north of the current Queen Street (then called Lot) to the north. Outside this area—west to Dufferin Street, east to the Don River, and north to Bloor Street—lay the "liberties," out of which new wards would later be carved. North of Bloor, local brewer Joseph Bloor and Sheriff Jarvis were already drawing up plans for the village of Yorkville.

As more immigrants arrived, the population grew more diverse, and demands arose for democracy and reform. Among the reformers were such leaders as Francis Collins, who launched the radical paper *Canadian Freeman* in 1825; lawyer William Draper; and, perhaps most famous of all, fiery William Lyon Mackenzie, who was elected Toronto's first mayor in 1834.

Mackenzie had started his *Colonial Advocate* to crusade against the narrow-minded Family Compact, calling for reform and challenging their power to such an extent that some of them dumped his presses into the lake. Mackenzie was undaunted and by 1837 was calling for open rebellion.

A severe depression, financial turmoil, and the failure of some banks all contributed to the 1837 Rebellion, one of the most dramatic events in the city's history. On December 5 the rebels, a scruffy bunch of about 700, gathered at Montgomery's Tavern outside the city (near modern-day Eglinton Ave.). From here, led by Mackenzie on a white mare, they marched on the city. Two days later the city's militia, called out by Sheriff Jarvis, scattered the rebels at Carlton Street. Both sides then turned and ran. Reinforcements arrived, pursued the rebels, and bombarded the tavern with cannonballs. Mackenzie fled to the United States, and two other leaders—Lount and Matthews—were hanged. Their graves are in the Necropolis cemetery.

Between 1834 and 1884 the foundations of an industrial city were laid: Water works, gas, and later, electrical lighting were installed, and public transportation was organized. Many municipal facilities were built, including a city hall, the Royal Lyceum Theatre (1848) on King near Bay, the Toronto Stock Exchange (1852), St. Lawrence Hall (1851), an asylum, and a jail.

During the 1850s the building of the railroads accelerated the economic pace. By 1860 Toronto was at the center of a railroad web. It became the trading hub for lumber and grain imports and exports. Merchant empires were founded; railroad magnates emerged; and institutions like the Bank of Toronto were established.

Despite its growth and wealth, Toronto still lagged behind Montreal—which had twice

- **1903** The dramatic short film *Hiawatha* is the first movie made in Canada.
- **1904** Great Fire burns much of downtown.
- **1906** First autos produced by Canada Cycle and Motor Company; Toronto Symphony founded.
- **1907** Bell strike broken. Royal Alexandra opens. The Lord's Day Act forbids all public activity except churchgoing on Sunday.
- **1909** Florence Nightingale Graham drops out of nursing school in Toronto, changes her name to Elizabeth Arden, and founds the first cosmetics empire.
- **1911** The founding members of the Group of Seven meet at the Toronto Arts and Letters Club.
- **1912** Garment workers' strike broken; Royal Ontario Museum founded.
- **1914** New Union Station built.
- **1914–18** World War I; 70,000 Torontonians enlist, and 13,000 die.
- **1920** The Art Gallery of Toronto hosts the first Group of Seven exhibit.
- **1921** Population 521,893.
- **1922** University of Toronto researchers Frederick Banting and Charles Best discover insulin.
- **1923** Dr. Banting is awarded the Nobel Prize in medicine. Parliament passes the Chinese Exclusion Act. Ernest Hemingway moves to Toronto to become a reporter for the *Star*.
- **1930s** Depression; thousands go on relief.
- **1931** Maple Leaf Gardens built as home base for the Maple Leafs.
- **1938** Toronto native Joseph Shuster creates Superman.
- **1939** Canada enters World War II; thousands of troops leave from Union Station.

continues

- **1940–45** Toronto functions as war supplier.
- **1947** Cocktail lounges approved.
- **1950** Sunday sports allowed.
- **1951** Population 31% foreign-born.
- **1954** Metro created; Toronto becomes a model for urban consolidation. Toronto native Marilyn Bell, 16, becomes the first person to swim across Lake Ontario. In October, Hurricane Hazel kills 83 people in Toronto.
- **1959** York University, Toronto's second major institution of higher education, opens.
- **1960** Movies are shown in Toronto on Sunday for the first time.
- **1961** Population 42% foreign-born.
- **1963** Ryerson Polytechnic University founded.
- **1965** New City Hall at Nathan Phillips Square is unveiled. Canada and the United States sign the Autopact, creating boom times in Toronto and Oshawa.
- **1966** U.S. draft dodgers start fleeing to Canada; many settle in Toronto.
- **1970s** Influx of immigration from Asia, Africa, India, Pakistan, the Caribbean, and Latin America.
- **1974** Mikhail Baryshnikov defects from the USSR during a trip to Toronto.
- **1975** Toronto International Film Festival founded. CN Tower becomes the world's tallest freestanding structure.
- **1980s** Creation and expansion of the Greater Toronto area, including nearby cities of Hamilton and Oshawa.
- **1981** Population 3,898,933
- **1984** City's 150th anniversary.
- **1989** SkyDome opens, drawing wide criticism of its

continues

Toronto's population in 1861—but increasingly Toronto took advantage of its superior links to the south. That edge eventually helped it overtake its rival. Under the Confederation of 1867, the city was guaranteed another advantage when it was made the capital of the newly created Ontario, which, in effect, gave it control over the minerals and timber of the north.

During this mid-Victorian period the growth of a more diverse population continued. In 1847 Irish famine victims began flooding into Toronto, and by 1851 and 1852 the Irish-born were the city's largest single ethnic group. While many of them were Ulster Irish Protestants who did not threaten the Anglo-Protestant ascendancy, the newcomers were not always welcomed—a pattern that was to be repeated whenever a new immigrant group threatened to change the shape and order of society. As the gap between the number of Anglicans and Catholics closed, sectarian tensions increased, and the old-country Orange and Green conflicts flared into mob violence.

LATE- & HIGH-VICTORIAN TORONTO

Between 1871 and 1891 the city's population more than tripled, shooting from 56,000 to 181,000. The increasingly large urban market helped spawn two great Toronto retailers—Timothy Eaton and Robert Simpson—who moved to Toronto from Ontario towns to open stores at Queen and Yonge streets in 1869 and 1872, respectively. Eaton developed his reputation on fixed prices, cash sales only, and promises of refunds if the customer wasn't satisfied—all unique gambits at the time. Simpson copied Eaton and competed by providing better service, such as two telephones to take orders instead of one. Both developed into full-fledged department stores, and both entered the mail-order business, conquering the country with their catalogs.

The business of the city was business, and amassing wealth was the pastime of such figures as Henry Pellatt, stockbroker and president of the Electrical Development Company and builder of Casa Loma; E. B. Osler; George Albertus Cox; and A. R. Ames. Although these men were self-made entrepreneurs, not Family Compact officials, they still formed a traditional socially conservative elite, linked by money, taste, investments, and religious affiliation. And they were still British to a tee. They and the rest of the citizens celebrated the Queen's Jubilee in

1897 with gusto, and gave Toronto boys a rousing send-off to fight in the Boer War in 1899. They, too, had a fondness for clubs—the Albany Club for the Conservatives, and the National Club for the Liberals. As in England, their sports clubs carried a certain cachet—notably the Royal Yacht Club, the Toronto Cricket Club, the Toronto Golf Club, and the Lawn Tennis Club.

The boom spurred new commercial and residential construction. Projects included the first steel-frame building—the Board of Trade Building (1889) at Yonge and Front, George Gooderham's Romanesque-style mansion (1890) at St. George and Bloor (now the York Club), the provincial parliament buildings in Queen's Park (1886–92), and the city hall (1899) at Queen and Bay. Public transit improved, and by 1891 people were traveling 68 miles of tracks for horse-drawn cars. Electric lights, telephones, and electric streetcars also appeared in the 1890s.

FROM 1900 TO 1933 Between 1901 and 1921 the population more than doubled, climbing from 208,000 to 521,893. The economy continued to expand, fueled by the lumber, mining, wholesale, and agricultural machinery industries, and after 1911 by hydroelectric power. Toronto began to seriously challenge Montreal. Much of the new wealth went into construction, and three marvelous buildings from this era can still be seen today: the Horticultural Building at the Exhibition Grounds (1907), the King Edward Hotel (1903), and Union Station (1914–19). Most of the earlier wooden structures had been destroyed in the Great Fire of 1904, which wiped out 14 acres of downtown.

The booming economy and its factories attracted a wave of new immigrants—mostly Italians and Jews from Russia and Eastern Europe—who settled in the city's emerging ethnic enclaves. By 1912 Kensington Market was well established, and the garment center and Jewish community were firmly ensconced around King and Spadina. Little Italy clustered around College and Grace. By 1911 more than 30,000 Torontonians were foreign-born, and the slow march to change the English character of the city had begun.

It was still a city of churches worthy of the name "Toronto the Good," with a population of staunch religious conservatives, who barely voted for Sunday streetcar service in 1897 and in 1912 banned tobogganing on Sundays. As late as 1936, 30 men were arrested at the lakeshore resort of Sunnyside because they exposed their chests—even though the temperature was 105°F! In 1947 cocktail lounges were approved, but it wasn't until 1950 that sports could legally be played on Sundays.

Increased industrialization brought social problems, largely concentrated in Cabbagetown and the Ward, a large area that stretched west of Yonge and north of Queen. Here, poor people lived in crowded, wretched conditions:

C\$570 million (US\$388 million) cost.

- **1992** Residents of Toronto Islands win 40-year struggle to retain their homes. Blue Jays win World Series for the first time.
- **1993** Blue Jays repeat as World Series champions.
- **1995** Progressive Conservative Government elected; focuses on budget cuts.
- **1996** *Fortune* magazine names Toronto best city in the world to live and work in. University of Toronto professor John Polanyi wins Nobel Prize in Chemistry. Population 4,263,757.
- **1997** People protest in Queen's Park against social-service cuts and the passage of Bill 103, creating a megacity.
- **1998** Toronto becomes a megacity anyway.
- **1999** Researchers at McMaster University in Hamilton discover unusual characteristics of Einstein's brain. The new Air Canada Centre becomes home to the Maple Leafs and the Raptors.

Housing was inadequate, health conditions poor, and rag-picking or sweatshop labor the only employment.

As industry grew, unionism also increased, but the movement, as in the United States, failed to organize politically. Two major strikes—at Bell in 1907 and in the garment industry in 1912—were easily broken.

The larger, wealthier city also became an intellectual and cultural magnet. Artists like Charles Jefferys, J. H. MacDonald, Arthur Lismer, Tom Thomson, Lawren Harris, Frederick Varley, and A. Y. Jackson, most associated with the Group of Seven, set up studios in Toronto. Their first and now-famous group show opened in 1920. Toronto also became the English-language publishing center of the nation, and national magazines like *Maclean's* (started in 1896) and *Saturday Night* were launched. The Art Gallery of Ontario, the Royal Ontario Museum, the Toronto Symphony Orchestra, and the Royal Alexandra Theatre all opened before 1914.

Women advanced, too, at the turn of the century. In 1880 Emily Jennings Stowe became the first Canadian woman authorized to practice medicine. In 1886 women were admitted to the university. Clara Brett Martin was the first woman admitted to the law courts. The women's suffrage movement gained strength, led by Dr. Stowe, Flora McDonald Denison, and the Women's Christian Temperance Union.

During World War I, Toronto sent 70,000 men to the trenches; about 13,000 were killed. At home, the war had a great impact economically and socially: Toronto became Canada's chief aviation center; factories, shipyards, and power facilities expanded to meet the needs of war; and women entered the workforce in great numbers.

After the war the city took on much more of the aspect and tone that are still recognizable today. Automobiles appeared on the streets—the Canadian Cycle and Motor Company had begun manufacturing them in 1906 (the first parking ticket was given in 1908), and one or two skyscrapers appeared. Although 80% of the population was of British origin, ethnic enclaves were clearly defined.

The 1920s roared along, fueled by a mining boom that saw Bay Street turned into a veritable gold-rush alley where everyone was pushing something hot. The Great Depression followed, inflicting 30% unemployment in 1933. The only distraction from its bleakness was the opening of Maple Leaf Gardens in 1931. Besides being an ice-hockey center, it also was host to large protest rallies during the Depression, and later such diverse groups and personalities as the Jehovah's Witnesses, Billy Graham, the Ringling Bros. Circus, and the Metropolitan Opera.

As in the United States, hostility toward new immigrants was rife during the '20s. It reached a peak in 1923, when the Chinese Exclusion Act was passed, banning Chinese immigration. In the 1930s antagonism toward Jews intensified. Signs such as NO JEWS, NIGGERS, OR DOGS were posted occasionally at Balmy and Kew beaches; and in August 1933, the display of a swastika at Christie Pits caused a battle between Nazis and Jews.

AFTER WORLD WAR II In 1939 Torontonians again rallied to the British cause, sending thousands to fight in Europe. At home, plants turned out fighter bombers and Bren guns, and people endured rationing—one bottle of liquor a month, and ration books for sugar and other staples—while they listened to the war-front news delivered by Lorne Greene.

Already prosperous by World War II, Toronto continued to expand during the 1940s. The suburbs alone added more than 200,000 to the population between 1940 and 1953. By the 1950s the urban area had grown so large, disputes between city and suburbs were so frequent, and the need for social and other services was so great that an effective administrative solution was needed. In 1953 the Metro Council was established, composed of equal numbers of representatives from the city and the suburbs.

Toronto became a major city in the 1950s, with Metro providing a structure for planning and growth. The Yonge subway opened, and a network of highways was constructed. It linked the city to the affluent suburbs, which were populated by families who were buying cars, TVs, barbecues, refrigerators, and washing machines—all the modern conveniences associated with house-and-backyard suburbia. Don Mills, the first new town, was built between 1952 and 1962; Yorkdale Center, a mammoth shopping center, followed in 1964. Much of the growth was also fueled by the location of branch plants by American companies that were attracted to the area.

The city also began to loosen up. While the old social elite (still traditionally educated at Upper Canada College, Ridley, and Trinity College) continued to dominate the boardrooms, politics, at least, had become more accessible and fluid. In 1954 Nathan Phillips became the first Jewish mayor, signifying how greatly the population had changed from earlier days when immigrants were primarily British, American, or French. In 1947 the Chinese Exclusion Act of 1923 was repealed, opening the door to relatives of Toronto's then-small Chinese community. After 1950 the door swung open further. Germans and Italians were allowed to enter, adding to the communities that were already established; then, under pressure from the United Nations, Poles, Ukrainians, Central European and Russian Jews, Yugoslavs, Estonians, Latvians, and other East Europeans poured in. Most arrived at Union Station, having journeyed from the ports of Halifax, Quebec City, and Montreal. At the beginning of the 1950s the foreign-born were 31% of the population; by 1961 they were 42%, and the number of people claiming British descent had fallen from 73% to 59%. The 1960s brought an even richer mix of people—Portuguese, Greeks, West Indians, South Asians, and Chinese, Vietnamese, and Chilean refugees—changing the city's character forever.

In the 1960s, the focus shifted back from the suburbs to the city. People moved back downtown, renovating the handsome brick Victorians so characteristic of today's downtown. Yorkville emerged briefly as the hippie capital—the Haight-Ashbury of Canada. Gordon Lightfoot and Joni Mitchell sang in the coffeehouses, and anti-Vietnam protests took over the streets. Perhaps the failure of the experimental, alternative Rochdale College in 1968 marked the demise of that era. By the mid-1970s Yorkville had been transformed into a village of elegant boutiques and galleries and high-rent restaurants, and the funky village had moved to Queen Street West.

In the 1970s, Toronto became the fastest-growing city in North America. For years the city had competed with Montreal for first-city status, and now the separatist issue and the election of the Parti Quebecois in 1976 hastened Toronto's dash to the tape. It overtook Montreal as a financial center, boasting the greatest number of corporate headquarters. Its stock market was more important, and it remained the country's prime publishing center. A dramatically different new city hall opened in 1965, a symbol of the city's equally new dynamism. Toronto also began reclaiming its waterfront, with the development of Harbourfront. The city's new power and wealth came alive in new skyscrapers and civic buildings—the Toronto Dominion, the 72-story First Canadian Place, Royal Bank Plaza, Roy Thomson Hall, the Eaton Centre, the CN Tower—all of which transformed the 1930s skyline into an urban landscape worthy of world attention.

Unlike the rapid building of highways and other structures completed in the 1950s, these developments were achieved with some balance and attention to the city's heritage. From the late '60s to the early '80s, citizens fought to ensure that the city's heritage was saved and that development was not allowed to continue as wildly as it had in the '50s. The best examples of the reform movement's success were the stopping of the proposed Spadina Expressway in 1971 and the fight against several urban renewal plans.

During the 1970s, the provincial government also helped develop attractions that would polish Toronto's patina and lure visitors: Ontario Place in 1971, Harbourfront in 1972, and the Metro Zoo and the Ontario Science Centre in 1974. Government financing also supported the arts and helped turn Toronto from a city with four theaters in 1965 to one boasting 22 in 1976, and more than 40 today.

The city's growth has continued, with the 1989 downtown opening of the SkyDome, the first stadium in the world with a fully retractable roof, and the Air Canada Centre stadium in 1999. Construction of commercial and residential buildings continues to boom along. A new subway line is being tunneled down under Sheppard Avenue, and an extension of the Bloor-Danforth line is under consideration (the plan would take the subway all the way out to the airport). There is strong interest in revitalizing the Toronto Waterfront, but firm plans have yet to be finalized.

Index

See also Accommodations and Restaurant indexes, below.

GENERAL INDEX

Abyssinia, 157
Accommodations, 50.
  See also Accommodations Index
  best bets, 5
  reservation services, 51
Addresses, locating, 40
African Lion Safari (Cambridge), 238
Afternoon tea, best bets for, 8
Air Canada Centre, 4, 7, 18, 128, 138
Airfares, 21–22, 24
Airlines, 21
  Web sites, 27
Airport. *See* Pearson International Airport
Algonquin Island, 40, 114
Allan Gardens, 48, 129
Amadeus Choir, 187
American Express, 14, 159
American Falls (Niagara Falls), 228
Amish, the, 214
Amtrak, 22
Angus Glen Golf Club, 136
Annex, the, 41
Antiques, 160
  Harbourfront Antique Market, 114, 142, 161
Archer, The (Moore), 115, 125, 148
Area code, 45
Argonauts, 35, 128, 138
Arriving in Toronto, 36
Art galleries, 34, 162

Art Gallery of Ontario, 4, 115, 131, 154
  movies at, 208
  restaurant, 78
Ashbridge's Bay Park, 134
ATM networks, 14, 30
Atwood, Margaret, 8
Auditoriums, 189
Auto racing, 138
  Molson Indy, 17, 138
Avon River, 210

Baby-sitting, 45
Ballet, 150, 189, 192
BamBoo, 124, 193, 195
Bank of Montreal, 150
Banting, Frederick, 9, 130
Barker, William, 130
Bars, 199. *See also* Pubs
  gay and lesbian, 206
  hotel, 205
  wine, 204
Baseball, 4, 15, 35, 138
Basketball, 35, 138
Bat Cave Gallery (Royal Ontario Museum), 116
Bata Shoe Museum, 121
Bathurst Pier, 114
Bau-Xi, 154, 162
BCE Place, 128, 149
Beaches, 34, 134, 232
Beaches, the (neighborhood), 42, 123, 134
Beardmore Building, 150
Beauty supplies, 176
Bed & breakfasts, 51, 215
Beer Festival, 17
Benson & Hedges Symphony of Fire, 17

Berkeley Theatre, 187
Best, Charles, 130
Bicycling, 45, 135
  North American Cycle Courier Championships, 16
  tours, 133
Billiards, 203
Black Creek Pioneer Village, 121, 131
Black Swan, 195
Bloor Street, 38
Bloor Street West, shopping, 159
Bloor-Yorkville Wine Festival, 16
Blue Jays, 4, 15, 35, 128, 138
Blues music, 194
  Great Canadian Blues Festival, 17
Board of Trade Building, 245
Boat travel and cruises, 133
  Niagara Falls, 228
Boating, 134, 214
  jet, on Niagara River, 220
Bonnie Stern School, 174
Bookstores, 166
Brown, George, House, 154
Buddies in Bad Times, 187
Buses, 44
  to Toronto, 22
  to/from airport, 36, 37
  tours, 133
Business hours, 45, 159
Butterfly Conservatory (Niagara Parkway), 231

Cabbagetown, 41, 245
  guided tours, 134
Cabs, 36, 44
Cafes, 208
Calendar of events, 15
Cambridge, 216, 238
Campbell House, 126, 148
Canada Blooms, 15
Canada Day, 15, 17
Canada Life Assurance Building, 149
Canada Permanent Trust Building, 147
Canada Sports Hall of Fame, 128
Canada's Wonderland, 120, 130, 191
Canadian Aboriginal Festival, 19
Canadian Broadcasting Centre (CBC), 132, 143
Canadian Imperial Bank of Commerce, 147
Canadian National Exhibition, 18, 33
Canadian Open, 18, 136, 138
Canadian Opera Company, 7, 150, 189–190
Canadian Stage Company, 187
Canadian Warplane Heritage Museum (Hamilton), 237
Candy, John, 9, 193
Canoeing, 134, 214
Car racing, 138
  Molson Indy, 17, 138
Car travel, 44
  driving rules, 45
  Niagara Parkway, 228, 230
  parking, 45
  rentals, 44
  to Toronto, 22
Caribana, 17
Caribbean Corner, 157
Carr, Emily, 120
Carrey, Jim, 9, 192–193
Casa Acoreana, 157
Casa Loma, 125, 131
Casino Niagara (Niagara Falls), 232

Cavalcade of Lights, 19
Cave Spring Cellars (Jordan), 227
CBC Centre, 132, 143
CBC Museum, 132
Cemeteries, 130
Centre Island, 4, 40, 114
  beaches, 134
  Dragon Boat Festival, 17
Centreville, 114, 131, 134
Ceramic Art, Gardiner Museum of, 116
Challenge, the, 133
Chapters, 167
Château des Charmes (St. Davids), 222
Chihuly, Dale, 166
Children
  accommodations, best, 5, 58
  restaurants, best, 8, 83
  shopping for, 167, 171, 181
  sights and activities, 130
Children's Festival, Milk International, 16, 130
Children's Film Festival, 130
Children's Own Museum, 131
Children's Village (Ontario Place), 111, 131
Chinatown, 41, 123
  guided tours, 134
  restaurants, 74
  shopping, 160
  walking tour, 153
Chinaware, 168
Chinese New Year, 15
Christie, Agatha, 188
Chudleigh's, 131
ChumCity, 132
Church Street, 41
Cinemas, 207
City Hall, 19, 125, 137, 148
  Old, 125, 147
Classical music, 190
Climate, 14

Clothing, 171
  department stores, 171
  discout shopping, 170
  furs, 175
  lingerie, 178
  malls, 178
  outlet mall, 171
  vintage, 4, 18, 182
Club Monaco, 171
CN Tower, 4, 34, 114, 131, 143
  restaurant, 6, 75
Coffeehouses, 208
Colborne Lodge, 127
College Park Shoppes, 179
College Street, restaurants, 74
Comedy clubs, 4, 192
Concert halls, 189
Consulates, 11, 46
Contemporary Canadian Art Museum, 122
Cookbook Store, 167
Cormier, Jim, 130
Cosmetics, 176
Country music, 193
Courage My Love, 157, 182
Craft galleries, 169
Craft Studio, 111, 141
Cronenberg, David, 9
Cross-country skiing, 135
Cruises, 133
  Niagara Falls, 228
Cullen Gardens & Miniature Village (Whitby), 131
Currency, 12, 14
Currency exchange, 46
Customs regulations, 12, 30
Cybercafes, 31, 207
Cycling. See Bicycling

Dance clubs, 195
  gay and lesbian, 206
Dance troupes, 191. See also Ballet
Dancemakers, 191
Danforth, the, 42, 123
Danny Grossman Dance Company, 192
Dentists, 46

Department stores, 171
Design Exchange, 122
Dining. *See* Restaurants
Dinner theater, 189
Dinosaur Gallery (Royal
    Ontario Museum),
    116
Disabled travelers, 20
    accommodations,
        best, 6
Discout shopping, 170
Dixie Outlet Mall, 171
Doctors, 46
Documents for entry, 12
Dollar, Canadian, 12,
    14
Dolls House Gallery
    (Fort Erie), 232
Don Valley, 135–136
Downtown, 39
    accommodations, 51
    restaurants
        East, 86
        West, 74
    sightseeing, 114
    walking tour, 149
Dragon Boat Festival,
    17
Dragon City, 123, 156
Dream in High Park,
    186, 188
Drugstores, 47
Dry cleaning, 47
Du Maurier Downtown
    Jazz Festival, 17, 194
Du Maurier Ltd. Open,
    18, 139
Du Maurier Theatre
    Centre, 111
Dufferin Islands, 232
Dundurn Castle
    (Hamilton), 238

Earl Bales Park, 137
East End, 42, 123
    restaurants, 99
East Toronto, accommo-
    dations, 67
Eaton Centre, 125, 160,
    179
Eaton, Timothy, 244
Edwards Gardens, 129
Eglinton Avenue, 42
Egoyan, Atom, 9
El Mocambo, 158, 194
Electricity, 46

Electronic goods, 166
Elgin Theatre, 186
Embassies, in Ottawa, 46
Emergencies, 46
Entry requirements, 12
Ernest Thompson Seton
    Park, 137
Estée Lauder Spa, 135
Exchange Tower, 133,
    146
Exhibition Place, 18–19,
    128, 138, 189

Factory outlet, 171
Factory Theatre, 188
Farmer's markets. *See*
    Markets
Fashion. *See* Clothing
Ferries, 45, 114
Festivals, 15
Film Festival, Toronto
    International, 1, 18
Financial District, 40
    accommodations, 51
    walking tour, 142
First Canadian Place,
    146, 179
First Night Toronto, 19
Fitness centers, 135
Folk music, 193
Food, shopping for, 174,
    219. *See also* Markets
Football, Canadian, 35,
    138
Forest Hill, 42
Fort Erie, 232
Fort George National
    Historic Park
    (Niagara-on-the-Lake),
    220
Fort York, 17, 127, 131,
    241
Fringe Festival, 17, 186
Furs, 175

Gardens
    Allan Gardens, 48,
        129
    Cullen Gardens
        (Whitby), 131
    Edwards Gardens, 129
    Kew Gardens
        Park, 134
    Royal Botanical
        Gardens (Hamil-
        ton), 238

Shakespearean Garden
    (Stratford), 212
Toronto Sculpture
    Garden, 152
Gardiner Museum of
    Ceramic Art, 116
Gay and lesbian travel-
    ers, 20, 31
    accommodations,
        best, 6, 66
    nightlife, 206
    Pride Celebration, 17
    theater, 187
George Brown House,
    154
George R. Gardiner
    Museum of Ceramic
    Art, 116
Gift stores, 175
Glassware, 168
Glen Abbey Golf Club
    (Oakville), 18, 136,
    138
Glenn Gould Studio,
    189
Globe and Mail, 33, 37,
    47
Golf, 136, 231
    Canadian Open, 18,
        136, 138
    miniature, 111, 121
Gooderham Building,
    150
Gould, Glenn, 130
Gowdy, Barbara, 9, 16
Grange House, 115, 242
Great Canadian Blues
    Festival, 17
Great Gorge Rapids
    (Niagara Parkway),
    230
Greek restaurants, 73
Greektown, 42, 123
    restaurants, 4, 6, 99
Group of Seven, 115,
    120, 246
Guelph Line, 139
Guided tours. *See* Tours
Gyms, 135

Haida, HMCS, 111
Hamilton, 236
    accommodations,
        239
    restaurants, 239
    sightseeing, 237

Hanlan's Point, 134
Harbourfront, 4, 40,
111, 130, 248
  bicycling, 45
  canoeing and kayak-
    ing, 134
  International Festival
    of Authors, 1, 18,
    114
  jogging, 137
  Milk International
    Children's Festival,
    16, 130
  Reading Series, 16,
    114
  Toronto Festival of
    Storytelling, 15
  walking tour, 140
Harbourfront Antique
  Market, 114, 142, 161
Harbourfront Canoe
  and Kayak School,
  134
Harbourfront Centre,
  40, 111
Harbourside Boating
  Centre, 114, 134
Hard Rock Cafe, 200
Harness racing, 139
Harris, Lawren, 115,
  246
Hazelton Lanes, 179
HealthWinds, 136
Helicopter tours, 133
  Niagara Falls, 228
Henry Moore Sculpture
  Centre, 4, 115
Hepworth, Barbara, 146
High Park, 129, 135,
  137
  Dream in, 186, 188
Hillebrand Estates
  Winery (Virgil), 222,
  227
History, 240
Hockey, 18, 35, 138
  Hall of Fame, 128,
    131, 150
Holidays, 15
Holt Renfrew, 170–171
Holt Renfrew Centre,
  135, 179
Home furnishings, 176
Honest Ed's World
  Famous Shopping
  Centre, 124, 144, 170

Horse racing, 139, 232
Horseback riding, 4,
  136
Horseshoe Falls
  (Niagara Falls), 228
Horseshoe Valley, 135
Hospitals, 46
Hot lines, 46
Hotel bars, 205
Hotels. See
  Accommodations
Housewares, 176
Hudson's Bay Company
  (The Bay), 147, 171
Humber College, 137
Humber River, 137
Humber Valley, 136
Hummingbird Centre
  for the Performing
  Arts, 150, 189

Iberica Bakery, 158
Ice hockey, 18, 35, 138
  Hall of Fame, 128,
    131, 150
Ice skating, 137
IMAX movies, 111, 115,
  132
  Niagara Falls, 230
In-line skating, 137
Indigo Books Music &
  More, 167
Industrial tours, 132
Information sources, 11,
  37
  Hamilton, 236
  Niagara Falls, 228
  Niagara-on-the-Lake,
    219
  Stratford, 210
Inniskillin Winery
  (Niagara-on-the-Lake),
  231
Insurance, 19
International Festival of
  Authors, 1, 18, 114
Internet cafes, 31, 207
Inuit art, 34, 115, 120
  shopping for, 159,
    162
Inuit Art, Toronto
  Dominion Gallery of,
  146
Isaacs/Innuit Gallery,
  164

Islands. See Toronto
  Islands
Itineraries, 109

Jarvis, William, 152,
  242
Jazz, 194
  Du Maurier Down-
    town Jazz Festival,
    17, 194
Jet boating, on Niagara
  River, 220
Jewelry stores, 177
Jewison, Norman, 9
Joey and Toby Tanen-
  baum Gallery (Royal
  Ontario Museum),
  116
Jogging, 137
John Quay, 111, 141

Kayaking, 134
Kensington Market, 4,
  129, 153, 157, 180,
  245
Kew Gardens Park, 134
Kim Moon Bakery, 123,
  154
King's Bridge Park
  (Niagara Parkway),
  232
Kingswood Music
  Theatre, 191
Kitchener, 214
Kleinburg, 120
Knudson, George, 130
Konzelmann Winery
  (Niagara-on-the-Lake),
  222
Koreatown, 41
Kurtz Orchards
  (Niagara-on-the-Lake),
  231

La Cage Dinner
  Theatre, 189
Lakefront, 40
  sightseeing, 110
Large Two Forms
  (Moore), 154
Laugh Resort, 193
Laundry, 47
Laura Secord Home-
  stead (Queenston),
  231

Law Society of Upper Canada, 127, 148
Layout of Toronto, 38
Leather goods, 178
Legends of the Game, 144, 175
Lennox, Edward James, 9, 147
Lester B. Pearson International Airport. *See* Pearson International Airport
Lingerie, 178
Lionhead Golf Club, 136
Liquor laws, 47, 192
Liquor stores, 182
Little Italy, 42, 123, 245
  cafes, 4, 208
  restaurants, 74
  Taste of Little Italy, 17
Lost property, 47
Lower Don Valley, 135
Loyalist Village (Niagara-on-the-Lake), 220
Loyalists, 220, 240
Luggage storage/lockers, 47

Mackenzie, William Lyon, 130, 243
  House, 127
Magazines, 33, 37, 47, 178
Maid of the Mist (Niagara Falls), 228
Malls, shopping, 178
Manulife Centre, 179, 182
Maple Leaf (train), 22
Maple Leaf Gardens, 191
Maple Leaf Quay, 111, 141
Maple Leafs (hockey team), 18, 35, 128, 138
Marineland (Niagara Falls), 232
Markets, 129, 180
  Kensington Market, 4, 129, 153, 157, 180
  St. Lawrence Market, 40, 129, 150, 180

Martin Goodman Trail, 135, 137
Massey Hall, 190
McFarland House (Niagara-on-the-Lake), 231
McLuhan, Marshall, 9
McMichael Canadian Art Collection (Kleinburg), 34, 120
McPhail, Agnes, 9
Medieval Times Dinner & Tournament, 189
Meetingplace (St. Jacobs), 214
Mendels Creamery, 157
Metro Hall, 144
Metro Toronto Convention Centre, 15
Midtown, 39
  accommodations, 61
  restaurants
    East, 99
    West, 89
Mildred M. Mahoney Dolls House Gallery (Fort Erie), 232
Milk International Children's Festival, 16, 130
Milne, David, 120
Miniature golf, 111, 121
Minolta Tower Centre (Niagara Falls), 230
Mirvish Village, 124
Mirvish, Ed, 124, 144, 170, 187
Mohawk Raceway, 139
Molson Amphitheatre (Ontario Place), 111, 191
Molson Indy, 17, 138
Money, 12
Montgomery, Lucy Maud, 10
Montreal Bistro and Jazz Club, 88, 195
Moore, Henry, 125, 148, 154
  Sculpture Collection, 4, 115
Mount Pleasant Cemetery, 130
Mousetrap, the (Christie), 188

Movie theaters, 207
Museum for Textiles, 34, 122
Museum of Contemporary Canadian Art, 122
Museum of Television, 34
Music
  blues, 194
  classical, 190
  country, 193
  folk, 193
  jazz, 194
    Du Maurier Downtown Jazz Festival, 17, 194
  North by Northeast Festival, 16
  pop and rock, 191, 193
  reggae, 193
  shopping for, 180
My Market Bakery, 157
Myers, Mike, 10, 175, 192–193
Mysteriously Yours, 189

Nathan Phillips Square, 15, 19, 115, 125, 137, 147
National Ballet of Canada, 150, 189, 192
National Club Building, 147
National Helicopters, 133
National Post, 33, 37, 47
National Tennis Centre, 18, 139
Native Earth Performing Arts Theatre, 188
Necropolis, 130, 243
Neighborhoods, 40, 123. *See also specific neighborhoods*
New Asia Supermarket, 123, 156
New City Hall. *See* City Hall
New Year's Eve, 19
Newspapers, 11, 33, 37, 47, 178

Niagara Falls, 227
    accommodations, 233
    at night, 230
    information, 228
    money-saving pass, 228
    restaurants, 235
    sightseeing, 228, 232
    traveling to, 228
Niagara Falls Museum, 232
Niagara Helicopters, 228
Niagara Historical Society Museum (Niagara-on-the-Lake), 220
Niagara Parkway, 228, 230
    restaurants, 236
Niagara River, jet boat tours, 220
Niagara Spanish Aero Car (Niagara Falls), 230
Niagara-on-the-Lake, 5, 219
    accommodations, 222
    information, 219
    restaurants, 225
    Shaw Festival, 5, 16, 187, 219
    traveling to, 219
    wine and vineyards, 222, 227, 231
Nightlife, 183. See also Bars; Comedy clubs; Dance clubs; Dance troupes; Movie theaters; Music; Performing arts; Pubs
    current schedule, 183
    tickets, 183
North American Cycle Courier Championships, 16
North by Northeast Festival, 16
North York, 42
North York Symphony, 187

Oktoberfest, 18, 214
Old City Hall, 125, 147
Old Town, 40
Olde Town Toronto Tours, 133
Ondaatje, Michael, 10
One Front Street, 149
Ontario Legislature, 126
Ontario Place, 17, 34, 110, 131, 191
Ontario Science Centre, 4, 34, 117, 130
Ontario, Lake, 38
    beaches, 134
    swimming warning, 138
Opera, 190
Organized tours. See Tours
Osgoode Hall, 127, 148
Outlet mall, 171

Pantages Theatre, 186
Parachuting, 137
Paramount Canada's Wonderland, 120, 130, 191
Park Greenhouse (Niagara Parkway), 231
Parks
    Ashbridge's Bay Park, 134
    Earl Bales Park, 137
    Ernest Thompson Seton Park, 137
    Fort George National Historic Park (Niagara-on-the-Lake), 220
    High Park, 129, 135, 137
    Kew Gardens Park, 134
    King's Bridge Park (Niagara Parkway), 232
    Queen's Park, 41, 137
    Queen's Park (Stratford), 212
    Queenston Heights Park, 231
    Ross Lord Park, 135
    Sunnybrook Park, 4, 135–136
Partridge, David, 148
Pearson International Airport, 35–37
    accommodations, 68
Pearson, Lester B., 10
Pellatt, Henry, 125, 244
People Movers (Niagara Falls), 228
People Players Dinner Theatre, 189
Performing arts, 186. See also Dance troupes; Music; Theater
    current schedule, 183
    tickets, 183
Perola Supermarket, 158
PGA Tour Canadian Open, 18, 136, 138
Pharmacies, 47
Phillips, Nathan, 125, 148, 247
Pickford, Mary, 10
Picnicking, 4
    in Stratford, 219
Pier 4, 111
Pier, the
    Toronto's Waterfront Museum, 122, 131
Pineapple Room, 157
Plaiter Place, 156
Playdium, 132
Polanyi, John, 10
Police, 48
Pool halls, 203
Pop music, 191
Post office, 47–48
Power Plant Contemporary Art Gallery, 111, 141
Premiere Dance Theatre, 190
Prime Gallery, 153
Princess of Wales Theatre, 144, 186
Pubs, 202
Putti, 162

Queen Street, 123
Queen Street West, 41, 124
    restaurants, 74
    shopping, 160
Queen's Park, 41, 137
Queen's Park (Stratford), 212
Queen's Quay, 40, 111, 140, 179
    antiques, 114, 142, 161
    performing arts, 190–192

Queenston, 231
  accommodations, 234
  restaurants, 236
Queenston Heights Park, 231

Radio, 48
Raptors (basketball team), 35, 128, 138
Recreational activities, 134
Reggae, 193
Reif Winery (Niagara-on-the-Lake), 231
Reservation services, 51
Reservoir Lounge, 195
Rest rooms, 48
Restaurants, 71. See also Restaurant Index
  best bets, 6
  by cuisine, 72
  dinner theater, 189
  late-night, 102
  Web sites, 33
Ride Niagara (Niagara Parkway), 230
Riverdale Farm, 4, 132
Rivoli, the, 124, 193–194
Rock music, 191, 193
Rock of Ages (Niagara Falls), 228
Rock-climbing, 137
Rollerblading, 137
Rosedale, 41
  guided tours, 134
Ross Lord Park, 135
Roy Thomson Hall, 144, 180, 190
Royal Alexandra Theatre, 144, 187
Royal Bank Plaza, 126, 149, 179
Royal Botanical Gardens (Hamilton), 238
Royal Conservatory of Music, 190
Royal Ontario Museum, 35, 116, 131, 134
  restaurant, 91
Royal Trust Building, 146
Royal York, 6, 56, 149

Safety, 48
Sailing, 134

Salamanca, 157
Samuel Weir Collection and Library of Art (Queenston), 231
Sandra Ainsley, 146, 166
Santa Claus Parade, 19
Scadding House, 126
Scarborough Town Centre, 179
Scarborough, accommodations, 68
Science City, 182
Scotia Tower, 147
Seasons, 14
Second City, 193
Secord, Laura, Homestead (Queenston), 231
Senior citizen travelers, 20, 32
Sex toys, 180
Shakespearean Garden (Stratford), 212
Shaw (George Bernard) Festival (Niagara-on-the-Lake), 5, 16, 187, 219
Shoe stores, 180
Shopping, 159
  tax refund, 48, 160
Shuster, Joe, 10
Sigmund Samuel Canadiana Galleries (Royal Ontario Museum), 116
Silverware, 168
Simcoe, John Graves, 127, 240
Simpson, Robert, 244
Skating, 137
Skiing, cross-country, 135
Skydiving, 137
SkyDome, 4, 15, 34, 128, 138, 191
  tickets and tours, 128
Skylon Tower (Niagara Falls), 230, 235
Snow, Michael, 10, 125
Snowboarding, 137
Soto, Jésus Raphael, 126
Southern Po Boys, 195
Spadina, 127
Special events, 15
Sports, 134
  spectator, 138
  Web sites, 35

Sports collectibles, 144, 175
Sports Hall of Fame, 128
St. Andrew's Presbyterian Church, 144
St. Catharines, 226
St. Jacobs, 214
St. James Cathedral, 152, 190
St. Lawrence Centre for the Arts, 150, 187
St. Lawrence Hall, 152
St. Lawrence Market, 40, 129, 150, 180
St. Patrick's Cathedral, 190
St. Patrick's Day Parade, 15
Standard Life Building, 146
Stock Market Place, 133
Strachan, John, 152, 241
Stratford, 5, 210
  accommodations, 214
  information, 210
  picnicking in, 219
  restaurants, 217
  traveling to, 210
Stratford Festival, 16, 187, 210, 212
Streetcars, 44
Student travelers, 20
Subway, 42
  to/from airport, 37
Sun Life Centre, 146
Sunnybrook Park, 135
  horseback riding, 4, 136
Swimming, 137. See also Beaches

Tsui Galleries of Chinese Art (Royal Ontario Museum), 116
Tafelmusik Baroque Orchestra, 190
Tai Kong Supermarket, 156
Tam O'Shanter, 136
Tanenbaum Gallery (Royal Ontario Museum), 116
Tap Phong Trading Company, 156, 177

Tarragon Theatre, 188
Taste of Little Italy, 17
Taverns, 202
Taxes, 48, 71, 160
Taxis, 36, 44
Telephone, 48
Television Museum, 34
Temperatures, average monthly, 15
Ten Ren Tea, 154
Tennis, 138
    Du Maurier Ltd. Open, 18, 139
Textiles Museum, 34, 122
Theater, 4, 7, 186
    dinner, 189
    for children, 130, 188
    Fringe Festival, 17, 186
    Shaw Festival (Niagara-on-the-Lake), 5, 16, 187, 219
    Stratford Festival, 16, 187, 210, 212
    tickets, 183
Theater District, 40
Theatre Centre, 188
Theatre Passe Muraille, 188
Thomson, Tom, 115, 246
Tickets, 183
Tim Simms Playhouse, 193
Time zone, 48
Tobacco, 181
Toilets, 48
Tommy Thompson Trail, 137
Top O' the Senator, 195
Toronto Argonauts, 35, 128, 138
Toronto Blue Jays, 4, 15, 35, 128, 138
Toronto Centre, 122, 187
Toronto Consort, 190
Toronto Dance Theatre, 192
Toronto Dominion Centre, 75, 146, 168
Toronto Dominion Gallery of Inuit Art, 146

Toronto Exchange Tower, 133, 146
Toronto Festival of Storytelling, 15
Toronto Harbour Tours, 133
Toronto International Festival Caravan, 16
Toronto International Film Festival, 1, 18
Toronto Island Airport, 36
Toronto Islands, 40, 114, 131
    beaches, 134
    bicycling, 135
    boating, 135
    cruises, 133
    ferries, 45, 114
Toronto Maple Leafs, 18, 35, 128, 138
Toronto Mendelssohn Choir, 191
Toronto Public Reference Library, 124, 126, 158
Toronto Raptors, 35, 128, 138
Toronto Sculpture Garden, 152
Toronto Star, 11, 33, 37, 47, 183
Toronto Stock Exchange, 133, 146
Toronto Symphony Orchestra, 191
Toronto Truck Theatre, 188
Toronto Zoo, 34, 117, 131
Toronto's Waterfront Museum, 122, 131
Tourist information. See Information sources
Tours, 132
    by bike, 133
    by boat, 133, 228
    by bus, 133
    by helicopter, 133, 228
    industrial, 132
    Niagara Falls, 228
Toy stores, 181
Train travel, 22, 37
Transportation, 42
    Niagara Falls, 228
    to/from airport, 36

transit info, 44, 49
Web sites, 35
Travel insurance, 19
Travel Stop, 182
Travel Web sites, 24
Traveler's checks, 14
Travelers Aid Society, 51
Traveling to Toronto, 21, 36
Trinity Church, 126
Trinity/St. Paul's United Church, 190
Tsui Galleries of Chinese Art (Royal Ontario Museum), 116

Underground Toronto, 40, 160
Union Station, 22, 47, 140, 149
University of Toronto, 20, 41, 138, 190
    accommodations, on Scarborough Campus, 67
Uptown, 39
    accommodations, 66
    restaurants, 103

Varley, Frederick, 115, 246
Victoria University, accommodations, 5, 66
Village by the Grange, 153, 179
Vineland Estates, 227
Vintage clothing, 4, 18, 182
Virgil, 222, 226
Visitor information. See Information sources

Walking tours. See walking tours chapter
    guided, 133
War of 1812, 220, 231, 241
Ward's Island, 40, 114
    beaches, 134
Warplane Heritage Museum (Hamilton), 237

Water parks, 132, 232
Waterfront Museum, 122, 131
Waterloo, 214
Weather, 14
    updates, 30
Web sites, 11, 24, 38
Weir Collection and Library of Art (Queenston), 231
Welland, 226
Whirlpool Golf Club (Niagara Parkway), 231
White Water (Niagara Falls), 232
Wild Water Kingdom, 132
Wine and vineyards, 182
    Bloor-Yorkville Wine Festival, 16
    Niagara-on-the-Lake, 222, 227, 231
Wine bars, 204
Winter Garden Theatre, 186
Winterfest, 15
Woodbine Beach, 134
Woodbine Racetrack, 139
Word on the Street, 18
World War II, 246

YMCA, 135, 138
Yoga Studio, 135
Yonge Street, 38, 41
York Quay, 111, 141
York Quay Centre, 111, 141
Yorkville, 41, 124, 247
    guided tours, 134
    shopping, 5, 160
    Wine Festival, 16
Young Peoples Theatre, 130, 188
Yuk Yuk's Superclub, 193

ACCOMMODATIONS

23 Albert Place (Stratford), 215
Acrylic Dreams (Stratford), 215
Ambercroft (Stratford), 215
Americana, the (Niagara Falls), 233
Avonview Manor (Stratford), 215
Bentley's (Stratford), 214
Best Western Primrose Hotel, 58
Best Western Roehampton Hotel, 66
Bond Place Hotel, 58
Brunswick House (Stratford), 216
Cambridge Suites Hotel, 51
Comfort Inn—Airport, 70
Crowne Plaza Toronto Centre, 54
Days Inn Carlton Inn, 59
Days Inn—Toronto Airport, 70
Deacon House (Stratford), 216
Delta Chelsea Inn, 5, 58–59
Delta Meadowvale Resort & Conference Centre, 70
Festival Inn (Stratford), 214
Four Points Hotel, 70
Four Seasons Hotel Toronto, 5, 8, 58, 61
Gate House Hotel (Niagara-on-the-Lake), 222
Guild Inn (Scarborough), 68
Hilton Toronto, 5, 54
Hilton Toronto Airport, 68
Holiday Inn by the Falls (Niagara Falls), 234
Holiday Inn on King, 5, 59
Hotel Selby, 6, 66
Hotel Victoria, 60
Inter-Continental, 61
Langdon Hall (Cambridge), 216
Le Royal Meridien King Edward, 5, 54
Metropolitan Hotel, 5, 55
Michael's Inn (Niagara Falls), 234
Moffat Inn (Niagara-on-the-Lake), 224
Neil Wycik College Hotel, 60
Nelson Motel (Niagara Falls), 234
Novotel, 55
Oban Inn (Niagara-on-the-Lake), 222
Park Hyatt Toronto, 5, 64
Pillar & Post Inn (Niagara-on-the-Lake), 223
Prince of Wales Hotel (Niagara-on-the-Lake), 223
Quality Hotel, 60, 65
Queen's Inn (Stratford), 215
Queen's Landing Inn (Niagara-on-the-Lake), 223
Radisson Plaza Hotel Admiral, 55, 65, 141
Ramada Hotel & Suites Downtown, 60
Regal Constellation Hotel, 69
Renaissance Toronto Hotel at SkyDome, 57
Royal York, 6, 56, 149
Sheraton Centre, 56, 58
Sheraton Gateway at Terminal Three, 68
Sheraton on the Falls (Niagara Falls), 233
Skyline Brock (Niagara Falls), 233
South Landing Inn (Queenston), 234
Strathcona, 60
Sutton Place Hotel, 65
Toronto Airport Marriott Hotel, 69
Toronto Marriott Eaton Centre, 57
University of Toronto at Scarborough, 67
Venture Inn, 66
Victoria University, 5, 66
Village Inn (Niagara Falls), 234

Vintner's Inn (Jordan), 224

Westin Harbour Castle, 57

Westin Prince Hotel, 67

White Oaks Conference Resort & Spa (Niagara-on-the-Lake), 224

Windsor Arms, 64

Woods Villa (Stratford), 216

Wyndham Bristol Place, 69

RESTAURANTS

360 Revolving Restaurant, 6, 75, 115

7 West Café, 102

Agora, 8, 78

Amore Trattoria, 106

Annapurna Vegetarian Restaurant, 8, 96

Annona, 90

Astoria, 101

Auberge du Pommier, 104

Avalon, 74

Avenue Coffee Shop, 99

Avli, 7, 102

Barberian's, 8, 74

Bentley's (Stratford), 218

Betty's Restaurant & Tavern (Niagara Falls), 235

Bistro 990, 8, 89

Bloor Street Diner, 96

Boba, 91

Buttery, the (Niagara-on-the-Lake), 225

Café Brussel, 99

Café Garibaldi (St. Catharines), 226

Café Nervosa, 95

Café Societa, 78

Canoe Restaurant & Bar, 6, 75

Caribbean Roti Corner, 102

Casa d'Oro (Niagara Falls), 235

Cedar's, 97

Centro, 6, 103

Chiado, 6, 78

Christina's, 100

Church, the (Stratford), 217

Cities, 81

Citron, 81

Courthouse Market Grille, 86

Dante's, 108

Diner on the Green (Niagara Parkway), 236

Dufflet Pastries, 6

Ecco La, 81

Fans Court (Niagara-on-the-Lake), 225

Far Niente Napa Grill, 78

Fifth, the, 79

Flo's Diner, 99

Florentine Court, 88

Fran's, 8, 83, 102, 107

Free Times Café, 84, 102, 194

Gio's, 106

Goldfish, 8, 95

Goof, the, 99

Grand Yatt, 108

Hannah's Kitchen, 107

Happy Seven, 7, 85, 102

Happy Wanderer (Niagara Falls), 235

Hello Toast, 88

Hennepin's (Virgil), 226

Hillebrand's Vineyard Café, 227

Hiro Sushi, 8, 87

Il Posto Nuovo, 6, 91

Indian Rice Factory, 97

Iseya (St. Catharines), 226

Jacques Bistro du Parc, 95

Jamie Kennedy at the Museum, 91

Japan Deli, 97

Joso's, 95

Juice for Life, 97

Jump Café and Bar, 6, 79

Kalendar, 85

Kensington Kitchen, 83, 97

Keystone Alley Cafe (Stratford), 218

Kubo, 88

La Bodega, 81

La Bruschetta, 8, 104

La Cantina (Hamilton), 239

Lai Wah Heen, 8, 79

Lakes, 104

Lalibela, 98

Le Papillon, 89

Le Select, 82

Lee Garden, 85

Let Them Eat Cake (Stratford), 218

Lolita's Lust, 100

Lox, Stock & Bagel, 98

Mars, 99

Matignon, 96

Mediterraneo, 106

Mercer Street Grill, 80

Messis, 8, 96

Mezes, 102

Mezzetta, 106

Mildred Pierce, 82

Millie's Bistro, 8, 83, 105

Mistura, 91

Monsoon, 6, 75

Montreal Bistro and Jazz Club, 88, 195

Myth, 100

Nataraj, 98

North 44, 6, 8, 103

Octavia, 100

Old Prune (Stratford), 217

On the Twenty Restaurant & Wine Bar (Jordan), 227

Opus, 90

Oro, 80

Ouzeri, 103

Pan on the Danforth, 6, 100

Pangaea, 94

Penelope, 85

Perry's Restaurant (Hamilton), 239

Peter Pan, 82

Pho Hung, 98

Pinnacle (Niagara Falls), 235

Pony, 82

Quartier, 105

Queen Mother Café, 85

Queenston Heights (Queenston), 236

Rebel House, 107

Rinderlin's (Welland), 226

Restaurant Index

Ristorante Giardino (Niagara-on-the-Lake), 225
Rivoli, the, 85
Rodney's Oyster House, 88
Rosewater Supper Club, 87
Roxborough's, 105
Rundles (Stratford), 218
Sang Ho, 83
Scaramouche, 6, 104
Senator, the, 87
Senses, 6, 94
Serra, 8, 98
Shala-Mar, 86
Shaw Cafe and Wine Bar (Niagara-on-the-Lake), 225
Shopsy's, 83, 89

Skylon Tower Restaurants (Niagara Falls), 235
Sotto Sotto, 96
Sottovoce, 86
Southern Accent, 94
Splendido Bar and Grill, 94
SpringRolls, 98
Stork on the Roof, 6, 106
Swan, 83
Table Rock Restaurant (Niagara Parkway), 236
Taro Grill, 83
Terra Restaurant Oyster & Martini Bar, 108
Thai Magic, 105
Tortilla Flats, 86

Trattoria Giancarlo, 80
Truffles, 90
Tundra, 75
Tuscany Café, 84
Vanipha Lanna, 107
Veni Vidi Vici, 6, 84
Victoria Park Restaurant (Niagara Parkway), 236
Vineland Estates, 227
Wellington Court Restaurant (St. Catharines), 226
Xango, 81
York Street Kitchen (Stratford), 218
Youki, 84
Young Thailand, 89
Zola, 90
ZooM Caffe & Bar, 87

Restaurant Index

FROMMER'S® COMPLETE TRAVEL GUIDES

Alaska
Amsterdam
Arizona
Atlanta
Australia
Austria
Bahamas
Barcelona, Madrid &
  Seville
Beijing
Belgium, Holland &
  Luxembourg
Bermuda
Boston
British Columbia & the
  Canadian Rockies
Budapest & the Best of
  Hungary
California
Canada
Cancún, Cozumel &
  the Yucatán
Cape Cod, Nantucket &
  Martha's Vineyard
Caribbean
Caribbean Cruises & Ports
  of Call
Caribbean Ports of Call
Carolinas & Georgia
Chicago
China
Colorado
Costa Rica
Denmark
Denver, Boulder & Colorado
  Springs
England
Europe

European Cruises & Ports
  of Call
Florida
France
Germany
Greece
Greek Islands
Hawaii
Hong Kong
Honolulu, Waikiki & Oahu
Ireland
Israel
Italy
Jamaica
Japan
Las Vegas
London
Los Angeles
Maryland & Delaware
Maui
Mexico
Montana & Wyoming
Montréal & Québec City
Munich & the Bavarian
  Alps
Nashville & Memphis
Nepal
New England
New Mexico
New Orleans
New York City
New Zealand
Nova Scotia, New Brunswick
  & Prince Edward Island
Oregon
Paris
Philadelphia & the
  Amish Country

Portugal
Prague & the Best of the
  Czech Republic
Provence & the Riviera
Puerto Rico
Rome
San Antonio & Austin
San Diego
San Francisco
Santa Fe, Taos & Albuquerque
Scandinavia
Scotland
Seattle & Portland
Shanghai
Singapore & Malaysia
South Africa
Southeast Asia
South Florida
South Pacific
Spain
Sweden
Switzerland
Thailand
Tokyo
Toronto
Tuscany & Umbria
USA
Utah
Vancouver & Victoria
Vermont, New Hampshire
  & Maine
Vienna & the Danube Valley
Virgin Islands
Virginia
Walt Disney World &
  Orlando
Washington, D.C.
Washington State

FROMMER'S® DOLLAR-A-DAY GUIDES

Australia from $50 a Day
California from $60 a Day
Caribbean from $70 a Day
England from $70 a Day
Europe from $70 a Day

Florida from $70 a Day
Hawaii from $70 a Day
Ireland from $60 a Day
Italy from $70 a Day
London from $85 a Day

New York from $80 a Day
Paris from $80 a Day
San Francisco from $60 a Day
Washington, D.C.,
  from $70 a Day

FROMMER'S® PORTABLE GUIDES

Acapulco, Ixtapa &
  Zihuatanejo
Alaska Cruises & Ports of Call
Bahamas
Baja & Los Cabos
Berlin
California Wine Country
Charleston & Savannah
Chicago
Dublin

Hawaii: The Big Island
Las Vegas
London
Los Angeles
Maine Coast
Maui
Miami
New Orleans
New York City
Paris

Puerto Vallarta, Manzanillo
  & Guadalajara
San Diego
San Francisco
Sydney
Tampa & St. Petersburg
Venice
Washington, D.C.

FROMMER'S® NATIONAL PARK GUIDES

Family Vacations in the
   National Parks
Grand Canyon

National Parks of the
   American West
Rocky Mountain

Yellowstone & Grand Teton
Yosemite & Sequoia/
   Kings Canyon
Zion & Bryce Canyon

FROMMER'S® MEMORABLE WALKS

Chicago
London

New York
Paris

San Francisco
Washington, D.C.

FROMMER'S® GREAT OUTDOOR GUIDES

New England
Northern California

Southern California & Baja
Southern New England

Washington & Oregon

FROMMER'S® BORN TO SHOP GUIDES

Born to Shop: France
Born to Shop: Italy

Born to Shop: London
Born to Shop: New York

Born to Shop: Paris

FROMMER'S® IRREVERENT GUIDES

Amsterdam
Boston
Chicago
Las Vegas

London
Los Angeles
Manhattan
New Orleans

Paris
San Francisco
Seattle & Portland
Vancouver

Walt Disney World
Washington, D.C.

FROMMER'S® BEST-LOVED DRIVING TOURS

America
Britain
California

Florida
France
Germany

Ireland
Italy
New England

Scotland
Spain
Western Europe

THE UNOFFICIAL GUIDES®

Bed & Breakfasts in
   California
Bed & Breakfasts in
   New England
Bed & Breakfasts in
   the Northwest
Bed & Breakfasts in
   Southeast
Beyond Disney
Branson, Missouri

California with Kids
Chicago
Cruises
Disneyland
Florida with Kids
Golf Vacations in the
   Eastern U.S.
The Great Smoky &
   Blue Ridge
   Mountains

Inside Disney
Hawaii
Las Vegas
London
Miami & the Keys
Mini Las Vegas
Mini-Mickey
New Orleans
New York City
Paris

San Francisco
Skiing in the West
Southeast with Kids
Walt Disney World
Walt Disney World
   for Grown-ups
Walt Disney World
   for Kids
Washington, D.C.

SPECIAL-INTEREST TITLES

Frommer's Britain's Best Bed & Breakfasts and
   Country Inns
Frommer's Britain's Best Bike Rides
The Civil War Trust's Official Guide
   to the Civil War Discovery Trail
Frommer's Caribbean Hideaways
Frommer's Adventure Guide to Central America
Frommer's Adventure Guide to South America
Frommer's Adventure Guide to Southeast Asia
Frommer's Food Lover's Companion to France
Frommer's Gay & Lesbian Europe
Frommer's Exploring America by RV
Hanging Out in Europe

Israel Past & Present
Mad Monks' Guide to California
Mad Monks' Guide to New York City
Frommer's The Moon
Frommer's New York City with Kids
The New York Times' Unforgettable
   Weekends
Places Rated Almanac
Retirement Places Rated
Frommer's Road Atlas Britain
Frommer's Road Atlas Europe
Frommer's Washington, D.C., with Kids
Frommer's What the Airlines Never Tell You